Acclaim and Praise for Eminent Islanders

You have made a huge contribution to our province by penning the history of Eminent Islanders for posterity.

-Robert Ghiz, Premier of Prince Edward Island

A new book, Eminent Islanders, is the story of Prince Edward Island leaders... who have first and foremost made a lasting impression on this province.

- Mary MacKay, The Guardian

An engaging and sometimes provocative look at our past, with some thoughts on our future and a conclusion that many of us have always suspected: In the end, when you look at it, all history has an Island connection."

-PEI Heritage Award Citation

It is indeed, an interesting, pleasing, informative, and imaginative volume. Well done!

-Professor T.H.B. Symons,
Vanier Professor Emeritus, Trent University

I read it through over the New Year ... it is truly outstanding.

-John McArthur, former Dean, Harvard Business School, Boston

Prince Edward Island remains a powerful part of my consciousness and your book reinforces a cherished connection.

- Peter MacKinnon, President, University of Saskatchewan

Other Books and Monographs by the Same Author

The Strategic Challenge: From Serfdom to Surfing in the Global Village

Embracing the Future: The Atlantic Gateway and Canada's Trade Corridor

The Japanese Industrial System

Bridge Across the Pacific: Canada-Japan Relations

International Bidding and Productivity: A Study of Subways (with D. Horvath)

Culture and Nation: The Aston Program (with David J. Hickson)

Investing in Tomorrow: Japan's Science and Technology

Building Blocks or Trade Blocs: NAFTA, Japan, and the New World Order

Services: Japan's 21st Century Challenge

Eminent Islanders

by

Charles McMillan

Charles McMillan

authorHOUSE®

AuthorHouse™
1663 Liberty Drive, Suite 200
Bloomington, IN 47403
www.authorhouse.com
Phone: 1-800-839-8640

This book is a work of non-fiction. Unless otherwise noted, the author and the publisher make no explicit guarantees as to the accuracy of the information contained in this book and in some cases, names of people and places have been altered to protect their privacy.

First published by AuthorHouse 8/10/2009

ISBN: 978-1-4343-4614-8 (sc)

Library of Congress Control Number: 2007908303

Printed in the United States of America
Bloomington, Indiana

This book is printed on acid-free paper.

This book is dedicated to Reverend Francis W.P. Bolger, Catholic priest, university professor, Member of the Order of Canada, Professor Emeritus, and truly an Eminent Islander.

Moral of the Island Story,
And how the Past helps create the Future:

In Education – Excellence
In Economy – Innovation
In Health – Prevention
In Politics - Imagination

Table of Contents

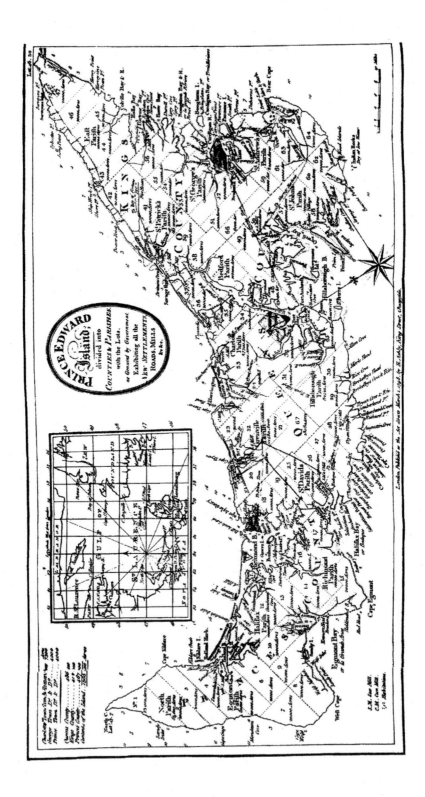

Preface

Eminent Islanders started from a small but growing bookcase on the history of Prince Edward Island. From personal stories to academic tomes, from diaries and letters to historic records, from governmental and legislative archives to personal biographies, the history of Canada's smallest province is an intriguing tale of the small among the great, of human endurance to great achievement. Her sons and daughters roamed the world, and brought renown to the councils of literary circles, the Church, the judiciary, academe, politics, and the professions. Aside from the good, the odd Islander warmed prison beds, feathered his nest from misdemeanors, everything from horse theft to stealing from private estates. The odd Islander also learned the worst from noble visitors, pompous men of action, and the great and near great, from one glass too many to slick rum running, from an over-weaning haughtiness to an exceptionally under-nourished verbosity. Small size and population put visitors under the microscope, and the Island has seen them all. Islanders are intensely loyal to their province and to their history. They know their own habits and prejudices, but they will extend their friendship and their charity far beyond what might be expected from such a small place where friendship is appreciated and extended without too much expected in return.

P.E.I., as it is affectionately known, is an island of some stature, known to many as *the* Island, home to *Anne of Green Gables*. As an Island, like thousands of other geographical places around the world, it is small by most features: acreage, people, economy, and diversity. Some called PEI *Spud Island*, or Canada's *Garden Province*, the *Million Acre Farm*, or the *Cradle of Confederation*. Islanders call it the Island, as if there is no other. But PEI is a legal and provincial entity, one of ten provinces in Canada, with its own legislative system and two hundred and fifty years of recorded government - from the domination of the French royalty, the heyday of the British Empire, to the very founding of Canada in 1864. From the thousands of geographical islands around the world, few have a protracted history of peaceful legislative evolution, without war, revolt, oppression, or military rule.

As a small colony, with only 5000 people in 1800, or 90,000 by 1900, PEI is roughly the same size as many independent states in the West Indies. True, some islands can be very large – Greenland, New Guinea and Borneo come to mind – and some Islands were once vast colonial Empires – Britain and Japan, for instance – but Prince Edward Island is in a unique situation by more than geography or population. It has gone through different phases of development, from a small outlet in the once vast French commercial Empire of North America, protected by the might fortress of Louisburg, to a British colony isolated in the vast British Empire and casually taken over by London as part of the British holdings in North America. For a hundred years, the colony struggled: it was dominated by a cavalier colonial administration and Governors more interested in pleasing London or serving as vassals to the absentee landlords. Gradually, through settlements, planned or otherwise, it gained stature by population and commercial success to warrant measures of responsible government. PEI avoided the worst excesses of other jurisdictions, from slavery to rebellion, religious persecution to ethnic cleansing. Responsible government gave rise to new leadership and new responsibilities, and gradually and reluctantly, this small island became a province of Canada in the new Federal Dominion. That was in 1873, almost 350 years after it was first discovered by the French explorer, Jacques Cartier.

Within Canada, and as part of Canadian history, PEI has carved its own place, sometimes benign, sometimes cantankerous, and sometimes stupendous. Geography plays a role - a truly magnificent site, ever the more so to first time visitors. George Brown, the Editor of the *Globe* and a leading Father of Confederation, taking a warm swim in the Northumberland Strait of PEI, remarked that the Island was "as pretty a country as you ever put your eye upon." Island geography has a heavy burden, because it largely shaped the economic, political and social life of the province. Like all British colonies, it fought for responsible government, not by the violent acts of 1789 in France, or the struggles in Ireland of 1798 or 1916, but the hardships were still real, and the land burden imposed by Imperial London were obtuse and objectionable and helped shape the Island's approach to friendship. More specifically, geography shaped its culture - its sense of distance even from neighboring provinces, its sense of isolation from events afar - from wars to cultural and political moods, from grand theories of industrialization and technology to protecting the Island way of life.

As in any grand proposal like Confederation in the nineteenth century, it is natural that the benefits of a union, however blessed or praised, were in the future; the costs, political and economic, were here and now. Collectively, the British colonies covered a vast territory, even more so when the lands of the vast wilderness of the Northwest were included. These colonies had abundant resources, including the coveted Atlantic fisheries, where the European Empires – Spain and Portugal, France, and then Britain fought and conspired for supremacy as far back as the days of Francis Drake in the sixteenth century. Two centuries later, the Americans from Boston and the British from the port cities of Liverpool, Grimsby, and Bristol coveted the Grand Banks where the fish were so abundant that schools of cod actually brought fishing boats to a halt. For their part, the Maritimes Provinces in particular, had over 100 years of British rule, a vast increase in the number of new immigrants, including families loyal to King George III, what became known as the United Empire Loyalists. The Irish famine drove hundreds of thousands from the Emerald Isle, most to the Boston states, but the Irish and other settlers increased the populations from the regular wars on the Continent.

Innately, Islanders know who is who, and who is from away. Islanders are odd that way - they have no sense that the province's citizens are inherently superior, in looks, talent, intellect or physique. In the same way, Islanders carry no wisdom or feeling of inferiority, by terms such as money wealth, gene selection, or class distinction. Bishop Francis Kelly, an Islander who became Bishop of Oklahoma and Tulsa, on loan as it were from his PEI roots, puts the Island mentality this way:

But, 'ware the Islander! He may look innocent but,
like Will Cain of New Perth, be an ex-school master

or school inspector turned back to farming. He may put a 'cargo' in Chicago but he knows his geography. He may exhibit curiosity about the Rockies, but he has a brother who made a fortune in Colorado. If he may be a Presbyterian, watch him, for it may be his near relative who had a fashionable church in Fifth Avenue, or was both President of Cornell and American Ambassador to Germany. A Catholic may have an archbishop or a professor of philosophy in his family. There are three living archbishops and three living bishops from the Island. Above all, 'ware the seeming guilelessness of the Islander! He is not a guileless Man. His humour is deep and he loves to enjoy it and the expense of the unperceiving stranger. If you go to the Island be humble, with the humility that is not carried as an ornament but as a safety belt.

The Island has seen its share of important people, from Queen Elizabeth and the Prince of Wales to Prime Ministers and Hollywood stars. But Islanders take it all in stride. Islanders feel confident that it is the Island who attracts them, not the reverse. As one British teenager, talking to a PEI dowager about the magnificent pageantry of the English monarchy, when asked if she had even seen the current Queen, responded, "Yes, on TV. Have you seen the Queen?" The Island lady responded with little emotion: "Yes, three times, in person."

Islanders are such people. Rich, in this sense, has several meanings - in natural bounty, in the arts, in beauty, in God's vision, whatever. In the North American scheme of things, where richness is measured on Bay Street or Wall Street by stocks and bonds, the Island economy scores near the bottom, measuring US states and provinces by the economic pecking order of financial wealth. To most Islanders, these economic figures don't mean much. What does count is what GNP figures may not account for - the annual roll call of lobster suppers enjoyed, the warm swims in real salt water, the longevity of grandmothers, the high presence of home ownership. Then there are the weekends, and especially Sunday, with packed car parks for church worship, and family gatherings, and rounds of golf outings.

In the scheme of things, PEI's capacity to manage its own economy has gone the way of the railroad, the telegraph, and the one room school. But Islanders have slowly, perhaps reluctantly, learned that real strengths - a proper education system, healthy lives, a clean environment - do bring advantages to the bottom line of wealth creation and personal longevity. Their heritage – mostly poor people from France, Scotland, and Ireland – mobilized their conservative instincts, their way of life, their attitudes to learning, their religious beliefs, their attitudes to the high and mighty (mostly distain) and to their real friends (exceptional warmth).

In 250 years of political development, half as a colony split roughly between the French and British empires, half as a self governing jurisdiction, first with its own system of responsible government, then as a province in the Dominion of Canada - Islanders have witnessed their share of fools, political and otherwise. From oppressed people through land control to inherited ignorance through limited education, Islanders have faced greater bodies in their midst and they have created their own. The Island's geography has its own impact - new arrivals tend to stay, outsiders are from away, the generations that inculcated the Island way of life.

The big issues come and go, the cycles of the economy go up and down. The political tides come in and they go out. Time passes but the clock doesn't stop. In so many ways, the Island has created its own heroes, some often unknown on the Island because their success is away. *Eminent Islanders* flows from this unique history, relatively unsullied by violent protest, political revolution, staggering poverty, and utter depravation from uprooted cultures displayed in such areas as the American colonies, Ireland, Scotland and England, where most of the population came from. The turmoil of these societies had their effects on the immigrants to PEI. Like many North American jurisdictions, the Island was also insulated by the desire to escape foreign environments, and to build a new society based on this Island's unique assets. These new Islanders left a legacy that now helps express the 'Island way of life'.

Lucy Maud Montgomery, who became not only the Island's most famous writer but Canada's, describes her enormous affection for her province and its links to the sea:

> *Much of the beauty of the Island is due to the vivid color contrasts – the rich red of the winding roads, the brilliant emerald of the uplands and meadows, the glowing sapphire of the encircling sea. It is the sea which makes Prince Edward Island in more senses than the geographical. You cannot get away from the sea down there...Great is our love for it; the tang gets into our blood; its siren call rings ever in our ears; and no matter where we wander in lands afar, the murmur of its waves ever summons us back in our dreams to the homeland. For few things am I more thankful than for the fact that I was born and bred beside that blue St. Lawrence Gulf.*

It might be presumptive to say that Island history mirrors historical views of the past, and the great sweeps of social, political, and economic history experienced in Europe during the eighteen and nineteenth century, in particular the battles for supremacy between Britain and France. History can be seen as a deterministic thrust, the great social forces that sweep the continental landscapes over the centuries, with individuals caught in the march of history. To some extent, PEI illustrates this deterministic perspective, from the wars of empire in the 17th and 18th century in Europe, to the momentous scientific and industrial changes that undermined the old schools of politics, economy, warfare, industry and commerce, and science itself. Many books have been written about this sweep of history and the choice of riding the new tides of history, or resisting these forces, by whatever means were available. The United States of America, with the frontier metaphor coined by Frederick Turner, personifies the forces of 'out with the old' and the creation of new institutions, constitutions, and rules to ride the tide of novelty, newness, and outright revolutionary thinking. In short, fate is in the hands of the stars.

Shakespeare, no stranger to the forces that sweep nations, taught this lesson in *Twelfth Night*:

> *Fate, show they force: ourselves we not owe.*
> *What is decreed, must be; and be this so!*

But there is another view of history. Fate may be important, but it is not the only teacher. Tidal forces are not necessarily deterministic. Chance and luck may have a role, but so do individuals. History, says Carlyle, is the essence of innumerable biographies. Thomas Carlyle, the grand Scottish scribe who coined such phrases as 'industrialism' and economics as the 'dismal science' and 'captains of industry' is the fashionable personification of the great man theory of history. For Carlyle, history is not the *deus ex machina* unfolding of drama swept by the hand of God or impersonal forces.

For Thomas Carlyle, who rewrote his study of the French Revolution after the original manuscipt was burned by accident, only strong and powerful individuals can control master events and direct their spiritual energies. When ideological 'formulas' replace heroic human action, society became dehumanised. Carlyle believed in the importance of heroic leadership. In his book *Heroes and Hero Worship,* the hero was somewhat similar to Aristotle's, *Magnanimous Man* – a person who flourished in the fullest sense. But for Carlyle, unlike Aristotle, the world was filled with contradictions, and all heroes, although flawed in their moral perfection, have heroism in their creative energy in the face of difficulties. These failings, far from weak attacks like the philosophy of those who seek comfort in the conventional, Carlyle called 'valetism', from the phase 'no man is a hero to his valet'.

Carlyle's sense of hero places a view of history on individual action and the role of heros. PEI has produced its own heros; this is the theme of Eminent Islanders.

Charles McMillan,
Bellevue Cove, PEI
August 16, 2007

Acknowledgements

"There is no strength," wrote Joseph Howe, "where there is no strain; seamanship is not learned in calm weather, and born of the vicissitudes and struggles of life are the wisdom, and dignity and the consolations." In writing this narrative on *Eminent Islanders*, I have been conscious that to some, as Henry Ford has testified, "History is bunk." That is a falsehood, but I am also aware that for Canadians, and for Islanders, as Professor Donald Creighton reminds us, "history can help men to understand their nation's distinctive character, and to recognize the main direction of its advance in time."

During the many years and months of preparing this book, I have been blessed with countless stories, helpful suggestions, and abundant readings on the lives and chronicles of *Eminent Islanders*. I wish to acknowledge the help and guidance of many friends, family, and complete strangers who provided me with references, letters, and documents on the Island story and, in particular, I want to thank the following individuals: Boyde Beck, Cathy Hennessey, Eileen Fulford, Wayne MacKinnon, Mary McQuaid, Harry O'Connell, Premier Alex Campbell, Premier Pat Binns, Fred Hyndman, the late Dr. A. D. Kelly, the late Rev. James Kelly, Frank Ledwell, Marion McArthur, Ed McDonald, David Mackenzie, Wade MacLauchlan, Senator Percy Downe, Hon. Marian Reid, Leo Walsh, Elizabeth Epperly, Pete Paton, Kevin Rice, Rev. Art O'Shea, Dr. T.H.B. Symons, Helen MacPherson, the Rt. Honourable Brian Mulroney, and Dr. Colin McMillan. In particular, I want to thank Tom Keeler, who read the entire text, and offered many useful and valuable suggestions. I also wish to thank Clara Kan, for much editorial assistance. I apologize in advance for any errors of omission or commission.

I am grateful to the Confederation Centre Art Gallery for allowing me to reproduce the following works: Robert Harris (1849-1919) Self-portrait, undated, oil on canvas, 39.5 x 30.5 cm, Collection of Confederation Centre Art Gallery, Gift of the Robert Harris Trust, 1965 CAG H-275; Robert Harris, Sketch for *Meeting of the*

Delegates of British North America, 1883, oil on canvas, 33.0 x 57.2 cm, Collection of Confederation Centre Art Gallery, Gift of the Robert Harris Trust, 1965 CAG H-79; Robert Harris (1849-1919) *The Rt. Hon. Sir John A. Macdonald*, circa 1890, oil on canvas, 84.4 x 66.2 cm, Collection of Confederation Centre Art Gallery, Purchased with funds from Hyndman and Company Limited and the late Margaret MacMillan Pratt, 1996 CAG H-8314; Photographer unknown, *Sir Andrew Macphail*, [1897] photograph mounted on card 18.0 x 15.0 cm (card), Collection of Confederation Centre Art Gallery, Gift of the Robert Harris Trust, 1965 CAG H-1821-D; Thomas Wright (1740-1812) *A Plan of Charlotte Town, the capital of the Island of St. John , delineated by order of His Excellency Walter Patterson Esq. By Mr. Tho. Wright, Surveyor*, 1771, pen and brown ink over pencil on beige wove paper, Library & Archives Canada/NMC-34291.

I thank yet again my wife Kazuyo, and daughters Aya and Mari, for their many kindnesses, and their tolerance of a messy desk, a cluttered bookcase, and copious notes and chapter drafts. They join with me in thanking many Islanders for their friendship and support. In particular, I thank the numerous Island teachers, professors, and historians of the Island's story, and one unique Islander, Rev. Dr. F.W.P. Bolger, to whom this book is dedicated.

C.J.M.

1

A New British Colony

Prince Edward Island, a Northern colony in North America, developed its colonial heritage and institutions during the European Age of Revolution. For two centuries, spanning the times of Charles I in England in 1688 to the era of Napoleon Bonaparte after the French Revolution a century later, Europe was struggling with the revolutionary ideas that would transform the world. Political ideas and the rights of man would dominate political thought and the methods of government – from codified human rights to the judicial system and role of judges. But revolutionary ideas were transforming science in all its forms – the study of geography and the mapping of the continents and oceans, biology and medicine, such as the first real scientific studies of plants, water, and the human body, including the circulation of the blood, scientific study of diseases, and new concepts linking the difference between religious beliefs and scientific study. The third revolution was the power and influence of political economy, the moral influence of wealth, the power of markets, the impact of free trade, the invisible hand, and the power of unfettered markets.

In the sixteenth and seventeenth centuries, the European empires vied for glory in the sea lanes of the known world. The three largest powers, Spain, France, and England all sought out the riches in territory, gold and silver, wonderful new addictions – spices, tobacco, and sugar, fish stocks, and scientific exploration. Their goal was China. From the days of the Roman Empire, countries had built their own navies, but the concept of entrepreneurial captains marked a new chapter for Europe, and less attention was paid to the loyalties to the monarch, and more to the money support of their finance backers.

The Mediterranean area was the first sophisticated sailing region. It had better ships, more efficient sails, better masts, superior navigation charts, and new instruments, like the compass, astronomical tables, hour glass, and simple tools such as the log and line. A log was simplicity itself, a piece of wood with a rope showing the lengths marked every six feet. Thrown overboard, the wood with the rope measures the depth of the water, and when trailing with an hourglass, provides the average speed of the ship measured in knots. It became a universal code – the ship's log.

From the Mediterranean to Africa, from Europe towards the Atlantic ocean, sailors, captains, pirates, explorers, hunters and slave traders pushed the boundaries of geography and the search for food, riches, new territory, and slaves. The leading explorers were primarily from Spain and Portugal, in part because King Ferdinand and Queen Isabella took personal interest in funding exploration voyages, with bountiful success. After all, Christopher Columbus toiled for this monarchy, but Columbus, who did reach the shores of San Salvador and Florida, was Genoese and cared more about financing than the monarchy he worked for. Columbus, like so many explorers before or since, from Francis Drake to John Cabot, was an indifferent mercenary at heart. Their exploits were early signs of multinational enterprise. Even the Papacy entered the exploration game. Pope Alexander VI, born in Xativa, Spain, whose mother was the sister of Pope Calixtus III, brought peace between Portugal and Spain, by a demarcation for the two empires, dividing the new worlds– the Americas for Spain, Asia for the Portuguese once Vasco de Gamma reached India in 1498.

John Cabot, a Venetian, sailing under the banner of Henry Tudor, who turned down the financing of Columbus' exploits of 1492, had his eye on China and the north-west passage. He sailed in May 1497 on his ship, the *Mathew*, only 50 tons with a crew of 20. He reached Newfoundland, witnessing the incredibly rich Grand Banks, and toured what is now the Maritime Provinces, calling the small island

Saint John. Cabot returned to England in August, knowing other explorers had been there before. The following year, he returned with four ships but died in a storm off the coast of Ireland. His son Sebastian, working for a corporate syndicate, the Company Adventurers of the New Found Lands, continued his exploration, again looking for routes to China. And in doing so, he visited the lands north of Greenland towards the Arctic, discovering the entrance to Hudson's Bay, finally returning home to new priorities – the rich mineral lands to the south.

The emphasis of European exploration shifted southward again, towards the lands where silver bullion was found in abundance. Here Spain was clearly ahead, with its vast multinational empire expanding to the Atlantic shores, to Mexico, Panama, Peru, and the great port city of Havana. Not to be outdone, the French monarchy picked up where the English left off, and funded the exploits of explorers like Jacques Cartier and Sieur de Robervalle. Cartier visited North America on several trips, his most notable in 1534, when he explored the St. Lawrence, naming the massive river on the day of its discovery, the saint's feast day, and named the mountain down the river Mont Royal. Later, he patrolled the Gulf of St. Lawrence and adjacent land areas, and calling the small, nested, and compact island to the south, Ile St. Jean.

On this voyage, in the spring of 1534, as recorded in his own report to the French King, in a document kept in the Imperial Library in Paris (two previously known records of his travels were verified, one in Italian, one an English translation), Jacques Cartier skilfully navigated down the Atlantic Coast, from St. Malo where he left on April 30, to Newfoundland, the Strait of Belle Isle, heading southward across the St. Lawrence towards Prince Edward Island. On June 30, 1534, he reached the Island's north shore, sailing ten leagues on the first day but found no harbours. On July 1, he landed from his two boats in several places, then traveled the whole length of the north shore of Prince Edward Island, finding a wide variety of trees, some known species (cedars, pines, white elms, ash, willows) and some unknown, as well as a full variety of peas, gooseberries, fruits, and corn, with many turtle-doves, wood pigeons, and other birds. He described the land as one of great quality, great warmth, bright skies, and glorious climate. "The finest land one can see, and full of beautiful trees and meadows," noted Cartier, "The fairest that it may be possible to see." With such words, Jacques Cartier discovered Prince Edward Island and claimed this fair island for France.

**

Throughout the hundred years of the eighteenth century, Prince Edward Island was an isolated island colony, thanks to the Treaty of Paris in 1763, when the small island was transferred from the French Regime, after General Wolfe defeated General Montcalm at the Plains of Abraham in 1759. All of North America was a mix of European colonial outposts: Mexico and California were Spanish, the so-called thirteen colonies of America and Newfoundland were British, most of the northern half of North America was French, centered in Quebec but extending southward to the vast territory of the Ohio Valley, west of the English colonies of Massachusetts, Connecticut and Virginia. These North American colonies reflected their imperial backgrounds: their mother countries influenced place names, capitals were called after kings and queens and prominent cities and people (Queen Charlotte, New Amsterdam, New York, Halifax and Manchester). Prince Edward Island was no different, where the names were strictly Georgian, from the name of the King's errant son to the three counties, Prince, Queens, and Kings.

In many respects, the colonies were miniature copies of the mother country's life style and social hierarchies: the government, the economy, languages and food, dress and clothing, personal habits, religious beliefs, and education. More importantly, the colonies reflected the institutions of Europe, their own aristocracies and land ownership. Power and influence in Europe varied by country, but was clearly hierarchical: the monarchy, the established church, the landowners, the army, the navy, and the clergy. Quebec was the center of the French order in North America, reflected France's strict social order, dominated by the Governor, appointed directly by the King of France.

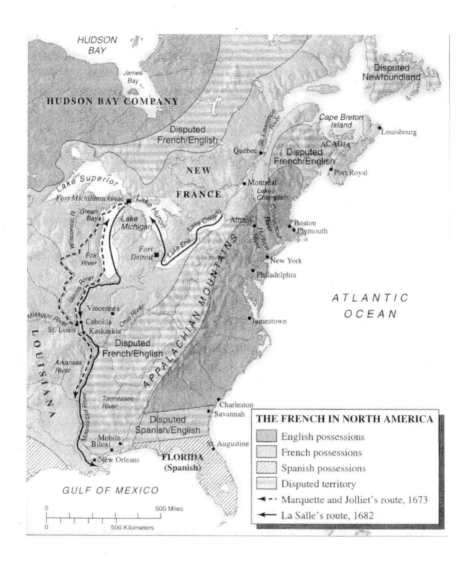

THE FRENCH IN NORTH AMERICA

- English possessions
- French possessions
- Spanish possessions
- Disputed territory
- ◄-- Marquette and Jolliet's route, 1673
- ◄— La Salle's route, 1682

Europe itself was a Continent divided, with competing empires of warring states, split by religion, languages, cultures. Many economic systems were rooted in slavery, from the landholding of peasant-based agriculture to slavery of imported blacks from Africa to European colonies like Haiti, Jamaica, Barbados and the southern British colonies of North America. In Europe, the nation state was organized by language and religion – Austria, France and Spain were Catholic, Italy was divided by city states with the Vatican centered in Rome, Germany was not yet united but Protestant Prussia was a rising power, most of Scandinavia was Protestant, Turkey was Islam, and Russia was Russia Orthodox. England was mostly, Anglican, with the Church of England as the established Reform Church established by Henry VIII, made paramount throughout Britain and colonial possessions thanks to the willful strength of his bastard daughter, Elizabeth I. Despite the tumultuous rivalry between Elizabeth I and Mary Queen of Scots, and the temporary reign of Mary's Catholic son James I, this Protestant religion was an institution imposed on Catholic Ireland and Scotland's Church of Scotland, with consequences that would last for centuries.

All European states were aristocracies; most were monarchies. From Louis XIV in France to Peter the Great in Russia, countries had absolute rule – *L'État, c'est moi*. The European system of empire states was slow to evolve as individual nation-based states. For almost 2000 years, Europe itself was governed by empires, from Alexander in Greece to the Roman Empire in Rome. These empires competed against the enormous land mass of the Mogul Empire of Genghis Khan to the Ottoman Empire in Byzantine (Istanbul) and the Chinese Empires in Peking. European states slowly emerged after the sixteenth century, as various stakeholders competed for power and wealth – the monarchies, which controlled armies, the Church, which controlled enormous land and patronage, the landowners who dominated the guilds and peasants. Servitude in all its forms was the watchword.

England and France were the two dominant military countries. Within Europe, there were both large and small countries, city states (in Italy), as well as the Vatican. For centuries, the European nation state needed social order, in part to maintain the aristocratic order to be sure, but also to pursue military and commercial goals based on mercantile interests. Armies, police, bureaucrats, and military conscription helped enforce security, law and order, and restrictions on rebellious behaviour. So too did jails, hangings, work houses, and various other institutions of indentured servitude, which included enforced jail sentences to penal colonies like Australia. Exceptions were the Tower of London, a condo-type jailhouse fitted for prisoners like Mary Queen of Scots; Paris' Bastille, and London's Newgate Prison, fitted out with small cells or comfortable apartments, depending on how much rent the convict could afford to pay.

By the 18th century, the nation state was the primary political body of Europe. Curiously, it needed two contradictory requirements. The first was social order, therefore a strong measure of legitimacy among its citizens. Kings and Queens appealed to the people to gain their allegiance, often by invoking foreign threats, a useful tool used both then and now. The threats of invasion were very real for a continent constantly at war (wars were measured in decades or centuries – Thirty Years War, Hundred Years War). Religious influences were often useful tools to gain domestic allegiances, in order to unite against the threat of heretical forces from non-Christian religions from the Arab states and from Turkey. The struggles within Christendom – the Protestants of England and Prussia, the Catholics from France and Spain, and Austria – allowed Britain itself to reinforce this religious divide with severe penal laws that banned Catholics from virtually everything – holding public offices, owning property, voting, and entering most professions.

Absolutist governments reinforced their monarchical dominance by banning most foreign influences that affected every day life, and went far beyond differences in flag waving, use of language, stamps and the postal system, currency and banking, and military uniforms. Throughout Europe, countries expressly cultivated their own music, architecture, books, food and cuisine, drink, weapons, and heraldry. Ale houses, inns, driving on the left side of the road, sports, clothing - all these issues reflected social influences to highlight national differences. Scotland was a known example: curling, the bag pipes, the kilt, the Gaelic language, the clan hierarchy, haggis, and the poems of Robbie Burns illustrated the clannish notions of the states of Europe, including England, France, and Spain.

The ruling classes relished in these national differences, and used such distinctions in power politics to elevate the disruptive influences of foreign powers, foreign religions, and foreign institutions. Marriages were convenient alliances of states and families, with little to do with the marriage bed, raising families, or romantic issues of love. Well into the twentieth century, national differences pre-occupied Europe. The best example was transport where, unlike in the United States, for instance, which could boast of a single currency, a single language, and a single legal system, roads and railways integrated disparate regions and people. European roads (and later, trains) were built on purely national boundaries, often with different tracks and control systems, to make sure that countries weren't integrated. (It took Hitler, learning from Napoleon, to realize that continental highways were also continental means to transport troops and armor, supported with heavy armored tanks.)

But if the nation state and its attendant institutions was one domestic requirement, the question remained how European states could cope with the second requirement, namely co-existence. Three developments slowly emerged. The first was power politics, namely a balance of power where no one country dominated, or wars developed to suppress the power of a single country. Britain best developed this approach to the international order, in part because Britain was an Island, and it had the largest and most powerful navy to protect its trade and commerce. From the aggressive advances of Louis XIV, the Sun King, to Napoleon and Hitler, Britain cultivated strategic alliances to diminish the power of any one country – Spain under Queen Isabella, France constantly, Germany after reunification in 1870.

The second proposition, aggressively gleaned from Machiavelli's famous book, *The Prince*, was that nations were not bound by the same moral code as individuals. They could do what they had to, simply because it was in their own interest to protect their integrity and sovereignty. The essence of Machiavelli's dictum was the new doctrine of state rights – or *raison d'etat*. In the extreme, which was unfortunately quite common, states could pursue their own ends, including the pursuit of war, whether justified or not, a clear ethical dilemma raised by philosophers from St. Augustine to Thomas Aquinas. The third issue was that economic growth and development – in commercial affairs, in plunder, in land conquest, in advancing national glory – required financial and military strength. Clearly, with European states divided, there was little opportunity for economic and social intercourse across the Continent. But this meant that states could expand abroad, using new techniques of shipping, movement of armies and navies for overseas territories, and also helping spread Christianity. This meant colonization.

From the seventeen century, the large powers of England, France, and Spain, as well as lesser powers like Russia, Holland, Austria and Turkey spread their wings. China and India were the elusive targets because of their supposed riches (spices, silk, opium, gold, and silver) but according to mercantilist doctrine, they wanted to lace their treasuries with free booty from distant lands. There was a scientific component to the colonial game, because various fruits, vegetables, and resources – notably fish and tobacco, later cotton and wheat – added to the strength of the mother country.

Colonization and the development of empires had other advantages. Although most countries had absolute rulers, which controlled all aspects of taxation, patronage, and land (hence timber rights, important for ships, bridges, transport, and many aspects of agriculture), the ruling class was not homogeneous, mainly because of the influence of the Church. Before 1648, with the Peace of Westphalia, Christendom was a unifying force in Europe, and the influence of the Crusades was a war against other religions. Moreover, despite its temporal features, the Christian religions placed great emphasis on the individual, his identity and beliefs, his sins of commission and omission. In time, countries had two loyalties – a temporal order, where the clear winner was the nation state, not the Church, and the spiritual order, which retains its power even today. So powerful had the Church become that even when Christendom itself divided, between the Church of England in Britain, the Protestant sects of Martin Luther in Germany and John Knox in Scotland, temporal leaders were forced to deal with religious leaders, in part because of spiritual requirements over most aspects of peoples lives, but also because most religious leaders were the best educated, the closest to people's lives, and lived in the real world of family life.

In this sense, the temporal leaders living in their secular side of power and money politics had to share power with religious leaders and their spiritual world of beliefs, churches, and the will of God. In time, the aristocratic class consisted of monarchies or Tsars, the landed aristocrats, the Church, and the Military. Collectively or individually, they controlled the guilds and artisan professions – painters, bricklayers, shoemakers, carpentry, gunmakers. The vast dispossessed – the uneducated peasants - filled both countryside and cities with growing numbers, and lived in poverty, disease, and hunger. Their plight left few real options. Servitude was the natural lot, because they had to feed their families. From Ireland to Russia, they existed on a subsistence diet, often living off a single crop – the potato – on land owned by aristocrats living in splendid homes and castles, unburdened with the depths of their despair.

The peasants had another route, with equal grounding in poverty. It was to join the army or the navy. From the seventeenth century, European navies and associated merchant ships conscripted thousands of young peasants. They toiled in the docks as shipbuilders, supply hands to make ropes, sails, anchors, and canons, and a vast supply of sophisticated sailing rigs. The British navy, for three centuries the largest and most sophisticated, was a rigid hierarchy, starting with the British Admiralty in London, run just like farm estates, where orders went down and obedience went up, where recruits started young and died young, and where loyalty was imposed, not earned. Some captains were exceptions – James Cook and Horatio Nelson stand out - because they excelled at extracting enormous loyalty from officers and their men.

The European empires differed in their forms of political control, in all its facets. France was much more centralized, with key decisions made by the King and his *Intendents*. The British Empire controlled its colonies indirectly by imposing local governors, usually for a fixed term, always for patronage reasons, sometimes as a 'gift' for military achievements. All empires had a mercantile economic thrust, i.e. to gain wealth from colonial riches like gold, silver, or various addictions like spices, tobacco, opium, rum, tea, coffee. The colonies themselves usually had an important military dimension, especially ports, even more so when products required slave labour. In the seventeenth and eighteenth century, colonies were pawns on the chess board of empire, traded or exchanged based on military conquests or defeats in Europe, worth not a great deal more than what Voltaire said about the French giving up its North American colonies to England, the loss of "some acres of snow".

In the British case, the colonial empire had its mercantile features. Mercantilism as an economic system was especially true for Africa and India, and the North Atlantic fisheries. In North America, and specifically in the southern colonies, where slavery and the cotton trade linked the north and the textile factories of England, military and naval issues worked in tandem. It was not just a slogan so say that Britain ruled the waves. From the great voyages of Captain Cook to numerous scientific missions like William Bligh of the *Bounty*, Britain saw its colonies as territorial outposts to maintain naval supremacy, and as conduits to transport its armies. Ironically, Britain itself was never part of the British Empire: the various colonies were possessions of England, and were ruled separately. Each colony received administrative support from London; the colonies in turn sold products to London, were forced to use British ships, and lived off British laws and regulations imposed on the colonial system. Clearly, as the British Empire grew in wealth, stature, and military predominance, England surpassed all of Europe for two centuries. The history of any one British colony, even for the rich American colonies which grew wealthy because of the slave trade, reflects how Britain and especially the London-based aristocracy viewed their colonial possessions.

***

George III

*Queen Charlotte of Mecklenberg-Strelitz
(May 19, 1744 -November 17, 1818),
Consort to George III.*

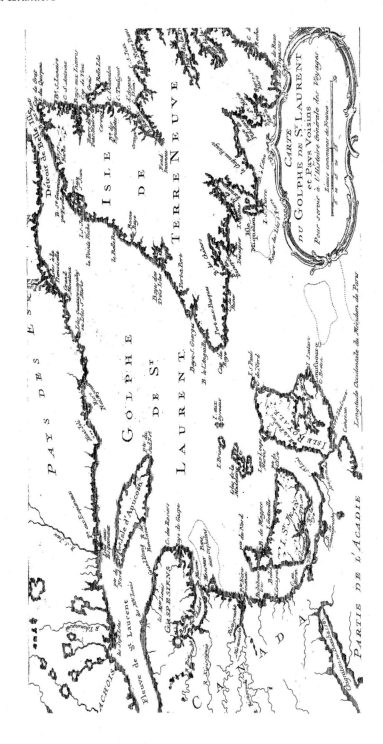

In North America, while Europe faced the Age of Revolution, it was the Age of Exploration on a grand scale. From the heights of Quebec City to the shores of Chesapeake Bay, the Atlantic seaboard states were extended south to the Gulf, westward to the Pacific, and north to the Arctic. On November 15, 1805, when the Lewis and Clark expedition reached the Pacific shore, Clark's often quoted words, "Ocean in view! O! the joy," had been mistakenly written a week earlier, in what is now Wahkiakum County, in the Pacific north west. It is now Washington State: wild, breezy country, and almost everything about the Northwest is wide, including the Columbia River itself, the mighty MacKenzie, and the roaming Saskatchewan across the Canadian prairies.

If Quebec became the center of the British Colonies, and Philadelphia the center of the American colonies, the Eastern seaboard is where the colonization truly began. The Mayflower, John Smith and Pocahontas, Champlain, Montcalm, the French and Indian Wars, Louisburg, Philadelphia, the Plains of Abraham, and Valley Forge and Yorkton, all are associated with the Atlantic landscapes. They cluster on the eastern side of the maps, French, British, American, or Spanish, where pirates, navies, rum runners, slave ships, and the mighty British Navy controlled the ports, the Atlantic Ocean, and the flow of ideas. From the days of Cabot and Cartier, explorers saw the one thing that Europe lacked, vast tracks of unexplored land, lands with mountains, land with plains, lands near rivers, lands heading in all directions, east, west, and north and south. These distances cultivated ideas so radically different from European circumstances. Geography and winter enforced ideas about separate government powers because no autocratic monarchies existed on the frontier. Ideas about equality under the law and individual liberty came from hardship, abundant land, and because everyone was an immigrant. Ideas about personal property came when land was the only currency that made people different.

Had Lewis and Clark gone in an Eastern direction, such signals would have been ominous, not uplifting; and indeed when they departed the teeming plains of buffalo, months of toilsome trekking and poor eating lay ahead. Yet they kept exploring, westward into the future. Like the French explorers, LaSalle, Jolliet, and Marquette, their journals are, for the most part, intensely optimistic. They were pursuing their happiness by demarcating the differences between the eastern seaboards of the Atlantic to the Western continental land mass. And what they mapped was indeed wide open. "I ascended to the top of the cut bluff this morning, from whence I had a most delightful view of the country," wrote Lewis a few months before reaching the Pacific, "the whole of which except the valley formed by the Missouri is void of timber or underbrush, exposing to the first glance of the spectator immense herds of buffalo, elk, deer and antelopes feeding in one common and boundless pasture." This was the unknown Continent of North America (North Dakota, actually); this was life itself, so completely different from Europe's aristocratic rule, crowded cities, indentured peoples.

On that mid-November day, two centuries behind new exploration to the solar system, Clark wrote, "Scarce of provisions, and torrents of rain pouring on us all the time." Private Joseph Whitehouse noted, "We are now in plain view of the Pacific Ocean, the waves rolling and the surf roaring very loud." What did he make of that fact? Did he exclaim his joy? Hardly. "We are now of the opinion," he continued matter of factly, "that we cannot go any further with our canoes, and think that we are at an end of our voyage to the Pacific Ocean." It was time now "withdraw a short distance up the river and provide ourselves with winter quarters." Winter, the bane of North America!

Was the Pacific the beginning of the end or merely the end of the beginning? North America has extended itself farther westward still, into Hawaii in the West, and Alaska and three Canadian territories in the North, bordering on Hudson's Bay, and southward to California and Texas, which were part of Mexico, torn by war from the Spanish in 1848. Curiously, if history had been different, British troops would have quelled the American revolt, but these British colonists were saved with French money and the French navy. All the same, the ocean marks a limit of sorts. "We cannot go any further with our canoes." And it is that generous North American spirit, attached to the land, the expanse of the mighty rivers – the Ohio and Mississippi, the St. Lawrence, the Mackenzie, the Columbia – that beckoned settlers, obscured European differences, populist nationalisms, religious vindictiveness. In this great expanse, small British colonies, French societies, and Spanish territories vied for wealth, territory, and conquest. One of the smallest, Prince Edward Island, peopled by French, English, Scottish, and Irish settlers, mostly poor and uneducated, is the story of political migration, from a small colony in the French territories belonging to Nova Scotia, then to a separate British Colony, and then, reluctantly, becoming the smallest province in the new nation of Canada, six years to the day after the Dominion of Canada's founding on July 1, 1867.

****

There are no statutes, no monuments, no plaques, and no memory of George III on Prince Edward Island. It is a curious lapse of memory, for no British monarch had more impact on PEI than George III. No monarch has been ignored in a colony so much as this King. There are monuments to Queen Victoria, government buildings and the hospital named after Queen Elizabeth II, and tributes to other Kings since Edward V. But not George III! Islanders, perhaps viewing their history from the prism of American history and all his alleged faults, real or imagined, as catalogued in the US Declaration of Independence, choose to ignore the historical significance of George III. Is the historic record so one-sided, against this complex king?

True, it was under his reign that the Island's territory, divided into 67 lots, hence the local word lottery, were 'auctioned' off on July 23, 1767 to 100 individuals. George III's patronage largesse truly defines the history of this period of Britain, the British Empire, and the North American colonies, which included the thirteen south of the 49th parallel. But the impact of geography is everywhere. It was under George III that the British colonies were surveyed, and PEI was the first of magnificent mapping by Samuel Holland, whose celebrated surveys and drawings allowed him to name almost 200 specific place names. His manuscript map, measuring about 8' by 5', still residing in London, is brilliantly detailed, and a work of art. So too does the demarcation of PEI – three counties - Prince, Queens, Kings - each divided into parishes, and place names of towns, hamlets, and the capital city, Charlottetown, plus Georgetown, Montague, O'Leary, Cavendish, and the main water bays, Egmont, Richmond, Hillsborough, and Cardigan, named after prominent members of George III's administration.

Samuel Holland, born Samuel Jan Holland in the Low Countries, served with the Dutch Army until 1755, and then transferred to British service in North America, starting in Halifax. At this port city, where the first planning of the attack of Louisburg took place, in part on the urgings of Governor William Shirley of Massachusetts, Holland toiled with another colleague, a brilliant cartographer, Joseph Frederick Wallet des Barres. He was a French Huguenot, meaning he was a Protestant, whose family departed from France, and received a commission in the Royal American Regiment. Together they compiled splendid surveys along the St. Lawrence, one inch to a mile, traveling on the ship, the *Canceaux*. So accurate were these surveys that they became critical to James Wolfe's capture of Quebec in 1759. (Montcalm's view of French maps was brutal: "... our best seamen or pilots seem to me either liars or ignoramuses.") One of Holland's close students of map-making, navigation tools, and surveying was James Cook, the sailing master of the *Pembrooke*, who learned the accuracy of map-makers, with their detailed and scientific examination of channels, water depth, ledges of rock, hazardous barriers, and landing places which could determine battles on land or at sea. History records that General James Wolfe, like James Cooke, were apt disciples of Holland's work.

Holland's surveys on the Island, building on the work of French maps, help describe the land settlements in PEI. The four decades of the French period of tenure, from 1719 to 1759, provided him with the superb drawings made of the Island's topography. The French had traveled widely and often adopted Mi'kmaqs (Micmac) names – *Cascumpec, Bedeque, and Melpeque.* In all, 46 names survive from the early French settlers: names like Belle River, deGros Marsh, DeSable River, Grand River, Morell, Pinette, Point Prim, Rustico, Savage Harbour, and Souris all reflect this French character. Sadly, as Andrew Clark notes, it is indeed regrettable that so many of the euphonious French names have been lost.

In August 1719, the first land grant was given to Comte Saint-Pierre. The first Commandant was Le Sieur de Gotteville de Bellisle, and the first priest on the Island, Rev. Réné Charles de Bresley, established the first Church, St. Jean l'Evangéliste at Port LaJoie. French settlements proceeded and reached 2,223, according to the first census, taken by Comte de Raymond, the Governor of Louisberg, which now controlled the colony from Isle Royale, now Cape Breton. Two treaties ended European wars, hence the division of the spoils in North America. The treaty of Aix-la-Chapelle in 1748 left mainland Nova Scotia to the British, and the founding of Halifax, the military port. The might of the British Navy would seal the loss of Louisburg, and soon after, under General James Wolfe, the fate of Quebec and the retreat of France from North America. The Treaty of Paris signed in 1763 turned over the French Maritime colonies of Acadia and Quebec to Britain.

When Captain Holland began his map-making in 1765, there were only 200-300 Acadians left on the Island. Holland himself named 191 places, many after prominent figures in King George III's administration: Amherst, Egmont, Murry, Carleton, Hillsborough, Howe, Cardigan, Percival, Wolfe, Rollo, Stanley, and Richmond. Other names would follow from notable British figures: Alberton, Cavendish, Derby, Gladstone, Roseberry, Victoria, Wellington, Churchill (the South African correspondent of 1900, not the British wartime prime minister of 1940), Primrose. Scotland, more than England, accounts for more place names, a function of the large, early settlements of Highland Scots: Afton Road, Annandale, Argyle Shore, Canavoy, Clyde River, Culloden, Dundee, Fort Augustus, Glengarry, Inverness, Keppoch, Kinlock, Montrose, New Glasgow, Scotchfort, and Strathgartney, are some of the 110 place names, but curiously some of the best known early names were dropped or changed: Glenaladale, Skyle Settlement, Gairloch, Gretna Green, Campbellton, or Raasa. Ireland, of course, provided a small number of names, including Belfast, Donagh, Irishtown, Kinkora, Monaghan, and Waterford. Regrettably, few Irish place names mirror the rolling pastureland of the Emerald Isle's own landscape, such as Loughaunenlugheask or SnuffhoconneclaghLough in Connemara from where so many Irish immigrants came to PEI.

Charlottetown itself is emblazoned with the kinship to George III. Like other North American colonial towns like Charlotte, North Carolina, the capital is named after George III's wife and consort, Queen Charlotte of Mecklenburg. Together, unlike many couples in the British monarchy, before or since, they had a very long and fruitful marriage of 45 years, fifteen children and numerous grandchildren. The first four governors - Patterson, Fanning, Desbarres, and Smith - were appointees of the royal patronage system and each contributed to place names and streets in Charlottetown: King, Queen, Prince, Sydney, Fitzroy, Euston, Great George, Dorchester, Cumberland, Pownal, Richmond, Weymouth all bear the hallmark of personages who adorned the high and mighty in the court of George III.

It is easy to castigate George III, as the Americans have done in their powerfully written Declaration of Independence. George III had a very long reign, and presided over great changes to Imperial Britain, with incessant wars with France, endless Whig infighting and political intrigue, economic and industrial transformation, especially the rise of manufacturing and urban life and, of course, the loss of America. George became the head of his family when he was only 22, and it is easy to forget that, despite his early reputation as someone who could scream across the corridors at Windsor Castle or chased ladies-in-waiting at Kew, he became a working monarch who steered Britain through five decades of turmoil, war, and political change. Despite his successful marriage, and a husband and father of earnest feeling, George III was not helped when the majority of his eight surviving siblings turned out to be a much ill-behaved family.

But many of the sins of George III were in fact the faults of the absolute monarchical government system throughout all of Europe. It was under George II, his grandfather (and the last British monarch to lead his troops in battle) that the absolute monarchical system began to change. There were numerous reasons, many inspired by events in Britain (the Revolution of 1688, the loss of the American colonies, the rights and prerogatives of the Royal Household, the rise of party affiliations in the House of Commons). There were also continuous antagonisms and conflicts within Britain based on land holdings and social privileges in Scotland and Ireland and, in general, grave misgivings by educated English men of the pure despotism of their Continental neighbours, where social, political, and religious aristocrats were largely divorced from the working class. Moreover, all the great writers of the Enlightenment could draw these class distinctions and looked to England and the moral contrast - Montesquieu and Voltaire, Rousseau and Beauchamais.

George III, despite his misgivings and his reliance on advisors like Bute, recognized the power of the House of Commons, the economic impact of the colonies (he was one of the first who wanted to avoid the *casus belli* of the American Revolution) and the rights of other religions, especially the Catholic faith. It is no accident that under George III, the constitutional Act of 1791, giving Quebec the right to practice its own religion and language, and enlisting powerful support of the French Cardinals and clergy, which included offering land to the French nobility in Prince Edward Island, show another side to this beleaguered but more pragmatic King.

In this sense, the early story of Prince Edward Island is the history of the life and times of George III. The colony was small, young, and dependent first upon Quebec and Louisburg under the French, and later London for its economic lifeblood. The basic institutions, namely the land grant system, its hierarchical administration centered on a Governor, and its economy as part of the imperial system set in motion how the colony would develop for the next 100 years. Unlike many of the American colonies, where leaders emerged to reject the British way of life, and to create their own institutions, including free land, free schooling, private universities, and responsible government, Prince Edward Island incorporated English institutions and English values. These included the paramount strength of English patronage, the English Church, a mercantilist view of economic life, and strict orthodoxy against democratic openness. Like most of the new British colonies in North America required, and what Prince Edward Island needed most, was people. Fortunately, the reign of George III created the conditions for emigration, and the emergence of a new land entrepreneur, Thomas Douglas, the Fifth Earl of Selkirk.

2

Early Settlements and the Colony of Thomas Douglas, Lord Selkirk

European Rivalry * Thomas Malthus * Scotland-A Land In
Trouble * Thomas Douglas * The Scottish Enlightenment *
Scotland's Clearances And Immigration
* The Polly and Prince Edward Island

As the new century dawned on Europe, a retrospection of the last hundred years would give many British some pause towards their future. The imported German Kings, George I and II, hardly spoke the English language, and the current king, George III, had gone mad, talking to a tree as the King of Prussia or reading Shakespeare's *King Lear*. Parliament was in a constant crisis. The American colonies were lost. The French Revolution deposed the monarchy, crippled its Church, and left French finances in anarchy. Napoleon now dominated the Directory in a post-revolutionary France, which had previously lacked a foreign policy because it couldn't afford one. Military rule was the result, and the Emperor wanted to dominate Europe, imposing the Continental System to blockade British trade. But events in the new century were unfolding in strange ways. So too for the small British colony, nestled in the Gulf of St. Lawrence, now renamed Prince Edward Island, after Crown Prince Edward.

At the start of the 1800s, Britain was retreating from Europe and becoming an imperial power. Her strength was not in land armies, which she was never especially good at. The Revolutionary War in the Americas proved that, as would future wars. But the world indeed was changing. If the eighteenth century was a global power struggle for empire, pitting Britain against France, like the previous century pitted Catholic Spain against Protestant Britain, naval power, not land wars, gave the British Empire unparalleled influence. Her Empire controlled all the key ports, what became known as the Rule of Seven, including the port of Halifax to guard trade in the North Atlantic, and Jamaica in the Caribbean. At home, despite the Continental blockade in Europe, the British economy was booming. The industrial revolution had commenced. Steam engines powered machinery that were starting to turn Britain from a nation where wealth came from land to a nation where wealth came from industrial exports.

Britain had other advantages. British industry had the key raw materials at home to foster the industrial revolution, starting in the textile factories of the north. The British navy, despite Winston Churchill's misleading comment about 'rum, sodomy, and the lash' was the only significant institution – though some might argue for the Church of England - that was organized with merit, discipline, and strategic considerations. The more the navy expanded, the easier it was to expand trade for British addictions – tobacco, pepper and various spices, tea, opium, sugar, and coffee. And the growth of the navy meant vast employment opportunities, including the need for timber, copper, and planks, all of which Canada could supply in abundance. And more ships meant more tracking of shipping, hence the growth in banking to capitalize shipyards, companies like Lloyd's to insure ships and cargo, and land transport to allow industry to export capital goods to England's port cities and towns.

Across the Atlantic, the new century revealed that slow political divorce was taking hold. The loss of the American Colonies, and war between the Americans and the British in 1812, could slow down the domination of England and her Atlantic colonies in Quebec, the Maritimes, and the Caribbean. Since 1799, George Washington had been acknowledged to have been "first in war, first in peace, and first in the hearts of his countrymen." Britain, now at war with France, fighting battles on land with Napoleon and sea battles in the Mediterranean, the Nile, the Caribbean with bigger ships and seasoned seamen, now dominated the oceans. At first blush, the American tirades on the 'democratic deficit', represented by the principle of 'taxation without representation' were directed at the British monarchy and George III in particular. In reality, these attacks had long lasting and unintended consequences for Britain and the British Empire. The loss of the American colonies had little direct economic consequence, but Britain decided to build a second empire, the Prime Minister and such key Cabinet positions as the Minister of Finance (and British banking) and the Foreign Secretary and such instruments as the British Admiralty and the Royal Navy. Even more paradoxically, the nineteen century would strengthen the British monarchy as never before – indeed, for most of the century, the whole world looked to Britain as the pre-eminent imperial power. Indeed, it was called the Victorian Era.

In North America, four countries fought for influence. Spain controlled Mexico and the Spanish provinces of California and Texas. The USA, representing the thirteen colonies but eyeing the great plains to the West, resented Britain's inclusion of the Ohio Valley with Quebec in the controversial Constitution Act of 1791, which protected the French language, religion, and culture of Quebec. The US learned from Britain how to become an imperial power, coveting the lands to the West, the south (Florida and the Louisiana Territories) and the British colonies to the North. From 1794, the Americans, judiciously using both France and Britain to advance her imperial cause, expanded her boundaries with border settlements with Florida and Canada, opened the Mississippi River for internal trade, and established commercial interests in the West Indies.

At the same time, the Americans, led by Franklin, Adams, Jefferson, and, of course, Washington, started plans to cultivate American institutions – universities, science, banking, a navy, and even a form of American English. When Noah Webster published *A Compendious Dictionary of the English Language*, he attempted to help shape the culture of the nation America would become. Webster was a brilliant polymath, in the style of Ben Franklin. When the USA was formed, British culture was still dominant. Outside government, most of the key institutions were copies from Britain or the Scottish Enlightenment. For people like Ben Franklin, it was imperative to steer clear of British rule, British habits, British culture, even if it was not yet clear what it meant to be American. Webster thought it was vital to shake off "foreign manners" and build an independent national culture. "Nothing can be more ridiculous," he wrote, "than a servile imitation of the manners, the language and the vices of foreigners." Webster Americanized British spellings in Samuel Johnson's famous dictionary, turning "defence" and "honour" into "defense" and "honor," and dropped the "k" from "musick." He added new American words like "subsidize" and "caucus," and left out hoary Britishisms like "fishefy." John Quincy Adams, son of President John Adams and a future president, was aghast by these "local vulgarisms," and doubted that Harvard, where he was a trustee, would ever endorse such a radical "departure from the English language."

France occupied the lands of the Louisianan Territories, but they were largely unpopulated and poorly administered. The sad exile of the Acadians in the Maritimes, some 7000 immigrants from Nova Scotia and New Brunswick, about 500 from Prince Edward Island, the first case of ethnic cleansing in modern colonial rule, left these families isolated in the woods of Maine, removed to Louisiana, or sent back to the Brittany areas of France. Napoleon dreamed of combining his French territories of North America with the Spanish-occupied lands of Mexico and Florida as a way to rebuild the commercial glories of Louis XIV, but to do that, he needed a powerful French navy. When Britain lost the war against the American rebels, who were aided by French naval forces at Yorkton in October 1781, just when it counted, the Royal Navy regrouped its operations, and infused its code towards a relentless will to win. Even Napoleon, who once saw his future as a naval commander, and even contemplated joining the Royal Navy, knew from direct military experience, as he later admitted, the "staggering destructive power of a British ship of the line in action."

With the resumption of war with the French, starting in 1793 as an outgrowth of the French Revolution, the Royal Navy cultivated a ferocious desire for total victory, and its ruthless killer instinct. The British Admiralty was aided by a brilliant set of naval commanders who knew seamanship and ship handling, aided by new signaling tools like Home Popham's magnificent flag signs, telegraphic signals or marine vocabulary, the Blackberry of its day, an instrument of profound naval advantage to a commander like Horatio Nelson, who absorbed intelligence with the compulsion of an addict. By this time, France was outgunned, outmaneuvered, and outclassed by larger ships, heavier canons, and superior military commanders, from Horatio Nelson in the 18th century to Jack Fisher in the 19th. The French, facing successive naval defeats in Egypt, the Mediterranean, and Quiberon Bay in France, ensured that French rule in North America was over for good. The French settlements in the British colonies, holdovers from the immigration settlement policies of Louis XIV and the *ancient régime*, were now abandoned by France and left to fend for themselves, a pattern that was to extend to most French émigrés throughout the world into the twentieth century.

The fourth country looking at North America as the new century dawned was Britain. France remained the major perceived military threat, long after she was no longer a rival. From Pitt to Canning, the British remained convinced that France was the only real threat to the British Empire, even if it meant conspiring with the Americans to keep Europe out of the Western Hemisphere. Napoleon himself understood the consequence of the Louisiana Purchase: "This accession of Territory affirms forever the power of the United States, and I have just given England a maritime power that soon or later will lay low her pride." Across the Atlantic, London's military concerns were brutally simple: keep the Americans down, the French out, and the British colonies in. The *Quebec Act* gave a certitude that French Canadians, despite military threats by the Americans, would remain on the side of Britain. The United Empire Loyalists, perhaps 100,000 people, located on free lands in Ontario and New Brunswick, would strengthen the British colonies. Halifax became the great naval base, designed by British engineers to take advantage of a fabulous natural deep water port and capital of Nova Scotia, the first North American colony to exercise responsible government.

But in Imperial Britain, not all was well in the United Kingdom. The problem was not in the port cities, of which there were thirteen, with their rising wealth, population, and bustling trade, led by London, Liverpool, and the naval bastion, Portsmouth, but in the North. The very far north, in the Highlands of Scotland.

**

"It was the best of times and the worst of times." So wrote Charles Dickens in his great story, *Tale of Two Cities,* a novel about the French Revolution. But he could be writing about Scotland and the horrible turmoil in the Highlands. Scotland in 1800 was a land in trouble. The United Kingdom, as it became known after the Union Act of 1707, when England and Scotland were joined, was anything but united. Extermination, eviction, and subjugation were the rule for the clans of the Scottish Highlands. Wars, rebellions, and Jacobite uprisings, first in 1715, then again in 1745, uprooted the clan structure of Scotland and transformed the society out of all recognition. It was called the Highland clearances. Conflicts between the Catholics of Mary Queen of Scots, the Jacobins, and the land-owning Protestants loyal to Elizabeth I produced civil wars. Clearly, disruptions and obvious difficulties from the religious scars, the uprising of Bonnie Prince Charlie in 1745, the Catholic son of Mary Queen of Scots, supported by the French, created backlash in defense of the English throne. But in truth, Scotland was at war with itself – the Highlands and adjacent islands had too many people on too much barren land, with far more four footed creatures called sheep than two footed animals called tenant farmers. Something had to give.

Was Thomas Malthus right when he concluded in *An Essay on the Principle of Population* that "the power of population is indefinitely greater than the power in the earth to produce subsistence for man"? The consequence, he believed, was starvation, vice, belligerence and misery. Malthus, an Anglican minister who became Britain's first Chair in Political Economy and helped train future employees at East India College for the East India Company (perhaps the first corporate university in modern history), was responding to the great prophets of technology, the perfectibility of man, social progress, and self-reliance. The American and French Revolutions were practical advances on the keys to the Enlightenment, and the chattering classes – in the coffee houses in London and Paris and the social clubs of Edinburgh - were all discussing the poor, the illiterate, and the expanding population. Malthus had forecast a population crisis, based on his calculations about babies and wheat yields: babies can make more babies, but each grain harvest leaves less land to cultivate more grain harvests. Malthus was asking serious questions: was over-population a crisis for landowners, for the aristocrats, for the Church, all of whom shared acres and acres of unattended land, with brooks and streams of teeming fish, and most peasants living on starvation diets?

This issue of land was not an idle question. The Irish rebellion of 1798 showed just how serious a starving population could upset a political order. Across the channel, the French Revolution became well documented, even more so when acts of God, from cold winters to rainy summers, could spoil the wheat crops and lead to food inflation. Some doctors in France also thought there was an additional complication of foul flour in the bread supply. France, like Ireland, showed another problem: in Dublin and Paris, thousands of peasants lived in the large cities, while aristocrats lived in the country. In Versailles, outside Paris, Louis XVI and Marie Antoinette lived in golden splendour, and they had to face peasant revolts from Paris, led mostly by women. In short, peasant starvation was the economic crisis of Europe, and each peasant rebellion had at its heart the dilemma of too many people, and too little food.

The population problem was the real issue to address, not the social order, the method of government, the entitlements of the rich. In Britain, the government had centuries of practice and legitimacy, based around the Monarchy, the Aristocracy, and the Military. There was some sense of Parliamentary government, when the aristocracy had to surrender certain powers to the House of Commons, but on most issues, the House of Commons and the House of Lords acted in concert, even more so when so many seats in the Commons were held by 'elected' MPs from rotten boroughs (eventually abolished in the 1832 reform bill). Unlike North America, Britain and most of Europe had a simple division: those few who owned most of the land, and those who were dependent on the land owners. Land, of course, was more than a piece of property. On land, all else flowed, from the timber for construction of homes and military vessels to all food production, and all the associated career streams, from skilled jobs of artisans, shipbuilders, furniture makers, to back-breaking jobs on the farm, indentured tenant farmers, to the low paid workers on His Majesty's Navy. Then, of course, there was also the army, a mix of low pay and a short life span.

Clearly, the issue of religion was not the main factor, either in Britain or in Ireland, since it was accepted that on all matters real, the Church of England was paramount. For the landed gentry, the political issue was the form of social order, and how best to feed the economic machine that kept the wealthy, well wealthy. Disease, poverty, starvation, and the military each did their part to hold down the peasant population, but it was hardly enough. What should be done with the Irish, the Scottish or the French peasants, and to restrain them from open rebellion? Even worse, how could the British prevent the French from invading England through Irish ports? What lessons from America did England learn about colonial rule, and the need to prevent Canada or the West Indian islands from seceding like the rebellious Americans?

Throughout Europe, agricultural slavery meant that the peasants lived off the land as tenant farmers: they could look after tracts of land but most of the profits went to the landlords. The land policies might differ – Ireland was the worst, because the land had too many families living off a single crop, potatoes. But the broad sweep of how the lands were administered, who controlled the crops, who were the preferred families – these issues were the exclusive decisions of the landlords and the aristocracy. In Scotland after 1745, the Highland Clearances largely destroyed the old clan system. More than a quarter of the population was cleared from land holdings. Except for wood products, the most valuable holdings were deer and sheep, so farmers and their families were displaced.

Curiously, it was never clear what should be done with the peasants. Scottish peasants made great soldiers – generally speaking, they were fit physically, they were available in abundance, and Britain needed soldiers for her many wars – with Spain, with France, with Prussia, with America. Starvation, of course, was an option – it worked in Ireland – and a move to the cities was also an alternative, but that could be dangerous, as the French Revolution had shown. Then there was emigration, a preferred choice for some Highlanders who left for the Carolinas.

Britain was slowly evaluating her British possessions in North America, while preserving her Caribbean islands – important for sugar, spice, rum and military ports. The Canadian colonies, brilliantly explored and well mapped by the French regime, had abundant land, fish, minerals, and valuables like fur. What Canada didn't have was people: a few remnants of the French Regime outside Quebec who hadn't been deported in an insane act of ethnic cleansing, the colony of New France with a population of about 60,000, another 100,000 loyalists from the American colonies, the local natives, and a smattering of British military posts. The United States had settled with Britain, signed a peace treaty with France's Napoleon, and settled in an era of doing what the quiet Americans do best, making money. Europe's trouble spots – London facing a Regency for the mad King George, Napoleon ruling France after the Reign of Terror, Austria faced with monarchical ambitions from Russia and Germany – opened up huge prospects for a growing population in the United States, which was doubling its population base every ten years, and was now bigger in land than all of Europe.

In short, what the British colonies in Canada needed was people. Lots of them. And Britain had plenty to spare, the castaways of the Highlands of Scotland, now that the land had been cleared for sheep, or the destitute of Ireland, where hunger, poverty and in-breeding was swelling the population by the millions. Perhaps the British people, as Adam Smith and James Boswell were to write, could be persuaded that losing the American colonists was one thing, but Britain had gained Canada from the French and Canada had vast territories, farm land, fishing, and animals of all description, and the new military base, like India, of her Second Empire.

In 1803, when a young Thomas Douglas, the fifth Earl of Selkirk was recruiting families in the Scottish Highlands to emigrate to his new land settlements in Canada, he was fully aware of population pressures in Scotland; indeed, his book, *The Highlands of Scotland,* sets out the very conditions that made change inevitable. His own solution was different: emigration. To Selkirk, Europe was a land in trouble, with Louis XVI and Marie Antoinette facing the guillotine, France and Britain at war, and Britain's loss of her American real estate due to the foolish King in London and his incompetent military advisors. The King was soon to become very foolish: in fact, he was to lose his mind. There would be five new Prime Ministers before the defeat of Napoleon in 1815 and Europe was to be awash in flames, terror, and starvation, as the Emperor sought European domination from the Pyrenees to the Urals. Selkirk's model was his settlements in Prince Edward Island.

***

Thomas Douglas-Earl of Selkirk

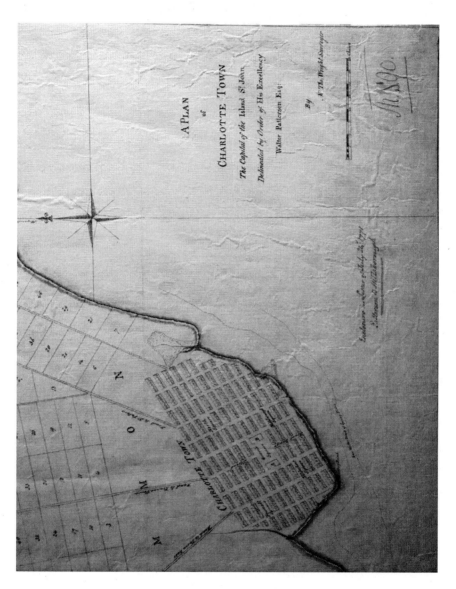

1771 Plan for Charlotte Town

The young Thomas Douglas – he was only 24 when he began his emigration plans for Canada, but then William Pitt became Prime Minister at 24 – was well traveled, and for his time, very educated. He had traveled not only throughout Britain and Ireland, but also Europe – France, Austria, Italy. Many people noted the obvious, the perilous political structures of entrenched monarchies, their aristocratic allies and their domination of land, the powerful role of the Church, with its control of vast land holdings. The French Revolution brought home to all of Europe just how vulnerable were the European monarchies and the supreme dangers of agricultural slavery. The tenanted peasants could indeed revolt, as the French Revolution had demonstrated. In the end, the peasants had one great advantage over the aristocracy: they had more people.

It was in these circumstances that Thomas Douglas, the fifth Earl of Selkirk, surveyed his new real estate in the Island colony. Through the Treat of Paris signed on February 10, 1763, King George III issued a Royal Proclamation dated October 7 annexing the Island of St. John and Cape Breton to Nova Scotia and a general survey of British North America was ordered. As a British possession, the Island was governed by the established church, the Church of England. By 1769, St. John's Island was made a separate colony from Nova Scotia, mainly on the landowners' urging. The British side of the Island's history was to unfold for the next 104 years.

Samuel Jan Holland
Major and Survey-General

The definitive map of PEI started with Captain Samuel Holland, who arrived on October 5, 1764. As already noted, Captain Holland with a team of engineers and surveyors (helped by Acadian guides), surveyed the Island in considerable detail, including the weather, pests, the rivers, harbors, the people, and the land acreage. He named almost 200 places, and his nomenclature includes well known French names that survive to this day. Perhaps he was inhibited by political correctness, prudery, or legal niceties. Unfortunately, there are few risqué place names, like Dimple Hole in New York, or Dildo or Gayside in Newfoundland, or Whorehouse Meadow in Oregon, not because Holland was a stickler for correct form, which he was, but because few Island place names had the advantage of the chance to cultivate political incorrectness. That was left to others, like politicians. As noted, Holland's survey and maps divided the Island into three counties - Prince, Queens and Kings, each subdivided into 20,000 acre lots, plus townships and parishes.

When the Island of St. John was established as a separate colony, an Order in Council stipulated that 'one hundred pounds be apportioned for the stipend of a clergyman'. The first Rector of the Parish of Charlottetown, the Rev. John Caulfield, held the position for four years. Like many landowners, he never set foot in the colony. Between 1768 and 1773, the Rev. John Eagleson spent time on the Island as a missionary for the Society for the Propagation of the Gospel. Theophilus Desbrisay became the rector of the parish in 1774. The next year, American privateers, after their attempts to plunder Charlottetown, took Desbrisay as a prisoner, but soon released him with no possessions. When he returned to Charlottetown, Desbrisey discovered he had no provisions, no salary, and no church. Dispite these forays to build a Protestant foothold on the Island, the Church of England did control church practices, including marriages, death services, and other rites, despite the presence of other religions, mainly Catholic, mostly Acadian families residing near Malpeque.

In England, the young George III was facing the first of many crises of his reign. Within seven years, from April 1763 to January 1770, five men held the office of Prime Minister: Grenville, the Duke of Cumberland, the Marques of Rockingham, William Pitt The Elder and the Duke of Grafton. It was an age of enormous political patronage, personal and financial, crown and parliamentary. In theory, the King controlled the court, the church, and the Army, and thus key matters of appointments, finances, land conveyances, and royal alliances. The Prime Minister's personal patronage was equally large, centered on privileges for parliamentary support, mainly through cabinet appointments and control of revenues.

Within this gluttony of political intrigue in London, the British Government accepted a plan for the Lords Commissions of Trade and Plantations to 100 individuals, fortunate by patronage and not by merit, gaining access to Prince Edward Island lots. In one short day, July 23, 1767, the Island's fate was determined by a lottery. An English novelist could write, in a rhyme as applicable today as then:

> *A lottery is a taxation*
> *Upon all the fools in creation*
> *And heaven be praised It is easily raised*
> *Credulity's always in fashion.*

George III's executive jobbery turned political direction away from Parliament to shameless control of all aspects of Britain and the Empire. It was a system bound by European political cross currents - the Magna Carta, the French concept of liberty, the rise of Parliamentary cabinet government, against the privileged royalty where one King lost his head, a second his throne, the third his American colonies. Notable voices saw through this chain of events - from Edmund Burke to Charles James Fox - and their appeals saw resonance in British North America, starting in Boston and cultivated in Philadelphia, particularly by the pen and voice of Ben Franklin.

Paradoxically, the early British Colonies were spared the worst excesses of George III's crass patronage and Royal sinecures. The 1774 Quebec Act provided great security of language and religion in Quebec, while new government brought a semblance of law and order with military establishments in Montreal, Halifax, St. John and Charlottetown. Despite the loss of the American colonies, together with William Pitt's initiatives - the abolition of slavery, reform of public finance, reduction of customs duties, Catholic Emancipation, and control over the House of Lords, the American Revolution had other consequences for Britain. There was the rise of a rejuvenated and powerful British navy, new technologies at home, and the shift of economic life from farm to cities. The transformation from agriculture to industry accelerated Britain's new heyday, while Europe by contrast was bonded by feudalism, absolute monarchy, and medieval guilds. But thanks to new industrial machinery, the power of her navy, the strengths of the London financial market, Britain was becoming a global superpower.

****

Eighteen century Scotland established many of the basic attitudes of modern Prince Edward Island. For 150 years, perhaps starting with the 1696 School Act, providing free and rudimentary schools and teachers, Scotland developed the tools and institutions for modern society - perhaps the first nation to do so. From schools and universities to the law courts and medical centers, Scotland cultivated an artistic and literary age that brought forth a powerful range of thinkers and doers - David Hume, Adam Smith, and Walter Scott, plus a host of intellectuals who frequented such social clubs as the Oyster Club, The Mirror Club, and the Select Society. Edinburgh and Glasgow teamed with this intellectual set, known and supported by a host of inventors (James Watt), scholars (John Millar), ministers (Adam Ferguson) and architects (Robert Adam).

The Scottish Enlightenment took old ways and refined them into new and fresh thinking. Pioneering philosophical tracts were slowly transforming Scotland, England and eventually the world, including North America. Smith's *Wealth of Nations*, and David Hume's *Theory of Moral Sentiments* brought together new ideas of individual virtue and societal enlightenment. Scottish history, English civilization, German enlightenment, the French Revolution, the American Continental Congress – this new thinking and political philosophies spirited the polite conversations in Edinburgh social clubs, and in the *Edinburgh Review*. Intellectually, they had influential friends, in government, in the military, and among erudite clergyman, who believed that a solid religious foundation needed a free and open society. A Spanish Jesuit, Francisco Suarez, had challenged the divine right of Kings; French aristocrats and military patriots like the Marquis Marie Jean Gilbert de Lafayette knew from the American revolution that rebels could develop a new political system, and observing that the cost of a grand ball at the court of Versailles would equip an entire regiment in America.

Into this world of Scottish ideas were three people as different from each other as their namesake. But they had similar core ideas and one in particular would influence PEI for 200 years. On June 25, 1759, in a small hamlet of Ayr Loch Lea, in a two room hut - a kitchen and a parlor, Scotland produced its most enduring bard. The words of Colonel Richard G. Ingersall, a pilgrim at Ayr, show his appreciation:

> *And yet I start within this room*
> *And fold all things in scorn*
> *For here, beneath this lovely thatch,*
> *Love's sweetest bard was born.*
> *And here the world, through all the years,*
> *As long as day returns,*
> *The tribute gets love and tears*
> *Will pay to Robert Burns.*

Twenty miles due west of Ayr, on December 4, 1795, in the village of Ecclefechan (near Dumfries), was born Thomas Carlyle. This small house was built by his father, a stone mason, just like Robert Burn's father William. The young Carlyle moved to the University of Edinburgh to prepare for divinity and to teach mathematics. He took up teaching and turned to writing, translating Goethe's *Wilhelm Minister* and a book on the German Fatherland's *Life of Schiller*. He was a private tutor for 200 pounds per year in Kirkaldy to Charles Buller. This student became a politician and belonged to the family of General Revers Buller, who later traveled to South Africa on the *Dunottar Castle*, a Castle Line ship as Commander in Chief of British Forces. His travel companion on the steamer was Winston Churchill. Charles Buller had his own claim to fame, possibly as the writer of the Durham Report. But that is getting ahead of the story.

Carlyle had a long career ahead - writing books on the French Revolution, a biography of Frederick The Great, and Oliver Cromwell. In *Past and Present* (1843) he attacked political and social conditions in England, a forerunner of the Victorian squalor themes of Charles Dickens. At Craigenputtock, Carlyle wrote his work on Robert Burns, part of which first appeared in the *Edinburgh Review*. Throughout his life, Carlyle was tormented by dyspepsia, a digestive ailment. Until his work, *The History of the French Revolution*, he faced financial burdens. Carlyle married in 1826. His wife was Jane Welsh, daughter of a Scottish physician. His first love was Margaret Gordon, whom he met when he was a school teacher and math tutor, in Kirkcaldy. She was nineteen; he was twenty-two. Margaret Gordon reminded Carlyle of his mother, self taught, with rare ability and an excellent talker.

Margaret and her sister Mary, despite their age, were well traveled. She was born in Charlottetown, P.E.I.; her grandparents were Margaret Hyde and Walter Patterson, PEI's first Governor. Her father was Dr. Alexander Gordon, one of PEI's first doctors. She was baptized on September 30, 1799 at St. Paul's Anglican Church in Charlottetown. Her father was moved to Halifax, but his regiment was reduced, and so was his salary, so he returned to England, but died on board the ship. Margaret and Mary went to Scotland with their aunt, Mrs. Usher. This guardian aunt was less impressed with the young Thomas Carlyle, whose fortune was likely to be typical of many teachers. Carlyle, himself, wrote about Margaret in his masterpiece, *Sartor Resartus*:

> *By far the cleverest and brightest, however, an ex-pupil of Irving's and genealogically and otherwise (being poorish, proud and well-bred) rather a kind of alien in the place, I did make acquaintance with (at Irving's first, I think though she came thither); some acquaintance; and it might have been more, had she, and her Aunt, and our economic and other circumstances liked! ...*

> *She was of the Aberdeenshire Gordons, a far-off Huntly I doubt not, "Margaret Gordon," born I think*

in New Brunswick where he father probably in some official post, had died young and poor – her accent was pretty English, and her voice very fine: - an aunt (widow in Fife, childless, with limited resources but of frugal, cultivated turn; a lean, proud, elderly dame, once a "Miss Gordon" herself, sang Scots songs beautifully and talked shrewd Aberdeenish in accent and otherwise) had adopted her and brought her hither over seas, and here as Irving's ex-pupil, she now cheery though with dim outlooks, was.

But Margaret, perhaps seeing Thomas' financial position, married a distant relative, Alexander "Sandy" Bannerman, son of a prosperous wine merchant, banker and wholesale merchant in Aberdeen. Prince Edward Island had not seen the last of this couple. Bannerman would return to the Island Colony as Lieutenant-Governor in 1851. Margaret was coming home. Carlyle's wife was not so lucky. In 1856, she would write: "I married for ambition; Carlyle has exceeded all that my wildest hopes ever imagined for him, and I am wretched."

To this group of "radical imperialists" or "colonial reformers" was a man who predated radical thinking in London. Indeed, if anything the loss of the American colonies under George III led to typical retrogression and cost cutting. For a century, Britain had two principal secretaries of state - one for southern Europe, one for northern Europe. In 1768, Britain added a third secretary, the Secretary of State for the American Department; the cabinet member become president or the first Lord of the Board of Trade. By 1782, with the loss of the American colonies, the Board of Trade was abolished. The Northern department became the Foreign Office, the Southern became the Home Office in charge of Ireland and the colonies. It retained the old Board of Trade and Plantations. It was a recognized custom to allow secretaries of state to manage patronage on a grand order - rich sinecures where real duties were to provide advantages for office holders. While new legislation passed Parliament in 1782, abuses were ignored from the past and more evaded in the future. This administrative nightmare was the context within which Lord Selkirk's plans for Canada were born.

Selkirk had a friendship with Edward Gibbon Wakefield, who was interested in land issues in the colonies, including in Australia, where he experienced immigration problems from a jailhouse in Newgate. Wakefield was the first of the colonial radicals, who regarded emigration as the key to success of the colonial empire. In 1837, Wakefield founded the New Zealand Association as a means to bring immigrants to match the growth in Australia, where the population surged from 130,000 in 1840 to over a million 20 years later. Buller, a close associate of Wakefield, became a member of the House of Commons, wrote the classic *Responsible Government in the Colonies,* and became secretary to Lord Durham. Indeed one fabricated rumour was that the Durham Report reflected the proposition that "Wakefield thought it, Buller wrote it, and Durham signed it."

Lord Selkirk's schemes for highland settlement in Canada had to be seen in a large canvas of political intrigue in London. By this time, Britain was at war with France led not by a Monarch but by a young, aggressive, and flamboyant Corsican, Napoleon Bonaparte. This was truly a new, global war, fought on many fronts beyond Europe, stretching across the British Empire in North America, the West Indies, Africa and India. It was total war that engaged all levels of British society, including the last years of George III and five successive Prime Ministers. The American Colonial war had shown Britain the real costs of empire - in treasury and in blood. At the turn of the 18th century, Britain was an economic mess, fighting expensive wars abroad. The French were soon to dominate the European continent under Napoleon, whose conquest were almost a direct copy of Hitler 150 years later. Britain was forced to go off the gold standard, while cash payments were suspended at the Bank of England, and rebellion and mob rule were a constant threat. Edmund Burke's treatise on the French Revolution and its reign of terror was a constant reminder of that country's slide into a calamitous abyss. Carlyle expressed the same warnings. After all, Queen Charlotte in 1796 was struck by a stone coming out of a theatre.

Within Britain, there was an age-old political debate: was Britain a great power because she had a colonial empire, or did she become a world power through the acquisition of colonies? Who was to pay for this greatness, in treasury, soldiers, and the Royal Navy? The American colonial experiment brought these issues into London with exceptional clarity. Edmond Burke's economic reforms through the Civil List Act had advanced Parliament's role in royal finance and control of patronage. Ironically, most of the reforms did not produce many serious results, except the number of places for Parliament - rich people who wanted the emoluments of office without the work or responsibility. As a solicitation with a seat on the Board of Trade had written: "a double list of candidates and clamorous for half the number of desirable places." With his own position abolished, the Solicitor retired to Lausanne to write his famous thesis: Edward Gibbon's, *The Decline and Fall of the Roman Empire.*

Parliament attempted to deal with institutions across the Empire, from India and the East India Company, to Canada and the Hudson's Bay Company. But it was Ireland that took hold of Britain's concerns. In 1785, as an apostle of free trade, Pitt wanted to complete trade and economic freedom through a link between Ireland and the British Isles. This proposal passed Ireland's Parliament but the English House of Common's defeated it. Pitt vacillated, Ireland drifted, and Wolfe Tone, the first modern Irish patriot, called for freedom. The Irish Parliament had been granted legislative independence in 1782. In 1793, this Parliament granted emancipation to Catholics and allowed them to hold military and civilian offices. The Irish - Protestants and Catholics alike - were fully aware of the American Rebellion – what America had achieved, Ireland could achieve. King George was tolerant - he had permitted the Canada Act of 1791 granting the freedom of religion in Quebec, a successor to the changes introduced in 1774. Indeed, he had given a secret pension to a French Cardinal during France's Reign of Terror. But George III was not that tolerant: the House of Hanover was committed to his oath to preserve the rights of the Church of England. Indeed, a statute passed in the reign of George III expressly kept Catholics banished from most positions of authority under the crown.

In reality, the King's veto was the real feeling throughout Britain and even Pitt knew emancipation would not pass the House of Commons. Told that emancipation for Catholics might apply to executive positions but not legislative, George III could respond: "None of your Scotch metaphysics" Like taxation of the American colonies a generation ago, Catholic emancipation for Ireland was not the only source of complaint against London. In the end, while the crown and its patronage suffered, the King's strengths rose. Pitt resigned. He was dead by 1806; it took four Prime Ministers to gain a peace treaty with Napoleon. By 1815 Britain found herself much like she experienced in 1945 - a country with an Empire, with great fear and envy, a country of lost hopes and overwhelming difficulties.

****

This was the political and social environment facing Selkirk when he entered Parliament as a Scottish representative peer, only one of 16 to do so. Ireland was the order of the day; French domination was the order of the battle. To gain favour in London, where Scottish earls were far down the pecking order – legacies of support for the Catholic prince, Charles Edward Stewart, Bonnie Prince Charlie in 1745 - Selkirk pushed initiatives to transfer Irish citizens to North American, such as Louisiana. But Ireland was no longer an acceptable focus, despite the population of four million living in the worst poverty within Europe, exporting some three quarters of a million pounds in land rents for absentee British landlords.

But the British government was not against some Scottish emigration, away from Louisiana or the Carolinas, or possibly towards Upper Canada. Lord Robert Hobart, Secretary of State for War and the Colonies, who would become the 4th Earl of Buckinghamshire, who was only too aware of landowner sentiments in Scotland, withdrew support for settlements in Upper Canada but allowed Selkirk's plans for Prince Edward Island. In contrast to many of the early settlers to the Carolinas and Pennsylvania, the 1803 Passenger Act required more daily rations per passenger on ships, and more space per tonnage. Selkirk had to be careful about his recruitment methods, his target areas of Scotland (including Catholics from South Uist), and his opponents among the lairds of the Highlands.

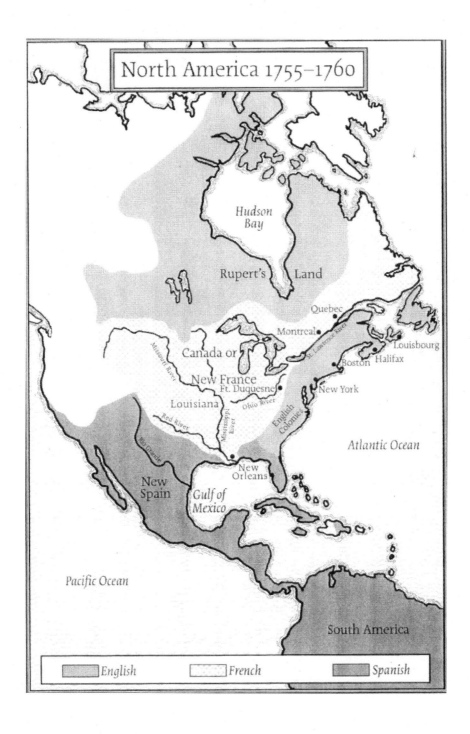

North America 1755–1760

Hudson Bay

Rupert's Land

Quebec
Montreal
Louisbourg
Canada or
Boston Halifax
New France
Ft. Duquesne
New York
Louisiana
Ohio River
English Colonies

Missouri River

Red River

Rio Grande

Mississippi River

St. Lawrence River

Atlantic Ocean

New Spain

Gulf of Mexico

New Orleans

Pacific Ocean

South America

English   French   Spanish

Opposition to Selkirk as a self serving promoter was becoming widespread. Even the clergy joined the fray. The Scottish lairds detested the emigration promoters, and the publication of a book, *An Inquiry into the Causes and Effects of Emigration from the Highlands and Western Isles of Scotland*, written by Alexander Irvine, a clergymen who defended the landlords and attacked people like Selkirk. By attracting emigrants from across the Highlands, from the Western Islands, from Argyll and Perthshire, to the northern shores of Sutherland and Kildanan, Selkirk was building a farm system, emigrants who would come to Canada and then attracted others to joint them in the new world. The Scottish establishment could turn on Selkirk, but the minor Scottish aristocracy could only look with envy at their English counterparts, who largely despised Scotland, with its Pretender to the Throne, its subservience to the French, and its alien religion.

Thomas Dunbar Douglas, the fifth Earl of Selkirk, inherited the title when his father died in 1799. It was another fluke in his life. He was the youngest of seven children, six brothers and one sister. Two brothers had died in infancy, a common problem then and now. Two brothers later died of yellow fever in the Caribbean, and two died of tuberculosis – a wretched, incurable disease. Thomas became the fifth Earl of Selkirk, formally known as Baron Daer and Shortclench, aged 28. From his father, he inherited more than the title: he became obsessively stubborn. His father was well known in Edinburgh, perhaps the learning capital of the universe. His friends included Walter Scott, and the intellectual giants of the university. At Edinburgh, students came from all over Europe, attracted by the Edinburgh Circle, men like David Hume, Adam Smith, and poets and writers like Walter Scot and Robbie Burns.

Selkirk also inherited a love for travel, for pushing the boundaries of his thinking. He was wealthy, ambitious, impulsive, and idealistic. In short, he thought outside the box. His father had many friends in London. The Selkirk tutor, William Lockheed, had a great interest in botany and natural history, and these were passed on to the Selkirk children. The fourth Earl promised the tutor a sea voyage to pursue his interests, perhaps taking a son on his travels. As it turns out, one son, Dunbar Selkirk, was interested in a worldwide voyage under the auspices of Sir John Banks. This expedition of Banks, now the pride of London, President of the Royal Society and close advisor to the King, George III, was a worldwide search for breadfruit seedlings in the far-flung Pacific Islands. The plants would be transported to the colonial islands of the Caribbean, to be used for the express purpose of quality nutritional food for the Negro slaves, on whose labour the sugar plantations depended. Banks supervised all aspects of the voyage, and was widely known in naval circles, having toured the coastal waters of Newfoundland and Labrador in 1764.

The captain carefully chosen for this expedition had sailed in these Pacific shores under the great Captain James Cook, who had learned much about mapping, surveying, and coastal waterways from Samuel Holland in Nova Scotia and Quebec. His name was William Bligh and his ship was called the *Bounty*. As preparations were underway, with crewmen being recruited and stores carefully prepared for the long voyage, Lord Selkirk visited this ship at Deptford Docks in Portsmouth, because he had a direct interest. His son, Dunbar Selkirk, was recruited as an 'able seamen' to travel on the *Bounty*. Bligh didn't appreciate Selkirk's inspection tour.

Selkirk knew something about ships. In 1778, five years before the Bounty was to sail, the Selkirk estate was raided by a small crew in the *Ranger*, which entered Kirkcudbright Bay and Saint Mary's Isle. The aim of the captain, a Scottish son of a local Kirkcudbright gardener, a man inflicted with both hubris and persistence, was to kidnap the Earl of Selkirk and exchange this peer for American prisoners held in English jails. Like many of his voyages, this escapade was a disaster. The Earl of Selkirk was away 'taking the waters at Buxton in Derbyshire', the mutinous crew stole the Selkirk silver, and scared Lady Selkirk and their children. The captain, now working with Ben Franklin, was John Paul Jones. Selkirk would later write to Jones:

Lord Selkirk to J. P. Jones,
Capitaine du Vaisseau Americain,
Le Ranger, à Brest:

> *I therefore would now allow myself to think*
> *with these people, that a man who professes*
> *honourable sentiments and is acting under an*
> *honourable commission, for what he thinks is*
> *supporting the Rights of mankind, would for*
> *the sake of a pitiful Ransom degrade himself*
> *to the low and vile character of a Barbarry Pirate,*
> *which can be the case if these people were right*
> *in the opinion they give, but I choose to judge*
> *more favourably of you and am, Sir ...*

Selkirk, first insisting that the silver be returned only through an American Act of Congress, accepted an offer from Jones to return the silver in person. On such merits, many view Jones as the father of the American navy!

On this inspection of the *Bounty*, Selkirk noticed numerous deficiencies. In a detailed letter to John Banks, whom he knew, Selkirk listed his concerns. The *Bounty* was only a cutter, not suitable for perilous voyages like a sloop of war. The Ship's company didn't include a Lieutenant or a company of marines. Bligh himself should be made a Captain, but his present standing was a lieutenant. Selkirk had reason enough to voice his concerns. His two sons were in the Caribbean, where hurricanes and storms were common. Selkirk's close friend, Richard Bentham, was father-in-law to William Bligh. Selkirk's letter to John Bank's had enough conviction to be forwarded to Lord Howe, first Lord of the Admiralty. But maybe the letter had little real effect, because down the road when the officers and men of the *Bounty* faced a court-marshal, there was little resolution to please Lord Selkirk. Neither Dunbar nor his tutor sailed on the *Bounty*.

Another inheritance from his father for Thomas Douglas was an innate capacity to go against the grain. Selkirk was indeed stubborn. His father wrote incessantly about the impact of the clearances, the destruction of the clan system, and the impact on the poorest of the poor. In 1792, at the age of 21, he traveled the Highlands and the outer islands, learning at first hand what he studied from history courses and close friends like Walter Scott at the University of Edinburgh. He even learned basic Gaelic, the language of the poor. On this tour, he saw the impact of destitution, poverty, and rampant child disease. Later, while touring Europe, he witnessed the impact of the French Revolution, the deep crevices between rich and poor, and the inherent barriers between the landed class and those without land. To further his own education, he worked on one of his father's farms, and took great interest in all aspects of farming, from seeding and farm management to the care of animals. His later writings, *Observations on the Present State of the Highlands of Scotland, with a view to the causes and probable consequences of Emigration,* published in London in 1805, brought him fame, if not fortune.

By 1798, when he inherited the title from his father, the Irish revolt was in full swing, a repetition of the revolts in Scotland in 1715 and 1745. On December 16, 1796, the Directory of France escorted 15,000 troops to Ireland as a prelude to a direct invasion, similar to the old battle plans of the Spanish Armada. The Irish leader, Wolfe Tone, promised total support from Catholics and Protestants alike. To their dismay, only one British ship stood in the way, led by Captain Edward Pellew and his 44 – gun frigate, the *Indefatigable,* celebrated in the novels, Horatio Hornblower, so admired by subsequent naval persons like Winston Churchill (seen reading the book on his way to Newfoundland to meet President Roosevelt). By the time the invasion actually took place in 1798, the British acted with a ferocious intensity, killing 12,000 Irish, dismantling the Irish Parliament, and instilling a Protestant Ascendancy that assured Catholics and Protestants would never work together, certainly for the next 100 years. London imposed harsh treatment on the Irish peasants sympathetic to the cries of revolution in France. Direct rule from London and an Act of Union, passed in 1800, made Ireland a British possession. Selkirk himself visited this troubled Island, and based on his updated thinking, submitted to the Colonial office his own prescription to deal with oppressed people – emigration.

John Paul Jones

But the Irish problems were now part of a much more serious military challenge for England, that being total war with France. England's defenses were based on naval supremacy, France's was based on large land armies, what Napoleon called the whale against the elephant. Selkirk's thinking was large in scope, daring and imaginative. His primary interest was the British colonies, and the movement of oppressed peoples. London's view was different. They were against large scale emigration. They saw the peasants as fodder for armies and chattel for the navy. Despite his plans for large scale emigration to what is now Ontario, centered in the Falls of St. Mary, based on the name of his birthplace, now known by the French name, Sault Ste. Marie, and to Prince Edward Island, the British Government was otherwise engaged and offered no real help. However, his plans for PEI were already underway, using his own resources to buy property (Lots 57, 58, 60, and 62) from absentee landowners, recruiting families who paid their own way (about ten pounds) and contracted three ships: the *Polly*, the *Oughton*, and the ship he traveled on, the *Dyke*. They reached PEI in August 1803, landing in Hillsborough Bay, due east of the old French capital, Port La Joie.

So, Selkirk's luck held. The new 1803 *Passenger Act,* proclaimed on July 1, 1803, following a report to the Treasury and Commissioner of Customs, was intended to prevent over-crowding of ships and guarantee proper provisions. In truth, it was a thinly disguised attempt to discourage emigration. In reality, however, it became a spur for faster movement of people (by 1828, when the Act was revised, thirty thousand people were leaving for Canada). In addition, Selkirk had sold some landholdings in Scotland. He thus had cash to buy more land in PEI from English land owners in the 1767 lottery, so he had an easy way round the land speculation problem. As much by accident as by design, Selkirk's settlers to PEI, not to Upper Canada, had another feature. They were not tenants of pure hardship and total poverty. Selkirk had recruited entire families, people who would choose to preserve a way of life on land they themselves would own. Many paid their own fares, and a few provided Selkirk with money to buy property. These settlers were acting with a conscious desire for immigration – indeed, they were the very people the Scottish lairds wanted to retain for their own farms. In once sense, it was compromise all around - the emigrants who chose PEI over Ontario, the British Government who accepted Selkirk's plan and timing, and Selkirk who provided the boats and a means to buy the land.

Selkirk traveled on the *Dyke*, which eventually steered into Hillsborough Bay on August 9, 1803. The other two ships were the *Polly*, a merchant collier built in Whitby in 1768 of 285 tons carrying the largest number of immigrants, many from Skye: some 280 adults, 120 children, and a crew of 17, resting in Orwell Bay after his arrival on August 7. The *Oughton*, the last ship to reach PEI, carrying passengers from Uist, arriving near the area now known as Point Prim, landed on August 27. The *Polly's* passengers disembarked on Lot 57, on land belonging to Captain Alexander McMillan, whose grandfather owned shipbuilding facilities with his brother Charles on the Susquehanna River in Pennsylvania. They were on the British side in the American Revolution, Charles being killed in battle. After the American war, McMillan was stationed at Charlottetown, serving as pay master for the British garrison. The *Polly* contained several key families, including people who met on the voyage and married on the Island. One such couple was the marriage of Samuel Nicholson to Flora McDonald, whose niece became the register at McGill University.

*****

The movement of 800 Scottish settlers to Prince Edward Island in the late summer of 1803 was not the first settlement from Scotland to PEI. The Selkirk settlers were clearly the biggest, the most successful of all the Selkirk initiatives – in New Brunswick, where the Earl bought land, Sault St. Marie, and of course, the Red River settlements in Manitoba, which was caught in the cross-frictions between the Hudson's Bay Company and the Northwest Corporation. Clearly, the fur trade barons did not want settlers or settlement to mar their monopoly trade rights. This issue was a generic problem throughout North America. It may be an over statement, but the Spaniards came to North America looking for gold, the French were interested in a commercial empire centered on the trade fur, and the British were interested in land settlements. Later, the same financial conflicts took place in PEI and throughout the Atlantic region between farming and shipbuilding, i.e. land settlements, needing long term development of farm lands and removal of trees, or ship yards and skilled labour to strip the forests for the yards located on ports.

The first significant settlement from Scotland came in 1772, more than 30 years before Selkirk's three ships landed on Lot 57. Captain John MacDonald, an aristocratic Catholic, organized a settlement that began on the Island with the arrival of the *Alexander* to Lot 36 at a place appropriately called Scotchfort, formerly the French hamlet of St. Louis. Selkirk's settlement was a direct consequence of the political difficulties in the post-Culloden environment of Scotland. While Bonnie Prince Charles failed in his attempts at the Stuart restoration in 1745, his strong supporters remained amazingly loyal to his cause. They were also mostly Roman Catholics. The Clan Chiefs, Selkirk later wrote in his diaries, "were reduced to the situation of any other proprietors, but they would not be long in discovering that to subsist a numerous train of dependants was not the only way in which their estates could be rendered of value."

As in Ireland two generations later, the British government imposed enormously harsh terms on the losers, including rigid controls on the Catholic religion. At the same time, many of the Scottish clans were now siding with the English from London, discarding the ancient rights of the Scottish clan structure, which included diminishing the strong *noblesse oblige* towards the poorest families (e.g. fishing rights, kelp farming) and lessening the ties to the Gaelic language, which slowly was confined to the Highlands and outer islands. Catholic teaching was disallowed in Scotland, so the Catholic Church began a series of Scottish schools on the Continent, for example in France (Douai and Paris), Germany (Colonne and Regensburg), and the Scots seminary in Rome. These schools taught lay students as well as seminarians, and had a curriculum rich in classical studies, languages, elocution, and legal studies. Scotland itself was starting to suffer the problem of absentee landlords, the Cheviot and Marino sheep graced the Highland estates, and the exodus of tackman and his people began, what Samuel Johnson called a 'fever of emigration'.

In general, the lairds were part of the economic process but few realized the consequences for the old social structure of Scotland.

One man who did understand was John MacDonald of Glenalladale, *Mac Iain Oig*, the son of Young John in the Gaeilic vernacular. "Emigrations are like to demolish the Highland Lairds, and very deservedly", he would write from Greenock before his own departure. Captain MacDonald graduated from the Scots School in Regensburg. He returned to Scotland and became the 8th Laird of Glenalladale, and a chieften of the Clanranald family, fiercely Catholic, stubbornly anti-land grabbers, and decidedly Jacobite. His family, like others (e.g. the Keppochs), were close associates of the Young Pretender. In the decades that followed, the victors took their revenge and started a campaign to impose various hardships, including renouncing their religion in favour of the Church of Scotland.

Perhaps the most extreme form came from Colin MacDonald of Boisdale. He forced religious convictions of the Presbyterian Church on his tenants of South Uist Island in the outer Hebrides by the use of a cane, earning him the title, the Religion of The Yellow Stick. This was not an idle threat. When Charles landed as part of the uprising on July 23, 1745, he landed with seven warriors – three Scots, two Irish, and two English – at Eriskay, South Uist, now known as Prince's Shore. The McDonald clan and the McDonells of Keppoch rallied to the cause, toasted the Prince, using the phase *Thearlaich,* son of Charles, or 'Charlie', hence the term, Bonnie Prince Charlie. McDonnell himself was killed and brutally burned by the will of the Duke of Cumberland, whose military attacks and subsequent brutality outraged even the English troops, which included James Wolfe.

For the losers at Culloden, out right killings, imprisonment, drownings by tackle, wandering families, and persecution were widespread, so emigration was the only option. Captain MacDonald first knew about Prince Edward Island from letters received from Scottish immigrants who settled there after the fall of Quebec, a group of disbanded Fraser Highlanders: four notable officers were Col. Simon Fraser, Lt. Col. James Abercrombie, Lt. Col. John Campbell, and Captain John MacDonnell. With secret support of the Catholic Church and the local Bishop, John MacDonald, he purchased land from the Lord Advocate of Scotland, James Montgomery. The settlers arrived in

PEI on May 1, 1772, led by his brother, with help in provisions purchased from Boston and Quebec. He called his expedition of 'opprest people', mostly tacksmen and lower tenants from South Uist, Moidart, and Arisaig.

The MacDonald clan, led by the Lord of the Glen, or in Gaelic as *Fear-a-Ghlinne*, John and his brother Donald, and his two sisters, Helen (Nellie) and the younger Margaret (Peggy) became a watchword in the eastern end of PEI, around the Tracadie and Scotchfort area of Lot 36, where they attempted to create a prosperous Catholic community. In the next two generations, they would build a growing settlement, and John's grandson William, with the money he made from the MacDonald tobacco business, would be a major philanthropist for McGill University, founding Macdonald College, and a MacDonald model school in PEI. Their first years on the Island were not easy. At the invitation of Lieutenant Colonel Allan Maclean and Major John Small, John and Donald, despite being Catholic, offered to help raise a Highland regiment from remnants of former soldiers among the various colonies, and John became a company commander. In the second battalion of the Royal Highland Emigrants (84th Foot), John and Donald joined a British regiment, the Royal Highland Emigrants, in the American Revolutionary War. While they were absent (Donald was a casualty of battle in 1781), Governor Walter Patterson was quietly using his position to take over lots from the absentee landowners, who had refused to pay the quitrents. John did not return to the Island until 1792, an absence of 16 years, and then had to appeal to the British Government to return lands seized by the Governor Patterson in his absence.

Until his death in 1810, John MacDonald endured a battle with the Island Governors, first Patterson, and then Edmund Fanning, who replaced him in 1793. The issue was the problem of quitrents, and who controlled the land sales for unpaid rents. Patterson and his Attorney General, Phillips Callbeck, formed part of an insiders club, eventually called the Family Compact, that seized land for unpaid rents. The King-in-Council issued instructions to Patterson to repeal the Quit Rent Act of 1774, annul past land sales and restore the lands to the former owners. Patterson refused to comply and the Colonial

Office appointed Edmund Fanning as his replacement. Fanning sought to settle the arguments between the tenants, who paid rents, the proprietors who issued leases to farmers, and the Government, who had to enforce the law. The plan was to have a court of escheat as a tool to settle land claims.

MacDonald, however, was deeply suspicious of Fanning and the insider government officials, and accused them of promoting a Levelling Party, with a view to stripping the proprietors of their land and subdividing the lots into smaller acreages, a replay of what had happened in France during the French Revolution, and what Irish leaders wanted in Ireland. The main leader in the Levelling Party was a member of Fanning's own administration, Chief Justice Peter Stewart. Fanning referred the issue to the House of Assembly, which the Governor controlled, since he appointed them. The Assembly sent the Sergeant-at-Arms to MacDonald's house in Tracadie, the Lord of the Glen refused to appear, but penned a letter outlining the pernicious background of the Assembly members, which drew resolutions condemning MacDonald's charges. Only Joseph Aplin and James Douglas among the landowners stood with MacDonald. Arguments continued until the arrival or Lord Selkirk, but by this time, the Napoleonic Wars shifted the concerns of the Colonial Office. While in England in 1805, MacDonald tried to sell his Island properties. His sister Nellie was not well, and she and his new wife remained on unfriendly terms (Nellie was referred to as the 'Queen of Tracadie'). By this time, his financial affairs deteriorated, and he received financial support from Lord Selkirk. He died in 1810.

This McDonald emigration to PEI served as a prelude to the Selkirk settlements, but the 1803 influx had a better class of people, according to the complex clan system of Scotland, which became known as the Celtic Patriarchical System. The Clans consisted of native men and broken men. The native men had blood ties and were related to the Clan chief, while the broken men were individuals or families from other clans who sought protection of a clan. Each clan had a chief, the tanist, the chieftens, the captain, and the daoin'-uaisle, i.e., the general body of the clan. The Chief's duties differed in peace or war, but his overall main duties were to dispense the law, to allocate land,

and to help administer the rents paid to landlords. The tanist was second in command and held the clan lands together during wars. The Chieftens were the heads of clan houses, while the Captain, often the same person, was the Chief of the family clan. When they differed, the captain was called the *Toiseach* (a term similar to what is used today to describe the office of Prime Minister of Ireland). The clan structure quickly broken down after 1745, as British justice prevailed and the social customs of the clans retreated to the Northwest of Scotland, preserving the Gaelic language and the total loyalty of the bonds of clanship. "Kindred to forty degrees, fosterage to a hundred," illustrates the incredible power of the clans, and the impact of fosterage, the exchange of young children to be reared by other families, including the children of the Chief. These were the norms and customs that Scottish emigrants brought to Prince Edward Island.

*****

Selkirk's tour of the Island, and his two separate trips taught him the immense potential of the British colonies, if only they could be managed successfully. His own comments about the Island government, and Fanning, the Governor, illustrate that their real interest was in themselves and the administration of patronage, both their own and their bosses in London. Governors, as a general rule in the British Empire, were appointed by London, together with a limited number of officials chosen by the Governor but approved by the Colonial Secretary. London granted each colony a financial allowance or appropriation to pay for salaries. The main preoccupations of the colonial governors, beyond local administration like courts, roads and harbours, education and public health, were primarily military and commercial. The colonial governors, viewed by London, were the eyes and ears of the Colonial Office for the gigantic British Empire, linked by the seas and oceans by the might of the Royal Navy.

The Royal Navy had to have priority, and ports like Halifax and Quebec were part of the global network of strategic ports, linking the commercial empire and the British merchant ships and the enforcement of the Navigation Acts to the great ports of London on the Thames and Liverpool. Colonial capitals, usually port cities protected by the British military and cannons, served the Royal Navy – repairs to ships, hosting the officers, refitting and restoring equipment, reprovisioning the cargo hulls with food, alcohol, fresh vegetables, clothing, and a range of sundry supplies, from furniture to gunpowder. The commercial side came from the Navigation Acts, where Britain imposed tariffs on non-British ships and payments (in money or in cargo) for use of the harbours and ports. In theory, if the Governor did a good job, he was rewarded with a pension or sent to another posting. If he did not do a good job, the Colonial Office brought them home, sometimes in disgrace. But the Royal Navy knew the social hierarchy – after all, no less than Horatio Nelson was clandestinely having an affair with the Governor's wife, Lady Hamilton.

In most of the colonies, there was a legislative assembly, a quasi-advisory group that, whether elected (as in the British North American colonies) or appointed, had an executive council of the appointed officials. The assembly was a venal instrument, representing the elites, but with little real control over what counted, namely money. Or, in the more elegant phrase of government, appropriations. In theory, the system worked. The revolt of the American colonies exposed the problems of the Navigation Acts and taxing the colonies without representation, but a more enlightened approach to the colonies, plus free trade, began to shift the economic calculus towards the colonies. Ireland as usual was a sore point: it was mainly Catholic, it was highly taxed, and most of the land was held by English aristocrats. England imposed direct rule, despite the opposition of the giants of Irish politics, Daniel O'Connell and Henry Gratton.

Selkirk, now celebrated on the Island as a true friend of the immigrants, was remarkably insightful about his passengers, the challenges they would face, and the practical challenges of living in a new world:

> *I found the people scattered about along a mile of shore, a few in barns, etc., belonging to three authorized settlers, the rest in hovel or wigwams built oblong like the roof of one of our European cottages and thatched in general with spruce boughs, some of them very close and fit to turn a good rain...*

We called in at an Indian wigwam, a Micmac who never drinks rum, his wife is from one of the Abenakivillages near Quebec and speaks French as he does good English... this man received us hospitably and presented us with berries in a birch bark bowl – he gave Dr. McAulay two wild fowl and refused to take any payment.

These immigrant groups defined the values of PEI. Captain MacDonald's settlers centered on the region of Scotchfort and Tracadie, and Lord's Selkirk's immigrants, so much larger, started in Orwell Bay and Point Prim but dispersed eastward towards Brudenell, northward to St. Andrews and St. Peter's, and later to Stanhope. Collectively, they were a mixed lot, Catholic and Protestant, dirt poor and not so poor clansmen who purchased`their land directly from Lord Selkirk, and varied widely on their skills as farmers, fishermen, or house builders. In general, they were separated by religion, although at the time there were no churches or clergy. Some of the land had been occupied by Acadian settlers, so French was common. Gaelic was, of course, the main language.

Clearing the land was a real challenge, because instruments were few and land clearing was necessary for agricultural production. From Point Prim in the south, northward towards Tracadie and Mount Stewart, there were natural wetlands, including salt marshes. These regions, described so poetically in the works of Longfellow's Evangeline or Bliss Carmen's *Low Tide at Grand Pré*, had more than natural beauty, as soon recognized by the very practical and shewd Lord Selkirk. The salt marshes, such as those at Mount Stewart and the tidal marshes on Alexandra Bay, carry a huge variety of vegetation, mussel mud, animals and flowers, including the abundant wild rose, whose blooms and rose hips were used as medicines and for tea. The first Acadian settlers brought a strong tradition of farming marshlands, mainly by a clever system of dykes and drainage ditches. Still easily seen today, these early engineering feats show the settlements in the census of Sieur de la Rogue in 1752, and the areas where Captain MacDonald and the Highland Scots settled in Tracadie and Scotchfort in 1772. Both Lord Selkirk, who had traveled extensively through France, and

John Stewart, in his *Account of Prince Edward Island*, recognized the value of the salt marshes, especially for the marsh hay, a source of nutrition for cows and other animals during the long winters.

Conclusions

Lord Selkirk has become minor legend in Canadian history - a good guy who developed the most successful first settlement from the Upper Highlands, a man who overcame the deep religious divisions of this country, a man who became the largest shareholder in Canada's biggest company - the Hudson's Bay Corporation. For PEI Selkirk was more than a pioneer immigrant landowner; he was the first to lay the seeds of Island self-reliance. The Immigrants wanted freedom - freedom from both oppressive government, and freedom from colonial survitude. Their experience on PEI exposed the circumstance of their wretched homeland and constant poverty. Their voyage was a one way flight for a better life, no matter how primitive was their new homeland.

It was not obvious at the time but Selkirk and PEI was part of what Tolstoy called the unstoppable march of history - the hordes of European masses either marching towards rebellion and revolution, in Ireland, in France, in Germany, in Russia - or marching to the empty spaces of North America. Whether in the isolated British colonies, or the fragmented states of the USA, whether the governments were free and open or whether they were autocratic and colonial, the movement of people could be delayed or could be slowed but could not be denied.

Selkirk's PEI lands were a model of respectability for the Island in three respects. First, the rents were fair for the tenant farmers. Second, the rental agreements to assume tenant ownership were not onerous. And finally, the settlements were remarkably economical. It would take other groups and people in future generations to deal with the land issue at large, and to build the institutions – such as schools, churches, and communities - that Selkirk so desperately wanted. When Selkirk left PEI for the last time, the settlers had only two memories. The first was one of a man they much admired, who understood the Scottish Highland spirit, and all its woes. Selkirk saw for himself what PEI brought to the settlers, not just new land, trees, fishing, and good robust soil, but a sense of what the settlers lost in their native land. He assumed a leadership based on trust and integrity. Selkirk had their respect. As others soon showed, many leaders didn't, and Islanders cultivated a deep, lingering, and lasting sense of skepticism towards public authority.

His departure from the Island in 1804 left a deep impression on the Highland population, and his various agents, including Charles Wright, never retained the deep affection of the Selkirk settlers. However, another Scotsmen quickly did win their affection, and indeed everyone who came in contact with this unique emigrant priest. His name was Angus MacEachern.

3

The Missionary Priest – The Work Of Bishop Angus MacEachern

A New Priest From the Highlands * Missionary Impossible –
Shortage of Priests * The Politics of a Young Church
* A French Visitor * The Brothers Calonne *
The French Revolution * The Struggles for a Responsible Church
* MacEachern and Higher Education

It was a beautiful August day on Prince Edward Island, the year 1790, and an immigrant ship reached Island shores, sailing northward up the Hillsborough River, to a Highland settlement at Scotchfort. Normally such ships stopped near the main ports, settled customs matters, and organized the passenger lists for accommodation and military inspection. But this ship was different: the captain knew exactly where to go, and a crowd awaited the passengers, tired but excited by the greetings in Gaelic emanating from Highlanders standing on the shore line. In this instance, there was one passenger that all awaited: a well-built, athletic and much acclaimed 31 year-old who, even before he landed, had a reputation for greatness. The passengers on board knew who he was and they relished the greetings from the assembled group on shore. Dressed in simple, unostentatious clothes, this gentle man was the first to disembark, not because he was important, but because it was a homecoming. Angus Bernard MacEachern, priest, scholar, missionary, friend, adept in languages, landed on Prince Edward Island, never to see his native Scotland again, but rejoiced as he greeted his mother Mary, who he had not seen in 18 years. Professor Bolger describes the heart-warming scene:

> *The spirits of the heavy hearted passengers, dulled by home sickness and the tedium of the slow Atlantic crossing, must have soared as they saw hundreds of their countrymen gathered on the shores to greet them, and heard their welcome shouted in the melodious cadence of the Gaelic tongue. Among the first to disembark was a tall, handsome, thirty-one- year-old priest clad in the somber homespun of the period. Men bowed, women courtesied, children clapped, and all knelt by the track that he walked, to be blessed as he passed. He moved through them quickly to lift from her knees the mother he had not seen since he was thirteen years of age. Father Angus MacEachern had come home to his own.*

For 45 years, Angus MacEachern dominated life on the Island. He outlasted four governors, the Family Compact, the merchants, the would-be politicians, even his fellow clergy, both Protestants and Catholics. He knew everybody. He traveled the Island like he owned it, in winter and summer, blazed new trails, literally, like the Quebecois *courier de bois*, leaving signs for those who followed, traversing rivers with his horse or his celebrated boat. Well after dusk, he could stop at a farm house, be totally welcomed, regale the family with stories, and offer a lecture on the lessons of the Good Samaritan. He was a master letter writer: copious notes of his work, his needs, his wishes, were sent to Rome, where his classmates held important positions at the Vatican, themselves totally impressed with his stylish and elegant Latin. He sent letters to Quebec, where a succession of Bishops wished him well but offered little in return. He wrote to his fellow priests and later Bishops in Halifax, Kingston, and Montreal, and to the local government that actually put him on the payroll – a road builder and inspector.

Mgr BERNARD-ANGUS McEACHERN,
Premier évêque de Charlottetown
1759-1835

In England, when the great Sir Christopher Wren died and was buried in the majestic St. Paul's Cathedral in 1723, there is a Latin inscription on his tomb: to see his works, look around. This epitaph could be that of Angus MacEachern. On the Island, his works are everywhere. He was the leader in building Catholic Churches across the Island, from Tignish and Cascumpec in the west to Rollo Bay and Saint Margaret's in the East. In Charlottetown, St. Dunstan's Cathedral is located on the site personally chosen by this august immigrant, the highest point in the capital, on land purchased from a shoemaker, Christopher Hartell, for £75, of which he contributed ten pounds. He founded the first university, St. Andrew's in 1831. This small institution, opening with 20 students, five from Nova Scotia and 15 from PEI, eventually became St. Dunstan's College and then St. Dunstan's University. St. Andrew's fostered among all immigrants, Catholic and Protestant alike, the value of education in all its forms, and reflected MacEachern's own upbringing. He was from a relatively poor family in Scotland, but blessed with an education in Spain, where he personally cultivated friendships among his classmates that dotted the known landscape. Indeed, he ordained the first Catholic priest on the Island, because clergy were in short supply. Two generations later, his pioneering work cultivated not only more Island priests, as Island clergy became bishops across Canada and the US. One Island priest, James McGuigan, a graduate of St. Dunstan's, became the first English Cardinal in the Catholic Church in Canada, and became Archbishop of Toronto.

Politics was not the vocation of Angus MacEachern, but during the pioneering years of Canada and the young colony of Prince Edward Island, political action was hard to escape. Before responsible government arrived on the Island in 1851, the Governors lorded over the colony, representatives of the British Government, but most lorded over their own patronage system on the Island, in close conformity with the Family Compact. MacEachern, as a young boy, learned the elements of the British system in the Highlands of Scotland. The fact that he stayed in Scotland after he was ordained in Spain, both toiling in the Highlands and ministering to his people, fostered an element of optimism when most suffered utter pessimism. Throughout his 45 years on the Island and the neighbouring colonies of Nova Scotia and New Brunswick, he tolerated the shenanigans and the scheming of the local British administration, knowing full well even Imperial London would see the evil of their way. But he understood as well, as most Islanders did not, that Britain operated with its strict penal laws against Catholics, and he walked a fine line between rigid acceptance of British authority and open defiance of patronage rule, especially when the French Revolution placed French Catholics in a precarious position.

No understanding of the political makeup of Canada, and its division into federal and provincial jurisdictions, is complete without comprehending how the Catholic Church in Canada, for 150 years, was run in a highly centered fashion by the Bishop of Quebec, starting with Bishop Laval. It was a centralized, unitary structure adopted in most Catholic countries with a small geographic base. But this was Canada, a land of vast distances, differing climates, a mix of seven months of Arctic winter and five months of hot summer. As the Atlantic provinces doubled in population, and the area now known as Ontario, once Upper Canada, grew tremendously compared to Quebec, with Catholics being either the first or second in relative numbers, it became increasingly difficult to administer the Church from Quebec: it was more than a language problem, although most Quebec priests' first language was French.

It was a geographic challenge. Vast territories of the Canadian colonies were bigger than England or Italy, with poor, boggy roads, ice and snow six months of the year, and a constant shortage of priests, which at the time were key to hospital treatment, education, and legal work, since only the clergy were literate enough to deal with government officials. To Rome, to Quebec, to his classmates, he appealed for help, for changes in the church structure, and for more autonomy to deal with the local governors. No doubt, despite his formal politeness, he undoubtedly exasperated his superiors. Finally the Vatican and the Bishop of Quebec relented: the Catholic Church would become a Canadian federated organization of five regions: Quebec, and four new Bishops, including the new Bishop of Rosen, for the Diocese of Charlottetown, encompassing all the Maritime provinces and the Magnalen Islands.

MacEachern needed priests, and he wasn't going to be fussy about where they came from. The various Bishops of Quebec were reluctant to surrender Quebec clergy, so the only other option was to import them from Europe, or to train young boys to become priests, which meant he needed a school. By coincidence, a priest did come to PEI, but not from the usual places like Ireland or Scotland, but from France. This priest, not of ordinary birth or circumstance, stayed four years on the Island, and obviously spent a lot of time with Angus MacEachern. His name was Joseph de Calonne. His brother was the Minister of Finance just prior to the French Revolution. On such a career did Angus MacEachern become a legend on the Island, revered by his parishioners, and celebrated by the community. The *Royal Gazette*, in its obituary notice, had this to say about his passing: "...Beloved, respected and esteemed not only by those of his own persuasion, but by every member of the community, this truly pious and estimable Prelate, has, by his departure, from this sublunary scene, after a long and laborious life spent in the unwearing discharge of his official duties, and distinguished by numerous acts of unostentatious benevolence, left a void in society that will long be felt by those who had the pleasure of his acquaintance, and a character as a man and a Christian beyond all panegyric...."

**

If Lord Selkirk was the first eminent Islander to change the face of PEI through immigration, and to enjoy a mystical reputation among the Highland settlers despite his short sojourn on the Island, who was this Scottish man of letters, this missionary priest who gained such a prominent reputation? Raised in a poor Scottish family, MacEachern was to become a born leader in Prince Edward Island, an ecumenical priest who would become one of the first non-Quebec bishops of the Catholic Church, a powerful supporter of education in the new colony, a man of immense charm who could speak Gaelic, write in quality Latin, converse with the Bishop of Quebec, and win loyalty with his political masters in Charlottetown. By dint of circumstance, he also joined his pioneering family, emigrants from Scotland who arrived on the *Alexander* with Captain John MacDonald in the early summer of 1772 at the Magdalen Islands.

The story of Angus MacEachern is a miracle of unintended consequences. Nothing in his life was predictable. He was all but abandoned by his family, who emigrated to PEI in 1770. At eleven, he was left in the care of the Vicar Apostolic of the Highland District, Hugh MacDonald and, on his death in 1773, to the local Bishop, John McDonald. For the next 62 years, as a student in Scotland, as a seminarian and priest in Spain, as a clergyman in the Scottish Highlands, and as an immigrant priest, educator, first Bishop of Charlottetown, MacEachern's life was a record of staggering achievement. On the Island and throughout his life, for Father MacEachern, diplomacy and hard work were his style, saving souls his lifetime mission. This priest became widely known throughout the small province, as being equally at home in the church or around the camp fire, an excellent horseman, a strong swimmer, and a man of languages and culture.

His life in the Catholic Church is really the story of the early years of PEI. No leader - French or English during the French Regime and the British takeover - captured the popularity of MacEachern among Catholics and Protestants, among those who ruled and those who followed. Perhaps more than anybody, Angus MacEachern served the province as much as he served his Church. He was an early ecumenical leader, served in key positions with the government, where he knew the colonial officials, and developed linkages with Nova Scotia, New Brunswick and Quebec. He wielded this influence tactfully, first as an immigrant priest, then as Bishop of Charlottetown, one of only five Catholic Bishops in all of the British North American colonies.

Like Lord Selkirk, MacEachern had a big view. He was a man of letters to be sure, but he was also a man of action. He knew Scotland, and he knew the complex relations between the lords and the tenants, the Protestants and the Catholics, the Scottish Lords and the English monarchy. MacEachern was born February 8, 1759, the same year that Quebec was to fall to the British, at Kinlock Moidart, in the west side of Scotland, son of Hugh (Ban) MacEachern, guardian to the Laird of Kinloch. The parents and six of the eight children emigrated to Prince Edward Island in 1772, arriving with captain

John MacDonald, Laird of Glenaladale and Glenfinnan on board the *Alexander*. Among the 210 emigrants, many of whom were Catholics, was the Reverend James MacDonald, who alone kept the Church alive on PEI, administering to Highland Catholics and the Acadians. He died in 1785.

Angus MacEachern was raised by the local Scottish bishop, Hugh MacDonald, and spent five years at the Catholic College at Samlaman, Moidart, learning basic classics and commercial education. The Bishop arranged to send MacEachern to the College of St. Ambrose, founded by the Jesuits in Valladolid, Spain. This seminary was named the Royal Scots College, because the Spanish Crown expulsed the Jesuits and turned the administration to the Scottish bishops, who had no seminary of their own in Scotland. In Catholic scholarly circles, Valladolid had a strong reputation and was widely known because of the influence of Francisco Suarez, a Jesuit theologian and philosophical jurist. Among his works, written in 1613 at the Pope Paul V's request, was the text, *De Defensio Catholicae Fidae*, a refutation against the theory of the divine right of kings.

The young MacEachern spent ten years at Valladolid, and was ordained a priest in August 1787, his 28th year. Clearly, his stay in Spain was an eye opening experience, with more than the weather to contrast against the hardships of the Scottish Highlands and the robust farm areas of north-west Spain. MacEachern was a natural linguist. The West Highlanders all spoke Gaelic, and English spread fast among the educated, as many Lairds catered to the dictates of the English masters. Latin, of course, was the language of the Church, history and philosophy, and the sacred orders, and as his future career would attest, MacEachern's capacity to write, and to use the Latin language with gusto, impressed many people, including his superiors in Rome. In Spain, he also learned French, the language of the Bourbons, and the *lingua franca* among educated people throughout Europe. But languages, theology, and reading were not his only passions: he remained a man of action, a person who learned trades, who could hunt and swim (a curiously rare skill in those days). He was also interested in practical subjects like carpentry, and gained some notoriety and fame as a boat builder – a feat which had some significance when the "enormous boat" he constructed at the seminary saved many inhabitants in Valladolid during a spring flood in 1788. Later in life, he built a boat at his home in PEI to carry his missionary needs, and it was equally celebrated as it was used as a boat, carried with a horse, or adapted as a sleigh. (It still exists, and it is on display at St. Dunstan's Cathedral in Charlottetown.) But MacEachern remained a modest person, unlike many who have much to be modest about. Already, people looked up to him.

The modern university was still to take shape, but MacEachern made friends with his classmates, perhaps on the expectations that he would need a contact some where, or could call on a favour. One classmate of MacEachern at Valladolid was Alexander Macdonnell (1760-1840) from Inchlaggon near Glengary, Scotland. He was later to found the Glengary Fencible Regiment with himself as Chaplin, the first Catholic Chaplain in the British Army since the Reformation. Like MacEachern, he too came to Canada, in 1804, and served as Chaplain at a time when there were only two Catholic priests in Ontario at the time in the war of 1812 against the Americans. He became the first bishop of Kingston in 1826, appointed to the Legislative Council in 1831, and died in Dumfries, the home of Robert Burns, recruiting Scottish emigrants for Canada West.

MacEachern left Spain in 1789, an auspicious year in France and returned to his birthplace as a missionary priest. For two years, MacEachern laboured in the western Highlands, working under the tutelage of the Right Rev. Alexander MacDonald, Titular Bishop of Polernard. The weather, the poverty, and religious prosecution were the main stay of the Scottish highlands, without mention of the muck and rain of the coastal invaders and military stopovers. As a clergyman and a man of the cloth, Angus MacEachern knew his priestly calling. He also knew the position of Catholics in his native Scotland, and knew of the church-state relations in Catholic Spain, where the Jesuits were banned not only in Valladolid but in several European cities like Paris and Vienna. As an educated man, he calculated the poor position he was in, with the Catholic population ebbing through emigration and having few priests and fewer churches.

For Catholics in the Highlands, in was an era of persecution. From 1744, Bonnie Prince Charlie had conspired with the French to begin an uprising in Scotland and an attempt to return to the Stuart Throne in London. The first attack from the Straights of Dover was thwarted by a disastrous storm - the "Protestant Wind", as it was called. The French soon lost interest. Bonnie Prince Charlie decided on an overload route from Scotland, arriving on July 23rd, 1745 via South Uist, closed to the very birthplace of Angus MacEachern. A group of clans supported the Prince, including the McDonalds of Keppoch, whose grandson Alexander moved to Prince Edward Island and purchased a waterfront property near Charlottetown.

The Stuart uprising was a failure, as many of the Scottish clans were neither Catholic nor pro-Stuart. In the end, it was Britain's modern army - fresh artillery, bayonets, swords and muskets – that routed the ragtag remnants of the clansmen, many of whom had not been paid, had no food, and had no supplies. The Battle of Culloden was led by William, Duke of Cumberland, but the engine of victory was Duncan Forbes, who used bribery, smarts, clan loyalty, and guile. There was no uprising of the clans, and Cumberland could exercise his position as "Butcher". Forbes could eventually see changes to the hereditary jurisdiction of the clan chieftains, and London could allow the Scots to bear witness to the Forty Five and the Prince's supporters.

One such man was Alexander McDonald of Boisdale, raised a Catholic, yet married to a Protestant, who turned on his Catholic tenants with a vengeance. The tenants were forced to renounce their faith, to avoid all contacts with priests, and sign a document proving their rejection of the Church. Some tenants agreed to the terms, yet many more decided to emigrate to North America. This was the sad picture that Father MacEachern faced in Scotland when he returned from Spain in 1789. His own family had left in 1772 with Captain John MacDonald for Prince Edward Island and he received correspondence from relatives about their plight in the new world.

In short order, MacEachern received permission to emigrate to PEI. His mentor, Alexander MacDonald, provided him with a letter for the Bishop of Quebec, dated at Samlaman, July 6, 1790. His plan was straightforward: he would join his parents and continue his priestly mission in this new land. Whatever beauty the Island laid out for the new priest, he knew that the colony had few resources - a nomadic school teacher, few priests, no industry other than limited shipbuilding, primitive agriculture with few instruments, and sparse transportation. When MacEachern arrived on the Island, the population was scarcely 3000 people - a mix of Acadian French who had arrived 50 years ago, recently arrived Scottish emigrants from Scotland, and a list of Irish peasants from the West counties. Under the then Governor and a mix of colonial officials, MacEachern had few associates to work with - no priests, no churches, few souls of high standing. The Island population was limited to a thousand souls in Charlottetown, some along seaboards and the coastal beaches: Scotch Protestants scattered in small hamlets, Catholics in Georgetown and St. Peters, Acadians in Rustico and Fortune Bay, Micmac Indians, and American Loyalists in Bedeque.

MacEachern knew that the Protestant governors from London would prefer the ascendancy of the Church of England to papal tenure in PEI. Even Governor Edmund Fanning, who was born in the USA and graduated from Yale, fully recognized that his plans for Catholicism on PEI – meaning more priests, education, and churches - had to fit into the plans of the Colonial Government in London. Emigration from Britain was a priority – the local assembly passed a resolution suggesting a plan to attract 500,000 immigrants for the Island, and this assembly knew the colony and the colonial administration had to earn its keep. Military security was a constant challenge. There was the French government (which at great cost had previously backed the American rebels) or from the Americans themselves, who resented British sea power and who controlled, through the Canada colonies, all the lands west of the Ohio. British military and colonial administrations may not have been brilliant, but they weren't stupid either. The British still banned American ships from Canadian ports, meaning that American products had to be transported in British ships. Above all, the Americans coveted the Atlantic fisheries, further adding to tensions.

MacEachern had another worry: the Catholic clergy centered in Quebec. The Catholic Church was more than a mission for God; it was an extremely powerful political force, an organization which outlasted sundry empires, uprisings, revolutions, Kings and tyrants. It was really an organization of great mystery with the Pope and the Vatican serving as the epicenter of a truly global organization with an implicit policy of *"divide et impera"* – or divide and rule, boasting an amply educated curia and its "privy council," and an immense organization that, even to this day, has only four hierarchical levels - the Pope, cardinals, bishops and priests.

In Canada, the Catholic Church was not without influence, which was reflected in the gains the church had made through the Quebec Act of 1774 and the Constitutional Act of 1791. The British governor might formally approve this or that appointment, or this or that new parish, but the historic division of labour held - render to Caesar the things that are Caesar, render to God the things that are God's. For MacEachern, who learned a great deal about dealings with governments in Scotland, Spain, London, PEI, his primary concern was with Quebec. He desperately needed priests, to bolster support for his growing Island parish, not just in PEI, of course, but in Nova Scotia where he had sisters at Judique, Cape Breton. He then turned to the Quebec Bishop for assistance.

***

MacEachern's first priority on reaching the Island was to send a letter to the Bishop of Quebec, whose responsibilities included the Island, Nova Scotia, New Brunswick and the Magdalene Islands. The Catholic hierarchy in Quebec, despite protracted letters between MacEachern and Bishop Plessis, was too concerned with local Quebec issues, focusing instead on the entry of a new Chateau Clique consisting of merchants in Magdalen and recently arrived United Empire Loyalists, or American Tories, and the desire to use the Jesuit estates, traditionally devoted to Catholic schools, for general revenues for the government. MacEachern's primary concern was to get more priests to come to PEI. This proved to be a tall order given the penal laws enforced through the British Empire, compounded by the shortage of priests outside Catholics countries like France, Spain and Ireland, and the remaining priests understandable desire not to cross the Atlantic ocean. As it turned out, there was a surplus of Catholic priests in of all places, England. France had overthrown the French monarchy of Louis XVI and by 1790, the reign of terror had started. Many Cardinals, bishops and priests left France (George III put one Cardinal on a pension from his own resources), and many moved to London.

By good fortune, one French priest residing in London decided to emigrate to PEI. Abbe Joseph Calonne spent four years on Prince Edward Island, from October 1799 when he arrived from Halifax to October 1803, when he departed for London, before returning to Quebec in the autumn of 1807. In London and in Liverpool, he coped with both his own finances and those of his brother, an intelligent and educated man who knew very little about personal finance. Joseph left a trail of letters, mostly to Bishop Denault and his successor, Bishop Plessis, which are now in the archives of the Urseline Convent in Trois Rivieres, where he died on October 16, 1821, aged 80 years. Clearly, by his own descriptions, by the laments of his letters, and his personal struggles, his time in Canada was lonely, reclusive, and aloof. He remained a European royalist in a land of pioneers, a castaway in the North American precinct, so distant from the gilded lifestyle of Paris or London, the royalist courts of Europe, or the precious time with his adored brother, Charles. Who was this French priest? Unknown to most people, Abbe Calonne, through his brother, put the Calonnes at the heart of the French Revolution, and helped shape Angus MacEachern's thinking for the rest of his days as a pastor, early architect of the Island school system, and strategist for major changes to the organization of the Catholic Church in the British colonies. Yet again the Island's history was shaped by events outside the control of its small population.

Abbe Calonne's brother, Charles Alexandre de Calonne, had been Minister of Finance under Louis XVI, who faced the guillotine on January 21, 1793, ten days before Britain and Spain declared war on France. The British court gave Charles Calonne 500 acres in PEI, close to Charlottetown on land that became known as the Warren Farm, near what became Rockey Point at the entrance to the Charlottetown harbour. Abbe Calonne himself decided to come to PEI, and began correspondence with Rev. Pierre Deauld, a priest

Abbe Joseph Calonne

in Montréal, who spoke about Father MacEachern, the Scottish missionary priest. At this time, civil administrative notices had to be given through circuitous channels, from Bishop Plessis to PEI's Governor Edmund Fanning, between Fanning and MacEachern, and between the Quebec bishop, Pierre Denault and Father James of Halifax. Unknown to anybody, Prince Edward Island was now at the center of key players in the French Revolution. What is the background of this twisting journey?

The Calonne brothers were born in Tournai, Belgium, a year apart, Charles in 1742, Joseph in 1743. Their parents, although not rich, were accomplished citizens. The family had great interest in the law, the arts, and the Church. From their parents and their teachers, the two brothers became well read. They enjoyed the company of the ambitious, and cultivated the life style of the rich, even if both remained poor throughout their lifetime. The Calonnes originated in Tournai, located in the low plateaus of central Belgium, about 25 kilometers due east of the French city of Lille. They were an ordinary bourgeois class, climbing the social ladders to occupy a part of the noble class by 1621. The parents of the two Calonne brothers became well connected in society. The father, Louis-Joseph Dominique de Calonne was a squire, advisor to the King, and President of the Parliament. Their mother, Anne-Henritette de Franqueville, belonged to a long line of noble families, many with 'squires' and knights' in the family history, thanks to their active military engagements and officer roles, dating to such ancient battles like Mons en Puelle (1304). With the two sons, the Calonnes were a proud, literate and reasonably comfortable family, advisors to the nobility in Flanders, and close to the Scots College at Douai. At this time, Belgium remained under the control of Austria, thanks to the settlement of the War of Succession in 1713. Almost all of Belgium at this time was Catholic.

Joseph was born on April 9, 1743, and baptized on November 20. He grew up in comfort, and was educated in law and elocution. He was a young man of considerable talent and socially popular, and as brilliant as he was frivolous. At 23, he became an advisor to the local assembly, where his father served as President and his brother Charles was a member. But Joseph decided he liked the eccleasistical life, and entered the Grand Seminary d'Arras, the fortress town in northwest France. The local Bishop wasn't sure about Joseph, thinking him too worldly. In fact, the two Calonne's were indeed dandies: well educated, with polished manners, sophisticated collectors of art, witty, and, above all, appreciative of women. So with his Father's cooperation, Joseph was enrolled at the Saint-Sulpice Seminary in Paris, where he studied theology and Holy Scripture. He was ordained a priest on June 1, 1776. (By coincidence, this was the same seminary attended by Rev. Charles deBresley, the first Catholic priest in PEI. The Community of St. Sulpice, loosely affiliated with the Court of Louis XIV, was active in Quebec and once had plans to build a seminary in PEI, or Ile St. Jean, as the Island was then called.)

Abbe Calonne moved to Cambrai, and soon became vicar general of the diocese. Under the old regime dating from Louis XIV, the Archdiocese of Cambrai had forty-one abbeys, eighteen of which belonged to the Benedictines. Cambrai was only a bishopric, but its jurisdiction was immense, including Brussels and Antwerp. The English college of Douai, founded by William Allen in 1568, was well known in Catholic England, and was affiliated with the Religious of the Holy Union of the Sacred Hearts, whose mother-house was located there.

In 1783, helped by his brother Charles, Joseph moved to the Abby of Saint-Père in Melun, declining the office of Bishop in Cambrai. He was undoubtedly a man on the move. But his real preference was to be in Paris, possibly in the office of the King's Library. While Jacques-Ladislas-Joseph quit his law studies and entered the seminary of Saint-Sulpice, Charles moved up the Court hierarchy. Charles Calone had spent his career in the service of the monarchy, starting as a member of the Noblesse de Robe, an elite civil service for the French King.

Under the Bourbons, France had a model of central government inherited from Colbert, the administrative genius behind King Louis XIV. A key appointment was the *intendants* who administered instructions from the royal council, usually with confrontations against military governors and local nobles. Charles had served as an Intendent in both Metz and Lille. This work was an important post responsible for troop movements, hospitals, highways and bridges, and maintaining law and order. The center was the crown, chained together by the three estates in the guilds and corporations, the universities and academies, and finally the courts and tribunals. In this way, Charles Calonne developed contacts with key people in French monarchical circles.

Charles quickly gained a reputation for monetary matters, including public finance. Coupled with his engaging personality and administrative talent, Charles, together with his brother, used his civil contacts to make direct acquaintance with such notables as Pierre-Augustin Caron de Beaumarchais, who, like Rousseau, was the son of a Protestant watchmaker, adventurer, dramatist, and secret agent to the Americans (who were seeking funding for their revolution against Britain). Both Charles and Joseph befriended Beaucharmais, author of the celebrated plays, the *Barber of Seville* and the *Marriage of Figaro*, and publisher of the complete works and manuscripts of Voltaire, who was decidedly anti-monarchist. Beaumarchais's *The Marriage of Figaro*, written in 1773, was held back from performance by court censors, as the King found it subversive. Beaucharmais worked secretly with Benjamin Franklin, the American Ambassador in Paris, to help finance the American war effort. On November 10, 1783, King Louis XVI appointed Charles to a singularly high office, the Controller-General of France. In short, Charles was now the finance minister, in charge of a country rapidly going bankrupt.

****

In the convoluted, ramshackle administrative model of the French Government, the *anciene regime* of absolute monarchical rule, Charles Calonne inherited the finance job from a hard-headed Swiss banker, Jacques Necker. Necker in turn replaced Anne-Robert Turgot (1774-1776), a brilliant finance theorist, close friend of Voltaire and student of the Physiocracy (led by Quesnay, the court physician and his partner, Marguis de Mirabeau, father of the Revolutionary orator). Turgot was the proponent of vast economic reforms, including lower tax rates in general, and a laissez-faire attitude towards French commerce in contrast to the industrial monopolies operated by the

Charles Calonne

Nobles, sparking pervasive changes to financial administration within the French bureaucracy.

Turgot, appointed on the eve of the coronation of Louis XVI and his new wife, the Dauphinesse from Austria, faced ever growing public obligations, including those for the Royal Household, such as the new gold crown for the young Prince. France's fiscal system was centuries old, but now created dangerous tax differences between towns and the countryside (whose farmers produced food), and enormously costly public corporations such as the Paris Water Company, which delivered no water, and fire and insurance companies, which insured no lives. Turgot was not inclined to support the Americans in their revolutionary war, on the simple premise that while a revolt might hurt England and help France, it didn't make sense for Royalist France to assist rebels against their sovereign, George III! Financial support to the Americans was part of a series of military conflicts that the Bourbons inflicted on a grand scale, such as the War of the Austrian Succession and the Seven Year's War. This global strategy was too burdensome, excessive, extravagant, and expensive. Few could see that these wars necessitated vast increases in tax because of spiraling military costs for both navies and armies, amidst diminished military success.

The new King, Louis XVI (1774-1792), an inexperienced former prince of only 20 years, lacked intelligence, courtly presence, and political will. Thomas Jefferson, a future US President, thought the King was a fool. But Louis XVI was a more complicated person, despite his age. Like many at court, he was an excellent rider, preferring deer hunting to his royal duties, and had real talent both as a blacksmith and at lock-making. He developed a great interest in geography, tracked British imperial voyages, and had read all of Captain Cook's published diaries. Naval matters interested him greatly, and he fostered illusions of a vast imperial navy, yet he never saw the ocean, and visiting only one port, Cherbourg, where he spoke and swore like a sailor, much to the delight of the sailors he met. The King was a strong linguist, speaking Latin, Italian, and English (later, while on trail, he would keep busy reading English newspapers). But in the end, Louis XVI disliked his royal duties, tired of political in-fighting and, as the financial challenges mounted, he preferred hunting to administration. (It is a paradox of history that at the same time, the English King, George III, instead of being a royal, wanted to be a Whig reformer and *did* attend to administration!)

The King's young wife, Marie Antoinette, the sister of Emperor Leopold of Austria, became the closest advisor to this absolutist Bourbon. In time, her own spending habits at Versailles, including her role in the celebrated diamond necklace affair, quickly became the subject of royal gossip in the Paris coffee houses and especially among the women at a time where grain had to be imported from the countryside. Yet unlike his predecessor, the unmourned Louis XV, the new King was widely acclaimed throughout France when he inherited the throne. At his lavish wedding in May 1775, there was an auspicious omen: a stray rocket ignited a depot of firearms at the Place Louis XV and 133 people were engulfed in flames.

Turgot, Necker, and now Charles Calonne all faced the perpetual dilemma of French finance: rising costs, mostly military in nature, coupled with static revenues, based on an inefficient, unfair, and a corrupt system of tax collection. For over a century, French finances were intended for two main purposes: to wage war to augment the French empire, and to support the French monarchy through a complex morass of royal patronage. The monarchy operated in a social class structure, representing the crown and a hierarchy of orders or estates, each legally defined with their own rights and responsibilities, each operating with tacit compromises and alliances based on personalities, family ties, and national circumstances. The first estate was the clergy; their allegiance was both to the French monarchy, but also to the Pope in Rome. The clergy were not taxed directly, but donated a free gift, a *don gratuit*. The second estate was the nobility, who were unquestionably loyal to the Monarchy, and subject to a form of income tax contribution, the *vingtième*, roughly amounting to one-twentieth of the tax payer's revenue. They were exempt from the direct tax, the *taille*, and they enjoyed a monopoly over administrative offices in Church and State, from bishoprics to army commissions, and administrative offices of the French state. The third estate were the lay commoners, consisting of some very rich professional and commercial classes, but most were the French peasants, perhaps over 90 per cent of the population, which carried the real burden of taxation.

This was the French social order: the Monarchy and the nobles provided secular protection in times of war and unrest, and the Church provided comfort to the simple souls of the peasantry, en route to the Kingdom of Heaven. The poor were taxed twice, by the Government through the *taille* and feudal dues to the nobles, and through the *tithes* paid to the Clergy. It was an awkward and complicated financial system, with much room for abuse, both by the peasants wishing to avoid the vast arsenal of dues and side payments, and by the nobles wishing to preserve their social privileges in isolation from monarchical largesse and extravagance in Versailles.

In August 1786, with France facing financial ruin, Charles Calonne presented to the King his famous document, *Precis d'un Plan pour l'amelioration des Finances*. His assistant in this budget, which was intended both to reform French finance, but also to advance political support for the King, was Charles Talleyrand, the citizen Bishop of Auton, and alumnus of the Seminary of Saint-Sulpice, a devotee of Voltaire, now exiled in Switzerland.

Before 1786, Calonne increased government credit, stimulated government spending, and set off a stock market boom. He devoted huge sums for sanitation, roads, canals, and harbours, including the great new docks at Cherbourg on the Normandy Peninsula, visited by the King himself, three to four hours from the British naval base at Portsmouth. The new King had illusions of a naval empire, one stretching beyond the Atlantic, and perhaps an Oriental Empire. There were enormous naval investments: French navy costs alone were 147 million in 1781, the year of Yorktown, while total costs that year for America's war were 227 million. Indeed 91 per cent of the American campaign came from expensive loans, some 1.3 billion livres between 1776 and 1783. France's annual debts climbed significantly during this period, by an estimated 651 million livres. Much of this debt came from the financial policies of Necker, who borrowed to support the Americans in their War of Independence. In fact, from 1615 to 1770, France had to renege five times on its debt payments. But the financial chaos couldn't last as the government was broke, with bankers calling. It was decided that new taxes were needed to keep the treasury afloat.

To encourage some administrative action with the notoriously indecisive King, Calonne proposed two fronts. The first were massive reforms to the entire fiscal and administrative tax system: land taxes for all landowners without exception, including the lands of the Catholic Church; extension of the Stamp Tax; reduction of the salt tax; and various measures to reduce the King's (and Queen's) spending prerogatives. The second front was much more political in nature, and was intended to install a real system of public credit, or what today would mean a department of internal revenue.

For decades, France imposed a convoluted system of tax collection from private individuals with the receivers-general responsible for direct taxation, and a syndicate called the Farmers-General responsible for indirect taxation, creating a state within a state. Needless to say, it was a model of vast inefficiency, waste and corruption. By contrast, the British system had a degree of openness, in that there was a national bank supported by the monarchy to obtain loans, backed by the representatives of the British nation. France actually had less public debt than Britain, but France's opaque financial system meant that loans were almost twice the cost of England's debt payments. In Britain, Parliament passed taxes sufficient to pay interest on its public debt, roughly seventy million pounds in 1751, and 450 million pounds in 1801. For the French monarchy, the largest and most entrenched in all of Europe, with the expressed aim for military and diplomatic glory of France, sound public credit was a sine qua non of France's honor.

Calonne presented his sweeping and ambitious reforms to the King on August 20, 1786. He had already commenced major reforms. A national lottery initiated by Calonne raised 100 million livres. The Clergy itself donated 18 million livres, in part because Calonne persuaded Beaumarchais not to publish his edition on Voltaire, the notorious scourge of the Catholic Church. In order to cover shortfalls, he borrowed more from bankers, but the more he borrowed, the more interest he had to pay. Only new taxes and a reformed tax system could save France's credit.

Louis XVI totally endorsed Calonne's revolutionary program, including the vast administrative changes to tax collections. To achieve these objectives, Calonne reached back 160 years to an expedient of Cardinal Richelieu, the calling of the Assembly of Notables. Calonne's plan was to consult the notables, without allowing them any specific rights to accept or reject the new plan of taxation. On February 22, 1787, Calonne spoke with frankness and candor to the 144 Notables: 11 clergy, 48 nobles, 12 from the Royal Council (including the King's brother, Compte Artois), 38 magistrates, 12 deputies from the regions, and 23 municipal officials, a veritable galaxy of France's best and brightest.

Their deliberations were provocative, and indeed revolutionary, touching upon ideas of free trade with Britain, strengthening French commercial interests, including spiriting British entrepreneurs like Mathew Boulton and James Watt to France (they did visit Paris), and imposing a single tariff on foreign trade, the so-called Single Duty Project. Calonne's kitchen cabinet – Talleyrand, Honore-Gabriel Mirabeau, the phisiocrat writer Dupont de Nemours, and Isaac Penchaud, a Swizz Banker and foe of Necker - also learned many things about their mentor, including that he was seriously ill (some said from a life of debauchery). In addition, they bore witness to his taste for prodigality, and a spectacular collection of paintings, along with his opulent kitchens in his two country chateaux and his house on rue Saint-Dominique. As Calonne remitted the currency in 1785, through adjustments to the gold-silver ratios, he gained infamy for personal extravagance and for extorting good money after bad. The scurrilous pamphleteers had a field day. As a result, Calonne's reputation was associated with the extravagance of the Court, cloaked in personal self-indulgence and excessive opulence.

In the end, while Calonne's reforms, if passed, might have prevented the French Revolution, the Notables, once they assembled and deliberated, had no intention of accepting Calonne's reform measures.

MacEachern's Letter in Latin, December 12, 1826

85

They were truly shocked at the extent of the financial deficit, and quickly blamed Calonne, in part because Calonne lacked the political tact to win approval, and part because Calonne himself was seen as a high spender. Thomas Jefferson, lobbying the French Government with his colleagues Benjamin Franklin and John Adams, was asked what he thought of the Assembly of Notables by his friend, the very rich French hero of the American Revolution, the Marquis de LaFayette. Jefferson's answer was that they be called the 'Not ables'.

By most accounts, Calonne was not the man to push such radical reforms on this reluctant group of notables, especially when the financial measures would impact them personally. The Notables were also astonished when they learned the real state of the country's financial state. Yet they did accept some reform measures, such as reductions to the salt tax, tolls on internal commerce, and free trade in grain. They also ended the dreaded *corée*, a cruel form of forced labour for municipal projects. However, Calonne had other problems, including opponents in the Paris Parlement. However much he enjoyed the King's favour when he first presented his sweeping measures, he had lost the confidence of Marie Antoinette. More significantly, perhaps, he lost her friendship. He had supported her extravagant ways, increasing the finances for the Royal Family by 100,000 livres per year, as well as extending support for her friend, Compte d'Adhemar, who became Ambassador to Britain. More tellingly, he disapproved of the purchase of Saint Cloud, at a cost of 6 million livres. This was to be the personal property of Marie herself, located so close to Paris and emboldened with a large "La Reine" on the pass key, what Baron de Breteuil called 'a ring on the Queen's finger'. Breteuil and Calonne detested each other from disputes dating back to 1784. Their paths would cross again, but in more dire circumstances as counter-revolutionary brothers in arms.

But the Queen's general disfavour was not auspicious for the Monarchy. Rising literacy among the middle class meant two great arts of the French were in full array – the power of the pens and the power of French gossip. Among women, especially, Marie Antoinette was always viewed with suspicion, 'that Austrian woman' as she was called, even as the Queen made fun of the older dowagers with their black dresses at the Royal Court. But malicious gossip about the Queen, involving her alleged sexual promiscuity, coupled with her innocent ignorance of France (she always called France 'this country' in her copious family correspondence, preferring the word *patrie* for her native Austria) underscored the line from the book *Les Liasons Dangeruses*: "Old women must not be angered, for they make young women's reputations." Events would soon show the wisdom of this aphorism.

Despite state censorship now common throughout Europe, where a license was necessary for printing (hence the Stamp Act), the French excelled at a new form of publishing, the pamphleteers. One of the most famous, a 47 page tract entitled *Common Sense*, written by Thomas Paine, endorsed by Benjamin Franklin, led to the Declaration of Independence. (Later Paine himself would end up in judgment of Louis XVI, suggesting the King be sent to America rather than be martyred.) The pamphleteers, or libellists as they were known in France (hence the word 'libel') often threw truth and consequences to the wind. Because most pamphlets were illegally printed and imported clandestinely into France across porous borders from Holland or England, they were widely popular.

Royal insiders quickly recognized that the Queen disliked Calonne as a person. She despaired at his elegant manners and good looks, his charm with women of the Court, and his intellectual airs in financial matters. Calonne himself recognized the problem: for his side, he resented the people around the Queen, and he disliked her presence with the King when he was discussing the precarious state of France's finances. The fact that Calonne was right in calling into question the acquisition of Saint Cloud, and what it did to the sense of extravagance of the Royal household and the Queen herself, did little to save his position. With this assembly, Calonne spoke as if the King supported all his measures, which was not the case. Calonne appealed to the public by publishing his speeches, which the Notables resented. LaFayette distrusted Calonne, and openly challenged him for 'monster speculation', by selling off royal real estate. LaFayette won the argument. The Clergy disputed a new tax on land, since it would require a national survey.

In the end, the King had to make a choice: should he continue to back Calonne, who deceived him on several treasury matters, or should he find a new Controller-General who would not appeal to the masses? When his Queen intervened and suggested that Calonne be dismissed, the King relented. On Easter Sunday, April 8, 1787, the King, ever the irresolute and indecisive authority figure, his own position weakening by the day, fired Calonne in a feeble attempt to please this 144 member group of the rich aristocracy. As one wit noted about Calonne's tenure, "He was applauded when he lit the fire, and condemned when he sounded the alarm."

Calonne's successor was another Notable, a free thinker, who six years ago was a candidate to be the Archbishop of Paris. The King protested the appointment: "We must at least have an Archbishop who believes in God." But Calonne's departure was now the key to the King's undoing. The days were numbered for France, as debts mounted, and political storm clouds gained height, not to be helped in the next year by a disastrous harvest and the coldest winter on record. Louis XVI withdrew from day to day administration, spending more time hunting by day and card playing at night. He put on weight, became careless in his pretensions, and disoriented with his associates, including Calonne's successor, Etienne-Charles de Lomenie de Brienne, Archbishop of Toulouse. Brienne was personable, a man with political savoir faire, as clever as Calonne without his vanity. The King's depression enhanced Marie Antoinne's role as personal advisor, while Brienne attempted to modify the extent of Calonne's taxation measures. He appealed to the 17 regional parlements but constitutional wrangling, indecisive Royal leadership, and appeals for the recall of the Estates General, a more regal and magisterial body, set off a train of events that culminated in the French Revolution in 1789. The Assembly of Notables was dissolved in May 1787.

*****

Charles Calonne, at first willing to resign if his reform program was approved, was savaged by the Court, denounced by the Notables and unmissed by the Queen. Like Turgot before him, he left in *disgrâce*, was stripped of his blue riband of the Order of Saint-Esprit, and burned in effigy on the Pont Neuf. Ever the optimist, hoping that his exile would be short-lived, he rented space from a monastery near his house and stored 1000 bottles of expensive wine. Charles left for Holland and then London accompanied by his brother, Abbe Calonne. At home, the struggle was now political: would the Third Estate, representing about ninety per cent of the population, have the same number of deputies as the first two estates combined, as Calonne had offered. Would votes be decreed by order of the three estates, or by the whole assembly, or voting by head? This was the core of revolutionary fervor, centered on whether the King would approve the *Estates-General* voting along aristocratic principles, dominated by the first two estates, or on populist principles, dominated by the Third Estate.

In these crucial months, France now faced what England faced in 1688 – the shift from an absolute monarchy to a constitutional monarchy. Would France's King go the way of Charles I of England? The indecisive King decided to let events unfold. Tensions mounted and Versailles, not Paris, became the focus of political intrigue. Necker had returned as Finance Minister. France chose her Estates General, 300 clergy, 291 nobles, and 610 representatives of the Third Estate. Both Charles and Joseph wanted to be members, yet only Abbe Calonne was successful from Cambrai. Tellingly, Mirabeau, rejected by the second estate, the Nobles, turned to the Third, the people, and was elected.

The French Revolution, and the fate of the monarchy, caught Europe by surprise. Its ferocity had far more implications than the distant revolt across the Atlantic. It unleashed enormous tremors that remain today, within the dynamics of nationalism, including the bitter feud between revolution and religion, and the new gospel of democracy. Louis XVI and Marie Antoinette, after a failed midnight escape from Versailles, were returned in ignominy to Paris, where they faced separate court charges, and ultimately both met the guillotine, separately and with little public remorse. The Estates-General, representing the nobility, the Church, and the commoners, soon lost control of political events and the Reign of Terror took over. Some 250,000 people were publicly charged and met the guillotine, a surgical instrument of profound instantaneity. This device, associated with Dr. Joseph-Ignace Guillotine, became the indiscriminate if spontaneous retribution, a measure of social equality in the face of instant death.

Louis XVI faced the scaffold on a foggy Paris morning of January 21, 1793, ten days before France declared war on Britain and Spain. "I don't think that this can be the eighteenth century," wrote Queen Charlotte, reflecting on the terror in Paris, "for ancient history can hardly produce anything more barbarous and cruel than our neighbors in France." Calonne was obviously well known; the British Prime Minister, William Pitt had visited Versailles and the French Court, and Britain, like many of the European monarchies, were horrified by the French Revolution and the Reign of Terror. The possibility of a possible Regency for Louis XVI's son had some merit, and Charles Calonne was seen as a possible prime minister in waiting.

In the years after the revolution, the Calonne brothers worked tirelessly to restore the French monarchy. They traveled extensively, published widely, spent profusely, and attempted to lobby the Courts of Europe. They toured European capitals in search of measures to protecting the French Monarchy and save the French King's life. At times, Calonne often put his own career on an equal footing as the leader of the counter-revolutionary forces. The Calonne brothers traveled to Venice, Cologne, met Emperor Leopold, conspired with the King's brother, Compe d'Artois, but the Army of the Notables, as this group became known, couldn't deliver. The Compte, brother to Louis XVI, actually led an expedition from Portsmoth to France in 1797, assisted by Horatio Nelson. However, the European Monarchies refused to come to the aid of Louis XVI and his forlorn queen and each facing court hearings and possible conviction and the guillotine.

Abbe Calonne, working with publicists, wrote pamphlets like *Courrier Francais*, at a cost of over 500 livres of borrowed money that he didn't have. As political tensions mounted, many Cardinals, bishops and priests left France and escaped to other Catholic countries, with many departing to Rome and the Vatican precincts. Virtually all the corps of bishops and court families left for London, taking furniture, treasure, and art. London developed a sizeable colony of French citizens, horrified by mob rule, the Revolutionary Tribunal and the reign of terror. Many notables became too relaxed about so much pent up populist anger, with concurrently indiscriminate use of the guillotine, and desire for revenge against centuries of aristocratic rule. Over six per cent of those killed were clergy, and many more were nuns, frequently executed for protecting priests or hiding holy objects to say mass.

But their work was all in vain. Charles Calonne, ever the optimist, thought he would return to lead the counterrevolution. Indeed, by 1791, Calonne was becoming the prime minister of counter-revolutionary forces, spanning a network from Normandy to Avignon. Still, the Army of the Nobles was ultimately a costly, futile failure. The Calonne brothers were playing a high stakes political intrigue. In England, where reformers and the Parliamentary circles were joined, it was not so in France. King George III put one French Cardinal on a pension from his own court resources; many French clergy moved to England. From the Continent, the Calonne's returned to London, living on borrowed money and help from court friends. Afraid of the guillotine, many clergy committed suicide, including Charles Calonne's successor, the Bishop of Toulose. Many departed to the US colonies, such as Charles Talleyrand, who spent time in New York and Boston before returning to France, courtesy of Napoleon Bonaparte. Charles married a well off French lady, Madame d'Harveluy, but like many aristocrats, she was asset-rich, and cash poor. In addition, Charles had incurred enormous debts for his counterrevolutionary mission.

The British court attempted to help. Parliament, listening to Burke, slowly learned the full terror of revolutionary France. Many civil liberties were curtailed, and possible war with France, which retained its immense army and navy in a country so much larger than Britain (26 million vs. 15 million) was both a warning to the monarchies of Europe, and a signal retreat from too much democracy. Even in England, civil repression was widespread: the great scientist, Joseph

Priestly, his life work ruined in England, departed for the United States.

The Prime Minister, William Pitt, was a disciple of Adam Smith and reformer of British finances. He had met the King and Queen and other notables, including Jacques Nector, in 1783, yet remained suspicious of England's arch-enemy, refusing any considerations of paying an enormous ransom to release the French monarchy. Remarkably, he kept his Cabinet at bay. Yet many of the French clergy pressed for financial support. One senior clergyman from Brittany, Jean François de La Marche, Bishop of St. Pol de Léon, took refuge in England in 1792. He organized material assistance for the émigré clergy, as well as spiritual comfort for the many French prisoners detained in England. Through his contacts, he obtained a grant for the Castle of Winchester as a home for émigré French priests, and gathered there no less than eight hundred of them. He died in 1806.

******

The Calonnes were only too aware of the published speeches and writings in Britain from such illustrious statesmen as Edmund Burke and writers like Thomas Carlyle, who had visited Europe and saw the Reign of Terror first hand. To Burke, now a distinguished Parliamentarian and widely admired, the French "destroyed all balances and counterpoises which serve to fix a state and give it steady direction, and they melted down the whole into one incongruously mass of mob and democracy." In Parliament, Burke decried the horror, and the architects of ruin: "In one summer, they have done their business... they have completely pulled down to the ground their monarchy, their church, their nobility, their law, their revenue, their army, their navy, their commerce, their arts, and their manufacturers."

Not by coincidence, the British Government tried to help some notables, and offered them passage to the various British colonies. Charles Calonne had considered moving to the British colonies, possibly bringing members of the London émigré colony with him, including French clergy. He was given 500 acres in PEI, as part of the crown lot not sold as part of the infamous lottery of July 1767.

This property, in Lot 65 close to the Charlottetown Harbour and near the site of the old French center, Port La Joie, became known as the Warren Farm. But ill-health and ill-fortune kept Charles in London. His brother, Abbe Calonne, knew that his career in his homeland was finished, with War with England underway and Napoleon ruling France. Reluctantly, he left his beloved brother, and moved to the newly acquired Calonne land in PEI. Angus MacEachern had a new priest.

Abbe Calonne, with his legal background and his awareness of the 1791 Constitution Act which protected the French language and religion in Quebec, wrote Rev. Pierre Denault, Bishop of Quebec, which in turn led him to write on the 5 February 1799 about PEI, the land which his brother owned, and inquiring as to the possibility of bringing up to a dozen émigré French priests. Calonne knew that he needed the Bishop's intervention with civil authorities to come to PEI. That meant formal letters to PEI's Governor Edmund Fanning from Bishop Denault, and letters in turn from Governor Fanning to Angus MacEachern, the sole Catholic priest on PEI.

Abbe Calonne corresponded from London. The new Quebec bishop, Pierre Denault, contacted Father James Jones in Halifax, who knew French clergy in Île de Orleans, acquainted with the famous Calonne brothers. Abbe Calonne arrived in Halifax on August 1799 with Father Amable Pichard, and then moved to PEI. Father Pichard, older and somewhat retired, settled in Tracadie under Father MacEachern's guidance. Abbe Calonne, now 55, wrote the Bishop on May 28, 1800, and noted that the Acadians in PEI lived in three areas - Malpeque, Rustico and Fortune Bay. They were well grounded in their religion and the discharge of their Catholic duties. The Scots spoke only Gaelic, and were Father MacEachern's responsibility. Further,

> *The abominable vice of drunkenness brutalizes the people and makes them indifferent to everything. In order to ingratiate myself with them, I ask no remuneration for my likeness: only too happy would I be, did they respond to my efforts. They are attached to their faith. They would suffer death rather than abandon it, but they don't observe even*

> *one of the Commandments. It would be easier, if I*
> *may so express myself, to make of them Martyrs than*
> *Christians.*

The good father's description was close to a visiting doctor, who said of Charlottetown, "In a few minutes, I found Charlottetown to be wicked enough for a large place; swearing and drunkenness abounded." From his small abode in Charlottetown, Father Calonne kept up a series of letters to the Bishop, describing the division of labour among the Irish, Acadian, and Scottish families and at times, offering unflattering descriptions of his flock. The Bishop himself visited the Island in 1803 and made Father Calonne his Vicar General. During this visit to PEI in 1803, a year later than he wanted, Bishop Denault was greeted by Abbe Calonne and Angus MacEachern. They toured the Island, planned new Churches, and met Governor Edmund Fanning. But Bishop Denault appointed Abbe Calonne, not MacEachern, as his Vicar General, possibly because this Scottish priest was so much a man of the people with a reluctant iron whip. But in this appointment, Bishop Denault and Abbe Calonne lacked subtlety and understanding of the changes taking place in London. Britain was not only at war with France, but Catholic Ireland, which was in open revolt in 1798. This Irish rebellion – there would be more - Ulster Presbyterians joining Catholics in Wexford, assisted by troops from France – forced Pitt the Prime Minister and George III the King to be unequivocal. What was Pitt to do: allow Catholic emancipation in Ireland, which was three quarters Catholic, or preserve the Protestant religion and establishment in Britain? Two kingdoms or one?

Since 1688, Britain had been ruled by Whigs, with all their blemishes. Unlike France, Britain had slowly built a tolerant style of government, a constitutional monarchy, in contrast to France's absolutist monarchy, that even clever American rebels admired. At its heart was the dictum of the Protestant establishment, the supremacy of the state over the Church. In Scotland, this meant Presbyterianism, in England, Episcopalism, in Ireland, anything but Catholicism. In truth, the colonies could be many things – a source of raw materials, a place for undesirables or patronage for sons of the aristocracy without provision. But now Britain and the Whig aristocracy made a decision on Ireland, cruel, pernicious, and unequivocal: Britain was to be an imperial power, Protestant, expansionist, isolated from Europe, and protected by the Royal Navy.

In distant PEI, or in Quebec City or Montreal, Bishop Denault and Abbe Calonne lacked the subtlety and personal diplomacy to see these imperial changes. Bishop MacEachern, brought up in the wilds of Scotland, where churches were underground with a price placed on Catholic priests, knew only too well the changing British landscape. Since his first arrival in PEI, he made friends with the colonial government, established a rapport with Protestants and the Governor, and practiced personal ecumenism long before it was accepted demeanour. Later, as Bishop, he would receive a government stipend and financial support for his new college. Through classmates in Europe, he knew the opinions of the Colonial office in London. The French Revolution meant that there was no hope for the Catholic Church in the British colonies without a measure of cooperation, and MacEachern had the grace and wisdom to understand the profound changes taking place in Europe, with immediate consequences for the Island colony. Abbe Calonne clearly learned from MacEachern, despite his own disparaging letters to the Bishop. Most of Calonne's personal initiatives proved unsuccessful, including a decision to establish a group of French Trappist monks on PEI.

In 1803, the French priest went back to London to settle family debts incurred by their expensive counter-revolutionary campaign to restore the French monarchy. He returned to Quebec four years later. In his absence, Captain John MacDonald, supported by his brother Augustine, became embroiled in a small quarrel over the location of the new church at St. Andrews - the captain preferring the use of his own home. He wrote a rather pompous letter to the Quebec Bishop, a wearisomely solecism, setting out the low-life perversity of the Scottish peasants towards external worship, and a diatribe against Acadian "dithyrambic ecclesiastic" praise. When asked to referee Captain MacDonald's epistolary dispute with the Scottish priest, Calonne came down solidly for MacEachern and his parish work was underway.

PEI remained a small colony with a tiny population, colonial administrators and a collection of Scottish, Irish, and French peasants. The few churches were little more than an unkempt barn, and religious objects, a tin cup, not a gold chalice, was a far cry from the rich embellishments of Calonne's upbringing in Douai or Cambrai. Moreover, the position of the Catholic Church was far different in the British Colonies than in his native country. Both Bishop Denault and Abbe Calonne were somewhat naïve about the changing currents in Britain. Both knew that the Constitution Act of 1791, a controversial measure that preserved the French language and religion in New France, but equally gave huge land holdings in the Ohio Valley to Quebec (a preview of American expansionism advanced by Ben Franklin for the American Government). In truth, the Catholic Church was prescribed. Most appointments, even when approved with Papal bulls from Rome, required acceptance by the Colonial Governors. Even Abbe Calonne's correspondence with Chief Justice Robert Thorpe, a somewhat officious bureaucrat on the Island, warned about British penal laws:

> *This act declares by statue the revocation of clandestine marriages. It prosecutes Catholics who attend schools without informing the court of the names and places, and they can't instruct any child of Protestant families.*

Father Calonne was an exemplary priest, a close colleague of Angus MacEachern, who welcomed Bishop Pierre Denault, the Archbishop of Quebec, to the shores of Prince Edward Island. His work and his correspondence elevated MacEachern's stature in the eyes of the bishops in Quebec, and helped rethink the organization of the Catholic Church in the British colonies. It would take time, because the Diocese of Charlottetown, with its own bishop, was relatively small, even with the neighbouring provinces included. On the larger canvas, the Calonne brothers is an intimate tale of intrigue at the highest levels of French politics, and an example of the long term influences of Europe on the welfare of Prince Edward Island. In remains a great 'what if' question if Charles himself had come to PEI, coinciding with Lord Selkirk and his 800 settlers a few years later.

Together could they have reorganizing the land question, instilled better local administration, and accelerated more formal schooling on this small colony?

Abbe Calonne's last years were spent in the Urseline Convent in Trois Rivière, attending to the sick, the meek, and the humble. It was a far cry from the heady revolutionary days of Paris, or the industrialized community of his home town in Tournai. At times, Calonne must have considered the extreme ironies of his situation. He was living in Canada in the land that Voltaire had dismissed as 'some acres of snow,' his language and culture protected through the Quebec Act by an English King, and the influence of French writers – Voltaire, Rousseau, Montesquieu – who were widely known among the educated elites of North America, including in French-speaking Quebec.

Calonne's early training as a student of elocution in Tournai and Douai never left this solitary priest. His sermons sometimes touched his counter-revolutionary fervour with the aura of the French monarchy, where political change produced the irreversible: the passions of the mob leading to the guillotine and extreme violence. Calonne would reflect on his brother's work, and the two tempers of hyperbole – the visceral, brutal, and rhetorical cries of freedom, and what he and his brother Charles so much wanted, a predictable, continuous, rational, and cerebral order. Paradoxically, this is what Canada offered him when he died on October 16, 1822, aware that priests, nuns, and his parishioners knew which temperament he so much favoured.

****

The visits of the two Quebec bishops - Bishop Denalt in 1803, Plessis in May 1812 – offered first hand evidence of the extensive territory that Angus MacEachern had to serve. In May 1812, Bishop Plessis visited the Maritimes, touring the Island, and met Government officials, including the former and current governor, as well as seeing parishes at close hand. He soon recognized first hand the differences among the Catholic flock in the Maritimes, as regards the diverse geography, the ethnic mix, and the languages spoken, which were mainly French, English, and Gaelic.

Joseph Ostave Plessy's was Quebec's eleventh bishop. He became Archbishop in 1819 and was a key figure in Lower Canada. A born diplomat, he played a strong role in rallying French Canadian Catholics against the American invaders to Quebec in the War of 1812. The English (and Protestant) government provided extensive leeway towards the extension of Church rights and vicarages throughout Quebec, and consistently defended Church rites, particularly in education. In the US, President James Madison had passed a half dozen resolutions with the Republican Congressional majority. The cry of Manifest Destiny was in the air. Henry Clay, Speaker of the House, boasted that "the militia of Kentucky are alone competent to place Montréal and Upper Canada at your feet" but this was mostly talk. The British took Detroit on August 16, 1812, the threats to Montreal were repulsed, and French habitants halted Major General James Wilkinson up the St. Lawrence.

Over the years, despite his constant pleas to Bishop Plessis, MacEachern's patience had waned, notwithstanding his long letters and solicitations. By 1825, he became indignant:

> *What has Canada ever done for this Island since the conquest? What provision for the Acadian settlers in spirituals before our people arrived on the Island? And what has been done for us since? And can your Grace for a moment say that we ought not to have a share in the wealthy of the Canadian Seminaries.*

In reality, MacEachern's exasperation was understandable but circumstances elsewhere weren't much better. The Catholic Clergy in Quebec were having their own internal political machinations. There was certainly the reluctant role of the Bishop of Quebec over the Maritime colonies. Now there were new conflicts between Quebec City and commercial interests in Montréal, and new arguments with the growing population in Upper Canada. As corporations far and wide were to learn, how much authority should be centralized, and how much to decentralize? Bishop Plessis, when he took over the Diocese of Quebec from Bishop Hubert, laid out the organizational challenge in 1806 to a colleague in London:

Examine the Map and you will see that it is impossible for one Bishop to extend his solitude with any degree of success from Lake Superior to The Gulf of the St. Lawrence. That territory contains more than two thousand Catholics, and yet there are only one hundred and eighty priests to addend their spiritualists. Add to this the difficulties arising from the entanglement with a Protestant population, and which is constantly making new efforts to establish the Royal Supremacy.

Bishop Plessis himself visited Europe in 1819, staying for the best part of a year in London. The British Government understood the issues at hand but wanted to deal with only one Bishop in the British Colonies on Catholic matters, not the new proposed plan for four. Plessis himself was elevated to become Archbishop that year so the organization plan was to have one Archbishop of Quebec, and four "suffrages"- equal in church authority as Bishop *in partibus infedelium.* Joseph-Norbert Provencher was appointed for the North-West (Bishop of Juliopolis), Alexander MacDonald for Upper Canada (Bishop of Rhensina), Jean-Jacques Lartique for Montreal (Bishop of Telmesse) and Angus MacEachern for the Maritimes (Bishop of Rosen). On June 17, 1821, in a scene only the Catholic Church can assemble, with majesty and pomp, Angus MacEachern was consecrated in Quebec at the Church of St. Roch. The Governor's consort, Lady Dalhousie, attended the ceremony: it was the first time ever that four Canadian Bishops were assembled in this elegant installation.

The elevation of Bishop MacEachern had many impacts. As a personal representative of the Church, it was not significant - his flock witnessed the same active priest, his same ease of languages, his same workaholic pace and zest for life. Personally, he worried about the very challenge that greeted him when he came to PEI in 1790, limited *tithes* or church collections for his travels and upkeep of his church, and his constant need for more priests. But in other ways, the mood *had* changed. In Quebec, MacEachern made representations about PEI's autocratic governor, Charles Smith, perhaps the Island's worst ever Governor - a man who managed to annoy everyone, including his own officials. In the next quarter century, the Island indeed had also changed. Emigration flowed, new churches were built, two Quebec Bishops visited the Island, and both the Catholic and Protestant faiths built up a strong base: churches, schools, and places of worship. To a surprising degree, it was a relatively ecumenical community – a strong group of churches in Charlottetown and a group of over 50 places of worship, community by community. Many churches still stand, or were replaced when fire or disaster struck.

****

Two of MacEachern's priorities besides seeking priests were the education and political emancipation of Catholics. In 1822, he supervised the first Island Catholic to become a priest, Bernard Donald MacDonald. He was ordained in Quebec and eventually become MacEachern's successor, and the second Bishop of Charlottetown. Catholic emancipation almost became a reality in 1825, when a formal resolution was submitted to the Island assembly, but the vote ended in a tie. The Speaker, John Stewart, voted against the petition, on the reasonable grounds that the issue had not been settled in England. Catholic emancipation became a five year running political issue on the Island, with venomous claims made on both sides. It was not for the first time that theological issues had been put aside and needless political claims were advanced that did little grace to either side of the religious divide, Catholics and Protestants alike.

Bishop MacEachern rose above this controversial dispute but remained frustrated by the new climate that was created, which he knew would raise problems in imperial London. When the British Parliament finally accorded Catholic Emancipation in 1829 within Britain as part of Prime Minister Robert Peel's reform leadership, the Island finally accepted emancipation in 1830. Not for the first time was the Island ready to follow, not lead. Not for the last time were religious sentiments ready to embrace politics and political action in secular jurisdictions. Ironically, the Assembly provided Bishop MacEachern with a stipend of 50 pounds for his "meritorious services," payable each year until his death. It was a measure of the remarkable personal esteem that the Legislature, all Protestants, had for this venerable priest.

There is no precise date to determine the start of formal educational facilities on PEI, but the year 1804 is a useful start. At that time, Governor Edmund Fanning provided trustees in Charlottetown new lands for the education of Island youth. The name chosen for this college was Kent College, named after Edward, Duke of Kent, commander of Halifax. Throughout the British Empire, education was anything but a duty of government. In Europe, the Catholic Church had developed high schools and universities. Indeed this was the Church's mission, to provide education and priests through its extensive seminaries, from Ireland to Poland and Catholic missionaries and activist orders like Opus Dei and the Society of Jesus. This latter order, The Jesuits, had become a global institution, with missionaries as distant as Chile, Japan and the Baltic States.

In Scotland, far in advance of England, the levels of literary and academic learning influenced all of Europe, with its great universities of Glasgow, St. Andrews, and Edinburgh. Citizens like Robert Burns or Thomas Carlyle were literate in French and Latin and knew the works of Shakespeare and John Locke. Protestants from across Europe came to study in Scotland, while Catholic Highlanders like Angus MacEachern studied in Scottish schools in Spain and Germany.

In the United States, literacy was promoted by religious figures imported from Scotland, and American universities like Harvard, Yale, Dartmouth and Princeton had received Royal Charters – eight, in fact, from George III. Boston and Philadelphia were leading centers for book selling, printing, newspapers and the "ink industries" – Philadelphia alone had more newspapers than London. Britain, of course, was not a land of public education - schooling for Kings and the aristocracy was a private affair. The bourgeois was an appendage to the rich, with special schools which were paradoxically called public but in fact were rich, private and exclusive. These were the boys' schools for the military, senior ecclesiastics, lawyers and colonial governors, a curriculum of some (but not too much) Latin and Greek, a little reference to the British Empire, literature, and a great wad of bullying, homosexuality, and ignorance.

In PEI and in the British Colonies, education in the first third of the nineteenth century was a church and religious affair. Books were scarce, libraries non-existent, newspapers few in number, mainly due to the shortage of paper. Presbyterians placed great emphasis on literacy because a literate person had the capacity to read the Bible. Catholic schooling was focused on literacy but the curriculum was also devoted to training priests, and this was a constant refrain in the letters MacEachern sent in Episcopal reports to the Bishop of Quebec. The Colonial administrations provided some money for education, comprised of a school house in Charlottetown, allotted £500 pounds and six school masters, two per county at £50 pounds in the budget estimate of 1806. But a lackadaisical administration assured that education was not a priority, a worrying problem for MacEachern. The new Kent school, or the National School, was under the control of the Governor and the teachers were paid by the families of students, plus a small grant of £10 pounds per year. There were other private schools across the Island, including those in the French parishes of Rustico and Tignish, but the capacity of people to write and sign their name was limited indeed.

The summer of 1813 brought a new Governor to PEI. In Europe, it was the close of the France-Britain wars. In North America, the War of 1812 revived old rivalries, between the aggressive Americans who sought Canadian lands, the Montreal merchants who wanted to reclaim their monopolistic fur trading empire in the Canadian West (with Lord Selkirk, now the largest shareholder in the Hudson's Bay Company), and the French Canadians, now loyal to the English Crown, and in particular, to Prince Edward, the Duke of Kent, the son of George III, who had been stationed in Quebec from 1791 to 1794 before moving to Halifax in 1796. The Americans had held off British and French Canadian forces, but soon the British force would attack Washington, set fire to the White House, and General Andrew Jackson would save Louisiana with a decisive victory in the Battle of New Orleans. War was everywhere on both sides of the Atlantic - treasuries were drained, while New Englanders were threatening to secede from the Union. The decline of the Napoleonic era, despite the Emperor's short comeback and his defeat by Wellington's forces at Waterloo in 1815, left Britain in a far weaker position politically and economically than most British understood.

In PEI, the small colony was largely aloof from the wider world. The new Governor was in place, Charles Douglas Smith. One of his first acts was to send a letter to the Catholic priest, Rev. Angus MacEachern, notifying that any marriages he performed would require a license issued under the seal of the Governor. MacEachern's position as Commission of the Peace was also revoked, a fate similar to another Catholic, Major Alex McDonald. In this single act, Governor Smith had planted the seeds of bigotry and religious intolerance that would become an Island curse for 150 years. The Governor himself would make few friends, Protestant or Catholic, educated or uneducated, men of means or men of the soil. Smith, in short, was a tyrannical despot, an overbearing Governor with no tact, no diplomacy, an author of deep distrust in an era where tact and diplomacy would have advanced the Colony's well being. Why was Smith given this job?

Smith's brother, Sir Sidney Smith, was the hero of Acre, an important battle in the Mediterranean Sea. Charles Douglas Smith's claim to this position was the fact that he was the brother of this famous Admiral, whose own eccentricities in behaviour and dress were passed on to all his brothers, without Sidney's naval competence. Admiral Smith, fluent in English and French, was the flamboyant naval hero that defended the Port of Acre in Palestine in 1799, just when Britain trembled at the fear of a French invasion. At the Siege of Acre, Smith's exploits destroyed the French Army led by Napoleon Bonaparte himself. Unfortunately, Bonaparte managed to escape on the *Muiron* for the French naval base at Toulon, then launched a coup d'état against the Directory and made himself the First Counsel of the French Republic. If only Smith had captured Napoleon at Acre – no Trafalgar, no invasion of Russia, no Austerlitz and French domination of Europe, and no C.D. Smith as Governor of PEI. History is a landscape of what ifs.

Both Smiths were friends of the Earl of Bathurst, chosen as Colonial Secretary by the new Prime Minister, the Earl of Liverpool. (From

1801-1820, there had been six Prime Ministers, the forgotten Prime Ministers of British history.) The Earl of Bathurst had to face problems of both organization and finance. The Napoleonic Wars turned out to be extremely expensive, as much of Britain's overseas trade was threatened by the Continental system, a trade blockage of European ports against British ships. Napoleon's armies amassed across the English Channel, keeping the Continent secure for France, and London was worried by an imminent invasion. When the war was over, Britain was broke. George III was incapacitated; colonies like Australia were governed by a despot like Governor MacQuarrie, who ruled a society of convicts. To this point, the Canadian colonies were relatively quiet, thanks to more representative institutions. But peace at home meant that Britain had no real intention of introducing democratic legislative forms in the North American colonies.

Britain was an imperial power, a conqueror of peoples – in Ireland, in India, in the West Indies, and in North America. The American colonies remained on shaky grounds, so Britain could resume her historic imperial role through her control of the oceans and seas with her powerful navy, a shrewd policy of a balance of power on the European continent, and an economic system where the colonies provided treasury and wealth to England, controlled by the crown, Parliament, and the Aristocracy. For Father Angus MacEachern, the dictates of the Governor of PEI were in one sense a needless diversion. This coy priest – knowing the ways of such people like Governor Smith - simply accepted the letter sent to him, then knowingly did a diplomatic shuffle. He simply ignored it, characterizing it openly as a 'penny paper' of 'obnoxious dye'!

In 1829, MacEachern undertook his own new initiative, the establishment of a Catholic college. This college was a priority from his first days on the Island, where he understood the challenges of basic illiteracy even among parents. His own experience - in Scotland and in Spain, coupled with his observations of Catholic education in Quebec at the College of Nicolet - had taught him that other issues were at play, including government support, finding teachers, and ensuring parental support. There were other problems. Nova Scotia, as a British colony with its own legislature, no longer corresponded to the ecclesiastic boundaries of the Church. Indeed, Cape Breton and the Highland Catholic immigrants from Scotland, was run from Charlottetown. MacEachern knew that a Catholic college would add strength to his diocese, but he then needed monies to finance it. At the same time, PEI had established the Central Academy, and a Board of Education was established in 1830. The Legislature provided an annual grant of £50 pounds for his new academy, the College of St Andrews.

But time was now running out for MacEachern. By 1829, he was in his 70th year. His constant travels throughout the Maritimes, along with his unstinting work for his parishioners, his incessant search for new and innovative ways to support his Churches, his University, and his love for the community took a toll. He faced regular political challenges. Despite his zest for action and his big dreams for his adopted country, he had access to few resources. In truth, government officials gave him much encouragement but not for the first time, offered him little direct help. He encouraged links with the Protestant community and he rejoiced at a visiting Catholic preacher fresh from Ireland, Father Edward Walsh. A brilliant orator, a man who could hold a crowd with his use of words and rhetorical flourishes, Walsh was to become the first rector of St. Andrew's. MacEachern invited him to address a mixed assembly on a cool, inclement Sunday. He spoke at St. Dunstan's church, with Protestants in attendance, including the Lieutenant Governor, Aretas W. Young, in 1831, drawing a full house and an attentive audience.

His new College took a personal toll, as it opened with twenty students, fifteen from PEI, five from Nova Scotia. All the land and church property had been assigned to the College, and an Act of Incorporation passed both branches of the Legislature and received Royal Assent on April 6, 1833. Time was indeed pressing on this missionary Bishop, and he succumbed to a deadly stroke at the home of Dugald MacIsaac in St. Peter's. Curiously, he was speaking to a young girl about political events in Spain. Suddenly he fell to the floor, unconscious, and help soon arrived. Notice was sent for medical assistance, and the Bishop was moved by horse and sleigh to his own house, accompanied by huge crowds who learned of his precarious state. He died at 3 pm, Wednesday, April 22, 1835.

Conclusion

The long service of Angus MacEachern is notable in three respects for this young colony, and for Canada generally. MacEachern, like Lord Selkirk, left an indelible imprint of Scotland and Scottish culture and values in the British colonies. Whether Highlanders or Lowlanders, the Scottish immigrants cultivated through their families, their Church, the Military, and their education optimism and a fundamental value of loyalty that remains to this day. On the Island, the Scottish influence is everywhere – in place names, in monuments, in an abundance of family names. No one every doubted Angus MacEachern's Scottish background. History records that few Islanders, immigrants or native born, had such a profound influence on all he met, the immigrants from Europe, the Irish settlers, the Micmac tribes, and French Acadians. The stories are legendary of how this simple man, so educated and yet so practical, impacted all the families that he met. From his earliest days on the Island, as a young 31 year old, now re-united with his parents and family, he pursued his vision for his new home. Saving souls and advancing education were his goals, and all else were the clever means to these ends.

His letters, in Latin, French, or English, are masterpieces of clever words and intended meaning. He often opened his letters with a joyous greeting: "Here I am soul and body, sound and hearty" and a description of his recent travels. How must the priests in Rome, living in the gilded Halls of Vatican City, who knew so little about this Scottish immigrant other than tales from his classmates at the Royal Scots College at Valladolid, wondered about the distant land that they didn't understand, and marveled at MacEachern's detailed descriptions of the Island and the neighbouring territories which he described in his Latin epistles!

Angus MacEachern was a master story teller, and his frequent and unexpected visits to farm houses and campfires offered him many occasions to relate the unfolding events in distant Europe. The

French Revolution and the incessant wars on the Continent meant for MacEachern that the only real ally of his, for good or bad, was the British Government, and he cultivated good relations with the various Governors and their associates. As he discovered shortly after his arrival on PEI in 1790, his own views were precisely those of the hierarchy of the Catholic Church in Quebec, who knew, at times publicly, but also privately, that the France of the past, the France of the pre-Revolution monarchy, had abandoned the French citizens of Quebec and the Maritime colonies. Whatever the Imperial Government in London did, the colonies of British North America were now locked into a tight grip of British colonial administration. If Britain loosened its tight grip on Catholics through its rigorous penal laws, as it did, leaders like MacEachern would be the winners. On the Island, when Catholic Emancipation almost was approved – it was a tie vote, broken by John Stewart, who wanted to see what Britain would do – it would have been the first colony in the British Empire to grant Catholics the right to hold administrative office.

MacEachern had another powerful influence on the young Island colony, which he shared with his fellow clergy, both Catholic and Protestant. Throughout its long history, unlike so many British Colonies, the Island was a remarkably peaceful place. Bigotry and youthful foolishness may have been common, at whatever levels of society, but the few instances of violence and killing – the Belfast Riots that occurred later, for instance – are remarkable because there are so few examples. Unlike many colonies in the Caribbean and later in Africa, there were many instances where violence could start, and had to be suppressed at great cost in men and treasure. On the Island, the horrible problem of the land question tested the patience of the tenant farmers and the squatters, especially when the land owners acted through their Island agents. The Clergy had a calming influence, and the power and dignity of MacEachern instilled a powerful value system that allowed peaceful dialogue, especially before the arrival of responsible government in 1851.

MacEachern wanted to raise the literacy of the Island people, and his constant attempts to cultivate schools and his new college, St. Andrew's, was a reflection of the Scottish respect for education.

It is particularly relevant that his school was open to Catholics and Protestants, and when the first Catholics were elected to the Legislature, even the *Royal Gazette* was moved to remark that the principles of tolerance and forbearance were due to the impact of Angus MacEachern. Dr. James Conroy, who was at MacEachern's bedside when this gentle priest suffered his mortal stroke, said on an earlier occasion when he became Bishop, that "any eulogy he might pronounce on the Bishop's character could not add to that esteem and veneration they all felt towards him, the dignity of whose office was adorned by the piety of the man..."

Soon, a new voice of reason and tolerance emerged in PEI, another immigrant, but this time from Ireland. Curiously, he lived quite close to MacEachern's home, but he traveled in different circles. He started as a newspaper publisher, then became a politician. His practical cause was responsible government and later the merger of all the British Colonies in North America. This eminent Islander was Edward Whelan.

4

The Move to Responsible Government: Edward Whelan

A Young Irish Immigrant * The Island's New Editor * A Political Career * George Coles and Responsible Government * The Charlottetown Conference* The Aftermath of Confederation

In a windy, poorly kept graveyard on Longworth Avenue in Charlottetown, there is a small brass plaque with a short narrative placed by the Canadian Historic Sites and Monuments Board. It marks the grave site of Edward Whelan, editor of *The Examiner*, member of the Legislature, delegate at the Confederation Conference in Quebec City, a pamphleteer against the Island's Family Compact, and a willing conspirator to bring responsible government to this small British colony. Edward Whelan joins the pantheon of Islanders who, like Lord Selkirk and Angus MacEachern, brought an outsider's perspective to this tiny colony, helping to shape its political destiny, and leaving a legacy that survives to this day. Born in County Mayo, Ireland in 1824, Edward Whelan was one of the youngest pre-Confederation era politicians, a man who, whether through displaying his brilliant oratory and Irish wit, or with his editorials and speeches, could, as an Irishman, teach the English how to use the English language.

Whelan had a busy life. He lived well and died young, at 42, economically destitute, and politically crippled. In the end, he suffered the fate of so many people in Island politics – or is it a plight of Canadian politics?- destroyed by his friends, ignored by his enemies, and left in a vacuum due to the power politics of rapidly changing events. Despite a short career, and through his writings, speeches, and essays, Whelan touched on all the issues of PEI. His primary economic concern was the land question. Like all Irish in the 19th century, whether Protestant or Catholic, it seemed simply unnatural to have so few gentry landowners control so much property and English proprietors at that! Whelan remained poor throughout his career on the Island, but he remained a constitutionalist, a firm believer in the rule of law, and the right of people to make their own laws. Even during the Irish famine, like the Scots Highlanders, the Irish chose not to revolt, to seek change by constitutional means, and that meant their leaders had to fight in the political realm.

Whelan moved to PEI, started a newspaper, and entered politics. As Editor of *The Examiner*, his second publishing venture, Whelan was at the center of political and reform movements on PEI, where he met all of the delegates to the Charlottetown Conference and was in turn a delegate to the Quebec meetings in October 1864. Unfortunately, like some other Island delegates, Whelan's personal and private papers were lost in a fire in 1876, but many of his speeches, writings, and letters have been retained, as well as records of his principal speeches and electoral addresses. His notes and speeches on the issues surrounding Confederation are central to the unrecorded side of this historic meeting. The true measure of his influence and legacy does not come from his idle religious practices (a noted historian on the Catholic Church in PEI, Rev. John C. MacMillan could write that "A rumor ... was in the air, that Mr. Whelan had grown somewhat indifferent in matters of faith, and had been for a time utterly neglectful with regard to the practices of his religion") or his personal habits. As Thomas Kirwan records in an obituary, "he was a fast liver, and fast livers do not generally attain to patriarchal age." Whelan, above all, was Irish, and remained tormented all his life by the maltreatment the English accorded his homeland, from the indignity of occupation to the brutal and harsh impositions on the poor, sometimes aided by the callous Church hierarchy. Whelan felt he needed few lessons on democracy and responsible government from Catholic bishops.

Nevertheless, on the secular role of government policy, and on many social issues, Whelan was consistently in favour of a legal and political settlement for responsible government, free public education, and peaceful resolution of the land question. He well understood the tactics and actions of the Tenant League, a group which emerged in the 1860s out of deep frustration with the Island's absentee landowners, and whose actions Whelan deplored, although sympatizing with their aims. At first, Whelan was not keen on Canadian Confederation. Not without reason, he felt that it was an Imperial scheme for legislative union of all the colonies. However, once he learned that it was an initiative by the diverse Canadian leaders who *had* achieved responsible government and a plan for political confederation, he became an early convert to the confederation plan of 1864. He supported Confederation, even while recognizing that PEI would have a diminished role from its separate status as a British colony, with relatively few members sent to the Federal parliament.

As an Irishman, only too painfully aware of the appalling conditions England had imposed on his homeland, Whelan remained faithful to constitutional means and the rule of law. Some of his speeches on Responsible Government are almost verbatim thoughts lifted from the great speeches of Edmund Burke, a fellow Irishman. As a Catholic, and an Irish immigrant to boot, where Irish Catholics at home had only the lone potato to eat, while priests administered prayers for the dying and forlorn hope for the living, Whelan was against public grants for Catholic schools and the Island's small Catholic university. In the Colonial structure of legislatures used throughout the British Empire, Whelan's voice was not against the Colonial Governor, as weak or incompetent (or both), as they inevitably became. He saved his invective for the Family Compact, that band of local politicians who were middlemen, land agents, and hucksters who dominated the Legislative Assembly, serving with the conformity of the tenant's discomfort. In modern terminology, Whelan had little use for political correctness: "The evil that men do lives after them; the good is oft interred with their bones."

Sketch of Edward Whelan

**

That said, Edward Whelan was an Irish orator, a raconteur, and a fiery politician of the old school who, despite his youth, taught the landed gentry where to find the bull in the China shop. He was born in the small hamlet of Ballina, in the Connaught district of Ireland, but immigrated to Halifax in 1831 with his widowed mother. According to William L. Cotton, who would eventually succeed Whelan as Editor of *The Examiner* and then start the first daily paper on the Island, *The Daily Examiner*, the first person the young Whelan met on the docks of Halifax was Joseph Howe. Howe was out for an evening stroll. He ran into the young lad of seven, exchanged some banter and, with his Mother's approval, "took at once to his heart, his home, and his printing shop."

In January 1840, Whelan enrolled at St. Mary's, a school linked to St. Mary's Seminary, and run by its first superior, Rev. Richard Baptist O'Brien. He also took a job as an apprentice for the local newspaper and print shop, headed by the redoubtable Joseph Howe. Schooling and the print shop, coupled with the influence of his Mother, gave Whelan the best of these three mentors. From his mother, Whelan acquired a deep and lifelong concern for the poor and the uneducated. From his Irish teacher, Whelan obtained a life long passion for learning: not only from reading books, committing his thoughts in writing, and listening to reform-minded people. From Joseph Howe, Whelan gained an unexcelled capacity for strong words and fiery oratory. As a politician, he needed all of these skills in his journalistic and political career on Prince Edward Island, where he took on the cause of responsible government, attacking religious bigotry, even against his own Bishop, and advancing the cause of public education. He started as a reluctant advocate for both Maritime Union and Confederation. As he learned more about the Island's limited tools to deal with the land question, Whelan became a strong advocate for Confederation. Throughout his life, he preferred constitutional means for change, as opposed to protest and violence, and for him, Confederation was the tool to address the one issue that held back PEI, the cause of land reform.

From his work at the printing office of Joseph Howe, who, like Benjamin Franklin two generations previously in Philadelphia, was a printer of note, Whelan learned the trade from the master, including the value and power of a well placed phrase. As historian Ian Robertson notes in his biographical profile, Whelan's Irish character easily crossed the Atlantic and he became active in local Irish societies. He succeeded Father O'Brien as director of the *Register*, an Irish Roman Catholic newspaper, liberal in orientation, meaning it had a Liberal bias, which argued for the repeal of the forced union between Ireland and England, enacted in 1805. Like many young people of the time, Whelan took great interest in elocution, the same subject taken by the Calonne brothers in France. These oratorical lessons clearly took hold in the clubs of Halifax, where later a colleague wrote that as an orator, Whelan was "brilliant, impassioned, exciting. He had the faculty of seizing at once upon the minds of his hearers, and carrying them along with him. ... His language was always correct, well chosen, and gracefully delivered."

At this time, the new era of Queen Victoria, it was the age of newspapers, cheap but popular broadsheets that shaped public opinion, fed by a strong editorial stance, an opinionated editorial, a simple printing press, and sufficient adverting and subscribers to pay wages and keep the Editor out of jail. From Howe, Whelan got the press bug. He attempted to start his own new publication in Nova Scotia, the *Spectator,* but failure led him to move to PEI, on Howe's urging. He managed to raise money for a new semi-weekly, the *Palladium,* which published its first issue on September 4, 1843. The motto of the paper was "The Liberty of the Press is the *Palladium* of the Civil, Political, and Religious Rights of a Briton". In one of his first promotions, Whelan advocated the idea of a police force for Charlottetown. As in Ireland, where the absentee land question was the central political issue, Whelan's preoccupation was land reform on PEI, as he believed that without land reform, all other issues, from responsible government to education and schooling reform, could not be settled. Whelan had little money, political backing, experience, and influence. His one wealth was in the power of words, and he lost no time in addressing his cause, namely "to investigate and assail, if not remedy, the evils which have grown out of the Landocracy

System, a system whose principle is 'monopoly,' whose effect is oppression."

But how was the goal of land reform to be achieved on the Island? The Family Compact, representing the elite business groups (who controlled trading with Britain), the landowners (most of whom lived in Britain), and a succession of Governors, from Walter Patterson to the Lieutenant Governor Sir Henry Vere Huntley, preferred the present system, in part because the Governors were typically landowners. In England, the various Colonial Secretaries had no desire to change the land tenure system, and brushed off reform measures by the simple argument that the Island was too small to have responsible government. Even worse, the Island did not speak with a single voice.

The Reformers on the Island lost the 1842 election, but sent one of their representatives, William Cooper, to London. He failed to persuade anyone with serious office to provide a hearing. The Imperial Government was content to continue to muddle along in its approach to colonial rule. At any rate, the government in London was preoccupied with much more immediate issues. England itself remained a social hierarchy, governed through a triangle of interests including the Monarchy, the aristocracy, and Parliament, with half the Cabinet ruled by members chosen from the House of Lords. Despite the passage of the Reform Bill in 1832, the majority of members were sons of peers and baronets, 217 in 1830, and 187 in 1865. England itself was being transformed by the industrial revolution, and as Britain began to develop a large and growing middle class in the large industrial cities, the political pre-occupations were fixed on Ireland, Free Trade and the Corn Laws, and domestic political reforms (the moral issues of slavery, Catholic Emancipation, the Chartists).

By 1840, thanks to the foresight of Lord Selkirk and his emigration initiatives, PEI had a growing population of 43,000, up from 5000 at the turn of the century, and was increasing steadily as more immigrants from Ireland and Scotland arrived (the population would be 62,600 by 1848). Roman Catholics were the largest in number, at 27,000, while Presbyterians mixed with Baptists and Bible Christians numbered 20,000. Despite having only 6580 members, the Church of

England dominated the executive and legislative bodies, whose main priorities reflected the political values of Victorian England. With the immigrants came pressure to clear more land, in order to exploit the British market, where free trade meant rising prices for colonial food supplies. Charlottetown itself grew, and rural families, despite the hardships of the land system, were not greatly politicized. The newspapers could be vitriolic, but each paper and each editor had pronounced views, so the public at large discounted what they saw or read. Political parties were in their infancy, and real power rested in a few executive positions and the financial elites who backed them. All British North American colonies looked to direct links with London for trade, not to their geographical neighbours. It was easy to see how the Family Compact could divide and rule the population, using religion and regional politics to anchor their own positions within the government of each colony.

It was not a great surprise to Whelan that the *Palladium* printed its final run in May 10, 1845. The printing and publishing industry of the time was a hit and miss affair, especially in this small colony where subscribers were hard to come by, and paper was in short supply. When Lieutenant-Governor Edmund Fanning first sent a request to the Colonial Secretary to hire a printer, the Island received one in the person of James Robertson, born in Perthshire, Scotland. Robertson had immigrated to Boston, where he lived a peripatetic life during the American Revolution as a pro-royalist pamphleteer, before embarking to the safety of Shelbourne, N.S. with a group of refugee loyalists. Moving to PEI with his printing press, he started *The Royal American Gazette and Weekly Intelligence of the Island of Saint John* on September 15, 1787. The paper had a longer name than it had a subscription base. Another newspaper venture at the time was the *St. John's Island Miscellany*, which started in 1790, lasting only two years. Robertson returned to Edinburgh in 1789, and was replaced by William J. Rind, who published the *Royal Gazette and Miscellany*. After a few years, James Douglas Bagnell replaced him. The *Royal Gazette,* without the advantage of a post office to help its circulation, was described as follows: 'this primitive journal was a light set up in a dark place.'

By 1823, Bagnell gave up the printing job for a life of farming and was replaced by his nephew, namesake, and pupil, James Douglas Hazard, who proved to be the first successful printer and publisher on the Island. He worked for the *Chronicle* in Halifax, learned to publish complicated state laws in Rhode Island, and cultivated subscribers from the expanding Island population. In addition, he published the *Prince Edward Island Register,* in conjunction with several other publications such as *The Prince Edward Island Calendar,* published annually, books and pamphlets including extended sermons by Protestant clergymen, *The Gospels in the Micmac Language,* and various editions on Latin, such as *The Works of Horace*, which were printed for the headmaster of the Central Academy, Edward Rupert Humphreys, who was recruited from Magdalen College, Cambridge, England.

Clearly, being a publisher had its risks, based on the simple equation of circulation and advertising revenues against weekly costs. Whelan, £400 in debt, decided to depart for greener pastures, deeply disillusioned by his Island experience. To Whelan, his cause was right, but his reform voice was decidedly weak. Depressed by his turn of bad fortune, departure from the Island seemed his only option. To his surprise, Whelan became the editor of the leading Island paper, the Tory *Morning News,* published by E.A. Moody, a supporter of the Family Compact and a friend of the Governor. Why? As in England, the political class was no longer uniform in views and outlook, and the Island social elite disliked the Lieutenant Governor, Sir Henry Vere Huntley. Clearly, the local oligarchy had a growing rift with the Lieutenant Governor. Whelan assumed he could, as editor, promote the reform cause. He believed the Reformers could exploit this feud for their own benefit, using the *Morning News* as the propaganda broadsheet for liberal reform on PEI. Unfortunately, Moody died in October, 1845, and the Family Compact bought the newspaper to maintain the status quo. Whelan had now lost this editorial option as well.

Suddenly, there appeared another. The political controversy with the Governor changed Whelan's fortune, and his career. He became a politician, and in August 1846, Whelan won election as an assemblyman. He was only 22, and was now the elected member for St Peter's in Kings County (the French site, Havre St. Pierre, was the old fishing village where Angus MacEachern spent so much time, and not far overland from his house in St. Andrew's). On August 7, 1847, only a year after his election, and with help from friends, Whelan started a new newspaper, *The Examiner*. Now he had the two tools he had always lacked, in a political pulpit to expound his immensely strong views, and a newspaper to allow him to express his views on land reform, the Family Compact, and free education. A new path to political reform had arrived, and within three years, PEI achieved responsible government. Political events were in keeping with the motto of *The Examiner*, taken from Euripides: "This True Liberty when Freeborn men, Having to Advise the Public, May Speak Free."

For Whelan, a rural seat was a natural political fortress against the merchant elites of Charlottetown, what he called in his fiery nomination address the "the numerous slanders" of "my Charlottetown enemies." While politics was his new life, his career remained devoted to political and social reform. With the editorial pages of *The Examiner* as his pulpit, Whelan re-launched the second aspect of his career adding a powerful editorial voice to address key political issues, centered around the need for social justice and land reform. Whelan established powerful local political identities to guard against the elites of Charlottetown, which remain even today. The press was his tool, not the Assembly, which he found rather boring and listless, with too many members docile. However, he did temper his voice, perhaps in part to gain more readers, but also in part to play down his commentaries on the Irish question. These commentaries were a perpetual thorn in the side of the Family Compact, a group so very comfortable in their ways, blind to the gross injustices that were part of the social hypocrisy which marked so much of the Victorian age.

***

In the imperial scheme of things, the British government was anything but radical. Responsible government, viewed from the perspective of the colonies of British North America, was the tool to hold the Empire together, the very glue for maintaining allegiance to the monarchy. According to the 1831 census, 28 per cent of the British population was employed in agriculture, with nearly half of the rural population working as blacksmiths, carpenters, bricklayers, traders and shopkeepers, forming the start of a new middle class. Seen from London and the Colonial office, responsible government was the first step towards an eventual break from the Empire, marking the path to dissolution. In the years running up to the grant of responsible government in 1848, there was widespread sentiment, especially in England, that the Empire would break asunder. This was the era of Little Englanders, where radical writers saw the filth, hunger, and stark poverty throughout Britain, made so much more obvious and visible by the new railroads and newspapers that vied for readers, and popularised by the novels of Charles Dickens, such as *Oliver Twist* and *Hard Times*.

The bleakness of the classic Dickens' tale, *The Christmas Carol,* reminds the reader that in Victorian Britain, the ethics of Mr. Scrooge are the ethics of the factory owner and the satanic mills of the cotton trade. Indeed, they stem from the utilitarian ethics of Adam Smith and Jeremy Bentham, existing unchecked by acts of benevolence, Good Samaritanism, or even simple Christian charity. Disease was rampant, and pestilences such as cholera easily spread from country to country, and port to port, leading to a pandemic that starting in Calcutta, headed to Moscow and the Baltic ports, and killed up to 50 million over 14 years. Contagious diseases had other consequences, not the least being the fear that disease meant associations with trade, foreigners, and much worse, the Irish. One of the scourges of the British Establishment was a young coroner in London who sought to expose why people really died, including the nepotism and wrong-doing of the London teaching hospitals. This coroner, Thomas Wakely, founded the medical journal, *The Lancet*, when he was only 28. He was elected to the House of Commons from Finsbury in 1835.

Another radical writer of the Little Englander school was William Cobbett. Born in Farnham, Surrey on March 9, 1763, the son of a tavern owner who taught him to read and write, William joined the British Army, where he spent time in Canada and the Maritimes. He saw corruption in the officer ranks, and he was viewed as a trouble maker when he tried to expose the scandals. He moved to France with his young wife, and then spent time in the US, where he taught English to French émigrés. In time, he started a newspaper, the *Political Register*, which gradually became more radical: by 1809, he was jailed for sedition and spent two years in Newgate Prison. On release, he moved to Long Island but continued to publish his newspaper, now a pamphlet with a circulation of 40,000.

Corbett was opinionated, independent-minded, and now hostile to emigration, viewing it as a cruel and dishonest substitute for long overdue domestic reforms, such as child labour and prison reform. Little Englanders wanted political reform to focus not on the British colonies but on Britain. They saw this as being an appropriate time, with a new King, William the Fourth, taking over from the long line of Georges that reigned since 1714. Corbett was explicit about the tyranny of sending prisoners first to the North American colonies, especially to the Carolinas, and then to Australia. His comments on Prince Edward Island give a flavour for his views of the colonies:

> *From Glasgow the sensible Scots are pouring out amain. Those that are poor and cannot pay their passage, or can rake together only a trifle, are going to a rascally heap of sand, rock, and swamp, called Prince Edward Island, in the horrible Gulf of Saint Lawrence; but when the American vessels come over with Indian corn and flour and pork and beef and poultry and eggs and butter, and cabbages and green peas, and asparagus for the soldier, and other tax-eaters that we support upon that lump of worthlessness, - and for the lump itself bears nothing but potatoes, - when these vessels return, the sensible Scots will go back in them for a dollar ahead, and not a man of them will be left but bed-ridden persons.*

The British North American colonies were influenced by the representation by population system of the United States, especially so in Upper Canada, which was rising fast with stern Loyalist traditions and an increased urban population, especially in comparison to Lower

Canada. It fostered a later preoccupation of George Brown, editor of the *Globe*, which stood in contrast to the constitutional straight-jacket of Britain. If anything, the Imperial Government understood that if the British North American colonies pushed the democratic urge too far, then other colonies might soon follow. Distance alone meant that the colonies needed to manage the issues that really counted, county by county. London was in no hurry, indifferent at best towards the colonies, and was often distracted by English concerns of changing circumstance, including religious upheavals and political revolts on the Continent. The colonies in North America had their own internal revolts, including commercial rivalry with the US, depression in the wheat market, changing economic trends as new immigrants increased the population, especially in Upper Canada, and political disputes between the merchant class based in the port cities like Toronto, Halifax, and Montreal and the farmers in the rural areas.

It came as a shock in London when the British colonies of North America had their own rebellions in 1837. It was one thing for the French Canadians to revolt; most French Canadians outside Montreal supported the Clergy, who wanted to preserve all elements of the old regime, the world of the 1791 settlement. It was quite another matter to have William Lyon Mackenzie King seize the capital, organize a militia, and declare a Republic. The Annexation Manifesto, signed by 1000 people at Montreal in 1849, tested the loyalties of businessmen and politicians towards the British Crown, as did the beckoning commercial wonders of the huge American market. The 1837 rebellions so perturbed Imperial London, immersed in its own Parliamentary political debates such as Catholic emancipation and extending the franchise, not to mention dealing with the challenges of a huge surge of Irish workers in London. To the initiated in London, the British colonies in North America had a proven avenue not open to the other British colonies – an escape clause from the British Empire, without even having to fight a war. Was the Colonial Office listening?

It was with reluctance that Imperial London sent Lord Durham across the Atlantic to study the political situation. He was an odd choice. "Radical Jack", John Lambton, the Earl of Durham, and son-in-law of Earl Grey, the Whig leader and former Prime Minister, was a reformer, preferring the Whigs to work with the Radicals to support Robert Peel's Reform Bill. By all accounts, Durham was hot-tempered, an unwilling team player, but also intelligent and decisive. Durham himself was part of a small group of people who were influenced by the earlier writings and speeches of Edmund Burke, who had urged that colonies could not be held by military force. Burke, of course, was speaking about the revolting American colonies (his son was a landowner in PEI, Lot 17) although Imperial London wanted to turn a blind eye towards the closest colony that was held by force, Ireland.

Lord Durham was given a free hand. His instructions from the Melbourne cabinet were direct yet vague, "To put things right". In the meantime, London suspended the Canadian constitution by an Act of Parliament. Durham was accompanied by two other 'secretaries', in Charles Buller and Edwin Wakefield. Together, they produced the Durham Report, otherwise known as the *Report on Canada*. Arguably, it is the most important study, magisterial in its implications, ever submitted to the British Government. Its recommendations helped determine not only the political framework of the British colonies in North America, but the future constitutional system of the entire British Empire which, after all, controlled about a quarter of the world's population. In one sense, the Durham Report was an accident of history.

The Little England theories present in mid-century Victorian Britain extended beyond these social issues. The commercial and economic unity of the empire was challenged by the introduction of free trade, building on the writings of Adam Smith and the political support of disciples like William Pitt and his intellectual followers in the Tory Party. Cobden, Bright, M'Croudy and J.S. Mill advanced the application of lower tariffs on food products to direct free trade, and *The Economist* magazine, led by the brilliant and polemical Walter Bagehot, held open the possibility that if Britain could have free trade against its colonies, the colonies could have free trade, or protection, against Britain. That was one of the reasons the Colonial Office was so reluctant to advance any measure of responsible government, despite the urgings of writers like Charles Buller, who coined the phase "Mr. Mother Country" as a scathing indictment of the policies of the Colonial Office and its permanent under secretary, James Stephen.

Except for a few writers like Thomas Carlyle, there seemed to be few serious colonial reformers, outside Lord Durham and a small, motley crew that visited Canada and corresponded with the leaders in the British colonies. Carlyle, perhaps now an arch-imperialist who wanted to retain the colonies, knew something about them, as his former beau was born in Charlottetown and was now married to Sir Alexander Bannerman, a fellow Scot, now the Island Governor. When asked later in life about the girl that declined to marry him, Carlyle commented: "I understand she has married a man who is lieutenant governor of some little island in the Gulf of St. Lawrence. "One thing that strikes a remote spectator," Carlyle wrote, "in these colonial questions: the singular placidity which British statesmen at this time, backed by M'Croudy and the British moneyed class is prepared to surrender whatsoever interest Britain might pretend to have in the decision." He could despair at the policy vacuum in London, where the faith in Imperial possibilities was drowned by the financial interests and imperial muddling disguised as colonial reform.

****

The Durham Report was a catharsis for the Imperial Government, shaking the lethargy of the British Cabinet. Various political leaders were now force to think again about the colonies and the Empire, especially those in North America where defense topics always trumped everything else, especially in the British Admiralty. Joseph Howe's own campaign in Nova Scotia, where the port of Halifax was never far from the concerns of the Royal Navy (the Admiralty was represented in the British Cabinet), was hard to ignore. Howe, himself, in his private discussions and correspondence with Charles Buller in 1846, left little doubt that if Britain were to treat the Canadian colonies in the manner they had treated the American colonies in 1776, the end results would be the same, adding that "the problem would be discussed in a different spirit, ten years hence, by the enemies of England, not by her friends."

As far back as 1838, Robert Baldwin warned Lord Durham that without responsible government, England would retain its colonies only with the military power of its troops. Howe gave Charles Buller the same message. Was Britain to be like the Bourbons of France, knowing little and learning less? Joseph Howe's four open *Letters to Lord John Russell,* were as elegant as they were pointed:

> *I have known a Governor bullied, sneered at, and almost shut out of society, while his obstinate resistance to the system created a suspicion that he might not become its victim; but I never knew who, with the best of intentions and the full concurrence and support of the representative branch, backed by the confidence of his Sovereign, was able to contend, on anything like fair terms, with the small knot of functionaries who form the Councils, fill the offices, and wield the powers of the Government. The plain reason is, because, while the Governor is amenable to his Sovereign, and the members of Assembly are controlled by their constituents, these men are not responsible at all; and can always protect and sustain each other, whether assailed by the representatives of the Sovereign or the representatives of the people.*

As it turns out, the British Government was indeed listening, at least for a time. Lord John Russell, the Colonial Secretary, had advised the Governors through a circular dispatch dated October 16, 1839 that "the tenure of colonial officers held during Her Majesty's pleasure will not be regarded as equivalent to a tenure during good behaviour." In short, Russell was saying that tenure terms were now restricted, with no assurance of retaining office, especially if there were problems of misdeed or wrong doing. The implementation of responsible government in 1848 in both Nova Scotia and Canada put pressure on PEI, but it was not clear London had much concern about this smallish place. In Charlottetown, the 24 members of the Legislative Assembly were in no mood to give up their places for a gang of reformers who intended to upset the status quo. The Coles-Whelan political duo was unrelenting in their campaign, and here they were pioneering new ground in electoral struggles. It was party politics in everything but name.

The rift between Huntley and the local elites taught Whelan and other reformers a lesson in the Imperial scheme of things, and opened the possibility that PEI and the Canadian colonies were starting to pull in the opposite direction, towards more self-autonomy and less executive control. In short, it was the political opening for the start of responsible government. Were the Canadian colonies to suffer the same fate as their American counterparts, and had London learned nothing from the loss of the thirteen colonies?

In PEI, thanks to earlier initiatives of other colonies – Nova Scotia, for instance, had a form of responsible government decades before North Carolina, well before the American Revolution – the Island Assembly requested the new Queen to grant responsible government. Victoria's coronation was in May, 1842. In this proposal, there would be an elected House, with an Executive Council chosen from among the elected members, not appointed by the Governor or from a list approved by the Imperial Government. The timing was auspicious. Political agitation throughout the Empire was of direct concern in London, and the rebellions in Upper Canada in 1837, which led to the appointment of Lord Durham in 1839, elevated responsible government as the great political issue of the day. In Nova Scotia, Joseph Howe was providing inspired leadership for responsible government, gaining the attention of London due to the strategic importance of Halifax as a naval port. From Montreal, Louis Papineau called on the Island Assembly for help in "procuring a better colonial system for all…".

Huntley, the Lieutenant Governor, was yet another in a long line of quarrelsome and decidedly autocratic governors that littered the Island landscape. Even worse, he weakened the position of Governor in the eyes of the Colonial Office and exercised passive and uninspiring leadership in the eyes of the local elite, surrounding himself with officials chosen by patronage or family connections. To be fair, responsible government was a radical departure from the status quo. When it finally came to PEI in 1851, it was responsible more in name than in fact. There simply wasn't a simple rule or formula to apply the adjustments to the Island's constitutional status. Precedent, of course, was on the side of the Governors, who preferred London to provide the civil list to pay salaries, a not inconsiderable preoccupation of the tenant of Government House. The usual pattern of British rule was that, unless stripped of the position for gross incompetence, governors stayed for a long time. Patterson, the first Governor, lasted 16 years, Fanning for twenty, Desbarres for nine, and Smith, the worst of a very bad lot, eleven. Besides, why would the Governors want to give up their powers, their serious administrative duties, to take on only ceremonial tasks, to become what a distinguished Catholic bishop called "old, white-harried, dignified, with plum aides beside them, and cannon firing salutes in the distance," or, as Walter Bagehot would later write, to manage the "seasonable addition of nice and pretty events"?

Despite mixed feelings in London, the colonies were serious about responsible government. However, the reasons for responsible government within the colonies varied. On the Island, Edwardian Whelan had another reason to moderate his fire and brimstone rhetoric, in George Coles. Together, despite their intellectual and social differences, they dominated Island politics for a generation, introducing real responsible government, dealing with the land question, and reforming the public schools. They were an odd pair, an Irish Catholic and a Protestant Englishman, a free wheeling man of character and a stern taskmaster who also owned a brewery. At heart, however, both were political pragmatists who saw the need for compromise on the issues facing the Island colony. Land reform was central to Whelan's political objectives, but perhaps more than most contemporaries in the Island's Escheat Party, he knew from the painful lessons of Irish history that political revolt, terrorist tactics, and social mayhem would lead to British reaction in kind. It didn't matter how spirited was the Irish rhetoric from Dublin, Galway, or London. Whelan was only three generations ahead of the same thoughts as Irish leaders like Michael Collins in the Edwardian era, where England's wars meant that colonial matters mattered.

The struggle for responsible government grew in intensity in 1850, particularly after the electoral victory of the Reformers in February, coupled with the subsequent refusal of the lieutenant governor, Sir Donald Campbell, to accede to their demands. Correspondence back and forth between the Island's Governors, Huntley and now Campbell, echoed the sentiments widely held in the Colonial Office that it was premature to start fundamental change to the colony's government. At best, the Island was too small, its resources too limited, and its land troubles too complicated. Even Lord Gray, the nephew of Lord Durham, very much a progressive reformer, could correspond with Governor Campbell that "the time has not yet arrived for any fundamental change in the manner in which the Governor of Prince Edward Island is not carried on." This view confirmed the general sentiment of Charles E. Poulett Thompson, M.P., who visited the Island en route to his new posting as Governor of Upper Canada. Thompson, a former Baltic timber merchant, and ex-President of the Board of Trade, was ambitious, shrewd, impatient, opinionated, and a close friend of Lord John Russell, the Colonial Secretary. He had a rare ability, like Durham and Lord Gray, to see in chaos the threads of agreement, or the central point in a convoluted argument. His views of the Island were anything but flattering, either as a Colony or regarding its government. Thompson, soon to be Lord Sydenham, was widely respected in Upper Canada, and became a friend of a young but rising politician, John A. Macdonald. Sadly, he was thrown accidentally from his horse and died on September 19, 1841, buried in Macdonald's district of Kingston, which Sydenham liked to call *Regiopolis*.

On the Island, with a new decade and a new Governor, responsible government was the issue of the day, dominating all other issues, including religion, land reform, and the growing problems of banking and money. Coles and Whelan pounded at the Family Compact, and carefully gathered a mix of voters who wanted change. Whelan relentlessly hammered away at the reform agenda. Whelan was everywhere, speaking at public forums, writing Editorials, and castigating the enemies of responsible government. He spoke at political meetings, and in late February decided to publish on a semi-weekly schedule in order to reach the public more frequently. In this highly charged atmosphere of confrontation, the *Examiner* was indispensable to the Reformist cause in explaining and popularizing the idea of responsible government. By the time it was attained, Whelan's stature in the Reform movement was second only to that of Coles. Coles and the Reformers won the election in February 1851. Hence it was no surprise that in April 1851 the 27-year-old journalist was named to the first Executive Council formed on the principle of responsible government. In July he was also appointed Queen's Printer, and hence editor of the *Royal Gazette,* which was the staid vehicle of official notices and proclamations. His installation forced the removal of the incumbent editor, James Hazard, who held the job for 21 years. "Of all papers the *Gazette* should, in our estimation, be *the* political paper," said Whelan, "the *Gazette* was to be the defender of the Liberal government *par excellence."*

Across the Island at this time, the reformers were a collection of diverse groups who sought reform for different reasons. The Acadian community, largely confined to Francophone villages like Rustico, Cascumpec (Alberton), Tracadie, Tignish, and O'Leary, were pushing for the sale of crown lands. The Acadian leaders found a champion in James Warburton, a Protestant land agent. Whelan, widely popular among the new Irish immigrants and the Catholic community in general, became a household name across PEI. Even as Editor of *The Examiner,* however much the Family Compact disliked him personally, this was a man who could not be ignored. His ally was a diametric opposite in George Coles, a Protestant, a merchant, distiller and brewer, a man with limited formal education but who had traveled to England (where he met his wife) and the US. He was, above all, a rising liberal politician who had seen from his own travels the need for literacy and education, and was unrelenting and uncompromising in his reform message. When Coles was invited to join the Island's Executive Council in 1847, he brought the reform agenda to the center of power.

The Cole-Whelan team guided the Liberal reforms of the 1850s, until their eventual defeat in the election of 1859. Whelan could draw on his European learning, not just in Ireland, to know that basic education and literacy would provide social justice. Among the Irish and Scottish immigrants, the level of education was extremely low, forcing them to rely on the clergy to provide assistance for secular issues. A remedy for this state of affairs was one of the main purposes of the Free Education Act, a Whelan initiative, of which Coles himself was a committed supporter.

Responsible government did indeed mean real change. The Governors that presided over responsible government before the Island entered Confederation in 1873 had their own peculiar and eccentric views of their roles, and relished giving their thoughts to the Colonial Office, much to the chagrin of the local Assembly. The boundary between newsy dispatches and outright interference was an open question, as was honest advice. Personalities often made a difference. It took until 1869 for the Island Assembly to provide £1400 sterling for the Governor's salary, which was subsequently raised to $7000 in 1872. What was to happen when the Governor departed? Who was in charge, the Governor, or the elected Premier? The Island's first Governor, Walter Patterson, set a precedent by naming the eldest resident Councillor as Administrator. When Huntley left the Island in 1848, the Island survived without an Administrator until Governor Campbell appeared on the scene. In 1853, when Governor Bannerman was visiting Boston, George Coles, the senior councillor, was in the peculiar position that as the first Premier under responsible government, he could advise himself to dissolve the Legislature, or govern as administrator on the advice of himself as Premier!

*****

George Coles and Edward Whelan recognized that fundamental political changes were sweeping the British North American colonies. Political action was moving away from the colonial practice of an elitist advisory council, preferred by Imperial London, to the real responsible government of an elected assembly. The elected Legislature now had real power, and the Premier in turn had real executive responsibilities if he retained the confidence of the elected representatives. That meant adjustments to the role of the Premier, to the Cabinet, and instigated a new meaning for electoral politics and the need for a legislative program. George Coles, the merchant turned politician, clearly understood these issues, campaigned for his programs, and was uncompromising towards the Governor and his own merchant class. For twenty one years, spanning from 1842,

George Coles

when he first espoused responsible government, to 1873 when the Island finally joined Confederation, Coles built the Liberal Party as the voice of reform – the Free Education Act of 1852, and the Land Purchase Act of 1853 are landmark reforms which transformed the way the Island was run, placing politics in the hands of the people. As individualists, the Scottish, French, and Irish peasant immigrants, many quite docile to political authority, were now in charge. Geologists might argue that there is no granite on the Island. They are wrong. The new political culture of self-autonomy was cast in granite.

Education reform exposed the low levels of enrolment in Island schools, but these enrolment levels on a per capita basis were no better or worse than other colonies. Even in industrial England, a young William Gladstone, himself a product of Eton, became Chancellor of the Exchequer, and was promoting school reform, the undesirability of science as a school topic, as distinct from a muscular Christianity curriculum. Coles took personal interest in school reform because he witnessed the comments of Islanders in Massachusetts and Ohio, which were now quickly industrializing. It is a pity that the Island chose as their model English education, rather than that of Scotland or the US. Education, of course, exposed religious influences and the issue of government support for denominational or secular schools. In 1851, Whelan spoke on this issue in the Legislature, in response to a large petition from Catholics looking for support for the new high school, St. Patrick's, ironically located across the street from the Assembly:

> *New schools have been established by private bounty, amongst the Catholics, for the purpose of affording education to the poorer classes. The tuition fees are very low, and are exacted only from those who can afford to pay them, but the generality of the scholars are taught gratis. ...I do not support the petition merely because it proceeds from that body of Christians of which I am a member, or because the aid for which it prays is for the support of schools belonging to, or under the superintendence and fostering care of*

> *that body, for I would with equal zeal support the*
> *claims of any other class of Christians having for*
> *their object the same laudable and charitable design,*
> *the diffusion of right knowledge among the children*
> *of the poor.*

Despite his background as an Irish immigrant, Edward Whelan could readily understand and relate to the harsh economic and social conditions on PEI and in his native Ireland. Vast tracks of land were held by absentee landlords, where the only difference between the two, as a French observer said, 'only magnificent chateaux and miserable cabins are to be seen in Ireland.' PEI had the dilapidated farm housing and unsanitary conditions, but with no chateaux.

Whelan also grasped the challenges of responsible government and understood the power of government to promote change. Why should the Island be different from Britain? From the Highlands of Scotland, and the rural lands of Ireland, to the farm lands of England, British lords and country squires owned and administered vast estates. The local parish church was a Sunday break for farm labourers and there was a clear link between the church and the state. In Ireland, the property-owning elite ruled, while the tenants paid rent, and the vast majority of people lived in a Malthusian river of population growth (Ireland had a population of eight million in 1845), with most living on a single crop, potatoes. In London, Irish famine, disease, and poverty were the foreign problems of a distant land, despite the fact that the British government included leading ministers from Ireland; Lord Palmerston owned most of County Sligo, and a full quarter of the British peers had Irish property. Palmerston, facing the horrors of famine and poverty, saw little advantage in relief, preferring Irish emigration to Canada.

It is no surprise that Coles and Whelan's Land Purchase Act was the primary focus of reform, but the issues at hand were more complicated. The new Act allowed the government to purchase land assets in excess of 1000 acres. Its only real success was the acquisition of the Worrell Estates, 81,000 acres in all, for resale to tenant farmers. When the government raised the stakes with a larger measure, including £100,000 for more acquisitions, the Imperial government disallowed the legislation. Besides, many proprietors like Samuel Cunard, who came to own some 200,000 acres, simply did not want to sell their property, based on his need for timber and regular cash flow from the rents. Only later, when his financial holdings were facing insolvency, Cunard decided to sell his Island estates to the PEI government.

Whelan zeroed in on the central issue facing the Island, his goal of real responsible government as the means to change the land system. As he said in a campaign speech, "the Executive Council - this family compact – these office holders, from whom have they derived their power? From unfaithful, unscrupulous representatives of the people." Ironically, Governor Edmund Fanning, who was appointed Governor to replace the disgraced Walter Patterson in 1793, had recognized "the existence of a family comport in the old councils." Unfortunately, by the end of the decade, religious bigotry was widespread. Political differences were not only those of party policy but of religion, and how religion influenced issues like education. Catholics had great faith in their Bishop and their priests, who were the only educated people that the rural families saw regularly. The two successors to Bishop Angus MacEachern, Bernard McDonald and Peter MacIntyre, were more than capable of stressing the power of the Church over their Catholic flock. The Bishop wanted to expand his influence over educational issues, such as the importance of denominational support for Catholic high schools and the new Island university, St. Dunstan's, the successor to St. Andrew's College established in 1831 by Bishop Angus MacEachern.

For the Island Protestants, whose numbers of 45,000 were split between Presbyterians, Kirk of Scotland, Church of England, Methodists and Baptist and other smaller denominations, there were strained relations with Catholic politicians like Whelan, and unsupressed agitation against the Catholic Bishop. There was open resentment against Catholic farmers who eventually became leaders in the Tenant League, which some Protestants saw as a parallel of the Irish Land League and the Irish Fenians, who were subsidized by Irish immigrants in the Boston states. The Editor of the *Islander*, a newspaper in competition with Whelan's *Examiner*, puts the matter squarely:

> *I believe that the time has arrive when, in the colony, every man who desires to live free from the degrading tyranny of Priests, who have sworn obedience to the Roman Bishop, should exert himself, regardless of what Baptists may say or do, in order to maintain a Protestant Government in this Colony. I believe Protestants are, at length, thoroughly alive to the dangers with which they are threatened. At this moment thousands throughout the land have associated themselves in Orange Lodges, and I trust are long to be able to inform you, that no township is without its lodge. These associates are now required.*

Catholic-Protestant animosities on Prince Edward Island were now deeply held convictions, but were not exclusively local. In Ontario religion played a much stronger role, where, for instance, a Roman Catholic would not become Premier for another 150 years. Religious differences were in many ways an elite phenomenon in Charlottetown, as Catholics became elites amongst the professions like teaching, law, and medicine, while Protestants were dominant in business and politics, Whelan's role notwithstanding. What, in fact, was the real concern on the Island was not the economy, nor issues tied to the British crown, nor religious issues but the land question and Confederation.

*****

Now that the British North American colonies had achieved responsible government, with a remarkably peaceful transition from Colonial rule, local politicians began to exercise significant legislative control over power, purse, and patronage. In the years leading up to the Charlottetown Conference in 1864, economic prosperity was in full bloom. New and better homes and buildings were constructed, while the shipbuilding industry and shipping prospered, with food and timber exports going to the Boston states and Britain. Immigration from Europe increased, but never on the scale of the United States. In fact, by 1880, immigration had ceased; there was now an exodus of Islanders to Central Canada and to the Boston states. Ontario was fast becoming the land of economic opportunity. Goods flowed back and forth, mainly on ships through Boston. In addition to the steady growth in primary sectors, the emerging export economy of PEI meant a rising middle class in Charlottetown, where most commercial activities took place, and in the shipbuilding centers, where the owners constructed large homes built with the best timber, hardwood floors, and the latest plumbing and heating appliances. Charlottetown itself, after the great fire of 1853, constructed a large supply of pre-confederation homes, most of which stand today, including the waterfront homes on Water Street and the row of office buildings on Richmond Street.

To furnish these homes, along with the grander buildings that included churches, Province House, and the bank establishments, as well as Government House, were collections of Island-made furniture, led by the master craftsman, Mark Butcher. Butcher was as prosperous as he was virile, fathering six children with his first wife, Margaret Chappell, and seven children with his second wife, Catherine Hooper. The Butchers came from England, born in St James, Suffolk in 1814, and immigrated to the Island in 1829. His family were traditionally cabinet makers, and it was natural that William, the father, set up a carpentry shop on Hillsborough Street in Charlottetown. Most furniture was imported from England, although some furniture had arrived as part of the personal belongings of colonial officials. Numerous American furniture makers published books on furnishings from English and European displays and drawings, and there were widespread variations depending on the availability of equipment and wood. Many primitive pieces were made as a by-product of the shipping industry, where employees learned how to use tools and the use of wood, combining, for instance, different kinds of woods to assure tightly fit joints. Maritimers felt prosperous, protected, and rather presumptuous about their future.

From the press, letters, and shipping interests, Maritimers were fully aware of the momentous events taking place in the Great Republic.

Directly, the American civil war had little bearing on the Maritimes or on PEI in particular. The generally accepted view was that the Americans were caught amidst a great clash between the North and the South, between the Confederacy, quietly supported by Britain, and the industrial North, with its slogans of manifest destiny. This clash was a bitter war between the slave-owning aristocracy of the South and the free states of the North, led by rich states like New York and Massachusetts, feeding off their superbly efficient textile mills and financial strengths based on cheap cotton. Samuel Cunard, that brash, daring Nova Scotian, well known on the Island as the largest landowner, won a direct mail contract with the British Post, and ran fast sailing ships like the *Britannia* linking London and Liverpool with Halifax and Boston.

Beneath these political and military divides were the pretentious expansion plans of the US, fed by tariff protection, and fuelled by enormous population increases due to immigrants from Continental Europe. In 1820, when only Jefferson and Madison remained alive from the original signers of the American Declaration in 1776, the US had a population of nine million people, which doubled every 20 years. By the 1860s, the US was producing, in each decade, the equivalent population of all Canada, a set of circumstances which lasted until the 1950s. The US was powered by public works on a grand scale, financing the construction of canals and railways, a Federal banking system, a national road system, and promoting an Imperial policy of Western expansion. Their sights ranged from Texas and California to Oregon and the Great Plains west of Kansas, going possibly as far north as Alaska, which was bought on the cheap from Russia in 1867. The Pacific coastline beckoned. So too did Canada.

American had new leaders, new spokesmen, and rival political factions – not just Democrats and Republicans, but a hodgepodge of names to confuse foreigners and confound new Americans, including Whiggery, Locofocos, Jacksononism, Tammany, Free Soilers and many others. There were barnburners, the Free-Sailers, and the Hunkers, providing a clear example of the comparative American

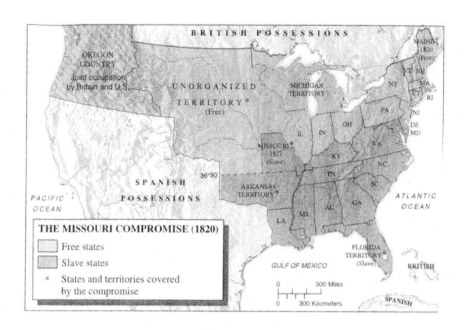

Free and Slave States

advantage in political lexicography, against the imported Canadian variety of Tories, Grits, Whigs, *Bleus*, Reformers, and Liberals. There was little concern in America about European affairs, or even the old nostrums and worries about British rule. The American navy and American merchant ships, no match for the Royal Navy on the oceans, protected US coastlines. American agriculture – wheat in particular – flooded Europe's markets, in part thanks to Britain's policy of free trade and suspension of the Corn Laws. North America, of course, had free land in abundance, producing agricultural food of all descriptions, including meat, fish, cereals, and fruit. Plantations, like that of Thomas Jefferson, produced candles, machinery, beer, and spirits. The fertile plains of the mid-West attracted poor Europeans as fast as ships could move them, and roads and trains could settle them.

But planted underneath this bursting, expansionist Continental economy were the seeds of moral terror. At its heart, the US Constitution is not really about the sins of George III, democratic ideals, or the divisions of powers between the national government and the states. For the original signatories of the Declaration, it was relatively easy to write the masterful words "All men are created equal…" and then ignore the implications, then or now. How could the separate American colonies be united, as a configuration of separate states organized as a Republic under God, led by a President, or a unified national government in charge of law and order, the military, and a national economy? Was the US to remain a nation forged with the vision of Washington and Hamilton, or to become a union of distinctly autonomous states, the preference of Jefferson? Or was the US to be a nation torn asunder by the issue of slavery?

For the American Founding Fathers, the real issue was the federal state, and the restraints imposed on the power of the national government, with its cleverly designed checks and balances between the executive branch, the Congress and the Judiciary. All three each had their own internal checks and balances; so too did the national government itself linked with the residual powers for the doctrine of state rights. Indeed, in 1776, there was a commonality among the 13 original signing states, which in fact were British colonies. Their inspired leaders, Washington, Jefferson, Franklin, Adams and Madison, then so accustomed to the style of the French and British monarchies, built around a caste system of the aristocracy, the military, and the church, became aghast at the sheer inefficiencies of imperial rule, and the inherent contradictions of imperial rule from the center without corresponding balances within the colonial structure. The US, in their view, could do better. By the 1850s, the US itself was in the midst of territorial expansion, its manifest destiny, first to Texas and California, coupled with corresponding industrial expansion of unprecedented levels, inspired by the British industrial revolution (steam railways, iron foundries, cotton and textile machinery, McCormick grain reapers) and the entry of new states in the West.

American expansionism tilted the geographic balance in the Republic away from the North-South merger of 1783, towards the south and the west, which remains true today (11 of the 18 Presidents from 1778-1900 were either born or spent their adult life in the Valley of the Mississippi). Demographics shifted dramatically: universal suffrage was adopted, and shrewd Americans saw the new economic and constitutional threats in the US system. Economic issues were (and are) always present in the tariff system, the federal bank, the sale of public lands in the territories, and the spoils system of patronage in Washington. But underneath this economic tinderbox was the issue of states rights and the plantation system of the South. British leaders could be indifferent to the US conflict, as they were to much of the British Empire, but in London and in the churches, the moral crusaders were on the political ascendancy.

In 1776, slavery and plantations were expected to decline and eventually disappear, especially once the elimination of forced indenture would remove its raison d'etre. Slavery was the only economic model in the South, resembling a system of feudal control (Russian serfs were being liberated faster than Negroes in the South). Slavery actually increased over time, from one million slaves to four million. When the US conducted its first census in 1810, a white family of four was valued at $350.00, while a slave was valued at $400.00. The lush acres of Mississippi and South Carolina were perfect for cotton fields that fed the textile factories of New England (and also the textile factories of Lancashire in England), helped by the middlemen and bankers of New York. In the south, there was the addition of the Protestant ministries – Baptists, Episcopalians, and Methodist churches – who fostered the slave trade; many Protestant ministers actually owned slaves.

These events forced the Americans to compromise, as only they can do, while ignoring the underlying political crisis. The Missouri Compromise of 1820 was a 'live and let live' truce, in that it allowed the slave states to retain their institutions. But over the next few decades, western US expansion created room for new states, in particular California, that forced decisions on whether the new states would be segregated, on the Jim Crow model of the South or 'free' on the model of the North. The great political orators – Henry Clay, John C. Calhoun, and Daniel Webster – raised the level of debate to new heights, but exposed the moral dilemmas for the American Union. To complicate matters, a new social force appeared. It was laid out in a stunningly brilliant book that opened a new fault line – the moral cause of freedom.

Harriet Beecher Stowe's monumental *Uncle Tom's Cabin*, published in 1852, was a national and international best seller. This book, in simple themes, stories, and language, exposed for all to see the underlying features of slavery and the slave trade – namely the human cruelties, the auction systems, the whipping establishments, and the break-up of families. *Uncle Tom's Cabin* was published in several languages (including a widely read French edition published in Quebec), and proved an instant success in England and throughout the British Empire. Slavery had been abolished in 1833, as the result of a huge popular movement throughout England and the Empire. However, the debate opened new political issues, and new fault lines on citizen rights. Who could vote? Blacks and Whites? Catholics and Protestants? Men and Women? Landowners and the masses? How does one principle, the right of land ownership, affect other rights, such as freedom from starvation? What legal protections exist for minority rights?

These were the issues facing the Americans, but it was a universal challenge for democracies that existed throughout the Victorian era.

Despite the rhetoric of Thomas Jefferson and the words of the Bill of Rights, it became clear that the Americans, by rejecting British rule, rejected learning from other countries. Fortunately, Canada could learn from the American experience and from countries across the Atlantic. Consider the case of slavery. The antislavery movement started in 1787, when Thomas Clarkson, an Anglican and Cambridge graduate, won a Latin essay contest with the beguiling title: is it lawful to make slaves of others against their will? A large man with thick red hair, Clarkson began a 12-man abolition committee at a Quaker bookstore in London. Slavery was a subject discussed but not raised publicly. Clarkson was a firebrand organizer who mobilized opposition so that 300,000 Britons were soon boycotting sugar imports, the main product from British West Indian slave plantations in Jamaica, Haiti, and Barbados.

Protests mounted, and nearly 400,000 signed petitions to Parliament demanding an end to the slave trade. Olaudah Equiano, a brilliant former slave, wrote a best-selling autobiography and embarked on a five-year speaking tour of the British Isles. Meanwhile Clarkson, aided by a young Tory, William Wilberforce, became a British Paul Revere, riding 35,000 miles on horseback, gathering witnesses for parliamentary hearings and setting up local antislavery committees. The Quakers, coupled with their preachers and lay supporters, pushed the arguments before the public. In 1792, the British House of Commons became the first national legislative body in the world to vote to end the slave trade, and by 1807, Parliament voted to end slavery.

That ban, however, did not become law, because the House of Lords balked, not the first time the Lords wanted to preserve ruling privileges. By the turn of the century, Britain and France, now led by Napoleon, began two decades of continental war that spread across the Atlantic. Wars are usually bad for social causes, especially one so economically entrenched as slavery. In the early 1800s, Clarkson toured the British countryside again, and in 1807, both houses of Parliament banned the slave trade, an unprecedented example of new coalition politics. The principal groups that people identified with in early 18th-century

England were religious sects such as Quakers, Anglicans, Baptists and Methodists, not the nascent political parties.

With the death rate on plantations in the British West Indies so abominably high, the abolitionists hoped that cutting off the supply of new slaves would quickly end British slavery itself. When this did not happen, Clarkson - now in his sixties - spent 13 months crisscrossing the English country side, this time by stagecoach, in 1823 and 1824. The next 10 years saw several new rounds of organizing, including large petitions, great meetings, skilfully coordinated lobbying, a rare street demonstration and, to widespread male chauvinist shock, the emergence of outspoken female abolitionists. In addition, there was the added pressure of a large, barely contained slave revolt in Jamaica, subdued at great cost to the British. Finally, after months of acrimonious debate, in 1833 Parliament voted to phase out slavery throughout the empire. When freedom for all came, just after midnight on August 1, 1838, a group of former slaves who were gathered in a Baptist church in Falmouth, Jamaica, placed a whip, chains and an iron punishment collar in a coffin, and buried it in the churchyard. Emancipation Day, August 1, has been celebrated ever since.

Time was now pressing on the American Confederacy. Their leaders and commercial interests had received quiet support by the sentimentalities of British aristocrats, feelings that spilled over to the Canadian colonial governors but conflicted with popular sentiments and in areas where the underground railway was operating, especially in Ontario and Nova Scotia. The former slave and abolitionist leader Frederick Douglass called August 1 "illustrious among all the days of the year." At the Concord, Mass., courthouse on August 1, 1844, Ralph Waldo Emerson gave a major speech against slavery. The writer, Margaret Fuller, sitting in the audience, described this speech as "great, heroic, calm, sweet, fair ... tears came to my eyes." On that day in 1847, 10,000 people assembled in Canandaigua, N.Y., to hear Douglass and others speak. Seven thousand people - free blacks and sympathetic whites - attended an August 1 rally in New Bedford, Mass., in 1855. Long before Abraham Lincoln's Emancipation Proclamation, Britain became the first nation to end slavery, mainly

Cunard Ship "Scotia"

Cunard Land Sale Agreement, June 29, 1866

because the mighty British navy could successfully enforce abolition in the colonies. Unlike American slavery, essentially brought to an end through the Civil War, the British antislavery movement perfected the use of virtually all the "new media" of the day: they created the first widely reproduced political poster, the first logo for a political organization (a kneeling slave in chains), and used political tools like whips, chains and handcuffs to dramatize political speeches. Like the dialogue in *Uncle Tom's Cabin,* activists learned that what attracted millions to read books and pamphlets was not religious and moral arguments, but vivid, eyewitness accounts and direct testimony.

Slavery was not unknown in the British North American colonies, including Prince Edward Island, mainly through American slave owners who moved north. Governor Edmund Fanning had slaves in Charlottetown, but the black community was tiny, and dwindled through marriages, mostly from illegitimate children of British soldiers. Canadians had a simple understanding of the American model, the southern slave states and the free states, but few appreciated the underlying constitutional dilemmas that propelled the US into civil war. George Brown of the *Globe,* himself a prominent member of the Toronto Anti-slavery Society, could warn his readers that, as they took leave of the year 1859, "the United States faced threats of disunion ringing in our ears."

By 1864, the carnage, the massive armies, the new artillery, the great battles, the mobilization of industries in the North to support the war effort, the army plans of attrition, maximum collateral damage, and untold suffering and destruction – all these were new concepts for the Canadian colonists who read their newspapers from a safe distance, cocooned within the confines of the British Empire. An uneducated Southern officer defined the art of war as "Firstest with Mostest", an inelegant but classic approach to war. Or as General Sherman put it, 'war is hell!'

The Great Republic, upon war's end in 1865, faced three-quarters of a million dead, the South in ruins, with her great cities plundered and burnt, the North reeling in debt, and furthermore, the ignominy of relying upon the British to finance her loans. Even in the 1850s, British politicians like Disraeli and Gladstone worried about defending Canada, only too well aware that American politicians from Jefferson to Calhoun were ready to invade the Canadian colonies. For Americans, the civil war did not stop the cries of manifest destiny. Cuba, Panama, Alaska, Hawaii, and the Philippines all stood in line of aggressive American military policies, even as far south as the A-B-C Powers – Argentina, Brazil, and Chile. And to the North stood the British colonies, with a land mass as big as Russia, centered on three oceans, and a population the size of New England.

******

This was the political environment of Canadian Confederation. Political deadlock between Upper and Lower Canada was now real. The Colonial Office became concerned about military defense of the British North American colonies. Paradoxically, growing economic prosperity within the Maritime colonies, now each enjoying responsible government, meant more autonomist political thinking, regardless of party stripe. To outsiders, this situation was a formula for chaos, even more so because the Colonial office had surrendered its control to local and largely unknown politicians.

The constitutional shape of modern Canada came courtesy of the smallest province, from the historic events of the Charlottetown Conference. Canadian Confederation came from the meetings in this small capital – Charlottetown was incorporated as a city in 1855. To many Islanders, it was now on par with the great cities of the world, truly the ideal capital of a united Maritime Provinces. Perhaps Charlottetown, a small city nestled on two rivers - the West and Hillsborough - with a tidy, protected harbour, was the perfect site even for the federal union's capital. After all, no province could gain an advantage through location, or in the railway and telegraph age, through geographical and economic strengths. The 1864 meeting was more than a conference born from deadlock between Upper and Lower Canada, based on the Constitutional Act of 1840, or from stalemate among the Maritime colonies where union was an unlikely political preference, despite what the various governors were suggesting to London, or even from fear of American imperialism, that aura of manifest destiny which rises and falls in the corridors of Washington.

The precise dates of the Charlottetown Conference were happenstance, merely isolated dates on politician's calendars. What turned out to be a meeting of 26 constitutional minds held over the first four days of September 1864 was favoured with fittingly gorgeous days and nights, a fine example where the early fall days of cooler weather were held in abeyance for the political meetings, private conferences and, perhaps appropriately for PEI, abundant food, drink, and spirited conversations. For the first time, the Island delegates had to think through their own future. Should they stand as a separate British colony, reaping the economic advantages of the civil war tearing apart the social fabric of the Great Republic, and the enormous economic growth of Britain and the British Empire? Or should they unite, in part to break the constitutional deadlock between Upper and Lower Canada? Opinion in PEI was clear: why rock the boat when this small Island dominion was truly on an economic roll?

The Charlottetown meeting was originally called to discuss Maritime Union. Typically, the Island was reluctant to take a lead. If anything, it was left to the Governor General, Lord Monck, now a close confident of John A. Macdonald, to force the issue. The main agenda was not the grand scheme for Confederation of all the British colonies, but the quite narrow focus on Maritime Union, or uniting the four eastern colonies. The leaders from New Brunswick and Nova Scotia accepted that the meeting be held in Charlottetown, a minor concession to the Island administration, but in fact, better Charlottetown than the humidity of Fredericton or the fog of Halifax. What better way to end the summer of 1864 than a holiday on the Island? Even better, the meeting was a happy concession to accept the delegates from Canada, where some form of union of the British North American colonies was very much on the mind of the British government, a thought that dated back to William Pitt.

Indeed, some measure of union of the British colonies in North America dates perhaps earlier, from 1775. Ben Franklin drew ideas from the New England confederation plans stretching back to the settlements of Massachusetts and Connecticut in 1643, and proposed "the United Colonies of North America," construed, it should be recognized, to operate as part of the British Empire or separately if the Empire broke apart. Richard Unijacke proposed a union in the Legislative Assembly of Nova Scotia in 1800. Then for sixty years, proposals came from all quarters, from London, the Governors, politicians, and even from the likes of Bishop Strachan in Toronto. Queen Victoria's father, the Duke of Kent, after whom Prince Edward Island was renamed, had his own proposals. So too did Lord Durham, and the British North American League, for which a young John A. Macdonald campaigned to the electors of Kingston, so that 'the Government will not relax its exertions to effect a Confederation of the British North American colonies.'

In the Maritimes, prior to 1864, the idea of a federation of the British colonies was floated by a wide number of people, including the Colonial Office, various governors, politicians, and the media. As early as September 1849, John Hamilton Gray, a polished conservative lawyer skilled in courtroom oratory (his grandfather was an Empire Loyalist from Boston, and his father had been in the British Navy) forwarded a motion to the New Brunswick Colonial Association in September 1849 in favour of "a Federal Union of the British North American colonies, prior to their immediate independence." The American civil war exposed how defenseless the colonies had become, and it was a concern where Britain's priorities were. There were also practical problems with economic expansion ranging from the need for a common decimal currency, to a railway to match the American and British transportation, with roads, tariffs and, of course, military defense. In Nova Scotia, the irrepressible Joseph Howe moved a resolution on federation, requesting a meeting of minds of the British Colonial Secretary, the Governor General, and the colonial governors.

Well before the Charlottetown Conference, the Maritime legislatures debated the pros and cons of both Maritime Union and federal union. As documented so carefully by Rev. Francis Bolger, the Maritime legislatures knew the issues, the entanglements, the pressures from the American Civil War and the feelings of the British Government. Edward Whelan opened the columns of *The Examiner* to discuss these union proposals. One politician who was quite specific, George Coles, is worth reading. Coles became the advocate of a federal model which was most opposed to the views of John A. Macdonald, although John A., through personal diplomacy, skilful work, and the power of his personality, carried the day both in Charlottetown and at the following meeting in Quebec City. It was there that the Coles formula, which proposed to invest residual powers in the provinces, was proposed and shot down by the Conference, including the Island delegation itself.

Coles categorically rejected Maritime legislative union. He also rejected a legislative union of all the British colonies, and wanted residual powers to be vested in the separate provinces, a model based upon the American constitution, where residual powers are vested in the states. Coles was favourable to a Federal Union of all the Provinces from the Atlantic to the Pacific, including the three Maritime colonies, Upper Canada, Lower Canada, and Central Canada, with each province being 'nearly equal' in their members to one chamber, the Assembly. Local legislation might be subject to review by the federal legislature but not reserved for Royal Allowance. Common issues, like "Lights and Light Houses, Postal arrangements between the different provinces, Crown lands, Currency, Steam Communications, and Railroads" - these would be the prerogative of a 'comprehensive system of government' and 'Charlottetown, no doubt, would become the place for the meeting of the United Legislature.' On the opening day of the Charlottetown Conference, the *Monitor* editorialized that "all attempts to bring about a 'legislative union of the Provinces will be stoutly resisted by the people and legislature of this Island'."

The Charlottetown Conference crystallized the thinking of all the British colonies. The American civil war left deep scars on the British colonies, as Manifest Destiny became seen as more than a slogan. The British government was running an unequivocal financial and military superpower, and the British cabinet was now concerned about how the colonies related to Imperial London. As Disraeli would later argue, "Self-government, when it was conceded, ought to have been conceded as part of a great policy of Imperial consolidation". Once again, wars on the Continent, military, civil, and revolutionary, pre-occupied the British Cabinet: Germany-France went to war in 1870, Ireland was in a perpetual dispute with Britain, the USA coveted the northwest of North America, and the Caribbean colonies, especially Jamaica, faced outright revolt.

Even in Upper and Lower Canada, the Confederation scheme was well known. Aside from the Colonial Office and various governors, it had strong advocates, including proponents like D'Arcy McGee and Thomas Galt, who would become the first finance minister in the new Canadian government. Among leading politicians, Georges-Etienne Cartier, and George Brown, the reluctant politician and editor of the *Globe*, were interested in a pan-merger of the British colonies. Brown, of course, preferred a legislature designed around population, where he saw Upper Canada gaining against Lower Canada with its static population. He was, of course, the arch enemy of John A. Macdonald. Brown detested John A's personal habits and political schemes, but knew that the combination of Quebec and Ontario in a single legislature was a formula for political stalemate. In the political circles of Toronto and Montreal, it was easy to see that the road to Confederation was the triumph of expediency over political deadlock.

Far from the Maritimes, on June 14, 1864, a motion of censure was put before the Canadian legislature. The amendment on a matter of supply, aimed at A.T. Galt, the finance minister in the Cartier-Macdonald government, brought down the government. The only choices open to the Ministry was dissolution and thus an election, or a reconstructed government, with a revised Cabinet. The defeat was wholly expected. As the Attorney General, John A. Macdonald told his followers, "If a disruption of the whole fabric is to be the price of John Sandfield's opposition, then woe to the constitution. We showed him no mercy; at his hands I do not think we now deserve mercy." Others saw it differently, but with the same outcome. As one writer noted, "It would be extremely unwise and unprofitable for a man suddenly to let virtue get the better of him while his party still held a majority of fifty men; but the case is reversed when the honesty-impulse can be exhibited while the party ship lies soggy in the water, and goes down with the defection of two or three of the virtue-stricken crew. Messrs. Dunkin and Rankin belong to this not uncommon class of politicians".

Macdonald evidently felt that of the two options, dissolution was the better one. But the day after the defeat, George Brown, who had no love for John A. or his Party, but a distinct hatred towards John Sandfield, a lukewarm Catholic, and the former Premier, had a conversation with two members of the government: J.H. Pope, member from Compton (and no relationships to the Popes from PEI), and Alexander Morris, the member from South Lanark. In a small fit of anger, Brown noted that the constitutional settlement of Upper and Lower Canada was at a crisis, that an election would not solve anything, and that a real settlement was necessary, "forever the constitutional difficulties between Upper and Lower Canada." Somewhat startled, the members asked Brown if they could pass that message to Macdonald with a view to a meeting. A meeting was indeed held, Macdonald invited Brown to join the cabinet, and the new cabinet would address the crisis that Brown noted, the 'sectional difficulty'; in short, the French and English, the regions of Ontario and of Quebec, simply couldn't get along.

Brown's only enduring interest was in a separation of Ontario from Quebec, with each having their own assemblies, voted on by population. To Brown, the union of all the British colonies was impractical and remote. Macdonald, together with Galt, agreed with Brown, but suggested that larger confederation would be the main goal. Failing that, he would seek a constitutional settlement for Canada alone. With these negotiations concluded, the session was prorogued on June 30, 1864, and Brown entered the Cabinet as President of the Council. Many of Brown's party members, mortified at the evildoers across the aisle, thought Brown had gone over "too cheap." It wouldn't be the first floor walk for members entering an alien Ministry.

What Brown had done was more than simply cross the floor, what Winston Churchill would later call the longest walk in the parliamentary system. Brown had raised, Lazarus-like, the inner thoughts of John A. Macdonald. This was John A.'s dream since he first entered politics, but John A was a realist of the finest type, a person who knew that advocating a big dream before the people were ready for it was to destroy any hope of success. He knew his strengths, knew his enemies, and understood that getting ahead of the people can be a costly error for a good idea. "The fruit is green and not fit to pluck" was an abiding motto of this master craftsman, but so too was another, *Carpe Diem* – and the day was upon him. He had a new cabinet, a new colleague in George Brown, and a new vista – the Charlottetown Conference. Strike now, strike hard, strike while the iron is hot. Charlottetown beckoned!

As in any grand proposal, it is natural that the benefits of a union, however blessed or praised, were in the future; the costs, political and economic, were here and now. Collectively, the British colonies covered a vast territory, even more so when the lands of the vast wilderness of the Northwest were included. These colonies had abundant resources, including the coveted Atlantic fisheries, where the European Empires – Spain and Portugal, France, and then Britain - fought and conspired for supremacy as far back as the days of Francis Drake in the sixteenth century. Two centuries later, the Americans from Boston and the British from the port cities of Liverpool, Grimsby, and Bristol coveted the Grand Banks. The fish were so abundant in these grounds that schools of cod actually brought fishing boats to a halt. For their part, the Maritime Provinces had over 100 years of British rule, and had a vast increase in the number of new immigrants, including families loyal to King George III, what became known as the United Empire Loyalists. The Irish famine drove hundreds of thousands from the Emerald Isle, most to the Boston states, but the Irish settlers increased the local populations, aided by refugees from the regular wars on the Continent.

Despite the dislocations caused by Britain's adoption of free trade, and with internal disputes on issues like public education and religion, coupled with the fear of American domination, for their part, the Maritime colonies were doing especially well in 1864. In one sense, Prince Edward Island was in the midst of a unique economic boom. Agriculture - oats, potatoes, hay - had an exceptional harvest and the American market, devastated by the civil war, provided ready customers. Wheat prices reached unprecedented levels. Shipbuilding and all its offshoots - ropes, furniture, canvas and sails, and assorted products, from anchors to watches, guns and powder to fine pottery

- was an economic cluster that created enormous prosperity. James Yeo and other ship owners, including Cambridge Owen, Angus MacMillan, the Peake Brothers, and James and Andrew Duncan, accrued real wealth. The enormous success of Island shipbuilding, equally shared by New Brunswick, especially in the Saint John region, but also in Lunenburg, Halifax and Pictou in Nova Scotia, was helped by the ready supply of timber - hardwoods and softwoods alike. Shipbuilding provided an enormous demand for skilled labour of all sorts, employing skilled tradesmen who could build sails, cut wood, design ropes, manufacture copper and iron for fittings, and joiners of all descriptions, including furniture and wood fittings.

The North American shipbuilding industry started as a small industry, and never reached the pinnacle of the sailing ships used by the Royal Navy. In the Maritimes, shipbuilding consisted of many small firms located near rivers and ports, and for over three centuries, was the largest single industry in North America. Nova Scotia alone was the world's fourth biggest producer of ships. In the early years of the British Empire, the Governors and the navy operated a monopoly in the transport of precious cargo, protected by the Navigation Acts, which forced all cargo and trade, a term that was often called traffic (and still is, at least for illegal trade in areas like drugs) to be carried on British ships. North American had an enormous cost advantage over ships made in Britain or the Continent.

The core feedstock, timber, was basically free and abundant. The technology was relatively simple, the core being in shipwrights who brought muscle power to the labour intensive process. Despite the heavy labour component, shipbuilding itself was an enormously complex process, reprieving a clever mix of skills: selection of the wood and timber, building the basic frame (starting with the keel), warning fore and aft with the planks added in close proximity, to be fasted with long tunnels (tree nails) wooden pegs prepared with huge augers. With this carpentry work completed, the arduous caulking process began. This task consisted of a mix of ookum (hemp treated with tar) which was pounded into the seams with large mallets to prevent water leaks. For most Islanders, political and constitutional issues had no real bearing on their economic future.

153

The details of the Charlottetown Conference have been amply documented, notably in a definitive book, *Prince Edward Island in Confederation*, by Rev. Francis Bolger, based on his thesis work at the University of Toronto. Today, the conventional wisdom is that the Fathers of Confederation met in Charlottetown, where the delegates from Ontario and Quebec, led by the cunning and shrewd John A. MacDonald, hijacked the meeting of the three provincial delegations called to discuss Maritime Union. Once the Maritime Union concept was thrown out, as it never had any chance of success, the grander scheme of a federation of all the British colonies in North America was seen as a possible reality. Indeed, once the meetings started, and the topic of Maritime Union was quickly set aside, the Charlottetown meeting became devoted to possible terms of a new federal scheme. The actual terms of Confederation were then decided six weeks later in Quebec City. It was, in short, a Central Canada idea, whose formal ratification was decided in Quebec City, not Charlottetown. In parts of French Canada, Confederation was a political pact between the two founding people, French and English. These versions are a betrayal of history and fact.

The conference proceedings were not recorded, in part because there was no notary, and the media were excluded. But there are some important records, notably by some of the participants like George Brown and Edward Whelan, who had the distinct advantage that they were editors of papers, with the according secretarial skills and tools, including shorthand, sharp powers of observation, and a retentive memory. Clearly, for the Maritime delegates, and for the host delegates from the Island, the Conference was a diversion from the issue they wanted to avoid, the dreaded topic of Maritime union. Since the Conference was held in Charlottetown, the Island could be presumptive enough to think the capital of the Maritime province would be Charlottetown, an assumption that was carried forward to the discussions later in Quebec City.

The second consideration at the Charlottetown Conference was the basic fact that until they met in Charlottetown on the evening of August 31, most of the delegates had never met each other, either personally or professionally. In this sense, the Charlottetown

Conference allowed the delegates to put personal rivalries aside, and to discuss the issues without the bias of political differences, or regional and ethnic prejudices. The Maritime delegates could put off the discussion of Maritime Union *sine die*, and allow the Canadian visitors to present the case for a larger merger, starting with Cartier on the first morning, and then followed by Macdonald in the afternoon. The rivalry between Upper and Lower Canada was the focus of Cartier's presentation, with the issue of political deadlock, and the need to allow Quebec to preserve its language and culture under the British crown. Cartier, in both his opening speech and his toasts and comments, and in subsequent presentations, never deviated from this central point.

But in many ways, the real story of Charlottetown is the emergence of John A. Macdonald as leader of the delegates. At the closing banquet, he escorted the Governor's wife in the opening dance. In a famous photograph, Macdonald is at the center, sitting on the porch surrounded by the delegates. He is also the focus of the celebrated oil painting, Harris' *The Fathers of Confederation*. Clearly, John A. knew his brief. As Attorney General, he knew British laws, regulations and political conventions, and he read widely, both in the British and American newspapers, along with the historians and biographers. At Charlottetown, John A. had low expectations of achieving any results. Indeed, prior to leaving Montreal on the *Queen Victoria*, Macdonald had greatly annoyed his colleagues, especially George Brown, for paying too little attention to the briefs prepared for the Conference. The reason was simple - John A. was on another bender. But that was his style. Even when the *Queen Victoria* arrived in Charlottetown on Thursday, August 31, he was not the least perturbed that the welcoming mat hardly matched Windsor castle or that, like Jesus and Mary in Bethlehem, there were no rooms in the house – all the 12 small hotels in Charlottetown were full.

When John A. signed the guest book at Province House, he wrote down his occupation as 'cabinet maker.' It was a shrewd choice of words. This is exactly what he was up to in Charlottetown, cabinet making. He was everywhere, carefully listening to his old colleagues, from both Upper and Lower Canada, and to his new colleagues

Robert Harris's Portrait of John A. Macdonald

from the Maritime provinces. He was challenging the convictions of the Maritime delegations, and testing what they really felt about the Confederation vision. Before coming to Charlottetown, John A. was a reluctant federalist in the conventional sense. His experience and sentiments, and his intuition, perhaps the most powerful instinct to this very crafty person, was that federal charters were inherently unstable – the US constitution he knew and studied carefully - and inherently subject to personal whims and forces outside the political realm, including ethnic tensions, religion, language and culture, and narrow commercial interest.

Macdonald's thinking evolved in these months of 1864, and the Charlottetown meeting further helped crystallize his own views of a federal Canada. Much is made of his arguments in favour of a unitary state, and a monarchical system, but he had already settled with George Etienne Cartier that Quebec would have all its powers accorded by the British settlement of 1791. He listened carefully to the presentations by Cartier and Galt, but more specifically, to the reactions by the delegates from the Maritimes. He slowly saw the ways of his Maritime counterparts, the nature of the differences in each British colony, and marked their abiding interest to protect their own turf. Prepared speeches and formal questions and answer periods, and even public announcements, don't give a true flavour of the Charlottetown meetings because, with ample time to discuss alone, to eat, drink and enjoy the weather, the delegates had to reveal their inner souls, and a lot more. Who would have expected a reformist liberal like the Island's George Coles, a man obsessed with political self-government, local autonomy, and the power of educational reform to emerge as the strongest voice for a decentralized union, with most of the reserve powers given to the provinces? In this sense, he was at the opposite end of John A.'s thinking towards a unitary rather than a federal model.

John A. thought carefully about these constitutional arrangements, and not simply because he was, as Attorney-General, in charge of the laws and the courts in the confusing political mix of the two Canadian provinces, a legacy of the 1791 arrangement and the issue addressed by Lord Durham's Report. As a Scotsman, Macdonald knew the history of his own country, absorbed by a 'charter' in the Act of 1707, and the depressing subsequent split between the Lowlands and the Highlands, with the ensuing treatment of Roman Catholics. More tellingly, he came from Kingston, with its own band of Scottish Highlanders who were suspicious of the new United Empire Loyalists and from other immigrants from the Continent. The Maritimes, and PEI, were full of Scottish immigrants who turned their back on their homeland, and were generally suspicious of outsiders. The differences between Ontario and Quebec were real and plain to see, as the French kept their own Church, language, and culture, including a curious mixture of the French legal code and British practices in areas like finance and insurance. Macdonald was, for instance, the director of an insurance company and had some personal knowledge of these affairs. He had unexcelled contacts in London, and he knew the private thoughts of leaders like Gladstone and Disraeli. Further, Macdonald was an inveterate newspaper reader, and he knew how politicians could leak their private thoughts to favoured journalists.

But it was the US republic that concerned John A. the most. Like many countries that would write a beautiful constitution - the USSR comes to mind - the American constitution was on paper a work of art, a carefully developed document with checks and balances, a powerful Commander in Chief, and a Congress consisting of elected representatives, chosen by population, with a Senate apportioning equality to the big and small states, nurtured through a Bill of Rights. In fact, even though many in the American Congress had ignored the Supreme Court after 1783, taking comfort that the Bill of Rights was beautifully written, "… All Men are Created equal…" but that was the end of that, and the reason for the American civil war. Moreover, since the days of Thomas Jefferson, the Americans had their own imperial designs, constrained to some extent by the British Royal Navy, but steady land acquisitions southward and westward meant that movement northward towards Canada itself was never far from American thinking. Moreover, until the US plunged itself into civil war, foreign territorial acquisitions allowed the Americans to avoid the terrible moral dilemmas inherent in the American union, the slave states or the free states. In addition, the British Empire, led by William Gladstone, was in moral fever, backed by the conscience of British liberals and the sanctimonious character of the British press.

But John A was a realist, a master tool maker who saw, as a young Attorney General in what was called Canada, the legal issues associated with the attachments to the Crown and Empire, including the spending powers, the rights and responsibilities of the legislative assembly, and the powers of patronage, both formal and informal. Macdonald's personal experience as an immigrant from Scotland taught him the peculiar instruments of the British system, the separate powers given to his native country in matters of religion, education, and the legal code, as well as the complicating features of the Protestant Churches in a formal Established Church. Like some of his colleagues, John A had excellent contacts in Britain, knew key players in the Disraeli and Gladstone administrations, and corresponded with the various occupants of Government House in Ottawa. Macdonald read widely, not just of British and American newspapers but the histories and biographers of England and the Continent, and the great works of Edmund Burke, MacAulay, Thomas Carlyle, Harriett Beecher, and Benjamin Franklin.

More than most politicians, whether in Imperial London or in the British colonies, John A. knew in his heart the reality of the North American landscape. Immigrants of whatever nationality that arrived in North America were not transplanted citizens from their own country. North America transformed people, uprooted their European DNA and transposed their body and soul to a new landscape. North America had wilderness, unlimited free land, and a vast expanse of rivers, lakes, mountains, plains, coastal waters, climates, coupled with staggering resources, both below the ground, in the water, on the fields, and in the forests. Where Europe was a mosaic of separate states, organized with absolutist principles of government, and separated by ethnic and religious lines, only Britain had survived as a constitutional monarchy, with an elected government choosing a leader and a Cabinet subject to the support of an elected assembly. Macdonald knew that the British North American colonies would pioneer their own system of responsible government, each sharing the common heritage of the North American landscape, and one that could be the model not only for the new dominion but for the other colonies of the British Empire, as later correspondence with Cecil Rhodes in South Africa would show. This is what appealed to Lord Selkirk and to Angus MacEachern, and this is what appealed to the vista of Edward Whelan when he visited Ottawa and Toronto. Macdonald also understood the power and influence of strong religious convictions, but for John A., like Winston Churchill, while he believed in religious freedom and tolerance, he personally believed in Churches from the outside.

At Charlottetown, Macdonald was in his 49th year, almost the same age that Winston Churchill became Chancellor of the Exchequer in 1926. He emerged as the leader not because of any formal position – he after all was an invited guest to the Conference. Despite his status as a gate crasher, Macdonald used all his time meeting the delegates personally, seeing the families of the Island delegates, cultivating friendships, and schmoozing with his good cheer and humour, no doubt amusing himself with the personal prejudices, biases, and jealousies of the individual delegates. Macdonald at Charlottetown was a great listener. He was anxious to know the views in favour of the federal scheme, but also wanted to learn about the reasons why they were against it. For the Island delegates, he listened carefully to the views of George Cole, who felt that a strong central government, let alone a unitary state, was not in the interests of smaller colonies like PEI. Macdonald listened to the catalogue of individual colonial concerns, including the land issue, the railroad, and continuous transportation links for PEI, for instance. Despite these provincial concerns, including the rep by pop arguments of George Brown, which was *his* central objective, and equal representation by province in a Senate chamber, from the Charlottetown meeting, Macdonald never deviated from his goal of a merger of the British North American colonies.

George Brown's letters to his wife Anne and Whelan's own papers give a vivid flavour to the Charlottetown meetings, and illustrate why this September gathering dramatically shifted all conventional thinking of the status quo. No longer was the separation of the British colonies a preferred option. The fruit was ready to pluck, and John

A. mapped out the way to formal agreement before gaining approval from London and the British Parliament. Later, after the Quebec meeting, Edward Whelan recalled the meetings of these two sessions, first in Charlottetown in September and then Quebec in October. To Whelan it was a form of confessional meeting, with each of the delegations lining up with their list of sins, cataloguing them as venal or cardinal, to see if through money or favours, they could obtain absolution. It was a fitting metaphor for the path ahead.

Conclusions

Whelan's death closed another chapter of the Island's story. From a small, lonely colony largely isolated from the tides of the British Empire, populated mainly by tenant farmers eking out a living on lands owned by absentee proprietors, PEI emerged reasonably unscathed by violence, extreme poverty, or the protests that caused revolutions throughout Europe or would soon tear the American Republic asunder. Whatever scepticism the Island population had towards their British rulers, they cultivated a political leadership that preferred responsible government and electoral politics to the extremism of many British colonies outside North America, including Haiti and Jamaica. In scarcely more than a generation, as the Island's population grew and the legacy of direct British control receded, not withstanding the peculiar religious controversies that the British elites tolerated in a divided Victorian era, Prince Edward Island adjusted to new circumstances, not of the British Empire but to the Confederation dream. Ottawa, not Imperial London, was to be the new center of power. Federal institutions, not Imperial designs, would guide the path to provincial rule. Sadly for Prince Edward Island, Whelan's death removed a future voice of reason and secular compromise.

5

The Post-Confederation Decades: From Louis Davies to Premier A.E. Arsenault

The Road to Confederation * the Land Commission *
The Island Railway * Better Terms *
The Island's Agricultural Economy * The Compton *
Island Banks * Georgetown's Social Whirlwind: A.E. Burke
* From Souris to the White House: John McCormick

How long does it take to create a country? Two generations ago, this question was not a theoretical issue, as the British Empire was slowly dismembered, new countries were sanctioned, and the United Nations, with five members of the Security Council and six rotating members (including Canada), went from the initial 50 countries in 1945 to over 100 almost overnight. When the Soviet Union broke up in 1991, fifteen separate countries were created. When the United States was created as an independent republic, it took about forty years – from 1783 to 1823 - to be a viable entity, and another 30 to be an ocean to ocean Continental Republic. Many of the signers of the Declaration of Independence, the actual parchment copy signed on August 2, 1976, overheard Benjamin Franklin, hearing from John Hancock that "there must be no pulling different ways; we must all hang together" retort: "Yes, we must indeed, all hang together, or must assuredly we shall all hang separately." Hancock doubted that the Republic could survive; the British hoped it would not.

By 1860, the Great Republic almost didn't. The civil war's end was approaching an agonizing closing as the Charlottetown Conference was underway, Lincoln had emerged as the powerful Northern leader, but the brutal battles, awesome killings, and savage warfare exposed how this war extended to class differences, sectional conflicts, and regional loyalties. To the delegates meeting in Charlottetown and Quebec, the internal issues of the Canadian federal structure, had to past another hurdle. There were the key institutions like the elected House of Commons and an appointed Senate, the judiciary, and taxation powers. The colonies were left to argue their favoured positions, knowing that the results had to be approved by their local legislatures. From Charlottetown, as the *Queen Victoria* carried the delegates to Quebec, with stops in Halifax and St. John, John A. Macdonald was thinking ahead for his great jury trial, the conviction that he could get approval from the Imperial Government. In fact, he became the great juggler of Canadian politics, in attempting to get at least two of the Maritime Provinces into Confederation.

He was comfortable that in the end, he could persuade Britain to approve the Quebec Resolutions. There would be negotiations, arguments over this clause or that, but the new country, the Dominion of Canada, was modeled in essence on the British parliamentary form, not the republican model of the US. Throughout his long career, he was an unwavering supporter of the British Parliamentary model. The Charlottetown Conference decided the basic framework, and to these core conclusions he was wedded. As he put it in 1881, "Independence is a farce … Canada must belong either to the British system or the American system. If we had to make a choice, between independence and annexation, I would rather that we should have annexation and join with the United States at once." He accepted that in the end, *he* would have to argue the case in London.

In Charlottetown, he came to admire William Pope, the Colonial Secretary of PEI, not only for his strong pro-Confederation convictions, but privately for his family, including Pope's eight children. Later, he would take on a young Joseph Pope as his personal secretary. He came to value William Pope as a colleague and private advisor, and they shared mutual British friends, literary men like Dickens,

Thackeray, Thomas Huxley and conservative political acquaintances like Lord Stanley and the Earle of Derby. He knew that all senior politicians in Britain of whatever political stripe had never visited North America. The British monarchy never gave passing notice that the Great Republic even existed – and it would take another 70 years before a prominent British politician, Winston S. Churchill, chose to visit Canada and in this case, Churchill was starting a long, lonely decade in political exile.

From the Charlottetown Conference in 1864 to Dominion Day on July 1, 1867, a period of only 1000 days, Macdonald forged the new country, placating the Imperial Government to pass the new constitution as an act of the British Parliament, the *British North America Act 1867*, establishing a new High Commission office in London and Washington (Quebec House, located in Piccadilly Square, was established in London in 1867 to represent that province's interest). For the next 25 years, from 1867 to his death in 1891, Macdonald outlived most of the Fathers of Confederation, stretched the geography of Canada to include Manitoba and British Columbia, bought the Hudson's Bay territories for only £300,000 pounds (George Brown worried that it would cost a million), and began the institutional architecture of a new Canada – a trans-continental railway, the courts, infrastructure, a police force, the start of an army, and a new financial system. But for six years, PEI was excluded from this new federal union. In 1865, the Island had rejected the terms of Confederation.

**

By the time the Island delegates returned to Charlottetown, some enjoying the sumptuous receptions and banquets in Montreal, Ottawa, and Toronto after the rainy days in Quebec City, it was clear that Islanders were unimpressed with the Confederation scheme. Two delegates, Edward Palmer, the Attorney General, and George Coles, the Liberal leader, were unalterably opposed to the final terms. They had the Island population with them. There were many reasons, and the debates in the Legislature, so well documented in Bolger's *Prince Edward Island and Confederation*, reveal the underlying dissension: a transfer of power to Ottawa, unequal treatment of small colonies (Rhode Island had equal representatives in the US Senate compared

*Robert Harris's Sketch for Meeting of the Delegates
of British North America*

to New York, one twentieth its size), no clear settlement of the land issue, doubts about a national railway, and the new and dreaded tax powers of Ottawa. On the Island, everyone dreaded taxes.

And everyone had an opinion. Town hall meetings were common, the editorial pages of the Island newspapers gave extensive coverage, and the Legislature debated the terms of the Confederation clauses. In truth, the Confederation terms were doomed for rejection. In many ways, it was a rational debate about the specific terms. For 100 years, certainly since the infamous land lottery of 1767, Islanders resented profusely the simple proposition that others knew best what was good for them. The Acadians had struggled against the British invaders who stole their land, their homes, and their life style. The Scottish immigrants had little use for the absentee landlords or the Island's own Family Compact. In the past, only Lord Selkirk and Angus MacEachern had the reputation, regardless of their religious differences, to seek the best course from the reluctant Colonial Governors. Catholics resented the Quebec Bishops who cared little about local conditions, and had ill-served this small Island diocese, with few priests, churches and schools. The new Irish and English immigrants were more interested in their rural livelihood that in the esoteric terms of Ottawa rule. Besides, now that they had achieved real responsible government, Islanders liked the Legislature they knew, their own, rather than the new one in Ottawa that seemed so far away. Island farmers and new immigrants felt that the Confederation terms were no different from the land owners, the Quebec Bishops, and the Family Compact, who were all interested in taking power and money away from Island voters. In the end, Islanders simply weren't persuaded. They were unwavering, even against better offers - $800,000 from the new Dominion to settle the land question, an offer of trade reciprocity introduced by General B.F. Butler to the US House of Representatives. They had their legislature, they had their pride, and no bribes would change their mind. For Islanders, they were more than an Island, they were isolated, what the *Islander* newspaper called 'our tight little Island'.

At the time of Confederation, despite the arrival of responsible government, the Island was still in the grip of the Family Compact, largely operating from Charlottetown. Indeed, there was a remarkable difference in the neighbouring provinces and even in Ontario and Quebec, between the rural country side and the cities. In the Maritimes, there were only three cities – St. John, Halifax, and Charlottetown - and their economic interests centered on commercial trade and banking with England, the shipping industry, and the new merchants. The rural economy was centered on small hamlets and villages scattered around the countryside, integrated by Ministers or priests, churches, the blacksmith, a tavern, a local doctor, and one room schools. For six months, the roads were impassable, a mix of rain and mud or ice and snow. A rail line was thought to be a better substitute for roads, and then there remained only the land question, the main question in the rural countryside.

For Island politicians facing their rural constituents, the land issue simply refused to go away. It affected everything, from the price of crops to banking, since money was a function of local currencies, the Halifax money rate, and the real price of British currency. The British proprietors now faced competition from new landowners, like Samuel Cunard, the Nova Scotia entrepreneur, ship owner, and budding ship builder, who joined with other land owners to suppress any real reforms, even when about forty per cent of Island land was held by tenant farmers and squatters. More specifically, the proprietors were against any Government initiatives that favoured escheat of their lands, i.e. a forced payment of taxes on land holdings. One of the largest land companies on the Island was a joint stock company called the Prince Edward Island Land Company. While in England to discuss possibilities of getting the British mail contract, Cunard was approached by George Young, a Halifax lawyer who would serve later as legal council for this PEI land company. Cunard joined forces with Andrew Colvile (agent for the 6th Earl of Selkirk, after Thomas died in France in 1820), Robert Bruce Stewart, and Thomas Holdsworth Brooking, Young's father-in-law. They acquired this large estate, some 60,000 acres in Prince County, with John Hill for £10,000. The group also took over the mortgage on the 102,000-acre estate of John Cambridge for £12,000 sterling; £8,400 was paid immediately, with the backing of London bankers Prescott, Grote, and Company and of the Liverpool Union Bank. Samuel and Joseph

Cunard held six-tenths of the shares, Andrew Colvile two-tenths, and Brooking and Young one-tenth each.

This syndicate joined with other proprietors to present a strong case against any escheat of their lands to the Colonial Secretary, Lord Glenelg. In August 1838 Young and Cunard went to Prince Edward Island to visit their new estates and to discuss the land tax with Lieutenant Governor Sir Charles Augustus FitzRoy. They offered assurances of "a common line of policy between the Proprietors and their tenants calculated to restore peace and to promote the prosperity of the Island." At a meeting of the Land Company, held in Charlottetown on October 20, 1838, Cunard and Young quarreled over the legal counsel, with Young wanting his own brother, Charles, and Samuel preferring his son-in-law, James H. Peters. Six months later, Cunard bought out his partners and became the largest proprietor on PEI. For the rest of his life, he was an uncompromising conservative on land tenure, true to his British aristocratic friends, who helped him gain an annual subsidy of £145,000 for a weekly transatlantic service of four steamships linking London and Liverpool, Halifax, Boston, and New York.

Cunard's experience in the financial jungles of Halifax, London, the Miramichi, and the West Indies, illustrated his approach to his Island land holdings. In essence, he wanted to use the timber rights to pay for the land holdings, using the timber rights for shipbuilding, or exports of timber. On the Cambridge estates, there were £2,535 in rent and his agent, J.H. Peters, was aggressive in seizing both cattle and land for late payments or in acquiring new tenants with more lucrative leases. Controversy surrounded Cunard's holdings. William Pope argued that the three estates purchased in Prince Edward Island in 1839 for £9,600 were resold in 1842 for £25,000. But tensions mounted as well, and many tenants disliked the aggressive approach to collecting rents. In one incident, close to where Edward Whelan would win an election, on Lot 45 in Kings County, 300 people had assembled on March 17, Saint Patrick's Day, took possession of a house and farm where the tenant had been legally ejected. It took 50 soldiers sent from Charlottetown to bring order to the Cunard Estates.

When responsible government arrived on January 1851, the Assembly had to listen to the grievances of the tenant farmers. The reformist Coles Administration, with Edward Whelan a constant thorn on the side of the proprietors – he later described Edward Palmer, a landowner and a land agent, as 'the steadfast apostle of the stand-still, the do-nothing, the Sleep Hollow School' – passed the Land Purchase *Act* of 1853, which in the end had little real effect (other than the purchase of the Worrell Estate). By 1860, with the Conservatives replacing the Coles government, Edward Palmer, unsure of a political strategy to deal with the agitated tenants, decide to adopt a common 'waiting game'. Palmer, who now owned most of Lot 1 in Prince County, wanted to appoint a Commissioner to study the matter, and sought guidance from London. The Secretary of State for the Colonies, Henry Pelham-Clinton, the Duke of Newcastle (and the eighth person to hold the job since 1854) suggested a three-man Commission, largely on the suggestion of Samuel Cunard: Joseph Howe from Nova Scotia, John Hamilton Gray from New Brunswick (representing the Crown), and J.H. Ritchie, also from Halifax (representing the proprietors).

Newcastle was close to William Gladstone, the Chancellor of the Exchequer and Liberal prime minister-in-waiting for the gerontocracy running Britain. Newcastle's predecessor, Edward George Lytton, took a personal interest in the colony of British Columbia and has a place named for him. He is notable as a novelist and the author of such phases as 'the Pen is mightier than the sword,' 'the pursuit of the almighty dollar,' and 'the great unwashed', a term that refers to the streets of Paris but could have referred to some of the British colonies. Newcastle also suggested that the Commission be free to form their own conclusions. Indeed, by 1860, Cunard had 1000 tenant farmers in 16 townships, paying one shilling per acre. His agent, now George W. DeBlois, found that rental arrears exceeded £17,000 per year. Cunard and the landowners thought that this three-man body would see their own views accepted but, to their surprise, this Commission – another would follow in 1875 – came out in favour of the tenant class.

Louis Davies

Premier A. E. Arsenault

Reporting in July 1861, the Commission, after intensive hearings, where Cunard himself appeared, recommended that properties be acquired according to the terms of the Land Purchase *Act,* with a guaranteed loan of £100,000 from the British Government. Despite efforts by the Legislature to enact the Report, Lord Newcastle, true to his aristocratic principles, refused to accept the Commission's recommendations. The Colonial Office agreed to Cunard's policy of non-interference, "in any manner different from that in which private estates in England could be dealt with", as Newcastle put it. The local bard, John Lepage, spoke for many with his satirical poetry:

> *Some say thou'rt governed by the Queen,*
> *And this doth please the Bard,*
> *Some 'praps' who say not what they mean –*
> *Say – by Sir Sam Cunard.*

For some of the Island delegates, whatever elation may have been left with banquets and parties as they returned on the *Queen Victoria* heading first to Halifax and St. John before turning towards Charlottetown, the formal resolutions crafted for the Imperial Government left politicians like George Coles and Edward Palmer utterly unimpressed. For them, it was straight forward: loss of autonomy in the federal government, reduced powers of taxation, too few seats in the House of Commons and no equality with the other provinces, unlike in the US Senate, and no superior offsets, such as in trade, in defense, or even in transportation, like a railroad. Only William Pope and Edward Whelan remained committed pro-Confederation advocates (paradoxically, none of the seven Islander Fathers would become Premier or members of the federal cabinet). Events in New Brunswick and Nova Scotia didn't help Macdonald's cause.

In Nova Scotia, Whelan's former mentor, Joseph Howe, used magnificent oratory for repeal. That colony managed to gain the recall of 18 of the 19 members sent to Ottawa, 36 of 38 members of the Nova Scotia Assembly. The Island election of 1865 was decisive for the anti-Confederation cause, declaring that the federal union "would prove politically, commercially, and financially disastrous to the rights and interests of the people." Only 94 Island electors could be found to send a vote of thanks to the Island delegates at Charlottetown and Quebec!

In Ottawa, Macdonald drew on the Advocates of Confederation, such as Brown and Cartier, Tilly and Tupper to present the formal resolutions to the Colonial Office. Brown laid the groundwork in London, including early negotiations on the Hudson's Bay territories (the Oregon Treaty with the USA in 1846 gave Vancouver Island to the British and extended the 49th parallel across the Continent to the Pacific), opening up the prospect of new provinces, more immigration, and aggressive Imperial nation building. By all means necessary, in John A's mind, he had to get the Quebec Resolutions presented to the British Government. Ontario was the big potential winner in the Confederation calculus, with its own legislature, a burgeoning population, and new markets opening in the lands to the west. Quebec had what its elites most wanted, protection for the French language, culture, religion, and legal code. Later, the Prime Minister could deal with the Maritime colonies, one by one. At the same time, he remained worried by the events to the south.

In 1866, the six Canadian delegates, led by Macdonald, converged for three weeks of slogging work at the Westminster Palace Hotel to negotiate the Quebec Resolutions with the Imperial Government. Clearly, Macdonald was the driving force, the center of visionary thought depicted in Harris' painting, the *Fathers of Confederation*. By this time, as Edward Whelan had noted, the Founding Fathers had gone to confession, it was contrition time, so to speak, and the delegation needed absolution and a blessing from the Imperial Father (despite Queen Victoria, it was very much a man's world, in Britain and in Canada). For Macdonald, it was a delicate balancing act. The four committed colonies were still on side. But each looked at the sins of the other colonies but suppressing their own, awaiting even the smallest concession to one without getting the same in return. Lord Blachford, formerly Sir Frederick Rodgers, the Permanent Under Secretary for the Colonies, described Macdonald's skills:

> *Macdonald was the ruling genius and spokesmen,*
> *and I was greatly struck by his power of management*
> *and adroitness. The French delegates were keenly on*

*the watch for anything that weakened their securities:
on the contrary, the Nova Scotia and New Brunswick
delegates were very jealous of concessions to the
arrièrée province; while one stipulation in favour
of the French was open to constitutional objections
of the part of the home government. Macdonald had
to argue the question with the home government
on a point on which the slightest divergence from
the narrow line already agreed on in Canada was
watched for – here by the French, and there by the
English – as eager dogs watch a rat hole; a snap on
one side might have provoked a snap on the other,
and put an end to the concord.*

For John A., it was not despondency that drove him on – he was
fully aware of Island sentiments and the limited euphoria about his
Confederation vision. As long as he had four colonies, now four
provinces – Ontario, Quebec, New Brunswick and Nova Scotia - the
others could wait. He stayed with his motto: "The fruit is green and
not fit to pluck." He was too much a politician to avoid the noises
from the anti-confederation crowd – that is why he was such a good
listener in Charlottetown and Quebec. He foresaw the future problems
and challenges to make the Federal union a meaningful concept with
the Imperial powers in London. He understood that he needed Nova
Scotia and New Brunswick, because of their Atlantic location and the
rights of the fisheries as a bargaining tool with the Americans. But
PEI, at least eventually, had to be part of the equation. Macdonald
wrote Lord Monck, the Governor General, who shared the letter with
the new British Prime Minister, William Gladstone:

*Canada is more directly interested in the immediate
acquisition of Prince Edward Island, from its
proximity to Nova Scotia and New Brunswick,
and the extent of its fisheries. Neither the Imperial
Government nor Canada can carry out satisfactorily
any policy in the matter of the fisheries under present
circumstances, and most unpleasant complications
with the American fishermen will ensue. It will,*

> *besides, become a rendezvous for smugglers, and, in*
> *fact, be as great a nuisance to us as the Isle of Man*
> *was in the days of old to England, before its purchase*
> *from the Duke of Athol. We must endeavor to get Her*
> *Majesty's government to help as much as possible in*
> *our attempts to conciliate the islanders, of which, I*
> *am glad to say, there is now good hope.*

It would, however, take time. The Island had its own interests and prejudices and Confederation was secondary to their local problems, especially regarding the absentee-owner question and the prospect of an Island railroad. It was a case where local prosperity and good fortune triumphed over Confederation. The former intoxicated Island politics with a certain pretension. Anti-Confederate Islanders could use the agreements determined at Charlottetown and agreed again in Quebec City as the Quebec Resolutions to argue for 'better terms' – a theme that exists to this day. It took John A. and the national outlook to eventually provide a modest and circumspect approach to the local economy. For Islanders, better the prospect of an Island railway linking Alberton to Souris than the distant chances of a railway from the Pacific shores to the Atlantic Ocean. Nothing illustrated this parochialism better than the Island railroad.

***

When Joseph Pope's Railway Bill was presented to the Island Legislature, PEI entered the railway age, the transport medium that was sweeping the industrial world. At the same time, it was the defining force that transformed modern society as much as the printing press had brought the literary world of the Bible, Shakespeare, and the poets 200 years before. In Britain, coal and iron production had doubled, speed of transport and annual doubling of industrial production became 'call words' for enterprising new entrepreneurs. By 1848, Britain had constructed 500 miles of railroads, new railway stations like Paddington and King's Cross, new book stalls and newspaper shops of W.H. Smith (who had a monopoly), and the wondrous new machines like semaphore signals, an early form of the Blackberry.

Premier Joseph C. Pope

William C. Pope

Railway tours and excursions, first organized by Thomas Cook, in part to promote temperance, extended the railway mania, and total investments accounted for 6.7 per cent of Britain's national income.

In the USA, by 1850, nine thousand miles of railways were built, opening the Great Plains to German and Irish immigrants. By the end of the Civil War, the US had 35,000 miles of track, which doubled in ten years, and doubled once again in 1890. Congress had granted millions of acres of land to the railway companies, which were funded by British capital, and three transcontinental railways were built, linking California in the West to Boston and New York in the East, with the railway companies becoming an integral part of the European immigration programs to attract settlers, an initiative enormously assisted by the Homestead Act, where a quarter section (160 acres) of public land was granted free to over a million settlers by 1890, west of the Mississippi.

A national railway linking the former British colonies was discussed both in Charlottetown and in Quebec; indeed, some of the delegates traveled by train from Pictou to Halifax while John A. and some of the delegates from Canada East and West continued from Pictou to Halifax on the *Queen Victoria*. The railway was a major priority for the new national government of John A. Macdonald, and so too were the Western lands owned by the Hudson's Bay Company, when George Brown began the negotiations with the Imperial Government on his trip to London in 1865. Ottawa secured titles to most of the land for the sum of £300,000, perhaps one of the greatest land deals ever consumed, certainly on a par with the deal transacted by the Imperial Government to secure controlling shares of the Suez Canal. The same year. But British banks proved more interested in squandering their capital in the US or Argentina than in the Canadian railways in the new Dominion. Perhaps they thought that the new federal union wouldn't last. It took high level finagling and patronage to get another Scotsmen, Donald Smith, to finance the fledging Canadian Pacific Railroad, Canada's first of two transcontinental railroads. As a result, British Columbia joined the Dominion in 1871, and Canada realized her motto, *ad mare usque ad mare*, from sea to shining sea.

Islanders became aware of the railway construction, and looked enviously at events taking place elsewhere. On the Island, by many standards, farm life remained a difficult existence. In one sense, the Island had everything: fertile land, abundant fisheries, plenty of trees, and wild life, fruit, and flowers of all kinds. No one starved, as they did in the big cities like London, New York, or Boston (Boston was referred to in Atlantic Canada as one of Canada's three cities). But it was a hard life nonetheless. Only hay and potatoes grew without much assistance – wheat, corn, or other crops needed lime, pesticides, fertilizer, or special equipment. The land question, of course, trumped all worries. Even the Belfast riots in 1860, or the early and tempting plots of John Stewart, where 800 people crowded the Market Square in Charlottetown in 1824, failed to arrest this horrible blot on the Island's economic development. And most immigrants were farmers by choice, since few jobs existed outside the agricultural economy.

To further add to these problems, there was yet another, in the Island soil. To outsiders, the red soil of the Island is a joy to see, a magnificent contrast to blues of the sky, the blue-greenish water, and the staggering shades of green, in the trees, grasses, and gardens. To Islanders though, even today, the red soil is a curse – dirty, muddy, a mix of water, soil and ice that can slow a two ton automobile to a standstill. Since there is no real rock or sub-soil gravel, Island red soil makes for terrible roads, an especially severe challenge for roads as the Island approached 100,000 in population by the start of the 20th century. It was this challenge that prompted the Island to construct a railway, entirely on its own, as its answer to rejecting the Confederation deal in 1865.

In 1871, Premier Joseph Pope, the brother of the strong pro-Confederation proponent, William Pope, now close friend and confident of Prime Minister John A. Macdonald, and his host during his delightful, two month extended visit in 1870, introduced the Railway Bill, which passed by the legislature and received Royal assent by Lieutenant Governor Robinson on April 17, 1871. If John A. is known as *the* Father of Confederation, and the prime proponent of the transcontinental railway (the National Dream, in Pierre Berton's felicitous phrase), the Island railway is the step mother of PEI's entry into Confederation in 1873. How did this happen?

The basic plan for the Island was to build a line from Cascumpeque (now Alberton) in the west to Georgetown in the east. It was to be a narrow gauge track, three feet six inches, with 40 lb. rails (i.e. 40 pounds per yard), 24 feet in length. The contractor, Schreiber and Burpee, organized as the InterColonial, was using 55.7 lb rails, which was standard gauge on the mainland. Fortunately for the contractor, while the construction fee was £5000 per mile, there was no mention of an upper limit, so the rail line went through every valley, passed near every politician's farm, and had lots of winding curves, which slowed down the train. Later, local wags would say that, both in Canada's largest province, Ontario, and the smallest, PEI, it took the train a whole day to cross the province.

The 165.5 mile PEI railway included wire fencing, seven foot spruce ties (5 inches thick, 8 inches wide), 2200 per mile, 32 telegraph poles per mile, and 32 glass insulators. There were 10 locomotives, 10 first class coaches, 6 second class coaches, six baggage and mail cars, three snow plows, and three flangers. Most of the interior furniture and rolling-stock came from the Mark Butcher Furniture Factory. Six of the ten locomotives, built by Hunslet Empire Co., in Leeds, Yorkshire in1872 turned out to be more ornamental than useful, and later went to Cape Breton and Newfoundland. The steam engines were powered by boilers, with water tanks located at Tignish, Alberton, Borden, Emerald Junction, Melville, Murray Harbour, Lake Verde, Royalty Junction, Breadalbine, and Bloomfield.

The terms of the financial obligations were for thirty years at four per cent interest, paid by PEI debentures, issued through the local banks. The operating assumption was that annual revenues from trade, passengers, cargo, and the post would cover annual costs. But the more relevant problem was political, in that the railway hadn't proceeded to Tignish, north from Alberton, or to Souris, north from Georgetown. Turmoil and agitation in the legislature led to an election, and the new government of R.P. Haythorne agreed to expand the branch lines with the same contractor. By this time, it was only too obvious that the Island couldn't afford the railway. Across the Continent, railways were a sure way to lose money, as shrewd Yankee entrepreneurs showed the sophisticated British financiers. On the Island, Premier Haythorne and David Laird traveled to Ottawa on February 15, 1873, to discuss Confederation terms, including the railway debt.

****

In the years following the 1864 Confederation Conferences, most Island politicians remained outside the pro-federal fold. Ottawa was a distant capital, the national railroad wasn't a reality, and trips to Halifax or London were an easy and enjoyable voyage, with ship connections from Charlottetown to Pictou or Halifax and onward to Liverpool or London. The educated elite finished high school at the Central Academy in Charlottetown, and finished their studies at Prince of Wales or St. Dunstan's, and then proceeding to further studies in England. This was a common path for the sons of the Family Compact, personified by Louis Henry Davies, later Sir Louis Henry, who became one of the Island's most famous sons, when he became Chief Justice of the Supreme Court of Canada.

Davies typified a lot of politicians who learned to change their mind. "Wise men changed their opinions when necessary," he later argued in the Legislative Assembly, "fools never did so." It seemed like an echo from another politician, Winston Churchill. He was born in Charlottetown in 1845. His father was Colonial Secretary in 1869, and he was a strong anti-federal union spokesman, introducing a motion at the Charlottetown Debating Club in February 1870 that the terms of union "are not just and equitable to PEI, and should not be accepted." Like many Island politicians, his strong suit was oratory, nurtured when he read law at the Inner Temple in London, when he was called to the bar in 1866, before working at the law office of Thomas Chitty. Unlike most Islanders, he became a first-rate cricket player, a sport which most Islanders would call Stone Age baseball.

Elected as a Liberal to the House of Assembly in the prosperous farm district of 4th Kings, an area which included lots held by absentee landlords, Davies opposed this new Island scheme, the provincial railroad. There were many grounds to oppose it – it was narrow gauge, and the contract had no mileage limit, which meant that it wound through every hamlet near a politician's home. Some argued it was a plot to sink the Island Government into debt. Then, and only then, would Ottawa bail out the Island, on Ottawa's terms. Davies joined with David Laird in the Assembly to challenge the Premier, J.C. Pope. But it was too late – the railway costs were too high, there was trouble floating the bonds in London and, despite protracted negotiations, the Island joined the Canadian Union on 1 July 1873. It was a bittersweet time for the Prime Minister. His comrade in arms, George Etienne Cartier, died in May in London, where he was treated for a serious case of Bright's kidney disease. Macdonald might be consoled that Cartier would see the dream of Confederation unfold from sea to sea. Cartier could also be comforted that this insular Island colony had finally acceded to "better terms". The Governor General, Lord Dufferin, traveling with Countess Dufferin on board the new Dominion yacht, the *Druid*, wrote the Prime Minister, seeing the banner on Pope's wharf in Charlottetown with the words, "Long Courted, won at last," that "the Island was in a state of jubilation, and quite under the impression that it is the Dominion that has been annexed to Prince Edward Island, and in alluding to the subject, I have adopted the same tone."

The celebrations on Dominion Day, accompanied by 19 guns salute from the battery at Fort Edward, a tour to Rustico and a luncheon at Ocean House, a Sunday service at St. Paul's Church, and a banquet and ball at the Colonial Building left a strong impression on the Governor General, and some politicians entered the federal fold. On September 17, 1867, the Island sent six members to the House of Commons: J.C. Pope and James Yeo from Prince County, David Laird and Peter Sinclair from Queen's, and Daniel Davies and Austin McDonald from King's. When John A. lost power that year, with the Pacific railway scandal brewing across the land, Prime Minister Alexander MacKenzie appointed David Laird as Minister of the Interior. Four Island senators were appointed: R. P. Haythorne, T.H.Haviland, Donald Montgomery, and G.W. Howlan.

In the first 50 years of Confederation for PEI, when Premier Joseph Pope led his Conservative Party to join the Dominion as the seventh province, from 1873 to 1923, when J.D. Stewart led his Conservative Government to victory, the Province had fifteen Premiers, one short coalition administration led by Louis Davies, 21 years of Conservative administration, and 24 years of Liberal governments. Not surprisingly, during this period, federal politics influenced Island voting. When John A. Macdonald died in 1891, provincial support shifted to the Liberals, and Liberal administrations governed PEI from 1891 to 1911, when Robert Borden, a Conservative, that shrewd Nova Scotian, regained power in Ottawa, after 15 years in the wilderness. He would be the last Maritimer to become Prime Minister. Provincially, J.A. Matheson and A.E. Arsenault (the first Francophone elected Premier; W. W. Sullivan was the first Catholic) ran Conservative administrations.

These five decades showed a continuing decline in the economic fortunes of the Maritimes, comprising a perfect storm of three issues: the decline of the leading export sector, shipbuilding; the gradual takeover of Maritime banks and the slow shift of the Maritimes as an exporter of capital; and finally a pernicious conflict between the need to invest in education and new technologies with the absence of any new government revenues at the provincial level. Both companies and the provinces had difficulty in raising capital, either in London or in Central Canada, so the only other solution was to deal with Ottawa. Clearly, the Canadian tariff policy, the main pillar of Macdonald's National Policy, was more than a tax surcharge facing imports. Tariff policy meant new revenues for Ottawa, so the Maritime Provinces were caught in a squeeze, and forced to seek 'better terms'. It was a spectacular spur to established industries, like home appliances. Home goods like fridges, washers, and stoves needed steel, aluminum, motors, and components, and these sectors were comfortably located in the big population centers, the profitable products for Central Canadian merchants: at one point, Eaton's supplied eighty per cent of all home appliances in Canadian households.

In the post-Confederation period, while the elites focused on railway financing, lawyers scrambled for patronage and federal fees, and newspapers argued the pros and cons of the Confederation calculation, rural life in PEI proceed apace, quite oblivious to the political scene. For Islanders in the small communities, it was a contented life of individual freedom and natural beauty. The country side abounded with wild flowers, recklessly protruding into the trees, fields, barnyards and country gardens. Imported species like garden lace, lupins, asters, sweet pea, verbena, sweet william, bush roses, lilacs, peonies, and wild roses and a wide range of flora dotted the landscape, while blueberries, raspberries and strawberries provided fresh fruit in summer and jams and cakes in winter.

But rural life was a struggle, even more so when the Maritime economy faced serious decline as export sectors lost traditional markets and, despite new sectors like lobster canning, little new investment was put into growth industries. Indeed, the Maritimes soon became a net exporter of capital, and outward migration would follow. From the very first settlers among the Acadians, to the Scottish Highlanders, agriculture in all its forms was a novel experience. This was not their background in Europe. They had little experience with soil conditions, fertilizers, pesticides, and animal husbandry. Worst of all, there was the Canadian winter. All too often the settlers learned about an Island winter – it comes early, and stays late. A winter in Canada defines the seasons: as the Quebec chanson suggests, *mon pays, c'est l'hiver.* Lord Selkirk, as soon as he stepped on shore in Lot 57 in 1803, quickly defined the essential challenge: be prepared for winter.

The Highland settlers faced the universal seasonal problem, so well known by the Indians and Eskimos: to design a structure like the igloo construction technique with ice and snow, or that used in Central Asian nomads with their yurt housing in the steps of Siberia, or the Indian tribes with the simple teepee – how to protect a family from the howling wind. On the Island, there was no shortage of wood, tools could be shared, and there were long months to mend the interior. But from October to April, cold wind was a challenge, as much for the animals as it was for people. Snow itself can be an insulator, as did newspapers, straw, and even seaweed. But the wind was everything, because it was primarily responsible for the real hardship of the Island winter, creating massive drifts, closing roads and lanes, and reducing travel to zero for days on end.

Government House 1860

Winter thus defines the rural calendar. Each month becomes a fixed piece in the schedule, with the winter determining how much food to store, the distance from home to barn, and sundry winter chores like ice fishing. Farm homes and barns were usually painted white, but barns were often painted a signature off color – a purple or orange or green – to allow a doctor or a priest to find the rural farm in the semi-darkness of a white snow. Barns, of course, were multi-purpose, both made for horses, cows, and sheep, but also dogs, kittens, chickens, and a workshop for the litany of farm implements, often made by hand.

The winters were the season for interior and exterior tasks. The long months after Christmas were devoted to equipment repair, home and barn improvements, furniture and tool making, usually assisted by the local blacksmith. Outside, there was no end of chores: felling trees for timber and firewood, and fixing board length wood for siding and floors, fixing logs for furniture, fence posts, hay storage, or lobster traps, or wood slats for wall insulation. Winter imposed a harsh drudgery on family life. Farmers faced a perpetual cycle of economic impositions – the more the land was cleared, more time was, in turn, needed for better horses and farm implements to be used for cutting hay, storing potatoes, gathering oats and taking produce to the markets in Charlottetown. In a real sense, winter defined the summer because everything had to be ready for the spring planting at the end of April and early May, from clearing the field, spreading manure, or using seaweed and Irish moss as a fertilizer. The French settlers were the first to use the seashores as a source for fertilizer on the soil – mussel mud stacked in the summer and dragged under the ice in winter, seaweed gathered immediately after late summer storms, and sometimes finely grained sea shells made small by the sea waves. (Ground shells were also used as food grit for farm fowl.)

The farm season started with planting in late April, with growth over June and July. The summer season imposed very long days for the entire family. The days and weeks were tiring and arduous (and often accident-prone): from milking cows in the early morning to working on the herring boats and setting lobster traps at the beginning of May to the harvest season, starting with hay in July and potatoes and vegetables in August and September. Even Sundays were workdays.

Rain and wind had a vital role in the harvest, especially for the potato crop, and visitors to the Island soon saw the native shrewdness of the farmers, who could do a quick calculation of the annual yield per acre, depending on the days of rain or sunshine. By the end of July, the harvest came on a regularized cycle: hay, the potato crop, abundant vegetables, flowers, and raspberry, strawberry, and blueberry crops. It was backbreaking work, non-stop from early dawn to night fall. Often fathers and sons worked in tandem; schools in the spring and early fall were given a break to allow the farm children to work in the fields. People in Charlottetown could always tell a farmer family – well tanned hands and arms and a diamond-like tan on the face and neck, with white skin every where else.

There was no end of tasks for the farm family. Unlike in Ireland, food was not a problem, particular in the fall and early winter. Fridges in most farms were a 20th century luxury, but by the 1870s, farm families cultivated the use of ice from the rivers and streams, and ice delivery was a cash crop for farmers living near Charlottetown. Farmers had learned from the military the century-old tools of meat preservation. Pork rather than meat from cows was the preferred long term winter food for storage, in part because it saved better, and its use for pork fat, an excellent by-product for daily cooking and soap-making. Pork was easy to cut for a single farmer, and hams, loins, shoulders and bacon strips were cured with a mix of Demerera brown sugar, salt and pepper, and salt peter. As in Ireland, there was a perpetual stew on the stove, with the customary FSB for the family to provide food for visitors (family stand back), or potted meats with leftover pieces from the cheeks, tail, and other odd bits thrown in. Often fowl meat was added – ducks, quail, partridge, geese, and sundry fowl caught on the fly – and these birds were equally useful for their wings for dusters, feathers for pillows and mattresses, and goose grease for backrubs.

Clearly, the farm life had its enjoyments, but the days were long, the nights short, and the summer season passed quickly. Each month had its own tasks. Consider the simple example of soap making.

Soaps had a universal need – from spring house cleaning to airing the winter cloths, night bedding, and other elements of the farm household. Soap making was a careful blend of fat scraps from cooking, plus the tallow dips of oil from the kerosene lamps, added as a chemistry of lye, hardwood ashes, and ash leach, mixed in a barrel or vat. According to some accounts, a barrel of ashes and 12 pounds of fat produced 40 pounds of soap. A hundred years later, it would take a posse of MBAs and a computer to make such calculations and reach the same conclusion. Besides, Canadian merchants now sold packaged goods, like Ivory soap, introduced in 1878, Jergen's soap (1882) and Sunlight Soap (1886). But too often, the poorest farms lived on the edge, where the best milk was diverted from the children to feed red foxes, a cash winner, so malnutrition was high and led to disturbingly high rates of tuberculosis.

The rural economy was a cash economy well into the twentieth century. The banks were incredibly cautious with money, providing cash outlays for mortgages and equipment, mainly tractors and hay bailers. Fisherman received money for boats and equipment. Farmers preferred the rural co-ops to the banks, and rarely saw the banks as a career for farm children. In addition to the staple potato, each farm yard had a large vegetable garden: beans, peas, onions, squash, pumpkins, cabbage, turnips, parsnips, carrots and tomatoes were standard products. A large portion of the farm output was for personal farm use, and a small portion was used for barter to pay off doctor's bills, keep the Church and God happy, and sundry bills like the blacksmith, a lawyer or the female teacher. The market in Charlottetown was a cash day, where real money was horded, even from neighbours.

Throughout the nineteen century, the absentee landowners were bought off and the standard Island farm was about 100 acres, supporting perhaps 16,000 farm families at the peak. More attention was paid to land cultivation and crop rotation – a challenge that farmers gave heed to but often ignored. The first Governor on the Island who took any real interest in Island farming, John Ready, established the Agricultural Society, with a view to improving live stock and seed. It was funded with £30 pounds, later £150 pounds, and renamed the Royal Agricultural Society under the patron, Prince Albert. For decades, the agricultural community lacked a coherent political voice in the Legislature, which was still dominated by the merchant elites.

The agricultural societies, even before Confederation, attempted to import new breeds of Shorthorn cattle and Leicester sheep from England, experimented with varieties of grain, and cultivated new seeds for various vegetable and horticultural crops. Starting in 1827, the Agricultural Society was an exhibit for live stock, farm products, home made articles, and cash premiums paid to local industries. In October 1867, this annual show became the Industrial Exhibit, and a major stimulus for improved agricultural production, located on the north side of Charlottetown, near the Hillsborough River, at the Exhibition Ground. Later, it became the annual Charlottetown Exhibition and Driving Park, held in August, since reorganized as Old Home Week. It was an exhibit of agricultural production in all its forms – horses, cattle, equipment, pastry and cooking, and breeding. Live stock and machinery were the main exhibit attractions, and the Fair included visiting lecturers (often from the Ontario Agricultural College, now Guelph University) and displays by equipment manufacturers like John Deere and Massey Ferguson. The most popular reading material in farm homes was *The Farmer's Advocate and Home Magazine,* published from London, Ontario, which had extensive coverage of farm life, animals, crops, fruit, and practical suggestions for farmers and their families. A review of the PEI Dairymen in 1906 is instructive:

> *The number of patrons supplying milk to cheese factories was in 1906, 2,999 and in 1907, 3,160, and increase of 161. The number of patrons supplying milk to butter factories was, in 1906, 672 and in 1907, 600, a decrease of 72. The milk contributed by each patron average, in 1906, 9,917 lbs., and in 1907, 8,528 lbs., a decrease of 399 lbs. per patron. The net average return to each patron was, in 1906, 78.66 and in 1907, 75.14, a decrease of 3.52. The gross value of cheese and butter manufactured in this Province was,*

in 1906, 357,302.86 and in 1907, 364,715.08 lbs, an increase of 7,412.22. ... This Dairy Association is crippled in its work for want of funds. The factories are already taxed all they will stand, the amount being $481, besides this the Association receives $300 from the local Government, and $300 from the Dominion Department of Agriculture, making a total income of $1,081 to pay for inspection, Secretary's salary, and other expenses. Nothing is over for milking competition or any educative work....

The Island's rural life style was depicted in local newspapers and in national outlets aimed at farm life. What was central was how the farm communities were integrated around small farm plots, with common dairies, cheese plants, and tanneries. A story in *The Examiner* describes the case of Crapaud:

Crapaud is well supplied with excellent mills, having no less than four, viz. Collett's, Stordy's, Leard's, and Howatt's. They are all supplied with French Burrs and other appliances for turning out first-class flower. Messrs. Collett and Howatt have saw and carding mills fitted up in the most appropriate manner... there are at Crapaud Corner two blacksmith shops, two harness shops, two tailors, two shoemakers, and a steam carriage factory. The thriving village of Hampton, about two miles east of Crapaud Corner, contains two forges, an agricultural implement factory and a tannery.

Crapaud was close to the village of Tryon, where Charles Edward Stanfield, an English immigrant from Bradford, Yorkshire, began a textile mill in Tryon in 1856 for carding, spinning, and weaving. Stanfield's first stop in North America was Philadelphia. Here he met a ship owner from PEI, who conveyed the news that the Island had no woolen mills. He explored the idea, sought capital from his uncle in England, and founded the Tryon Woolen Mills. An expert on machinery, he was a tinkerer in the mold of Thomas Edison. He soon owned a tannery, a general store, a hat factory, and a farm.

For ten years, he cultivated his determined business acumen. As the company expanded, Stanfield sold his business interests to his partner and brother-in-law, Samuel Dawson, and with his proceeds, eleven thousand dollars, he moved his family to Truro, Nova Scotia, with his house and factories located near the new Intercontinental Railway. Eventually his company was renamed the Truro Knitting Mills Ltd., and in 1906, it became Stanfield's Ltd. Its most enduring product was Stanfield's underwear, an ideal gift for mine workers in the Klondike, the footmen in the railway, or the troops in the army. Charles Stanfield's grandson was Robert Stanfield, Harvard law graduate, future Premier of Nova Scotia, and national leader of the Progressive Conservative Party. (As Opposition Leader, Stanfield campaigned in this homestead hamlet in the 1972 and 1974 elections, and his Party won the seat in both campaigns.)

This was the rural life of Prince Edward Island, where the province entertained a dual economy, the first involving the federal government and trade sectors like shipbuilding (and later lobster plants and fox ranching, led by stalwarts such as Charles Dalton, the Tignish entrepreneur), and the second involving farming and fishing communities. As noted by historian, Lorne C. Callbeck, "the farmers of the region had markets close by at which they could sell their wool and hides; mills to grind wheat flour, buckwheat flour, and oatmeal; mills to saw lumber and split shingles; tailors to make their suits out of cloth manufactured in local mills; shoemakers to make their boots and shoes out of leather prepared in the tanneries; harness makers to fashion harness for their horses. Carriages and certain farm implements were manufactured close at hand and blacksmiths were available to keep them repaired. Altogether, most of the necessities of life were within easy reach...."

By the turn of the century, PEI represented the ideal economic model of the family farm, the so-called mixed farm economy of multiple crops where farm families and community values were a shared partnership. On the Island, there was an equality of interest. The fact that the urban folk needed the farm produce and a community of interest because the farm family created the wealth at home, independent of international markets, bankers, and special interests like lawyers. In this mixed farm life, there was indeed a real social equality, the combination of the farm, the school, and the church, with a high measure of individual dignity and the absence of real poverty, the bane of the urban environment.

*****

The small scale of the Island economy led some groups to work together to advance cooperative enterprise for goods and services, for the home, the farm, and the community. One such group is the remarkable case of the Comptons of Belle River, located near St. Peter's, the political district which elected Edward Whelan. The Comptons had an energetic leader, Benjamen Compton, who incorporated a new venture, B. Compton Ltd., a partnership of founding families - the Comptons, the Humes, the Bears, and the Saunders. This arrangement allowed the families to pool their personal assets in such new enterprises as a large saw mill, a machine shop, a lobster plant, and an electric power mill. Any supplies needed for these ventures were brought wholesale and distributed to he family members. The Compton Company spread to a number of industries - fishing, farming, and various products from the saw mill. They produced fish boxes and butter boxes used throughout the Island, and a large supply of hardwood flooring. Their products were also sold to Glace Bay and Sydney in Cape Breton, using the Compton ship, the *Hataven*, a two-masted schooner bought in Lunenburg. On return runs, the *Hataven* brought back coal and gravel. Other products sold by the Comptons went to the Pictou region of Nova Scotia, a port for ships going to England.

At the peak, the Comptons numbered about 100 families. They were members of the Mcdonaldite faith, based on the principles of the Scottish Minister, Rev. Donald McDonald, whose religious tenants were those of the Church of Scotland. McDonald died in 1867 but his sermons and teachings were widely known not only in King's Country but across the Island. The McDonaldites held religious services twice a week in their homes, married within the group, and largely kept to themselves for social occasions like weddings and births. As a group, they differed from a commune, which was based on a mix of unrelated people. The Comptons, in fact, were related to United Empire Loyalists from New Jersey and Maine, and later from New Brunswick.

After Confederation, some of the Compton group moved to Western Canada as homesteaders. However, as crop failures and droughts in the West caused too much family hardships, most returned to the Island. For the period it existed, the B. Compton Co. was a remarkable success story, providing happy, prosperous, and well dressed families, with the children participating in school and social affairs. Newly weds were provided with a fully-furnished house and farm, owned by the Company, where the new couple would reap their annual harvests and add to the community wealth. In time, the prosperity of the Comptons, and their shrewd investments (which included rural electricity), attracted attention from other communities, as well as from places as far away as California, Ohio, Chicago, and New York, as well as Canadian cities. Young people were interested in jobs. Many outsiders saw the Comptons as an economic model to be emulated, especially as regards the availability of electricity for the saw mills. They were, in short, all but self-sufficient and sustainable.

But it wasn't going to last. Other Island communities wanted the Comptons to join in province-wide movements to deal with the potato crop, whose prices fluctuated, usually downward. The Comptons were not interested in government support. As one Comptonite told *The Guardian*, assistance from the government was "only taking money out of one pocket and putting a smaller amount in another for some is lost in administration." Ben Compton died in 1921, the result of a saw mill accident, and the new leader was "Big" John Compton from Bangor, Maine, replaced later by his brother-in-law, Hector Compton of Belle River in 1944. Both the First World War and then the Second World War caused many disruptions, and a disastrous fire in 1942 forced the families to break up, or move away. The Company was dissolved in December 31, 1947.

The Compton Company was part of the economic pattern in PEI, from Confederation in 1867 to the Second World War. Families operated as a "quasi-vertically integrated" community enterprises, sharing financial risks, and integrating the financial needs for food, homes, and supplies. Sheep farmers supplied wool for firms like MacAusland's Wollen Mills, as well as milk for dairies that produced cheese, bottled milk, and ice cream. But the problems for such enterprises on the Island were twofold. As the Comptons learned, even though they shared a common religious faith, and they felt immune for a time from outside forces, other issues were at play. "We ask for the things we need, no more. And these are given to us gladly. We do not abuse the system," said a Comptonite. Nonetheless, the second problem was more basic: outside forces were indeed at work - transportation problems, changing technology, and new methods of production - the old labour-intensive system could not remain self-sufficient - it had to grow or die. It was becoming a new world of mass production, where large companies had a cost advantage, and the smaller enterprises folded, merged, or closed shop.

This was the life that drove the political values of rural Prince Edward Island and propelled voters to reject the Confederation scheme of the Founding Fathers. Confederation was seen as solely for the business elites of Charlottetown, who were tied to dangerous outside interests and constant legal entanglements. Furthermore, the merchant class and the political elites were in favour of large scale industrialization, along with the modern urban life that threatened farms and took land out of production. PEI had preserved an ideal rural life, the life of the farmer and fishermen, the two keys to explaining the inner sense of the Island way of life. This was the celebration of writers like Andrew Macphail, the boy from Orwell Corner, a Selkirk settlement in Lot 57, whose masterpiece, *The Master's Wife*, described the Island lifestyle. It was a similar theme to another Island writer, Lucy Maud Montgomery, who cherished the one room schools, the farm families, and the rustic countryside of Prince Edward Island. To Islanders, they simply had a suspicion of big shots, the idle rich, and the sweet talkers who might threaten their rural life style and the family hospitality of the local community.

******

But Confederation entailed political adjustments. The Island sent federal representatives to Parliament, both as elected MPs and

New Brunswick, Nova Scotia and Canada are united in a federal state, the Dominion of Canada, by the British North America Act (July 1, 1867). The province of Canada is divided into Ontario and Quebec. The United States of America proclaims the purchase of Alaska from Russia (June 20).

The British North American Colonies, 1867

appointed Senators. Ottawa took over the Island railway, and cultivated new institutions, including the Post Office, the federal Courts, policing, and new taxes. The Land question was finally settled, after 107 years, when the lottery was first introduced. The House of Assembly passed the Land Purchase Bill of 1874, but it was reserved, so a new Act was passed the next year, which provided for a land commission to settle the claims of tenants and squatters. This commission heard from both sides, Davies representing the tenant farmers, Edward Hodgson representing the owners. Davies background in law and law proceedings allowed him to dominate the hearings: his basic aim was to challenge land titles, improper use of legal procedures, and lower the financial costs of improvements. To everyone's surprise, Davies settled on costs that greatly lowered what the proprietors had wanted. Some refused to accept the awards, and appealed to the Island's Supreme Court. The proprietors won their case. Legal arguments ensued but the Province appealed to new Supreme Court of Canada. In January 1877, the chief justice, William Buell Richards, argued against the Island's case, but the appeal went in favour of PEI, which did have the right to pass the Land Purchase *Act*.

The land question was only one of numerous adjustments that governments – the Island Legislature, and the new Parliament in Ottawa – had to make. The major one, of course was money and banking. From the earliest days of exploration and settlement in the British colonies, money was a problem. Some might say it still is. In matters of money, there are two core issues. The first is the role of money as a medium of exchange. In societies where money exchange is primitive, the medium of exchange is also primitive. This situation can exist even when societies reach a high level of industrialization, the old Soviet Union being the best case study. In these cases, the means of exchange is barter, a form of trading one product for another – arms for oil, diamonds for drugs, presumably in numbers that make the exchange roughly equal.

Historically, the North American colonies had several devices to apply barter exchange – wampum, corn, wheat, hides, beaver skins, cattle, horses. Initially, since the only hard currency was the money issued in Europe, the colonies had to rely on barter and other primitive means because there was a constant shortage of hard currency. In Quebec, perhaps the earliest use of paper money was the promissory notes issued by the Intendant, Jacques de Meulles in 1685. Five years later, the Massachusetts Bay Colony issued paper money, described not only as "the origin of paper money in America but also in the British Empire, and almost in the Christian world". Throughout the eighteenth century, the commercial empire of France in North America was led by the French West India Company. By 1721, it issued copper *denier* coins for circulation in New France. After the British conquest in 1759, the Treaty of Paris added a clause authorizing redemption of card money, discounted by 25 per cent of the issued value. Why?

The 1763 Treaty settlement typified the second problem of money. Coins and coinage date back to the Roman Empire and much earlier, probably to the use of decimal coinage in India. Coins, of course, have the notable advantage of convenience – they can be carried anywhere, often across oceans, borders, or military walls. Unlike beaver skins or cattle, coins were easy to accept, dispose, weigh, and trade. They were more durable than cattle, whisky, or a load of fish. But coins had one incurable weakness: whatever metal was used to make them, it was easy to debase them, by substituting a less valuable metal, be reducing their size, by adding a cheap substitute, even by a tiny fraction, or a combination of all these factors. Coins, in short, were easy to counterfeit. To this counterfeit dilemma, there was now added the second challenge, inflation, which could quickly debase the currency as a store of value. This, indeed, was the problem facing Charles Calonne in Paris before the French Revolution, and still remains a problem today for many countries.

In the British colonies, dating from the Treaty of Paris signed in 1763, as the population grew through immigrant settlements and high natural fertility, more trade and commercial transactions required a means for money exchange, hence a stable currency. The usual practice, whether under the French regime or the British, was to tie colonial trade to money transported from Europe. Curiously, the most stable currency was the Spanish milled pillar dollar, against which local colonial currencies could be established as a value or 'pegged.' In Halifax, the pillar dollar was five shillings, and was known as the Halifax currency. But in general, hard money was scarce, so local needs had to be met by alternatives, by barter of goods, for instance, by exchange of one colonial currency with another, but at a steep discount. In general, until well into the nineteenth century, all the British colonies faced a measure of monetary chaos.

This uncertainty flowed from two problems. As noted, most hard money, i.e. specie, came from Europe, either London or Paris, or from the Spanish gold and silver coins minted in the Americas. Some was stolen from Spanish ships by the Royal Navy or entrepreneurial pirate captains. One of the great strengths of the British Royal Navy was the capacity to move money from colony to colony in military ships, sometimes carrying bullion absconded as prize money from foreign vessels. When Lord Nelson, for instance, first traveled across the Atlantic to Quebec, his ship was carrying £100,000, a staggering sum at that time. Hard currency had to be transported to the British colonies, because they lacked a banking system, the one thing that would advance money circulation to augment trade exchange. The currency chaos is illustrated by two British colonies, Quebec and PEI. Prior to 1763, the Quebec Intendants issued promissory notes on playing cards to pay for various transactions, such as salaries for the military, for instance: 100 livres in the black cards, 50 livres in the red. These playing cards, used as a currency from 1711, were much inflated by 1763, hence the reference to a stable currency in the Treaty of Paris 1763.

Generally speaking, the exports of the British colonies went to Britain, but were discounted in value compared to imports of manufactured goods, again mainly from British manufacturers and transported on British ships. The value of colonial exports was in *specie*, usually promissory notes or bills of exchange. Colonial imports were paid in hard currencies, gold, silver, or even copper coins, and since the pay of salaries for the military establishment and colonial Governors and officials came from hard currency brought in from Britain, this pay expenditure provided the principal means of monetary circulation in each colony. The bigger the military payroll, the more the circulation of money. Without a strong military, there was less payment and thus lower circulation of money. Indeed, in Halifax, the oldest private bank, the Halifax Banking Company, founded in 1825 by a pre-revolutionary Loyalist, Enos Collins, had the expressed purpose of financing privateers and their bounty from sea battles. Among the backers of this Halifax Bank was Samuel Cunard, subscribing £5000 of a total £50,000 capital, which despite widespread dissatisfaction, was immensely profitable. Later it would become, through mergers, the Canadian Imperial Bank of Commerce, against its main rival, the Bank of Nova Scotia, founded in Halifax in 1832. Collin's own battle cry was 'loud war by land and sea'.

Quebec's scheme of playing cards acting as a currency, like many early tools of finance, was frowned on in official circles, but it served the perpetual challenge of public policy: what isn't disallowed must be necessary. PEI, with little hard currency, was a form of barter society, a cashless economy that relied on agricultural produce as the form of money circulation. As early as 1786, it was proposed that Island agricultural products, like fish, grain, or lumber be used as legal tender. Indeed, Thomas Desbrisay, PEI's first Colonial Secretary, was perhaps the first and only public official to accept fees for services, half in cash, half in produce, a practice that survived in the professional community well into the 20th century. When Bishop Peter Denault visited PEI in 1803, his pastoral letter prescribed that the *tithe*, the church tax, be paid in produce, either grain or in potatoes. (In Halifax, the military complained that their salaries should take the form of payments in rum!).

The currency problem led Lieutenant Governor, C.D. Smith, to address the circulation of money, given the limited availability of English and Spanish coins on the Island. This hard money was often amassed for hording, as an inflation hedge. Smith decreed that British coins be rated at one-ninth above their sterling value. Knowingly or not, Smith's action, while seeming to be a decisive move at the time, had two direct impacts. The first, by not taking into account that the new Bank of England tokens were underweight, and by giving them the status of legal tender (which they didn't have in England), he established the basis of currency depreciation, or debasement.

Second, by his autocratic and pernicious treatment of the Legislative Council, he built up government surpluses, which detracting from the money available in circulation.

The arrival of responsible government with the Whelan-Coles Government inspired Islanders to create new, local banks. Banks bring out the best and worst of people. It is for a good reason: that's where the money is found. For centuries, entrepreneurs – the shady kind and the wealth generators – understand the creative miracle of compound interest rates. It is a simple calculation: with annual interest rates, money doubles, taking the rate of interest divided into 72. This gives the years or months when the principal doubles in value. If a customer deposit in a bank is paid three per cent interest, the deposit doubles in 18 years, i.e. 72 divided by three. Even better, if the bank pays three per cent interest for deposits, and lends the money to governments or corporations at six per cent, the bank makes three per cent and bankers get rich fast. In Canada today, this is known as the 3, 6, 3 formula for bank success: accept deposits at three per cent, lend out at six per cent, and be on the golf course at three pm.

By nature, bankers are unpopular. Like the tax man, they take away money. That's why the head of bankers, the Central Banker, in this case the head of the Federal Reserve, was depicted as the ultimate Scrooge: just when the party is heating up, he takes away the punch bowl. Modern banking history is the story of taking away the punch bowl. From the early days of colonial history, bankers were unpopular. Bankers in London and Amsterdam financed the wars in Europe, usually at immense profits. Governments need money to finance their operations, conduct wars, fund commercial empires, and build navies and railroads. If they tax fairly and spend within their budget, bankers are happy. This, of course, was the quandry facing Charles Calonne in France, followed a line of Finance Ministers who recognized that the unfair tax system would lead to bankruptcy. The King refused to pay attention, the French Revolution ensued, and the King lost his head to the guillotine. John Adams, the second US President, worried about banks, feeling that when they issued paper in excess of the gold in their vaults, bank bills "represent nothing, and is therefore a cheat upon somebody."

Money, banking, and jurisdictional issues were central to the new federal scheme for Canada in 1867. At Charlottetown, and then at the Quebec Conference, Thomas Galt laid out the economic and financial aspects of the new federal union. But he did not address the specific point of banks and the issuance of currency bills. Yet the details of provincial responsibilities was the central debating point at both Charlottetown and Quebec. George Coles, on October 24, 1864 introduced a motion that "the local legislatures shall have the power to make all laws not given by this conference to the General Legislature expressly." As a merchant, a distillery owner, and a former Premier, he was a committed capitalist and a committed provincialist, like Edward Chandler of New Brunswick and Edward Palmer from Charlottetown. Coles lost this round, defeated by all the delegates, including the Island delegation.

In 1864, Prince Edward Island supported three banks: the Bank of Prince Edward Island, the Union Bank of PEI, and the Farmers Bank of Rustico, founded in 1863 by the brilliant and redoubtable Acadian priest, Georges-Antoine Belcourt. As far back as 1852, there were plans for an Island bank, the Bank of Charlottetown, a shadowy finance arm of Captain, later Lieutenant Colonel, Arthur Sleigh, a clear forerunner of shady banking practitioners on the scale of Bernie Cornfield, Bre-X, and Enron in later years. Sleigh had given notice that he purchased the large Charles Worrell estate in PEI for £17,000, the same estate sought by Samuel Cunard. Sleigh was a classic con-man, an inveterate promoter, who used the elite to give credence to his financial schemes. In 1852, he entertained the Governor General, Lord Elgin and most of the Cabinet in Quebec City on his new, 1100 ton steamer, the *Albatross*. Touring the Maritimes, Captain Sleigh entertained 103 of the Island elite in the Legislative Chamber, with abundant toasts and the local band playing "see the Conquering Hero Comes." Later he promoted, according to the *Standard London Times* of March 12, 1859, "the construction of a railway for India, without receiving any guarantees from the state." Needless to say, the Bank of Charlottetown didn't open its doors on the Island, even though it issued bank paper for Americans in New York.

Island banks were creatures of the elite, promoted by merchants and shipbuilders, with their supporters in the Island Assembly. For instance, the first incorporated bank, the Bank of Prince Edward Island, had shareholdings from James Peake and James Duncan, two of the most prominent shipbuilders, and merchants like John Longworth, Charles Stewart, Theophilius DesBrisay, and Thomas Haviland, who also was a member of the Assembly. George Coles, the Liberal Premier, was to be a shareholder but, according to *The Islander* of May 30, 1856, wanting to screen loan applications to see if they supported the government, alleged that "this bare faced attempt at grasping a grand engine of corruption having thus signally failed. George subscribed for a few shares, but suspecting that the shareholders would not have him as a Director, withdraw his name."

Banks on Prince Edward Island 1856-1906

Name	Year Founded	Circulation	President	Outcomes
Bank of Prince Edward Island	1856	£30,000	Ralph Brecken	Liquidated, 1882
Union Bank of PEI	1863	£61,000	Charles Palmer	Acquired by Bank of Nova Scotia, 1883
Farmers Bank of Rustico	1863	£21,200	Jerome Doiron	Closed, 1891
Summerside Bank	1865	£30,000	John R. Gardiner	Purchased by Bank of New Brunswick, 1901
Merchants Bank of Prince Edward Island	1871	£30,000	Robert Longworth	Acquired by Canadian Bank of Commerce, 1906

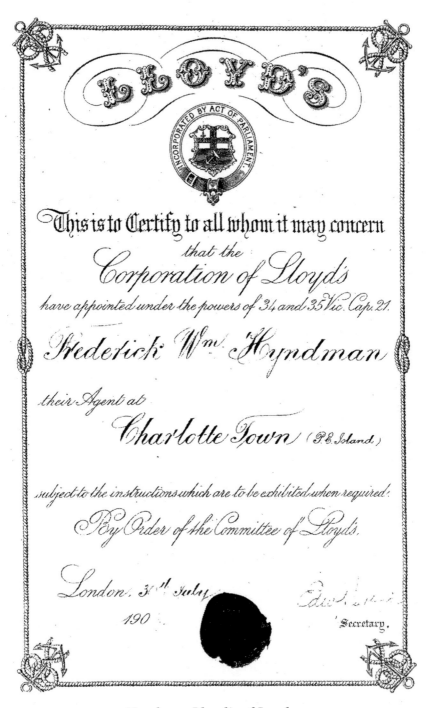

LLOYD'S

INCORPORATED BY ACT OF PARLIAMENT

This is to Certify to all whom it may concern

that the

Corporation of Lloyd's

have appointed under the powers of 34 and 35 Vic. Cap. 21.

Frederick Wm Hyndman

their Agent at

Charlotte Town (P.E. Island.)

subject to the instructions which are to be exhibited when required.

By Order of the Committee of Lloyd's.

London, 3rd July

190

Secretary.

Hyndman-Lloyd's of London

At the Union Bank, which would become the largest bank on the Island, shareholders included J.C. Pope, a future Premier and federal cabinet minister, Peter Hyndman, an insurance broker, William Lord, a merchant and member of the legislature, Thomas Dodd, William Dawson, a merchant and Mayor of Charlottetown, and Charles Palmer, younger brother of Edward Palmer. Indeed, the only bank that was not developed by the Island's elite was the Bank of Rustico. In 1882, the Hyndman Insurance Company was founded, which became affiliated with Lloyd's of London, and remains the oldest firm on the Island.

For more than a century, from 1759 when the British took Quebec, the Island's Acadian community attempted to maintain their isolated existence. Throughout the Maritimes, British troops rounded up Acadian families. What they didn't kill, they expelled to France; many moved to the Boston States or to Louisiana. Sixty Acadian families from PEI went to the defense of Louisberg in 1759. Still, the small Acadian community had few friends, and often moved to isolated areas to avoid detection. But their numbers grew and they developed their community structure in places like Tignish, Tracadie, and Rustico, the largest of the seven Catholic *parois*, or parishes. They had few friends outside their Church. Angus MacEachern was one, and he looked after their spiritual needs, including attracting French-speaking priests like Joseph Calonne. Despite their isolation, the Acadians persevered, their numbers grew, and they maintained their rural community culture.

In 1859, Angus MacEachern's successor, Bishop Bernard MacDonald, sent a new priest to Rustico, the energetic and formidable Georges-Antoine Belcourt, born in 1803, the same year that Lord Selkirk arrived in PEI with his band of Highland settlers. After ordination, this brilliant priest spent time in the Red River district, by co-incidence, another colony founded by Lord Selkirk. Belcourt befriended the Metis community, sought their political rights, and baptized their leader, Louis Riel. By aligning himself with the Metis community, he ran afoul of the major landowner, the Hudson's Bay Company. He moved to PEI, and then was transferred to Rustico.

A born organizer, Belcourt started a high school with a friend from Montreal, Israel Landry, as teacher. He established a library and opened an Agricultural Institute, for abstainers only. He discouraged the French practice of land division for the oldest son, preferring the English model of wider acreage for a viable farm. Like many travelers, he took great interest in mechanical machines. In 1866, he established a new machine, what locals called a diabolical invention, what Father Belcourt referred to as a 'mechanical contraption'. It was the first self-propelled vehicle on the Island, perhaps the first in North America, a single seated wagon powered with a steam engine. (It would take another fifty years before such contraptions were legal on PEI – by then they were called motor cars, legalized by the first Acadian Premier, A.E. Arsenault.) Since farmers needed capital for growth, the farmers needed a bank. Belcourt applied for the Farmers Bank of Rustico.

Finance interested Belcourt. He saw that in his travels to Western Canada, where Toronto bankers advertised cheap land on the Prairies for $8 an acre, with Toronto finance syndicates funding large tracks of land. At home, he noticed that Island merchants were quick to provide credit to farmers for their supplies – seeds in the spring, when the farmers were most impoverished from the long winters, or store goods during the growing season. What Belcourt recognized was the lesson of compound interest rates, that the exorbitant interest rates on this store credit was indeed usurious, that credit supplied was a form of unilateral dependence not only on the individual farmer but the entire community. This interest difference, what bankers respectfully called the *spread,* was what creates the miracle of compound interest rates. If the spread could be narrowed, and the money earned went to the farmers themselves, the profits would be turned into community development.

Belcourt was no Marxist, based on that dreary publication, *Das Capital,* that appeared at the same time in Britain, written in the Reading Room of the British Museum, the same room used by another writer, William Ewart Gladstone. Karl Marx, a German, wrote one of the finest depictions of the experience of the British working class, 80 pages of the dreary lot of the English worker and the inhuman conditions of satanic mills in Leeds, Birmingham, London, and Manchester. These factories were the same plots of *Great Expectations* and other novels of Charles Dickens, the scrooge-like behaviour of the capitalist class, but with a difference. Britain, unlike the countries on the Continent, had developed a capacity for change, for accommodation to new circumstances. Britain was enjoying a period of immense economic growth, thanks to the Age of Industrialization and New Machinery. It was also the age of savings, of investment incomes, of bank deposit income, as the new middle class started to save more than their daily wants. Only fifty years before, individuals acted as bankers, including Horatio Nelson, the hero of Trafalgar, who used his prize money to lend to his friends. In 1861, Britain had 645 banks, with total deposits of almost £42 million. Scotland and new Scottish bankers took the lead. In 1810, Rev. Henry Duncan started Penny Banks in Dumfries, near the birthplace of Thomas Carlyle, and banks blossomed into the Savings Bank movement, Trustee Savings banks, and Friendly Societies.

What Father Belcourt noticed about the Island merchants, as he took the time to digest their operations, was the reality that they were really bankers, managing the interest rate spread, between what they owed their suppliers and what they charged the Acadian farmers. Indeed, what was the Hudson's Bay Company, a giant monopoly trading company disguised as a bank, selling furs, giving the Indians and the Métis beads and trinkets in return for furs sold to the rich in London? Belcourt wanted the Acadians to become capitalists. This they did, subscribing to the Farmers Bank of Rustico, with shares at £1 each, and received Royal Assent at the Court of Windsor on April 7, 1864, the first cooperative bank in North America and a global pioneer in microfinance.

The Bank of Rustico prospered and enjoyed an unblemished record of loan repayment. Yet it faced larger problems, some outside its own control. Maritime banks were consolidating, or being taken over by banks from Montreal and Toronto. Ottawa payed attention to the need for economic stability, the new mantra of the Canadian bank industry, helped by the cartel features of the Canadian Bankers' Association, formed in 1890. Larger banks took over smaller companies and, despite increased overhead costs, was mitigated by 'over-competition' by removing interest rates as the basis of price competition. That lasted until 1964. When the Bank of Rustico sought a federal charter as a result of the bank reforms of 1890, Ottawa refused to accept its application, mostly for political reasons. It closed in 1901, after an eight year saga of dismay and recrimination. One witness to this affair was an obscure civil servant, Antoinne Desjardens, who worked part time for *Hansard*, the secretarial arm of the Parliament of Canada debates. He watched the Bank of Rustico's demise, and wondered about the implications for his own province, Quebec, where the bulk of small private banks were in small towns. He learned indeed a great deal from the Bank of Rustico episode and returned to Quebec where he worked closely with his namesake, Antoinne Desjardens. Together they did study the Rustico Bank, and soon, Antoinne Desjardens founded a new Quebec institution, the Caisses Populaire movement.

****

Throughout the Island's history, certainly for the first 250 years, aside from the men of medicine – there were no females – and a small group of the political elite – the most uniformly educated people were the men of the cloth. At first, most clergy came from Europe, from France initially, and then from Scotland and England, with a few from Ireland. The early French priests – some 47 in all from the time of the first settlements to 1759 – were educated in French seminaries, or at La Grande Séminaire de Quebec in the old quarter of Quebec City. French, of course, was their first language, but many spoke passable English, and all knew Latin; many also knew Greek. Until Angus MacEachern became the first Bishop of Charlottetown, the Island priests reported to the Bishop of Quebec, who had ruled the entire Catholic hierarchy in the British North American colonies.

In the staid circumstances of Island life, where the emphasis was to conserve the status quo, there were few rebels to upset the political elites of the rural lifestyle. Each group – farmers, merchants, politicians, clergy – accepted the premise of Island life, that what you have is what you keep. Catholics and Protestants lived in a social harmony, sometimes interrupted by cunning politicians who knew how to mobilize their supporters for their own ends, and the political elite, not wanting change, knew that the electoral system perpetuated the status quo if religious differences could be exploited. That explains why the likes of James Yeo, Edward Palmer and the Popes – James C. and William – fought over religious issues, including public support for Catholic schools and grants for St. Dunstan's College, often on the specious grounds of sectarianism or secularism, words that meant little to the family on the farm.

For their part, the Catholics tended to support their local Bishop, the third Bishop of Charlottetown, Rev. John MacIntyre, who succeeded Bernard MacDonald, on August 15, 1860. MacIntyre, like many of his ecclesiastical colleagues across Canada, was seen by Protestants as ultramontaignes – i.e. as a devotee to the primacy of the Pope on Church matters, long after these religious differences meant little in Protestant England. In England, there was a profound opposition to the Catholic Church, dating from the days of Elizabeth I, and a fear for the restoration of the Catholic faith, placing England as dependent on foreign powers. But Catholic Emancipation, and even the accession of High Anglican clergy, including the outstanding but subtle thinker, John Henry Newman, later appointed as a Cardinal, to Roman Catholicism, didn't break the new mood of toleration in Britain. If anything, the Oxford movement led to internal dissent and vigorous debate between Low Church and High Church parties and the English flock who weren't Anglican, such as Congregationists, Baptists, Presbyterians, Methodists, and Unitarian preachers.

These issues became much more pronounced in PEI, where rival Protestant sects fought over local prejudices of who really belonged to the Church of England, and the petty biases of "Pusseyites" in the Tractarian Movement within the Church of England. In Charlottetown, this controversy led to the construction of a new Protestant Church, St. Peter's, on land donated by William Cundall, who had been a prominent member of St. Paul's, on the expressed stipulation that this new church be free of 'pew rents' – a practice where congregational members had reserved seats in return for financial obligations towards church maintenance and salaries of clergymen. Members of St. Paul's expressed open hostility to the new church, and the local Pastor solemnly excommunicated anyone having to do with 'that church'.

Within the bosom of the growing Catholic Church, there was, at least in theological matters, by Island standards, a real radical, Rev. Alfred Burke. He did, however, became an expert on big issues, well beyond church matters, including the Island railway, agricultural education, relations with Ottawa, the ferry service and later, support for Ukrainian Catholics in Western Canada. On the Island, Burke was seen as someone with a measure of non-conformity. Within each Catholic family, the oldest boy was often seen as a potential priest, and the career paths led to high school, a degree at St. Dunstan's, and a seminary in Quebec. This was the position of a young Georgetown boy, A.E. Burke, who became a peripatetic priest who traveled widely, had diverse interests, visited the US and Mexico, spent time in Western Canada, and traveled to Rome, where he died on December 15, 1926. He could swear like a sailor, befriended people who crossed his life, and he made personal friendships with the great man in Ottawa, Sir Wilfred Laurier, despite his own background as a Conservative.

Burke was a writer, and knew the power of words, the bon mot and the bon jeste, and he used his writing skills to great effect. He was one of the first clergy historians on the Island, and his chronicles of PEI parishes and his authoritative profile of the first Bishop, Angus MacEachern, is as solid today as when it was written 100 years ago. His letters to Island newspapers, and especially to the *Daily Examiner*, the newspaper started by Edward Whelan and now a strongly Conservative organ fit well the political biases of Alfred Burke. (After PEI joined Confederation in 1873, most Island Catholics who were not Francophones supported the Conservative Party.) Burke's letters to the Editor were a mix of audacious humour, sharp scolding, and brutal invective, much in the style of a future inveterate letter writer, Eugene Forsey, or Gratton O'Leary. No misdemeanor was off limits for this clergymen with his peripatetic interests: the Post Office, train service, roads and transportation, or Catholic education. As one of his polemical letters noted, "somebody with an once of common sense in his head is needed in the railway offices at Charlottetown for a little while; or failing this the whole thing ought to be closed out and exhibited as a curiosity in these days of competent service and up-to-the-date travel."

A.E. Burke was born September 8, 1862, in Georgetown, two years before the Charlottetown Conference, and not far from the famous Three Rivers settlement of Jean Pierre de Roma. This area, where the Brudenell, Montague, and Cardigan Rivers converge, formed the base of a rich port town, with shipbuilding and shipping plying their way to Halifax, Sydney, and the Magdalen Islands. During bad weather, notes historian Art O'Shea, over 200 ships would rest in the harbour. Burke's parents were immigrants, the father the descendant of the Burkes of Tipperary, Ireland, and his mother, Mary Moar, from the Orkney Islands. There were seven children, with four boys, and three girls. It was an educated family, which was now typical of many Island families who placed a great deal of faith in personal and formal education, all graduates of the Georgetown High School, a three room school seen as the best in King's County. His youngest brother, William, became a graduate of St. Dunstan's College, and finished his medical degree at the University of New York in 1891, before practicing in Boston. He died at the age of 31, and was buried in Georgetown in one of the largest funerals ever in this growth community. His sister Minnie, married to J.C. Murphy, later a Senator, moved to Tignish, where she too died at a young age, 31, from childbirth complications.

Burke was educated in public schools in Georgetown, then to St. Dunstan's College, before entering the seminary at Laval University. After ordination by Cardinal Alexandre Taschereau in 1885, Burke became secretary to the Bishop of Charlottetown, but his personality led the Bishop to make him pastor of Alberton in 1888, which his friends noted was about as far away as possible from Charlottetown. His interests were indeed extensive, from horticulture to land cultivation, and he was a popular speaker with farm groups, winning national awards for his interests in soil, seeds, and land use. He wrote learned papers for *The Farmers Advocate*. He was the first cleric to sponsor afternoon teas to raise money for his church and his good causes, and Father Burke made sure that his Alberton teas and picnic were not only the best in the province, but were widely appreciated in Church circles, as when the Archbishop of Quebec spent his summer with Father Burke in 1894.

Like many clerics who saw the abandonment of local financial institutions, Burke took a great interest in a new initiative started in St. Mary's Parish, Niagara Falls, N.Y, i.e. the creation of a Catholic Mutual Benefit Association, in effect an insurance organization to provide widows and orphans financial help as beneficiaries to deceased members. The first organization was begun in 1876, but quickly spread to Canada, and by 1894, had ten thousand members, 238 branches, with Burke in charge of the first branch in PEI, started in 1893. Indeed nothing passed the scrutiny of this intellectually curious priest: fruit growing, dairy cattle, poultry, bee keeping, temperance, ferry service, a tunnel initiative to New Brunswick, and even Island forests. In fact, at the Canadian Forestry Association meeting in Ottawa, held in 1904, with the Governor General, Earl Gray, presiding, and Sir Wilfred Laurier serving as Chairman, Burke gave a rousing speech on the need for systematic reforestation, and called for federal help for PEI to plant valuable hardwoods like maple, birch, and walnut. Clearly his speech had some effect: Laurier personally congratulated him and the Governor General invited him for dinner at Government House. The Americans in the audience also were impressed: he received an honorary degree, as Doctor of Forestry, from the University of North Carolina.

His interests now extended to a new mission, when he became the first President of the Catholic Church Extension Society of Canada, 1908. This post was a two-sided coin, allowing him to mix with the senior Bishops in the Catholic hierarchy, but placing him in conflict with some of the more aggressive bishops, who had their own agenda. For example, at one point, Burke initiated a plan to turn St. Dunstan's College, his Island alma mater, as a missionary college, especially for the training of clergy for the deluge of new immigrants in Western Canada, especially for the struggling Ukrainian Catholics. He had the backing of both the Canadian Extension group and the American, the latter support coming from another Islander and mentor to Burke,

Bishop Francis Kelly (he added an 'e' to his name when he moved to the US).

Kelley was born in Vernon River in 1870, attending Queen Square School in Charlottetown, St. Dunstan's College, and then the seminary at Nicolet, Quebec. In time, he helped found the Catholic Church Extension Society in the United States. He had enormous respect for Burke's leadership and energy, even if Burke had some rough edges. On the Island, Charles Dalton, the fox rancher from Tignish and future member of the legislature, who won for the Conservatives in 1917, was a big Burke supporter. When the Archbishop of Toronto died and was replaced by Neil McNeil, a Cape Bretoner from Mabou, he had Burke in his site and wanted to have his own seminary, St. Augustin's. He wanted Burke removed from his Extension post. In the end, McNeil retired and returned to his flock in Newfoundland, where he once served, but not before there was bad blood within the Extension hierarchy. Clearly, Burke took it all in stride, and felt quite at home wandering the Ottawa corridors of power with the likes of federal cabinet members, the Chief Justice, Sir Wilfred Laurier, and Robert Borden. When the First World War broke out, Senator J. A. Lougheed, father to a future Alberta Premier, acting as Minister of Militia and Defense, appointed Burke as chaplain to the Second Canadian Division and honorary major. Indeed, at one point, when the Island's representation in the House of Commons was reduced, and there was further talk about Maritime Union, Burke was forthright enough to ask the Prime Minister if this might be a solution to the economic problems facing the Atlantic region. Laurier responded to Father Burke:

> *I doubt if any change will ever take place in the condition of things in the Maritime Provinces. You could no more induce Nova Scotia, New Brunswick and Prince Edward Island to drop their identity that you can get Rhode Island, Connecticut and New Hampshire to join together. Such communities are particularly tenacious of their autonomy. It is a respectable sentiment and one which must be recognized.*

On August 12, 1912, he resigned as President of the Extension Society. He was also relieved to hear that the new Pope, Benedict XV, elevated him to a Prothonotary Apostolic, which meant that he became known as Right Revered Monsignor Burke, allowing him to wear the purple robes on high occasions. Curiously, at the same time, his mentor, Francis Kelley, was appointed to a lesser post, but wiser counsel on the American side soon had the Pope personally making Kelley a PA as well. Bishop Angus MacEachern, with all his letters to Rome in his illustrious Latin script, must have felt comforted that his Island family had reached such heights in the Catholic hierarchy.

******

As noted, the rural setting of PEI, despite the booming economy at the time of Confederation, was a harsh life for this pioneer colony. It was more than the weather, which in winter could be brutally cold and forbidding, with many farms lacking insulation, wood was the main fuel, and roads were impassable with snow build ups and ice for months. Farming and fishing were also physically demanding, as trees invariably needed to be felled, land cleared, and marsh lands either dyked or refreshed (most marsh dykes were built by the French in the eighteenth century). Rural life in PEI, in short, was hard work, from dawn to dusk. Rural farms were isolated, roads were sparse, and many farm lanes took a long path to the farm porch. Trains, when they came to the Island after Confederation, were the only means of reliable transportation, not only for the population at large, but also essential for doctors, clergy, and country teachers.

Many people couldn't cope. On the Island, suicides were rare - this after all, was a Christian community, and suicide was a mortal sin. But there were other escapes, and alcohol was a primary vehicle. So was immigration, or going down the road, as Islanders (and Maritimers) called it, in search of greener pastures - to Boston, to Toronto, and much later, to Calgary. By 1880, emigration to the Island had all but stopped for the Maritimes and Quebec. Confederation had opened up new lands in Western Canada, Ontario became the economic juggernaut among the provinces, helped enormously by Macdonald's New Economic Policy of tariff protection. There also beckoned the Great Republic to the south, slowly setting aside the scars of the Civil War, and opening up the Western Plains with aggressive land grant schemes and educational openings of land colleges.

John A. McCormick

Joe McCormick is a classic example of an Island family which couldn't cope. He was born in Grants Crossing, a hamlet near Souris, on the Eastern end of the Island, in 1862. He was a precocious child in a poor region of the Island, and turned into a drunk and a rake. Unemployed and considered a n'ere do well, Joseph H. McCormick left for Maine and then moved to Boston.

His wife, Mary Ellen O'Brien, was born in Boston, of Irish heritage in a city full of Irish immigrants, thanks mainly to the Irish famine. Joe and Mary Ellen had eight children: two died in infancy, while six survived. Joe McCormick, poor, broke, and unemployed, was a stone mason, which meant they his only skill was the physical ability to crush rocks. (Much later, historians said he was a hod carrier, a term referring to a vee shaped shoulder tool to carry rocks and mortor.) Boston was no different from most immigrant cities: ethnic rivalries, political hatreds, and people moving constantly to avoid paying the landlord. The Irish in Boston knew Maritimers, and most had low status, seen there as 'two-booters' or 'herring chokers', an unwelcome sobriquet in this enthnically charged city. "Shut the doory. There's a heron in the bay" was an anti-Maritime refrain, much like the "Novey" term for Nova Scotians.

McCormick was neither a caring father, nor a good husband, nor a reliable employee. Around 1901, a pregnant Mary Ellen returned to Prince Edward Island, alone with her children, to escape Joe's alcoholic furies. She stayed with her sister in Souris, Kate McCormick Haley, in a small, crowded farm house, an unwelcome guest with her brood of sickly children. Domestic problems soon arose and multiplied. The meagre household was too small for this visiting family, and the children soon outlived their modest welcome. Mary Ellen miscarried, and the local priest refused to allow a burial in consecrated ground of St. Mary's Catholic Church. Worse, Joe had tracked down his family and returned to Souris. For her part, Mary Ellen returned with her children to Boston, leaving Joe on his own.

Joe opted for a popular 'poor man's divorce', forever leaving his family. Beset by his demons, he took the Boston and Maine Railroad to Waldoboro, Lincoln County, Maine - the ticket cost $2.50 - a small mining town where he found work in the granite quarries. It was work, but very dangerous work: cracking rocks all day, and filling his lungs with rock dust, the industrial equivalent of tuberculosis. Joe McCormick died on February 29,1904, buried in a paupers grave, with no wake, no funeral, no consecrated ground, no mourners.

Mary Ellen stayed in Boston, but her position was not much better. Her third child, James, died in 1911 of tuberculosis, aged 17. Catherine died at 19, from this same scourge of the poor. Mary Ellen herself died in 1913. The children were raised by the fourth son, John, now the eldest in his family. John McCormick rejected his Canadian heritage and his Island background, altered his name to McCormack, and started his long climb up the greasy pole of Boston politics. He represented South Boston at 25 at the Massachusetts Constitutional Convention, and then, at 28 in 1920, was elected to the Massachusetts House of Representatives, and later to the State Senate from 1923-1926. He ran as a member of the US House of Representatives to fill the vacancy caused by the death of James A. Gallivan. Eventually, he reached the pinnacle, becoming elected Speaker of the House of Representatives, first ever Roman Catholic on January 10, 1962, succeeding the legendary Texan and compatriot of Lyndon Johnson, Sam Rayburn. When President John F. Kennedy was assassinated in November 1963, for 14 months, this son of a dirt poor father from Souris, PEI was a heartbeat away from the US Presidency. His two closest colleagues in Boston and in Washington were the legendary Tip O'Neill, who coined the classic phrase of political warfare, "all politics is local", and Senator Ted Kennedy, the last surviving brother of the Kennedy clan. In 1964, Edward Kennedy received an honorary degree from St. Dunstan's University, proving yet again that what goes around comes around. All politics is local.

6

Lucy Maud Montgomery:
Lessons in Canadian Literature

Early Literature* John Howe * Henry Bayfield * Early Painters *
Jacob Schurman * Robert Harris – Portrait Painter * Montgomery's
Anne of Green Gables *Church Architecture – Critchlow Harris *
Andrew MacPhail * Basil King * Island Historians

In the post-Confederation period, from 1873 to the First World War,
the Island struggled for its economic salvation. There were many
problems with the provincial economy, albeit some deeper than
others. Indeed, a deep recession hit Maritime industries hard in the
1880s, despite the rapid increase in the Canadian population. But
there was little increase in population on the Island itself, and it was
more than economics alone. The shipbuilding industry, the Island's
largest export sector, had seen its peak, although there were few
people outside the industry who recognized the profound changes
taking place, which were due mainly to the rise of coal and steam,
and the attendant machinery to power ships. The Suez Canal, now
firmly in the hands of Imperial Britain, reduced shipping time to
India and the Orient by months. The great corporations and rival
governments, including companies such as Samuel Cunard's, wanted
bigger ships, faster ships, and sturdier ships. This meant that the days
of wind, wood, and sail were leaving an old industry in its wake.
The shipbuilding centers across the Island still employed a great

deal of people, so there was a certain conflict between the ways of these coastal communities, and the traditional agricultural and rural lifestyle, which was sometimes associated with small farms and co-op communities.

The Island's shipbuilding industry, associated in the 18th century with Britain's 1787 Navigation Act – and the designation of five ports of registry in the Maritimes, including St. John's Island - was a centuries-old drama of mapping, nautical instruments (the world's first fog horn was installed in Saint John in 1859, replacing guns and bells), and a sophisticated cluster of skilled people in all sorts of trades. There were experts in timber, carpentry, insurance and ship registers, custom agents, construction survey crews and light house keepers. Bigger and faster ships required ever larger shipyards, based on sophisticated iron and steel works. These ships, in turn, needed bigger ports and a strong population base for the workforce. The Edwardian era of Britain started an age of unprecedented size and scale of ships – military ships, transportation vessels, and new passenger carriers. Prince Edward Island, like the Maritimes generally, had great difficulty coping with these changes, even more so when the best Island timber stock was so rapidly depleting.

Tourism was not yet an important industry, but already people from the big cities started to arrive on the Island, escaping from the humidity and heat of Washington, Boston or New York, or even of Ottawa and Montreal. John A. Macdonald himself spent an entire summer on the Island in 1870, refreshed by the sea, the sand, and his Island friends, the Pope Family. He knew the Island was a place to refresh the body and the spirit, whether of the mind or of the bottle. When he arrived in Charlottetown that summer, he stayed at a place called Falconwood, which later became a lunatic asylum. His political opponents thought this was an appropriate fit. Other new residences included Dalvey-By-the Sea, a splendid summer home built for Alexander McDonald, a director of Standard Oil, which proved an imposing addition to the Island landscape for rich summer visitors, many of which were American. By the turn of the century, no less than three US Senators had places to visit on the Island. Sailing captains spent their summer holidays, telling anyone who would listen about their exploits in far off places, including the South China seas and the Orient.

American writers had published tour books about the Maritimes, indicating the places to stay, currency differences, and the hotels by the sea. The Rollins hotel and the Seabreeze in Rustico, the Keppoch beaches outside Charlottetown, the Stanhope hotel on the north shore, and Victoria were all seen as desirable resting places. Local gossip was that with some guests at least, there was involved not a little scandal. For some visitors, the local churches were interesting as tourist spectacles, as well as a Christian stop for Sunday services. The new St. Dunstan's Cathedral, the third church built on the site in Charlottetown, added to the mix of new buildings, and bolstered an ecumenical array of well-attended churches in the Charlottetown core.

There remained a wide disparity in economics, politics, and culture between the capital, Charlottetown, and the countryside. In the capital, new amenities were arriving, from central heating to the telephone, and typewriters to gas lamps, but the rural areas had to wait generations for similar luxuries. Nowhere was the void wider than in the school system, where in education and schooling, with three-quarters of the population living in rural areas, one room school houses and female teachers, poorly paid and with little family and professional support, kept the level of illiteracy on a par with rural Scotland or Ireland. In his painting, *A Meeting of the School Trustees*, where a young school teacher talks to the village elders (who can't read), Robert Harris depicts a Canadian affliction which persisted until well into the twentieth century. Many of these one room schools, which totalled 416 of the 472 schools on the Island in 1924, were badly built, poorly equipped, and lacked insulation, clean windows, good heating, or proper lighting. Rural electrification – the last mile to farm homes – came only in the 1960s with the Walter Shaw government. Alexander Bell's telephone arrived in 1884, but only in Charlottetown.

Local newspapers, abundantly political and partisan, were the main outlets for news and opinion. The most popular source of information for the Island was the Post Office during the week and the country churches on Sundays. It was an era without radio, with the telegraph too expensive, and it wasn't until the 1930s that telephones became accessible, albeit by way of rural country lines, with four phones to a common number. By the turn of the century, the *Farmer's Advocate and Home Journal*, published on a weekly basis in London, Ontario gave a rundown of agricultural news, science, fairs, international news, prominent affairs of state, and events across Canada and within the Dominion. Books and libraries were few, as there was no great Canadian, let alone Island, patron of libraries, such as Thomas Jefferson in the United States, whose private collection became the base for the Library of Congress. There were in the Maritimes no magnificent college libraries like the Ivey colleges of Harvard and Columbia. For Islanders, Boston was the Mecca of culture, Montreal the center of medical education, and Toronto a hog town surrounded by bankers and finance. Ottawa was still a distant place, although the new political culture was starting to impact politics on the Island.

The train became the main method of transport, rain or shine, in both summer and winter. The Island still relied on horses, carriages, and the skills of the local blacksmith and for much of the year, roads were abominably bad, covered by snow and ice in the winter, with a mix of mud and snow runoff in the spring, blowing red sand or mud in the summer. Sporting events were popular, including outdoor skating rinks in Victoria Park, and city schools played rugby and hockey. Harness racing was becoming popular, and included horse races on the frozen rivers. Even when cars arrived after 1910, with politicians, farmers and city folk all clamouring for laws for or against automobiles, Island roads were everybody's problem, and thus a great topic for governments, political patronage, and campaign promises.

Island literature and culture for most of the province was seen as an issue of no importance. Until Lucy Montgomery began publishing her novels, there was no national literary recognition of Prince Edward Island. In some ways, the same was true of much of Canada. Some writers would argue that a great national literature presupposes an advanced and integrated society, serving as a potent symbol of a separate national identity. In one sense, this may be so, but there

Lucy Maud Montgomery

seems little direct link between economic and industrial growth and a great national literature. As yet, there were no great intellectual circles in Canada, unlike Edinburgh that had brought forth Scotland's finest intellectuals. It was a mixed group, like David Hume, Adam Smith, Robert Adams, and Walter Scott, who collectively attracted the poets, story tellers, Ben Franklin, and the social critics that studied the arts, the sciences, medicine, economics and politics and became the wonderment of Germany, France, Poland and the United States. By 1900, Boston was a rising intellectual center that tended to attract more Island visitors than Montreal or Toronto. Boston writers and poets – the Concord circle – were attracting European attention, and became to rival the sales of the powerful novels of Walter Scott in Scotland, and Leo Tolstoy in Russia – works that stand in stature and awe over the centuries. And superb writers undoubtedly knew the works of their international peers. As Tolstoy, the great Russian author, wrote to his younger writer friend, Anton Chekhov, "Stop writing plays. They are as bad as Shakespeare's."

**

Canadian literature traces its history along colonial and geographic lines, beginning with the earliest explorers, including the letters and diaries of Jacques Cartier, Montcalm, and the French explorers and Jesuit priests who came in the service of the French King and the glory of God. Some historians argue that Montcalm was Canada's first painter. The colonial writers who moved to Canada, or who were born in Canada, became known as the Confederation Group (1867-1900), as the separate British colonies became more integrated to produce a new Canadian school. At the time, there were no national publishers, with newspapers being largely provincial or local. It would take great events like the First World War to recognize skilled Canadian painters, writers, and poets such as John MacCrae, author of the memorial poem, *In Flanders Field*, the same title of his book. Considering its size, the Island received more than its fair share of writing from early explorers, describing in letters, journals, dairies, and books the Island's natural beauty, including its unique red soil. A notable example of the genre is John Stewart's book *Prince Edward Island*, a tract written in part to attract British settlers.

Thomas Douglas, the fifth Earl of Selkirk, wrote a book entitled the *Highlands and Prince Edward Island*, which served as an amazingly accurate and realistic depiction of the Island's landscape and geography, immigrant culture, government, and economic potential – this from a very literate man who traveled extensively throughout Europe, Britain, and the United States. The early explorers in Canada – Champlain, de la Salle, Hudson, Frobisher, Baffin, Kelsey, MacDonald, and Hearne, for instance – typically follow the tradition of great naval captains – Cook, Bligh, Nelson – who described their journeys with detailed logs. Often they were joined by secretaries and engineers who also painted personal scenes, military sketches, and mapmaking for military use, but often using their free time to send letters to their relatives by returning boats.

These early explorers and military personnel may not have had the literary flourish of the great novelists, but they leave a legacy of rich characters, robust personalities, and shrewd observation. These in turn produced their own style, interest, and charm, and they later influenced writers and poets who drew upon these works. The colonial writers, say from 1760-1850, when Canada was stirring with the need for responsible government, were linked to the great battles of Europe, of international colonial rivalry, church politics and sectarianism, and social and economic controversies. Close to the Island, John Howe, a native of Boston, moved to Halifax and recreated his *Newsletter*, which he re-established in Halifax as the Halifax *Gazette*. In this move, this Loyalist printer founded the oldest newspaper in North America, paving the way for a new age of literature in the Maritimes. The *Nova Scotian* was founded in 1824, and allowed his son, Joseph Howe, blessed with a powerful voice, immense literary talents, and a rich vocabulary, to begin a new tradition of Maritime writing. As he put it:

> *I wish poverty, rebellion, and bravery could capture*
> *the poets and writers like Yeats and James Joyce.*
> *The Americans were more communicators, could*
> *attract writers, poets, and story tells like Mark Twain,*
> *Europe, of course, had lived for thousands of years*
> *around the patronage of the arts, with Kings, Queens,*

Emperors, Tsars and Popes writing the stories of success and accomplishment, while the emerging dismal science could spell out the failures.

Howe's *Acadian Magazine,* like the *Quebec Magazine* and the *Literary Garland,* enlivened a new stable of Maritime writers. Later the *Prince Edward Island Magazine* included works on Island history, poems, historical remembrances, and international affairs of state. These various journals were modeled to some degree on *The Edinburgh Review,* a favourite outlet for Thomas Carlyle, and covered controversial topics, including the church, school and faith, subjects that paralleled the sectarian pamphlets in New England. In doing so, they offered a compelling mixture of strong intellectual thought, clear cut argumentation, and rich invective. It was, however, largely imitative, and never reached the heights of British literature. In Nova Scotia, Howe's friend, Thomas Chandler Haliburton, became the first Canadian author of a book widely read in both Canada and in Britain, challenging his readers with his *Sam Slick* series, and serving as a model for other Maritime writers.

Throughout the Island's history, and certainly for the first 200 years, aside from the men of medicine – there were no females – and a small group of the political elite, the most uniformly educated people were the men of the cloth. At first, most clergy came from Europe, from France initially, and then increasingly from Scotland and England, with a few from Ireland. The early French priests – some 47 in all, ranging from the time of the first settlements to 1759 – were educated in French seminaries or at La Grande Seminaire de Quebec in the old quarter of Quebec City. French, of course, was their first language, but many spoke passable English, and all knew Latin, since the vespers, all masses, and the sacerdotal vows were conducted in Latin. Many Protestant Ministers born and raised in Scotland were also fluent in Gaelic.

Protestant ministers came from England and Scotland, and from diverse orders of Christian affiliations – Presbyterians, Baptists, Methodists, Episcopalians, Church of Scotland, and Anglicans. Some sects were unique to PEI – the Island's McDonalites, for instance, were a branch of the Church of Scotland centered in the Selkirk area of Lot 57. Most were Highland Scots. Many parishioners in the congregation were unilingual, speaking only Gaelic, a language that survived in some Island communities until the 1960s. The most famous of the McDonaldites was Rev. Donald McDonald, born in Perthshire, Scotland in 1783, who came to PEI in 1816. Like Angus MacEachern, McDonald was a man of many talents, and a skilled violin player, but ultimately discarded the violin for song writing, following in the tradition of Dugold Buchanan, his schoolmaster in Drumcastle. Curiously, his songs, printed as "McDonald hymns," were not used in worship or accompanied by music, and they were usually played at the start of service. He traveled widely across the Island, and even to Scottish settlements in Nova Scotia and the Miramichi area, where the Cunards were busy with the lumber trade. The diverse clergy of the Island served more than the spiritual needs of the early settlers, or later, the young province after 1873. Because they traveled, they also often wrote letters to friends and family, or to other clergy in Europe, the US, or Toronto. The clergy were more than a source of news, as friends sent them newspapers, journals, and other broadsheets from England and Scotland. Some clergy managed to receive Christian books and bibles that were presented as gifts, or given to the Public Library, which opened in 1824.

Among the clergy, Angus MacEachern was unique, a large man, athletic, a great story teller, and the source of news to all and sundry because he had excellent contacts in Rome, throughout Europe, and other clergy and his class mates. MacEachern was, of course, a great letter writer, and even Rome was impressed with his wonderful Island descriptions in Latin. Eventually, letter writers needed the PEI Post Office, their stock in trade. Postal service started in 1803 with Benjamin Chappell as Postmaster. The mail from PEI was sent via ship from Charlottetown to Pictou, although after 1828, some mail was sent via Cape Travese to Cape Tormentine, a nine mile route pioneered by Neil Campbell and Donald McGinnis and their ice-boats.

Early writers, artists, and poets kept to traditional Canadian themes, such as historical events, regional or provincial material, and bibliographic reference. But as more Canadian work was published, and more circulation outside Canada, there was recognition of a new Canadian craft, a skilled set of original writers who could shape personalities and character themes. But it would take time. As far back as the 18th century, the Loyalist migrations from the US brought new cultural traditions to the Maritimes, including literary journals like the *Acadian Recorder*, which was formed in 1813, theatrical performances, and reading societies, all of which added to the powerful oral literary traditions of pioneer Highland settlers. Religious figures like the Reverend Jacob Bailey and Reverend Jonathan Odell, two Tory satirists, focused their writings on the perpetrators of the American rebellion, and their impact, while not great in the first part of the nineteenth century, had enormous impact two generations later in the writings of Bliss Carmen and Charles G.D. Roberts, or even the literary progenitors of Thomas Haliburton.

In this scheme of things, Canada was a backward way-station, with little literature to offer, and only a few painters, such as Cornelius Krieghoff, who arrived in 1853 in Quebec, and Robert Field, who was perhaps the best painter in the Maritimes until Confederation. Even Halifax's Chess, Pencil and Brush Club, an outgrowth of Prince Edward's stay there, slowly cultivated interest in art and culture. In 1831, England had established the first Mechanics' Institute, and local clubs were set up after 1835 in Halifax, Charlottetown, and other centers, with a view to promoting self-education through lectures, evening courses, readings, and art exhibitions, ultimately forming the basis of a popular appeal for art, music, and literary performances. These initiatives followed in the tradition of the *Nova Scotia Magazine* which, although having a small subscriber base, had a profound impact throughout the Maritimes and read by local elites. In the US, Ralph Waldo Emerson, fresh from a trip to Europe and meetings with Thomas Carlyle, sharing together a progressive philosophy of self-reliance and defiance of old nostrums, called for a new cultural awakening, and an end to America's cultural apprenticeship to Europe, which he scorned as "timid, imitative" and "tame". It was a lesson still to be learned in Canada.

The history of painting in Canada dates to the earliest French colonies in Quebec and the leadership of Samuel Champlain. Most early

Canadian painters were students of European artisans, particularly from the Paris salons and from London. Unlike in Canada, European painters, like musicians, had patrons, often members of the Monarchy, the Vatican, or rich merchants and landowners who wished to bestow portraits on significant people, such as military heroes and politicians. In Canada, certainly until the late nineteenth century, the opportunities for artists were minimal, similar to the low fees paid to doctors. Clearly, both in Canada at large and in PEI, there was a strong interest in amateur painting, both in the natural scenic grandeur, like cliffs and waterfalls, rivers and lakes, but also in portraits.

One of the first people who cultivated painting and music on the Island was a woman, Fanny Amelia Wright. She was the wife of Henry Wolsey Bayfield, the prominent surveyor who mapped most of the Gulf of St. Lawrence and the coastal waters around the Maritimes, including Prince Edward Island. His tenure in Quebec coincided with a flourishing output of amateur painters, and Fanny Wright had the additional advantage of learning from British military artists and engineers, who sketched the various rivers, ports, and embankments that might have military significance. When the Bayfields moved to the Island in 1841, staying at a large new house in Keppoch overlooking the entrance to the Charlottetown harbour, Fanny became a teacher of art and painting, as well as music. On the Island, her special interest was in watercolours of wild flowers, where there was an extremely large assortment found in the fields, woods, and rivers near her home. Often her paintings and watercolors included a *sepia* trademark, a brownish tint later attributed to photography. Her works also included collections of moths, butterflies, and caterpillars, as well as early scenes of Charlottetown.

The late 19th century in North America showcased the tremendous pace of industrialization. Britain, of course, was the first country to industrialize, capitalizing upon a domestic advantage of abundant coal fields, and pioneering the use of the steam engine to power the staggering transformation of entire industry sectors, including railways, machinery, steel mills, household appliances, printing presses, urban buses, and powerful armaments. For the British, soon to be followed by Bismarck's Germany, the result was the creation of new and more powerful weapons, faster cruisers, and guns of all sorts. Most people forget that modern defense weaponry started as a 19th century industry. Britain's early industrial lead, which started in the 18th century, but quickly accelerated after the peace treaties of 1815, when Britain enjoyed an unrivalled century of banking and industrial supremacy, had truly become the workshop of the world. However, by the end of the 19th century, Britain's lead was rapidly evaporating, as Germany and the United States were themselves industrializing. Many historians might argue that by the First World War, Britain actually trailed these industrial competitors, especially in the case of the United States, which enjoyed a huge Continental market, benefiting from a common language and legal system, and promoting an expansionist managerial philosophy lifted from the robber barons, such as John D. Rockefeller, Andrew Carnegie, and J.P. Morgan.

It was a huge shift for these industrial countries in embracing a mechanized, urbanized, and increasing impersonal society, which seemed a long distance from the quiet rural life of the agrarian age. For the latter, time was calculated by the seasons, not the new march of industrial progress, filled with bureaucracy, urbanization, new machinery, and the 24 hour clock. Many rebelled against this theory of progress, and in time Islander writers, in novels, commentaries, and diaries, rejoiced at the rural setting of their native province, seeing the Island way of life the epitome of God's design for mankind. Nova Scotia's Reverend Thomas McCulloch was one of the first to wax eloquent about this theme, proposing a rural setting as the ideal environment, where man discovers his true relationship with nature, with a combination of hard physical work, Bible reading, and tough mental and philosophical discourse. McCulloch set out his views in a series of imaginary reports called *Stepsure Letters*, set in rural Nova Scotia, with strong attacks on the folly of individuals escaping hard work, getting rich by trade, and embracing the 'get- rich quick' schemes of New York and Glasgow. These themes were well known in French society in Quebec, surfacing in the writings of Louis-Adolphe Pâquet, and the study of the 300 hundredth anniversary of the arrival in Quebec of Louis Hebert, *La Terre Canadienne*.

A constant theme for Maritime writers, poets, and artists was the role of small communities, and how they can be connected to the larger, urban industrial world. Once societies and communities become large, urbanized, and geared to exude commercial values, a shallow existence results, and is filled with false friendships. This theme, of course, is not unique to Island writings – Hugh MacLennon, a Cape Bretoner by birth, and Rhodes Scholar, spent his time in England and New York before entering McGill University, explored the same issue. As he wrote, "is it possible for so few people to meet the challenge of this vastness and mystery, of this variety of the land when we live because the network of its rivers enabled a handful of explorers to claim it for us?" Lucy Maud Montgomery's view of heavenly peace is "walking on the shores or in the fields or along the winding red roads of Prince Edward Island in a summer twilight when the dew is falling and the old stars are peeping out and the sea keeps its mighty tryst with the little land in its bones. You find your soul then. You realize that youth is not a vanished thing that something dwells forever in the heart."

The Island landscape, of course, flowed from the veins of the French and Celtic settlers, from Ireland and the Scottish Highlands and the outer Islands, and many had very long family histories – the Montgomerys, the MacDonalds, the MacNeils, the MacEacherns, the MacPhees, the MacLauchlans, the MacKinnons, the McMillans, and the Campbells go back over 200 years and include family yarns, oral traditions, and often family diaries and letters. As a child, Lucy Montgomery remembers the storehouse of family and community memories: "I listened with delight of the many traditions and tales on both sides of the family as they talked over them around winter firesides." Like the Scots described in John Kenneth Galbraith's *The Scotch*, remembrances of his early days in Southern Ontario near Guelph, the families had an inner soul, what he described as religious and spiritual connections on religious matters, some politicians excepted, with strong support for their Church, their Clergy, and their public duty. They also knew their own culture, their individual and familial characteristics, their strengths and weaknesses, including the sparse use of their savings. Indeed, Sir William MacDonald, the grandson of Captain John MacDonald, who made millions from the sale of tobacco, refused to allow anyone to smoke in his presence.

In Nova Scotia, William Lyall explored the small communities and towns and their social emotions uniting all mankind in the eyes of God. His replacement at Dalhousie was a young Islander, a Baptist by religion and of Dutch heritage, whose ancestors had been United Empire Loyalists from New York, leaving in 1784. Jacob Gould Schurman was born in Freetown, a small village near Summerside, on May 24, 1854. He graduated from the local school, attended Prince of Wales College and, as a Baptist, went to Acadia College in Wolfville, N.S. He was an excellent student, and won a Canadian Gilcrest scholarship to study at the University of London. He received a BA in 1877, and an MA the following year, graduating with first class honours in mental and moral science. For three years, he studied in Paris, Edinburgh, and (as a Hibbert Fellow) in Heidelburg, Berlin, and Gottingen, and received his doctorate, a D.Sc., in 1878.

He returned to Canada, and became professor of English literature, political economy and psychology at Acadia College in 1880-1882, before moving to Dalhousie College in Halifax as Professor of metaphysics and English literature. But he was unhappy in Halifax, and so moved again to Cornell University, which is set in a rural setting in Ithaca, New York, in 1882 as Sage Professor of Christian Ethics. He felt that Cornell was an academic institution more likely to serve the whole community, rather than the privileged few, as he viewed his years at Dalhousie. He became Dean of the Susan Linn Sage School of Philosophy in 1891-1892. In 1892 he became the third president of Cornell University, succeeding Charles Adams.

His first book, which was published in London in 1881, *Kantian Ethics and the Ethics of Evolution,* attacked the theories of Immanuel Kant and Herbert Spencer. Despite their contributions towards morality and evolutionary ethics, Schurman argued that they didn't address why practical reason, the theory of conduct, needs to be informed by experience, otherwise it produces moral nonsense. He expanded these ideas in his book, *The Ethical Import of Darwinism,* showing how social context does make a difference. In 1889, Schurman wrote an article called "The Manifest Destiny of Canada," for *The*

Forum, where he describes the constitutional position of Canada, unifying the discreet and disparate parts of Canada, as a more flexible arrangement than the American counterpart, and opined that Canada's history flowed from the stream of Western civilization. Curiously, he also praised Canada's stimulating weather and climate. He recognized that Canadian constitutional principles were deeply embedded, and attacked American proposals to incorporate Canada into the American union, the old theories of Manifest Destiny. His ideal federal principle, shown by Canada, was a shrewd balance between common interests, healthy tensions, and flexible institutions. His later work, *The Balkan Wars*, on Bulgaria, showed how this country's intellectual culture, based on its Greek heritage, and its political culture, based on the Turkish Ottoman Empire, was similar to Canada and its relationship to the power of the United States.

As the third president at Cornell, he expanded the University, building a College of Veterinary Medicine in 1894, the Cornell Medical College in 1898, and the State College of Agriculture in 1904. During his 28 years, Cornell increased its enrolment from 1,538 to 5,765, and the campus grew from 200 acres to 1,465 acres. He was a strong supporter of academic freedom, scholarships for foreign students, and the rights of African Americans: "All university doors must remain open to all students irrespective of color or creed or social standing or pecuniary position." He became interested in public affairs, and did some work for the Republican Party. However, he was seen by contemporaries as from the conservative side rather than the 'progressive' politicians like Theodore Roosevelt.

Schurman saw the nation state as a conciliator of diverse interests. He wrote about the American experience on trust-busting, the regulation of railroads, and other measures to tame the excesses of American capitalism. To Schurman, individuals embodied moral principles, not the state. In an address to students in 1896, during the turbulent Venezuelan boundary dispute (with negotiations between Britain, British Guyana, and Venezuela) he felt that Canada, upon gaining full independence, would seek entry into the "American union," an ambiguous term which probably meant the Pan-American Union, an organization which Canada refused to join, and the predecessor to the current Organization of American States. Later, when the Spanish-American War ended, the United States took possession of the Philippine Islands, and he became Chairman of the First United States-Philippines Commission in 1899. Schurman felt that the US should not become a colonial power, and drew on his Canadian experience to transfer powers to smaller authorities. Schurman lost the fight, and the United States did become an imperial power in the Philippines. He wrote part of the official report to the US Congress, but gave his own, real views in his study, *Philippine Affairs – A Retrospect and an Outlook* in 1902. Schurman then spent forty years fighting for Philippine independence. His basic concern was to create a political framework capable of flexibility, with adjustments to political tensions, and an openness to change.

***

In the smallish, elite circles of Charlottetown, the professional and merchant class took the rural areas of the province for granted, much as in other neighbouring provinces. Indeed, throughout Atlantic Canada, the rural areas saw little direct impact after Confederation, as government spending was small, and concentrated in areas like banking, the Post Office, railways, and the courts. The primary concern of people in places like Charlottetown was their personal worries about family, education, careers, and the Church. There was a clear distinction between Catholics and Protestants to be sure, but rivalries within the Protestant groups could also be pronounced. There were, after all, two Protestant church groups in Charlottetown that disagreed, leaving two denominations at St. Paul's and St. Peter's to shape the family gatherings on Sundays. One Island artist who got caught in this mix was a young painter, Robert Harris, whose brother William, an architect, designed St. Paul's.

William Critchlow Harris was an Island architect who spent time in Winnipeg before returning home and becoming interested in church architecture. The first church he designed was St Paul's Anglican Church adjacent to Province House in Charlottetown, the first of more than 20 designed and built in PEI and Nova Scotia. Brick buildings are a rarity on the Island, but many churches were made of brick. St Paul's was different, because it was built with red Island sandstone, in contrast to the few buildings, including nearby Province House, made with Wallace stone imported from Nova Scotia. St. Paul's, adorned with paintings from his brother Robert, enormously impressed the citizens of Charlottetown and the clergy. The Church and attached glebe fill the entire block on Prince Street, its steeple rising on the North side of Great George Street, and the exterior design is elegant, with the windows and doors surrounded by Nova Scotia freestone, and the roof, supporting a rib-vaulted ceiling of spruce boards, made of imported slate.

During this same period, Harris, like his brother a high Anglican, desperately wanted to design the new St. Dunstan's Cathedral, located only two blocks away. Francis-Xarier Belinquet, an architect from Quebec, won the commission. On this occasion, however, religious affiliation was not a factor, because he ended up designing many magnificent Catholic Churches on the Island; indeed, he designed 17 churches on the Island and in Nova Scotia. By this time, Robert the painter was better known outside the Island, but the two brothers remained close friends. Both had musical talent, playing in the Orchestra that hosted John A. Macdonald and the Fathers of Confederation during the Charlottetown Conference in 1864, and both sang in the church choir and played the violin. Charlottetown was an elite community that enjoyed musical talent, but there was little formal support for the Arts, or even for church music. However, there were immigrant families who knew and appreciated the cultural life of European society. One such family was that of John Newberry, an expatriate Englishmen who graduated from Oxford, and married a wealthy Italian, Adele Travaglini. They lived for a time in Italy, moved to North America in 1860, where Adele died in New York. John took the children to PEI, moving near Charlottetown. A skilled amateur painter, he had the young Robert Harris as a painting student.

Robert Harris' first formal training was in Boston, where he arrived in January 1873. He spent a great deal of time studying this historic city, and undertook engravings of cityscapes for reproduction in Halifax newspapers. Between 1871 and 1875, he completed 61 portraits, including numerous merchants, the first Mayor of Charlottetown,

Thomas Heath Haviland, Joseph Howe, and Halifax Bishop Hibbett Binney, as well as the Speakers in the Island Assembly. In 1876, he enrolled in the Slade School in London, run by Alphone Legros from France.

Encouraged by Legros and his classmates from Boston, he moved to Paris. He enrolled in a French studio, the Atalier Bonnat, of Leon Bonnat, then considered one of the great French landscape painters, as well as his works of biblical subjects. Surrounded by students from around the world, Harris worked diligently at his painting techniques, and learned novel colour schemes. This hard work was lightened by many pranks and practical jokes, but the Atalier Bonnat was serious business, especially when the master, Leon Bonnat, made his trenchant criticisms to his students. From Paris, Harris moved to Toronto, the new art center of Canada, and received rave attention for his painting, *The Chorister*, completed on February 8, 1876. This work was recognized as Harris' diploma painting, and became part of the first and initial collection of the National Gallery of Canada, which opened in 1878. He also taught at the Art School in Toronto. Drawing on his European experience, Harris changed the School's teaching methods, and according to his young student, George Reid, caused 'great excitement.'

Toronto became the base of his formal painting career. Harris returned often to Prince Edward Island, not only to renew acquaintances, visit his family, and seek possible portrait work, but in part because he had severe eye problems and often needed rest. He still traveled often. He succeeded Lucious O'Brien as vice-president of the Ontario Society of Artists, where he encouraged young artists to study abroad, especially Paris, joined an American sketch club, and enrolled at the Académie Julian under Jean-Paul Laurens and Alexandre Calonel.

On May 15, 1883 a short note to his younger brother Edward gave some ominous news: "I'm just going to scribble this line to tell you that the picture for the Government to be all right. So I shall be able to work on it at home all summer. I suppose, which will be O.K." With this letter, Robert Harris, Island artist extraordinaire, announced a coveted new commission from the Federal Government, with the portrait to be called *The Fathers of Confederation.* Harris' painting was to become one of the best known works in Canada, and later was widely reproduced in stamps, calendars, posters, folk art, and other replicas. Unfortunately for Harris, despite a payment of $4000 for what he called 'the government painting', he did not receive the copyright, which left him embittered, despite the added fame and attendant rise in his public stature.

Excepting artistic circles in Toronto and Montreal, Robert Harris was hardly known beyond the small political elites of Charlottetown. Clearly, he desperately wanted this government commission, and he used important lobbyists to work for his cause. Senator J. S. Carvel, a prominent businessman, a former Mayor of Charlottetown, and close friend of John A. Macdonald, together with Joseph Pope, his personal secretary, advanced Harris' case. When the Prime Minister, John A. Macdonald, finally announced in the House of Commons, in response to a direct query from Wilfred Laurier, that the commission would bring honour to Canada, as well as to Harris, given Harris' prominence in Europe, he was unapologetic.

The *Charlottetown Examiner*, now a Tory voice, was especially enthusiastic:

> *It is a matter of great satisfaction to every Islander interested in the success of his fellow countryman, not the contract for executing. The proposed historical painting, commenting the Confederation of the British American Provinces, is to be warded to Mr. Robert Harris, of this city. Mr. Harris is a well known and highly talented Canadian artist, who for the past three or four years has been engaged in prosecuting his studies in the three Art centres of the world, London, New York and home. Among Canadian artists, it is readily admitted that he stands pre-eminently first. We congratulate Mr. Harris and hope that before long, his name will be as well and favourably known at the other side of the ocean as it is in Canada.*

Robert Harris self-portrait

Harris 61"X 41" portrait, hung in the Railway Committee room of the House of Commons, was displayed once (in Liverpool) outside Canada, before being burned in the great Ottawa fire of 1916, when tragically the House of Commons center block was gutted. Fortunately, there were many pictures made and a prominent replica hangs, appropriately enough, in the provincial legislative at Queen's Park in Toronto, where Harris was a founding member of the Royal Canadian Academy of Arts and had staged an exhibition with the Ontario Society of Arts. Like most Islanders, Harris developed an enormous interest in political events, both in Canada and in other provinces, due to the fact he knew so many of the players, including the influential Ottawa civil servant and fellow Islander, Joseph Pope. In Charlottetown, as an aspiring artist, he painted anyone who was anyone at that time on the Island, including present and retired politicians, in addition to a series of memorial paintings in his brother's architectural gem, St. Paul's Church.

Over the course of four decades, Harris was proven a pioneering artist in Canada, a man who wished to raise the profile of Canadian artists both at home and abroad. He courted politicians and businessman – George Brown often visited his Toronto studio. He painted people like Lord Strathcona, William Osler, Lord Aberdeen, and John Molson in Montreal, as well as other prominent religious and political figures. His portrait of John A. Macdonald is one of the best ever done. After the 1896 election won by Laurier's Liberals, he personally lobbied Wilfred Laurier to display Canadian paintings abroad, both in exhibits in Paris and at the Worlds Fair in St. Louis: "Many of our artists have studied there …. In the best modern art centers and under the best …, even though they are Canadians who prefer to live, if possible, on the scant encouragement furnished by their own home. It does not seem, however, that is difficult for people, especially in a new country, to have confidence in their artistic ….of their own …., produced under their own skies, dealing with the life and nature of their own land."

Harris' direct appeals to Wilfred Laurier received little encouragement. Laurier actually referred Harris' request to display Canadian art at the Paris International Exhibition of 1900 to Hon. Sydney Fisher, the Minister of Agriculture. It must have been depressing, if not discouraging, that the philistine philosophy of Canadian politicians was also to disregard Canadian artists in their own country. At this stage in his career, Harris was fully familiar with the great art galleries of Europe, had seen the museums and galleries filled with Europe's finest paintings, from the human forms of Michelangelo in Rome to the scenic countryside of London and Yorkshire. He realized that he who sponsors art records human affairs – military figures from Caesar to Bonaparte, Popes, Kings, Queens, Tsars, and the moneymen of the world. And now Harris in Canada was dealing with the Minister of Agriculture!

At the Paris Exhibit, the French objected to Canada's participation because "we are a Colony." Despite this pompous putdown, Harris himself exhibited his painting, *Mrs. D.E.L. Porteous and Her Children.* The artist received an honourable mention among the artists, and he also received a letter from Sir Joseph Chamberlain, the British Colonial Secretary, dated June 26, 1902:

> *I have much pleasure in informing you that the King has been pleased to accept my recommendation. That the distinction of the companionship of the Order of St. Michael and St. George should be conferred upon you; and I desire to take the opportunity of congratulating you on the flourishing condition of art in Canada at the present time.*

It was, records Harris' biographer Moncrief Williamson, the first occasion that a Canadian artist was so honoured. For Harris, the lesson was clear: Canada must be represented at future exhibits. For once, the Eminent Island artist won this round. It was not the first time that the artistic community carried the day for Canada, a lesson not unknown to fellow Maritimers, including the Prime Minister, Robert Borden, who would spend much time in Paris at the Versailles Peace Conference in 1919. During his adult life, sight had been a constant worry for Harris, and by 1919, he was blind. Shortly after hearing his diagnosis, Harris died. Canada and the Island lost a historic man of the arts.

****

The Lucy Maud Montgomery of *Anne of Green Gables* fame forms the best known part of her fabulous writing career, but she, too, like Robert Harris, had a larger side to her life. Maud was above all a Cavendish lady of P.E.I., despite her travels, friends, and celebrated status. To her friends, she was always called Maud. Cavendish in all its wants "is really the prettiest country I have ever been in. It is a long, narrow settlement, bordering on and following the art line of the north shore, whose wonderful waters, ever changing in here and sheen, now silvery gray, now shimmering blue, now darkly ....., now misty with moonrise or purple with sunset, can be seen from any and every point...."

Why was Maud such a good writer? Was it her schooling? Her teachers? Her family? A mixture of all of this? Or more? She gives much credit to the life and family environment of Cavendish: "A different environment would have given bias. Were it not for those Cavendish years, I do not think *Anne of Green Gables* would have been written." Lucy Maud's female friends, her schoolmates and her close chums played together, and wrote each other letters, many quite long and varied. They worked on essays together, refining their writing for submissions to newspapers and literary journals. Montgomery was the Tiger Woods of writing. She started composing at a young age, wrote every day, and through her correspondence and publications, perfected her craft. Rare was the day when she didn't put pen to paper, and her preferred place to write was her home in Cavendish.

Her family was a daily source of a labyrinth of tales and stories, running the gamut of family problems, Cavendish neighbours, the people of the Island, and influencing her personal thoughts and dreams and nightmares. Her grandfather was a walking encyclopedia of yarns and stories. Montgomery was an excellent listener, who loved to hear stories from sea captains about their distant travels, and she unfailingly copied their stories onto paper. Cavendish was at the centre of an extremely sophisticated literary society – meetings were well attended, books were read in advance, a proper delectation of the evening was prepared, and there was both lively debate and much fun and laughter. Even Deacon Arthur Simpson and his supercilious wife was an unwitting player in the literacy society. In one sense, Montgomery was much like Charles Dickens, in that she thought about children and family, and the world of children as seen by children, and of close friends and childish activities like play, innocent idleness, swimming, and farm amusements. It was easy to forget that in the industrialized Victorian world, most children, if they survived, by the time they were ten, lived in an adult world of hard work, long hours, and a rather brutish environment of hunger, loneliness, and poverty.

Montgomery's books on Anne, coupled with her marvelous poems, essays, letters, and other writings (including a song, the Island Hymn, written in 1908 and now the provincial anthem) illustrate the personnel odyssey of this celebrated writer, now adored by so many people from around the world. Montgomery had a hard and troubled life, with personal family problems, concern about finances, and worries over unscrupulous editors. In addition, she struggled with her growing fame, and often worried over what this meant for her few friendships. As she ascended the halls of fame, as shown in her autobiographical work, *The Alpine Way,* life was a struggle. "The Alpine Path, so hard, so steep, to true and honoured fame." Later in life, she would communicate to her true friend, Ephraim Weber: "I could not begin to tell you all the petty flings of malice and spite of which I have been the target of late, even among some of my own relations."

In both personality and behaviour, Montgomery could be the famous writer and author of renown, the story teller with a touching phrase. But she could also be much like her creation, *Anne of Green Gables,* more so than her photos would show, her personal decorum often well disguised. Montgomery's diaries, of course, often gave the real persona behind the face, analyzing her struggles with fame, confined family life, and time spent away from her cherished Cavendish. Her home life was a troubled affair, as she was married to a Minister who suffered from mental illness, with few friends and close companions outside her Cavendish home. Indeed, she was a women struggling with new roles and tasks inside her own household. For her, the diaries became an inner compass of feelings, filling over ten legal volumes in all of notes and letters. These diaries tell the real story of her inner, secret life.

A good example of the Montgomery personality, often taking on the Anne role model, was her 1910 visit to Orwell, PEI, where she had dinner with the Governor General at the Macphail homestead. Macphail was a Professor at McGill, but was born and raised in Orwell, and he arranged a visit with the Governor-General, Earl Gray and his wife. Lucy Maud met them at the Charlottetown train station, and the group traveled to Orwell, which was about 30 kilometers east, with the Lieutenant Governor and his wife (from the Rogers family), and the Premier and his wife (from the Hazards family, who she said, "did not care much for the Hazards"). Together, they arrived at the spacious Macphail homestead and had afternoon tea. Lucy Maud and the Governor-General then went for a stroll through the orchard and sat down in front of a neat little building painted white. "The GG never did let the conversation lag, over an hour and a half. He could ask a 'blue streak' of questions. He was totally delightful and asked for autographed copies of Kilmeny and her poems". They then proceeded to a fine dinner, with guests including the Canadian correspondent of *The Times*. What Montgomery didn't explain to the Governor-General was the fact that he had been seated on the Macphail homestead's W.C., otherwise known on the Island as a farm outhouse.

> *I recited and played a couple of pieces - much to the rage of Deacon Arthur Simpson who hates me almost as much as he hates music. He hates music because he was born that way; and he hates me because I belong to a family who have never given any indication of thinking even Arthur is the most wonderful man in the world. The Deacon is known to irreverent young Cavendish as "Pa" and his pallid, malicious wife as "Ma" because of their habit of addressing each other thus upon all occasions. I think Arthur Simpson is the one and only man in the world I hate with an undiluted hatred. I hate him so much that*

it is nice and stimulating. And it is such f...to do
things – perfectly innocent things which other people
like, such as playing on the Hall organ etc. – which
infuriate him!

Anne of Green Gables and its subsequent offspring have become renowned around the world, with a long list of authors and books exploring Montgomery's themes and life interpretations. What is especially interesting is how Montgomery's own lonely life fits into the memorial personalities of Anne. Despite her gifted talents and her celebrated Island fame, Lucy Maud became a well traveled author, but her mental focus remained on Prince Edward Island, with its mix of home, community, Island geography, and the Island people, with all their warts and prejudices on religion and politics. Montgomery's massive works cover a very broad canvas, ranging from feminism, war, American attitudes, Catholic-Protestant rivalries, French-English relations, her family, and mental illness, to name a few.

But these themes, while important, are not the central tenets of Anne's immense popularity around the world. Japan, of course, is the most obvious country to adopt Anne, where the novel is included in the high school curriculum. Thousands of tourists, many quite young, now make the Mecca-like trip from Tokyo to PEI, unencumbered by side trips to Toronto or New York. Cavendish is the home and birth place of Anne, represented by Avonlea, but to a wider audience, including the Japanese, PEI is Cavendish - it is the heartland of Anne's world, and it represents the sense of family and community that display the hallmarks of Anne's scrumptious innocence.

To the Japanese especially, but also to millions of fans from as far as Poland and Peru, Anne is a wonderful enigma wrapped in her own personality. Chosen as an orphan boy farm hand, Anne is an emotional, loveable, and ultimately irresistible eleven year old. For Matthew, the bachelor farmer who finds Anne at the railway station, it is love at first sight. His story is that of an over-worried farmer who can't wait to do things for Anne, from buying dresses to lecturing his sister, Marilla, and his neighbours about Anne's real needs. Marilla, a stiff Presbyterian spinster who carries the whip in the family, is the fall guy for Matthew's attention to Anne. She is constantly afraid to let Matthew or the orphan girl know that she really adores Anne.

Into this simple threesome – an aging farmer bachelor, a spinster sister, and an orphan school girl – Lucy Maud spins her stories, integrating the community of Cavendish, with the neighbours, schooling, fights, gossip, and churches, all typical of the rural life of PEI. It is a masterful story of PEI in a wider world – Scotland and the Scottish churches and Scottish ministers, the British Empire, Confederation, and the tribal and clan life of PEI. Like rumours in war, on PEI, there is gossip everywhere, often stemming from boastful and clever people leading unimportant lives, but much truth besides. Maud also knew that Islanders, and the Cavendish clans in particular, true to their Scottish heritage, operated on the principle that misplaced politeness was not a substitute for misplaced reputation. Arrogance and stupidity often go hand in hand.

Anne is an outsider who becomes family in this village. She is a woman in a man's world of farm communities, who has a temper, a streak of non-conformity, and a heart that is simply gold, both to Gilbert and her teachers, but especially to Matthew and Marilla. Matthew's gifts to Anne may be the stuff of puffed sleeved dresses, and pets, and core values like never giving up. By contrast, Mirilla is the education mama, to use a Japanese phrase, who knows that high school and university are the way to advancement, especially for women, but is reluctant to say the obvious, especially to reveal her deep affection to the precocious Anne.

A non-conformist in a man's world, a poet in a farm community, and a dreamer in a land of political conformity, Anne is talkative, self-reliant, fashion-conscious, opinionated, gossipy, and red-haired to boot. Throughout Montgomery's writings, Anne is a hidden role model, both a girl orphan without a family desperately seeking love and affection and a girl of immense vanity who knows too well that an orphan scorned is an orphan abandoned. She is a young girl seeking friendships and social approvals everywhere but with few real friends besides Diana Berry. Anne is the focus, but it is the threesome interacting in the family together. Marilla is transformed through the course of the novel from spinster to an adoring and emotional woman, while Matthew in turn is transformed from a semi-literate farmer to a visionary for Anne's emotions and dreams, with Anne ultimately transformed from an out-spoken teenager to a young adult agonizing over Mathew's death and serving as a new parent to a distressed Marilla.

The world of Lucy Maud Montgomery, as she grew up in the workshop of rural Prince Edward Island, was a curious mix of the local calendar and great happenings far away. In the distance, Islanders knew about but often didn't understand the pace of diplomacy, wars, and international rivalries, and how they might affect Imperial Britain and the colonies of the British Empire. Edward Whelan's brilliant speech in the Island Assembly regarding Britain's wars with Russia and Afghanistan is a telling reminder that distant wars are not time constrained, with many local young men conscripted. But Montgomery followed the path of writers like Charles Dickens, in that each shared a unique capacity to escape from a world of poverty, destitution, and unhappiness and see the world as a child, understanding some goodness in the wider landscape. Rural PEI was her laboratory and Montgomery saw the goodness as a child sees goodness, often in little things, and in God's natural bounty.

The centennial anniversary of Lucy Maud Montgomery's birth occurred in 1974, coinciding closely with the hundredth anniversary of Prince Edward Island's entry into Confederation on July 1, 1873. This Centennial produced an outpouring of books, anthologies, movies, and television programs on this most famous Island author, allowing an easy escape into the wonderful memories of the past. It was a simpler time, when the advance of industrialization had not yet pushed everyone for the demands of money and the time clock. Perhaps it is no accident that the Japanese, and especially young girls often traveling without the parents, trekked to Prince Edward Island to enjoy the delights of Cavendish, Anne's home ground. Their fascination could be seen as an attempt to avoid, even momentarily, the rush of Japan's urban madhouse of unstoppable work, family tension, and competitive stress. In a global world, Anne of Green Gables has universal appeal.

Cavendish and Prince Edward Island became code words, used to describe what was happening around the industrialized world, from Poland to China, and Ontario to Argentina, where the acute differences between the agricultural economy and the life style of small farms, small communities, and small scale, clash with the cult of bigness – big government, big industry and companies, big banks and universities, and bigness in all its ugly forms. Today, there is a universal struggle between big scale and the clash with the little guy, the little community, and the little thoughts of families, church, and nature. Lucy Maud Montgomery was not an economist, a sociologist, or a geographer, but her writings, like the paintings of Robert Harris, the architectural forms of William Critchlow Harris, and the novels and writings of Andrew Macphail shared this in common, that small scale in all its forms, from the school house to the farm, the church to the community, was something to celebrate, to cherish, and to preserve.

Islanders knew about distant lands in other ways. They understood from their earliest days as immigrants the folklore of Scotland and Ireland. To some degree later, they saw in north counties of Lancashire and Yorkshire, where in the mid 19th century, English settlers arrived, families like the Stanfields in Tryon, who later moved to Truro via Pictou to establish Stanfield's Knitting. They recognized the extensive fleets of schooners, brigantines, clipper ships, and brigs, which promoted trading in England and the U.S., but for local merchants as well. (Between 1860 and 1900, Islander merchants sailed the Atlantic by the score – Bob McLeod, of the firm Moore and McLeod, crossed the ocean 40 times to buy goods in London.) Enormous fleets, some commissioned for the British Admiralty, plied the trade routes of the Caribbean and South America. British Guiana, for instance, was often frequented to trade for sugar and molasses, a key ingredient for rum, in addition to the coastal parts of the U.S., the Boston States and, of course, England.

By the middle of the 19th century, Islanders became aware of the new world of global shipping, trade, and ship design. Britain clearly controlled the oceans of the world. British ships and the British navy were the lifeline of the British Empire, with England's security, trade,

Andrew Macphail

and colonial territories reaching as far south as India, as far east as Singapore, and as far west as Egypt and the Suez Canal. Emigration to Canada (and especially the Irish to the U.S.A.) was accelerating, but new vistas opened, both to Australia and New Zealand, and, thanks to Britain's voracious demands for new addictions, tea, peppers, silk and opium - to China. In the U.S., the California gold rush brought its own scores of immigrants, and the financial world of plunder, scandal, and manipulation.

In this frenzy, where passports and customs rules were scantily followed, it was a golden age of immigration, with a 'get rich euphoria' sparking the search for gold in South Africa, California, and the Yukon, a phenomenon which also motivated the merchant and naval mania for speed. When the *Marco Polo*, then the fastest sailing ship in the world - her namesake tells the story of trade, vast expansion for overseas commerce, and discovery - ran ashore in a fierce July 1883 windstorm on a reef off Cavendish, Lucy Montgomery had a vivid recollection of the wreck. Everyone on the Island knew the stories of the *Marco Polo,* and her astonishing feats of endurance and speed. In her prime, the *Marco Polo* beat a steamship, travelling from Liverpool to Australia, by a week. This ship spoke to the world about Maritime shipping prowess, as she was built in New Brunswick, but also brought the world to Islanders. Her crew was a lesson in diversity - what Montgomery called their "especial delight" - being comprised of Norwegians, Swedes, Dutchmen, Germans, Irishmen, Englishmen, Scotchmen, Spaniards and most curious of all for Islanders, two Tahitians, "whose wally heads, thick lips and gold earrings were a never failing joy to myself".

The sailing and shipping industry was a source of comfort, a link to the outside world. It was also a big source of employment, seasonal or full time on the Island and throughout the Maritimes. Timber – and all its impacts, from tree lots to timber prices, from wages to freight rates, from vessel production to navigation aids-markers, buoys and insurance - was a mainstay of local Maritime prosperity. It had global repercussions beyond industry, banking, the military, and trade. Local painters were attracted to water colour sketches and then oils of ships, captains and shipyards. The *London Illustrated*

News, a magazine that first started in 1842, was a popular source of international happenings and personalities, printing, and global shipping. Sketches and engravings became very popular, with scenes by Pooley, Woolford, Eager and Hickman widespread. William Bartlett, a British engraver, toured the U.S. and Canada, developing a sizeable following. Another lithographer, widely known on the Island although with no Island prints, was the U.S. Company, Currier and Ives. Soon a new influence would impact Canadian artists, in the military and the causes of war.

****

Andrew Macphail of Uigg, P.E.I., was born in 1864, the year of the Confederation meetings in Charlottetown and Quebec, and became a man of letters, a leading figure at McGill University, and a major player in the Canadian Medical Association. Like many Islanders who were raised in small communities schools, Macphail's heroes were his teachers, both in high school and in university. As he recalled, one of his professors, a Scot from Aberdeen, and gold medalist from Edinburgh, had tremendous strength of character. He had two hundred scholars under his control, and in two years he never administered to anyone so much as a rebuke, unless in whimsical bantering, or a reference to youthful folly that was construed as such. He treated the crude boys as if they were grave young gentlemen determined to become scholars, capable of winning, by their scholarship, any high place in the world.

The Macphail family had a long history (400 years) of participation as teachers or clergyman, but after some thought, Andrew chose medicine, deciding to attend McGill. It was a very good career decision: he graduated at 27 with a B.A. and an M.D., with twelve hundred dollars and no debt. He worked as a tutor in Montreal, earning more per hour than he earned per day in P.E.I., while also becoming a newspaper reporter, earning about $2000 per year. He wrote for the Montreal *Gazette*, the *Star*, the Toronto *Globe and Mail*, wire services and the New York *Times*. Like Winston Churchill in England and Gordon Sinclair writing for the Toronto *Star* in Canada, Macphail signed on as a traveling reporter, visiting countries as diverse as Britain, France, Egypt, Hong Kong, Japan and Singapore.

He practiced medicine for more than ten years. In 1903, Macphail became editor of the *Montreal Medical Journal* which merged with the leading *Canadian Medical Review* as the *Canadian Medical Association Journal.*

Macphail became a respected writer and prominent member of McGill society, the leading university in Canada and, thanks to the teaching of Sir William Osler, one of the great medical schools in the world. Macphail was the editor of the *University Magazine* at McGill. He became a close friend of Stephen Leacock, who was a frequent contributor to the *University Magazine*, as was John MacCrae, a physician and poet, and author of the immortal, *In Flanders Fields.* During Macphail's distinguished career at McGill, he was also close friends with the Dean of Arts and Science (and head of the English Department), Cyrus Macmillan, another Islander, and the Principal, Sir Arthur Currie, who led Canadian Forces in the Great War.

Even visitors to McGill became influenced by Macphail. Rudyard Kipling actually wrote a speech to McGill in Macphail's home. He was the first professor of the history of medicine. By 1905, and scarcely over 40, Macphail had published ten books. They ranged from a study of the Bible in Scotland, an English translation of the French novel *Maria Chapdelaine*, a lengthy drama, books of confessions, and the official history of the Canadian Army Medical Services in World War I. However, Macphail's masterpiece, a mix of autobiographical and intensely personal social criticism, was the *Master's Wife.*

Despite his travels, and notwithstanding his success at McGill, he remained in close contact with his community and his family. In P.E.I., Macphail was a man of eminence, a major in the Canadian Army, and was appointed a knight by the King at Buckingham Palace. His brother, Andrew, was a professor at Queens University. In P.E.I. they became active in community affairs, where they brought scientific methods to the potato industry, introduced tobacco growth to the Island, and literally founded the seed potato industry. When friends had approached Macphail to run as a Conservative candidate in Queen's county, there were rumours that Andrew might run there as an Independent. He did run in 1918 as a Conservative member in the Legislative Assembly.

The Macphails family background, like Lucy Maud Montgomery's and Robert Harris', showed their enormous love and affection for P.E.I. and the province's capacity to escape from industrialization and a stressed urbanization. For them, Prince Edward Island represented a preferred way of life, emphasizing the ideals of community, a direct link between man and nature, and a better combination of art and science. Macphail put the matter in this way:

> *Farming is a way of life. It is that and nothing else.*
> *It is not a business. If a man does not find his life and*
> *pleasure in his daily work, in the context of his fields*
> *and the compounding of his animals; if he does not*
> *enjoy his labouring words by stream and sea: if he*
> *thinks less of his daily bread, of the provisions for a*
> *severe and contented old age, and more of the profit*
> *he draws, he would be well advised to seek some*
> *other vacation.*

As a social critic, and a critic of university men "who prefer to sit in a well and gaze at the stars", refusing "to tell the truth", Macphail also rejected American influences, with "its process of urbanization, industrialization, and bureaucratization ... this economic approach had its own blights, the urban poor, deskilling of workers." It was a theme also picked up by other Island writers, like Basil King.

*****

Basil King, born in Charlottetown on February 26, 1859, was a writer of note, a Canadian clergyman who shifted careers and turned to writing. He became an influential author, with several best selling books, and was one of the founders of the Canadian Authors Association. His full name was William Benjamin Basil King. In 1881, he graduated from the University of King's College in Nova Scotia, and three years later he was ordained as an Anglican priest, serving the rector of St Luke's Cathedral in Halifax. His life in Charlottetown, including as Assistant Priest and Schoolmaster at St. Peter's Cathedral, and his strict religious upbringing inspired his writing. His book, *The Conquest of Fear* (1921), also made reference to his fears of blindness. He had good reason for this phobia. As a young adolescent, he had been slowly losing his sight, and he suffered from thyroid gland problems. Later he moved to France and spent an autumn at Versailles. Here, like many lonely painters, he was tormented with introspection and personal fears about a total loss of vision.

While in France, Basil King took to writing, thinking that spiritualism was his guide, and that a spirit personality could intone his books: "It is my blood, my breath, my brain." He traveled to Boston, which he made his home, and spent seasons writing in New York, Nice, Cannes, Munich, London, and Berlin. In 1892, King became the rector of Christ Church, Cambridge, Massachusetts, but his medical problems persisted, as did his eye problems. By 1900, he resigned as rector because of failing eyesight. He became an influential moral fiction writer, and his first publications included *The Inner Shrine* (1909), *The Wild Olive* (1910), and *The Street Called Straight* (1912).

In 1884, he married Esther Foote. For much of his life, King thought his life was a waste, but there were two major turning points. The first was sparked by some improvement in his thyroids, which stopped the loss of vision. A teacher also imbued him with thoughts about fate, Nature, and his own spiritualism, similarly effecting a transformation in King. Somewhat confident of his own fate, and the challenges that Life imposed on him, he decided to heed his own advice: "Be bold and mighty forces will come to your aid." His new works included *The High Heart* (1917), a book about the struggle of a young girl from Halifax who wants to be accepted into New England high society, and *The Dust Flower* (1922), a contrast between upwardly mobile Canadians in New York, and the poverty of immigrants. King had several best-sellers, almost all of which were set in the United States, but with Canadian characters. "My small experience in the conquest of fear can be condensed into these four words: Calmly resting! quiet trust!"

Rev. Basil King

But King's torments wouldn't recede. He returned to Cambridge, and there hosted many writers, including Lucy Maud Montgomery, but his spiritual worries and fears of failure constantly consumed him and poisoned his personality. King thought that he could trust his friends, but various misunderstandings ultimately led to more depressions. After two years, he felt his life didn't amount to much, despite the pretence of working: "Suspicion always being likely to see what it suspects, the chances were many that I was creating the very thing I suffered from." He decided to leave Cambridge, and started traveling again, but his spiritual side took over, in what he called a *metanoia* of sorts. This spiritual conversion made him realize that his life's role was not to control fate in order to avoid his worst fears, but to put his trust in God and let them work together. King's new lease on life led to *The Conquest of Fear* and his own concept of God:

> *'I am all right,'* is the unspoken thought in many a heart, *'so long as I am not overtaken by the Will of God. When that calamity falls on me my poor little human happiness will be wrecked like a skiff in a cyclone.'* This is not an exaggeration. It is the secret mental attitude of perhaps ninety percent of those Caucasians who believe in a God of any kind. Their root-conviction is that if God would only let them alone they would get along well enough; but as a terrible avenging spirit, like the Fury or the Nemesis of the ancients, he is always tracking them down. The aversion from God so noticeable in the mind of to-day is, I venture to think, chiefly inspired by the instinct to get away from, or to hide from, the pursuit of this Avenger. *'Fear was not overcome; I had only made a more or less hesitating stand against it; but even from doing that I got positive results.'*

In 1928, Basil King died in Cambridge, Massachusetts.

******

Curiously, there was little emphasis placed on academic writing on the Island, not even through the formative years at St. Dunstan's

College or Prince of Wales College. There was an outlet for local history and community affairs, in the *Prince Edward Island Magazine*, which started in 1898. Some professors and a few notable personalities wrote impressive articles on Island place names, the education system, or personalities like Bishop MacEachern. One notable exception, unknown to the general public, was the work of Rev. J.P.E. O'Hanley, a Professor of Greek and Latin at St. Dunstan's University. He translated from Latin to English the three volume work of Rev. Henrique Grenier's massive study, *Cursus Philosophia*, a textbook on the work of St. Thomas Acquinas, which is widely used in Catholic colleges and philosophy departments around the world.

The rapid development of Canadian higher education, and the concurrent explosion in scientific work after 1945, led to a number of writers using the Island as a place of rest, a reclusive spot for thinking through their deep thoughts, or simply as a place to write without interruption. Unfortunately, the Island has never pushed the envelope like Ireland, where there are important tax measures that help attract writers and artisans to work and live on the emerald Isle. One person who did spend a lot of time each year on the Island, perhaps up to a third of his life, was an academic from Princeton University, a man almost unknown to Islanders, and only familiar to a select specialty group in Canada, Julian Jaynes. Jaynes himself was a loner, a man who stayed at his family house in Keppoch, the *Redcliffe* three story house built for Admiral Henry Bayfield overlooking the Charlottetown Harbour.

Jaynes was born in West Newton, Massachusetts in 1920, but his parents had spent their summers on the Island since the 1890s. His father died that year at the Borden ferry terminal, traveling against his doctors' orders in a rush to make it to the Island one last time, feeling an instinct to return to his large, quiet property, close to the beach and the rolling waves of the Northumberland Strait. Julian Jaynes remained single all his life, and had few personal intimate friends, but acquired an immense following during his academic life in the psychology department at Princeton, where he taught from 1966 to 1990. His academic work is not easy to classify, but became of intense interest beyond psychology and philosophy. His undergraduate work was in the Department of Arts at Harvard University and at McGill University, and he received his masters and doctorate in psychology at Yale University, combining what President John F. Kennedy said about the best thing in American higher learning, a Harvard degree and a Yale education.

Despite his American background, Jaynes spent a lot of time on Prince Edward Island, often during the summer, but also through the long months of the early fall, where the Island weather and color can be at its best. He was a prolific author, and spent a great deal of time at other universities, not only teaching his core subject, psychology, but also in departments of philosophy, archaeology, and medical schools. Why? Jaynes' primary interest was in the workings of the human brain, and the stream of consciousness and mental structures that lead to behaviour. His magnum opus, *The Origin of Consciousness in the Breakdown of the Bicameral Mind*, first published in 1976 was, like many such tracts, instantly acclaimed as one of the great works of the century, and castigated by other writers as interesting but unimportant.

What interested Jaynes was the nature of the human mind, and his novel bicameral views of the human mind structure. In one sense, his work coincides with the pioneering work of Wilfred Penfield, an American Rhodes Scholar from Princeton, who built his career in the School of Medicine at McGill University, establishing the world famous Montreal Neurological Institute. As a great man, Penfield recruited good people, which can be the principal failing of weak people, and studied, for instance, how learning languages was an exercise of the mind, like physical labour was an exercise of the body. Jaynes' bicameral theory explored the left and the right side of the mind, and how one might lead to highly rational thought, exercised by the use of mathematics, while the other leads to creative tensions, seeing the big picture, and with less interest in smaller details.

Through his determined attempts to accurately define human consciousness, Jaynes introduced his revolutionary bicameral mind theory to argue that consciousness is a learned process, one that grows from experience, rather than something that began back in animal evolution. His bicameral mind theory had enormous possibilities for medical researchers and social scientists, who saw in his work implications for various medical problems, modes of thinking, and the controversial topic of consciousness. Various extensions flow from his thinking, including the capacity to remember things, modes of decision making of interest in political science and business schools (bureaucratic behaviour, autocracy in management, and creative mind sets) and a host of medical issues that are explored in journals like *Canadian Psychology, Behavioural and Brain Sciences*, and even *Art/World*. Jaynes died in 1997 and left his estate to the Prince Edward Island Heritage Foundation.

******

It might be said, that only a generation ago, there were many Canadian provinces that had no adequate literature, no adequate histories, and no prominent biographies. It might even be possible to argue that the same statement could be said of Canada. Certainly, this has been the problem of PEI, where for generations, too many people had little real appreciation, and even understanding, of the Island's history as it progressed from an isolated colony within the British Empire to become the Cradle of Confederation and a self-governing province within Canada. From Jacques Cartier's detailed diaries of his voyages in the Maritimes, to Lord Selkirk's own history of the Scottish Highlands and his trips to PEI, few people cared enough about Island history, and neglecting its role in the Confederation debates, and ignoring its writers, painters, and authors. As Frank MacKinnon, in his classic work, *The Government of Prince Edward Island* stated in 1955, "There is no adequate general history of Prince Edward Island".

Since the days of Confederation in the nineteenth century, there have been only two significant works on the history of the Island. D. A. MacKinnon and A.B. Warburton's treatment, *Past and Present in Prince Edward Island,* is an interesting overview of the province, with profiles of significant areas, including religion, medicine, invention, and politics. A.B. Warburton, a Charlottetown lawyer, Premier, and social commentator, gives an interesting profile of the Island's development in *A History of Prince Edward Island*, starting with the landings of Jacques Cartier in 1534, and stretching to the end of Colonel John Ready's tenure as Lieutenant-Governor in 1831. Rev. John MacMillan's two volume work on *The Early History of the Catholic Church in Prince Edward Island* and D.C. Harvey's *The French Regime in Prince Edward Island* help round out the early history, but with little emphasis on social or economic issues. James Pollard's *Historic Sketch of the Eastern Regions of New France, and also Prince Edward Island: Military and Civil*, covers events to Queen Victoria Diamond Jubilee in 1897, based on interviews and newspaper accounts. MacKinnon's own opus, *The Government of Prince Edward Island*, focussing on the the Island's government, and part of the MacGregor Dawson Canadian Government series published by the University of Toronto, is a powerful study of the evolution of the Island's government, covering from the colonial periods of the French and British regimes to the development of P.E.I. as a province. It was the first study ever written solely about the government of a Canadian province.

It was not until the centennial of the Charlottetown Conference of 1864 that a renewed interest in the Island story unfolded. As MacGregor Dawson points out, while "Prince Edward Island is, of course, by far the smallest of the Canadian provinces both in area and in population, but in terms of constitutional interest, it is well up near the top." The centennial celebrations both of the 1864 Conference and the 1873-1973 centennial when Canada joined the Island, at least in the view of many Islanders, led to an explosion of histories, biographies, and monographs on Island history. Many Islanders who took graduate studies at Canadian and foreign universities delved into the archives in PEI, in Ottawa, London, and Paris. The PEI Heritage Foundation, which was set up as a lasting monument in 1973 by the government of Premier Alex Campbell, publishes *The Island Magazine*, and spurred an enormous level of interest in Island history, folklore, family archives, Acadian settlements, Micmac communities, and industries and institutions like the Island co-op movement. Irene Rodgers' superb study of the architecture and construction of the buildings, *Charlottetown: The Life in Its Buildings*, including Government House, is a case study of the new found interest in the history of this unique province.

If there is one eminent modern historian of Prince Edward Island, it is the wise and erudite works of Professor Francis Bolger, a Catholic priest who made his teaching career at St. Dunstan's University. Dr. Bolger's outstanding book, *Prince Edward Island and Confederation 1863-1873,* (and a later volume, *Canada's Smallest Province*) sets out, through detailed analysis of official documents and private letters, the constitutional issues of the 1864 Charlottetown Conference, including the subsequent Quebec Conference, and examines how the very basis of the Confederation agreement was decided in PEI. He was the first Islander to trace the protracted letters and documents in the British archives, including the colonial records and official papers. Other works include studies of Lucy Maud Montgomery, Bishop Angus MacEachern, and the history of Vernon River Church.

Bolger's book launched a new generation of Islanders exploring all aspects of Island history. But it was Bolger's personal influence, coupled with his desire to get foreign documents placed in the official archives of Prince Edward Island and the St. Dunstan's University Library, which places him on the path set out by Joseph Pope. Above all, he knew the importance of archival documents, the plethora of letters, maps, and mementos that are so important to understanding history. His courses on Canadian History and Island History, including his magnificent, spell-binding speeches and his seminars to community groups, started a new tradition of Island history and record keeping that places this small province at or near the top of all jurisdictions in Canada for preserving historic archives.

Perhaps no area illustrates the wide range of activities of Eminent Islanders, and their influence on PEI and abroad, is the record of Island doctors and the practice of medicine.

7

Island Medicine: Nature's Helpers

Native Medicine * Military Influences * Natural Products *
Island Nutrition * Prohibition * Rural Medicine * House Calls
* McGill's Influence * Dr. John Mackieson* Hospitals * The
Nursing Profession * Public Health* Doctors' Clinics * Blue Cross
* Medicare * Hope

Morell, PEI is a small farm community located about 35 km northeast of Charlottetown, half way between St. Andrew's Church, the home of Bishop Angus MacEachern, and St. Peter's, the district that Edward Whelan once called his political home. In its heyday, Morell had many fine characteristics, including natural mussels, thriving farmlands, a distinctive political culture, and perhaps the finest home-made moonshine, renowned at political functions and marriage ceremonies throughout the Island. Today, it is the home of Crowbush Golf Course, considered one of the finest in Canada.

There were other advantages - a thriving French community, a major trading post linking Charlottetown and the port of Souris, a water system linking three rivers (the Morell, the Marie, and the Midgel with their own French engineered dyke system), tempestuous political rallies, and one of the first Catholic Churches ever built on PEI, constructed in 1751. Morell was also the birth place of an eminent Islander, Cyril Sinnott. To many Islanders, Cyril Sinnott was simply called Cy. Islanders have a funny way with names. People with respect are often called by their first name, not as a sign of informality or disrespect, but with a certain reverence. Father Angus MacEachern, later *the* Bishop, was often called Father Angus, or the Bish. The last name usually implies a certain reserve, almost implying that he is a suspicious character or, even worse, that he is from away. Cy received a very respectable education, starting with Island high schools, before shifting to employment in the Royal Canadian Air Force during World War II. When the war ended, he graduated *summa cum laude* at St. Dunstan's University, and finished with a quality medical education at McGill University. Perhaps against his wish, he returned to the Island and joined the Charlottetown Clinic, a thriving medical practice combining general and family medicine with specialty work in surgery, gynecology, urology, obstetrics and pediatrics.

How little many Islanders know of their own citizens! As it happened, a chance event brought home to a few Islanders how much they owed to this new wave of medical doctors who returned to PEI in the late 1950s and later. The essence of a Cy Sinnott story, like so many incidents in the saga of Island medicine, is an event that at first glance appears to be relatively straight forward. A tourist family from Toronto was visiting Island relatives at a farm in Morell. It was a cloudless PEI summer day, much like the Fathers of Confederation enjoyed in 1864. The visitors from Toronto were helping the local Morell family do their farm chores, enjoying an early breakfast, with the men already in the hay fields, the women in the kitchen making breads and brownies for the evening *Ceilidh*, and the young boys playing around the farm yard. For the Toronto family, it was a typical week, comprised of swimming in the Morell River, visiting the harbour at nearby Red Head, playing with the farm animals, horse rides, lobster feasts, and at night, after dark, a taste of PEI moonshine, reputedly the very best from Morell Rear. The young boy from Ontario was probably mystified why anyone would choose to spend their summers, let alone all year round, in places like Toronto. The idle hands of young boys, passing a lazy summer afternoon, could pass through the large barn. Then disaster struck! The Toronto boy, seeing some coloured grains in a bag, assumed they were for consumption, almost like a speckled candy. Within seconds, he was seriously sick - no colour, no strength, and no motion, lying on the floor of the barn.

The Morell farm boy did the usual act in the face of emergency - he went to his mother. A quick visit to the barn revealed the problem to be a very sick boy. Her response was motherly, in a hasty phone call to the medical scientist from Morell, Cy Sinnott. Using the telephone for long distance on a party line with an operator, a system used by Island Telephone until the early 1970s (usually old discarded equipment from Mother Bell), the Mother contacted the Charlottetown Clinic. Paradoxically, the busiest season for an Island doctor is the summer, not only because of the large number of tourists, but because there are so many accidents among farmers and fishermen. This call was different, and Dr. Sinnott hurriedly learned the simple details about the accident. Now aware of the problem, he could relate to his own farm upbringing in Morell, while aware of the doctors' usual warning: above all, do no harm. Cy Sinnott moved into action, quickly grabbing another phone for his medical needs. He also repeated his first command to the farm mother in Morell - stay in the kitchen and do not hang up the phone line to Charlottetown.

Cy Sinnott then assembled two Clinic colleagues, distinguished graduates of McGill's famed School of Medicine, a noted surgeon, the first a winner of the Holmes Gold Medal as well as the Lieutenant Governor's Medal, and the second, a noted pediatrician who had interned in Connecticut and at Sick Kids in Toronto, receiving the first ever certificate on the Island from the Royal College of Physicians and Surgeons. With their help and opinion, Cy Sinnott started the dirty work, grace under pressure.

He called his colleagues at McGill and the Montreal General Hospital, describing the symptoms, and then gave his diagnosis in fancy chemical language, asking for an antidote. In addition, he needed an immediate response, which, he informed them, in his quiet, coolly methodical way, couldn't be a complicated pharmaceutical prescription, to be purchased at a Charlottetown drugstore or a fancy package flown in from Montreal. There was simply no time. To add to the chaos, the antidote had to be made in a typical farm kitchen,

Dr. Cy Sinnott

from ordinary stock ingredients, in a rural farm setting away from shopping centers.

True to form, with Dr. Sinnott serving as a NASA-styled scientific coordinator, the McGill doctors came up with a strange cocktail of substances promptly referred to the country kitchen on PEI. Cy Sinnott, raised on a farm in Morell, where he and his brothers had horses but could not afford the money to buy a bicycle, was amused by children like his own who lived in cities and had bikes but wanted a horse. The telephone calls seemed to last hours, but it was in fact far less, and Dr. Sinnott now had his delicate prescription. He had to convey them to a terribly scared Toronto mother and a worried farmer's wife in Morell. Thanks to McGill and the farm experience of Cy Sinnott, the prescriptive remedies were provided like a recipe for baked blueberry pie: mix the various ingredients together, add lots of water on the side, and have the boy swallow the lot, force feeding if necessary, giving as much as possible as soon as possible. While the hours seemed interminable, the timing was amazingly short, curious because summer time in the summer in PEI is Island time, where clocks are used as furniture pieces, not time clocks. The diagnosis was amazingly accurate, as was the antidote, for the concoction worked, with the Toronto boy soon recovering, not much the worse for his simple mistake about barnyard consumables. As any farmer will tell you, fertilizer isn't good for the stomach or for human consumption.

**

The opening chapter of Island medicine, from the early years of the French regime in 1720 to the period up to the First World War, was very much the story of rural medical practice in Canada, usually the lone doctor, his small equipment bag, and his horse. What was true in PEI was largely the case for medical practice throughout the pioneer days of Canada. Most doctors were themselves immigrants, first from France, and then from Britain after 1759, mainly from England and Scotland. Dr. Angus MacAulay, a Gaelic-speaking academic, lay preacher, and physician, traveled with Lord Selkirk to PEI and eventually became speaker of the PEI Assembly. Two early doctors on the Island, Dr. James Cook and Dr. J.P. Sherlock, served aboard vessels sailing in Nelson's powerful fleet with his flag ship, *The Victory*, at Trafalgar in 1805. Many had experience as medical officers. As William Osler noted, "the military element gave, for some years, a very distinctive stamp to the profession. These surgeons were men of energy and ability who had seen much service and were accustomed to military discipline and reputation."

In a larger context, early medicine in North America pre-dates the French explorers who arrived with Champlain in 1604 at Port Royal, and then later in Quebec in 1635. The Europeans in general, especially those who could read, write, and keep dairies and letters, were surprised by the curiously sophisticated medical practices among the various Indian tribes. Training was necessary, including lessons in botany and pharmacology, and it was open to men and women. Early Indian practice knew concoctions of herbs, plasters, and nutrition. According to one account, notes Andrew Macphail,

> ... *they understood the use of emetics, purgatives, and diuretics. They gave broths in fever. They were especially versed in hydrotherapy, giving cold water to the patient enclosed in a sweat-tent; and in physio-therapy, using local and general message. They were familiar with the specific use of certain medicinal plants, using the roots and bark; and according to the Jesuit Relations (1635-6), they had a rude but somewhat efficient surgery.*

Indian medicine did not have the European formality of clinical experiments, anatomy, or scientific language but, like Chinese herbal medicine, it had other advantages, in that it cured people. In the cold winter of 1535-1536, when Jacques Cartier toured Canada on his lengthy voyage and stayed at Quebec, he was accompanied by the apothecary Franoys Guitault, a third of his men died from a company of 110, and all but three were hopelessly sick. Indian tribes came to succour them, prescribing their own medicine, the tree of life, and saving the Cartier mission. The remedy was called *annadda*, and the ailment became known as scurvy. *Annadda* was an infusion of spruce, hemlock buds, and bark. *Annadda* was the tree of life.

In this case, the French did not fully understand the power of these remedies. Over the ensuing decades, scurvy would take staggering losses from the French, British, and Spanish explorers, including many itinerant soldiers who took long sea voyages, before they understood the cure. Indeed, before James Lind, a Scottish physician, discovered in 1747 that scurvy was caused by the loss of critical vitamins, and could therefore be cured with citrus fruits like lemon or lime (hence the term *limey*, a malapropism for British sailors), some medical progress was made. Lind's experiment, dividing six sailors who took lime juice and six who didn't, to study the symptoms of scurvy – perhaps the first clinical trial in medicine - on board the *Salisbury*, appeared to be conclusive but it took the Admiralty time to accept his conclusions.

By 1769, when Captain James Cook visited the South Seas carrying citrus fruits like oranges and lemons, on Lind's suggestions, it was clear that a cure for scurvy was readily available. Yet it took another three decades to overcome the stupidity, obstinacy, and sheer ignorance of the British Admiralty before citrus fruits would become standard issue on British ships taking long voyages. Horatio Nelson, famous for his battles in the Mediterranean, Egypt, Denmark and the Baltic Sea, plus his most famous, Trafalgar, as well as his travels to the West Indies, Quebec and New York, assured that he and his 13 Band of Brothers, as he called his captains from the Battle of the Nile, carried proper supplies for his sailors, including fruit, lemons, quality meats, cognac and rum. A student of James Cook, Nelson was scrupulous about the need for a clean ship, and he ensured that sailors scrubbed the vessel to keep scurvy and typhus at bay. Sadly, the war ships on the Thames River were much cleaner than the streets of London, usually gray and dirty from the coal dust, and soiled by excrement from the horses and other animals traveling on the dusty pavement. About 250 tons of fecal matter entered the river water every day. By the mid-1850s, when Dickens wrote *Great Expectations*, London was so polluted that the drinking water was a repellent mix of toxic chemicals, decomposing body matter (people and animals), and putrid water. It took reforms and Bazalgette's exceptional engineering to build sewers and embankments to arrest the drinking water crisis, a problem which Napoleon had solved for Paris fifty years previous.

For the first 150 years of settlement, Islanders were served by doctors performing both general surgery and obstetrics, and very often dentistry. It was a profession of rural practice, with the family home being where babies were born, and sometimes died. It was an age before science took hold of the doctor-patient relationship - there were no anaesthetics, antibiotics, or asepsis. Public health knowledge was virtually non-existent. Farms and fishing villages had outdoor bathrooms, while running water came from makeshift wells, and the revolving seasons helped to purify the air. In places like Charlottetown, according to one report, "the streets were muddy and dirty. Up to 1863 sidewalks were virtually non-existent and when some were finally installed, there were made of hemlock plants subject to the usual rattling and breakups." Most milk deliveries in towns came from un-pasteurized milk until the 1950s; water was not fluoridated until the 1960s.

As the Island approached about 100,000 in population at the start of the 20th century, the Island averaged about one doctor for every 1000 people, scattered across the province, county by county. Until the first hospital was built in 1879 in Charlottetown, most doctors spent their waking hours on house calls, travelling from farm to farm, delivering babies, practicing therapeutic medicine (treating of blisters, bleeding, lancing boils), and surgery, such as setting fractures, amputations, hernias and appendectomies. Farm life, ship building, boot repair, and logging and construction, whatever their economic gains, were all enormously dangerous and doctors often attended to patients with damaged limbs and freak accidents. Diagnostic tools for medical practice were few, and medicine usually consisted of treatments to restore the natural balance of behaviours. Excretions, abnormal breathing, perspiration, and abnormal coloration led to observations about the patient's blood, temperature, pulse, urine, and bowel movements. Opium, quinine, alcohol, Madeira and other wines were widely used, as was mercury, salt peter, and arsenic. Europeans, of course, used various herbal medicines for their therapeutic qualities, including sedatives (cowslip, red clover), soporifics (lavender, carmamile), hallucinogens (poppies), anti-depressents (lemon balm, evening primrose), and plants to induce calmness (rue, penny royal), reduce blood pressure (hawthorn, mistletoe) and cure headaches (black peppermint). Larger sailing ships and increased trade introduced new medicinal aids, such as willow bark for pain relief, wild yams from Mexico of black cohosh for hormones, quinine for malaria, and digitalis for the heart. The ever present doctor's bag was as simple as a priest's ecclesiastic kit, containing a scalpel, simple instruments, some chloroform, cotton bandages, the stethoscope, and perhaps a prayer book.

Natural products were widespread in Island homes and farms. Spruce gum, rosehips, cayenne pepper, mustard, pinecones and barks, and even kelp and other berry ingredients were used to develop home remedies, usually in the form of a liquid concoction mixed with tea or hot water. As early as 1810, Thomas DesBrisay opened what was to become one of the oldest drug stores in North America, the Apothecaries Hall, on Queen and Great George Street in the center of Charlottetown. Records from orders placed by doctors show an amazing mix of materials, drugs and medicines, including test tubes, block tubing, adhesives, elastic catheters, Rochelle salts, ammoniated mercury, acetic acid, mentholated spirits, Collodion, croton oil, extracts of ergot, turpentine, glycerine spirits and the like.

Rural medicine was more art than science, based more upon home care than hospital care, and reliant upon neighbours and mid-wives as much as, if not more than, doctors and nurses. Most families were large, death at birth was common, and most people preferred family care to a doctor's visit. As one local account recalls,

> *Each district had one or more unselfish neighbours of practical skill, who prescribed simple remedies for the various ailments. Through their intelligent interest and devoted care many were saved, but the death toll from Tuberculosis, Diphtheria, Scarlet Fever, Croup, Pneumonia and epidemics that frequently swept over the country, was heavy.*

These men did valuable work, but the midwives of Belfast exhibited a skill beyond praise. They were equal to every emergency. They never turned a deaf ear to a call for help and without the thought of reward they braved miles of miserable roads and bitter storms. Finally, when they made way for modern practitioners, they left behind a record of unselfish care and shill, rarely if ever, equaled under similar circumstances.

For the Island, and for Canada generally, the nineteenth century was a pre-industrial age, free of the black stench of coal dusts spewing out of furnaces and cluttering up people's sinuses. What promoted healthy living and longevity was not the presence of doctors and medicine but the effects of weather and an outdoor life style. In Europe and Britain, the cities were massively polluted, with terrible water, no drainage, and no underground sewers – Napoleon's construction in Paris was a notable exception. In Europe, city life showed a dramatic discrepancy in mortality rates, with differences between the middle class and the working poor. In England, a study in 1842 showed that children under five made up 62 per cent of the deaths of working class families, and the average age at death was 22, compared to double that level for middle class professionals. People lived in dirty neighbourhoods and filthy homes, accompanied by the excrements of dirty streets. Bad air or a stinking smell produced a new medical term, miasma, and bad air brought disease, what the Italians later called *mal aria* – bad air. It was a stark contrast to the open vistas of Canada, with clean air and water, abundant fresh food and vegetables, and a wide choice of fish, game, and meat.

On the Island, despite the economic poverty, there was little outright destitution and families had easy access to food of all sorts. Fresh berries were wild and in profusion, while lobster was seen as a poor man's food. All Catholics ate fish on Fridays, but the low cost, if not the Bible, inspired many Protestants to have fish on Fridays as well. In general, a large breakfast coupled with a hearty supper meal were the normal eating habits of Islanders, refreshed by clean air, abundant fresh water, and little processed foods. Horatio Nelson, the hero of

Trafalgar, a man who constantly suffered from scurvy, dysentery, tooth aches, and skin problems, spoke for many British when he stayed in Quebec. As he wrote to his father, "Health, that greatest of blessings, is what I never truly enjoyed until I saw Fair Canada. The change it has wrought, I am convinced, is truly wonderful. I most sincerely wish, dear Father, I could compliment you in the same way."

Nutrition on the Island was a rich blend of meats, fish, and dairy products, coupled with a wide assortment of vegetables and fresh fruit of all sorts, including apples, cherries, strawberries, blueberries, blackberries, and raspberries. In addition to remedies made at home, there was a surprising inventory in rural areas of self-medication, prepared at the Apothecaries' Hall: Mustang Linament, Conditioning powder, Podophylin, Holloways Pills, Beales Pills, Bitumen of Antimony, Blue Pills, Tr. Cantharidis, soothing syrup, Chloral Hydrate, Pills Colocynth, Tr. Asofoedeta, Pills Cath. Co., pain killer, Syrop of Red Spruce Gum, Tr. Arnica, Robinson's Emulsion of Cod Liver Oil, Wilson's Pills, Nervine Electric Oil, and Indian Blood Syrup. Coffee was scarce, and tea was available, but considered a luxury.

At the turn of the twentieth century, Island medicine had 80 doctors and three hospitals, with the senior doctors often sharing their diagnoses and prescriptions. It was not yet scientific, but it was more professional, thanks largely to one the Island's best known physicians, born and trained in Scotland, John Mackiesen, who practiced in Charlottetown for over 60 years. He was widely known, not only by his peers, but he served both the rich and the poor. He kept detailed records of his cases, including the remedies and diseases, and his treatments. The second was Sir Andrew Macphail, originally from Orwell Corner, which was in the heart of the Selkirk settlements on Lot 57. He was the first editor of the *Canadian Medical Association Journal*, and so had the advantage of a teaching post at McGill, which he used to compare the evolution of Canadian medicine from the dual perspective of his travels and his Island homestead.

***

From the earliest days of settlement in North America, doctors had an air of mystery about them. They were men of superior education, sympathetic to God's natural order, witness to how medicines might help the patient, but always aware that nature might take its course. Unlike politicians and preachers, whose stock in trade was fiery oratory and the ambiguity of the clear statement, doctors spoke with quiet, clear and soothing voices, providing help and comfort in their home visits. Of course, it did not hurt that their black case was full of universal pain remedies like morphine, digitalis, and rum or whiskey. These were the doctor's tools and families understood the natural order. Doctor's prescriptions, scribbled with mostly illegible hand writing, probably learned in high school from badly learned MacLean method of writing with a Palmer script, further reinforced the barrier to comprehension with frequent use of metric weights and Latin notations. In surgery, doctors had few tools to work with, with anaesthetic agents such as ether and chloroform poorly understood and often mal-administered. As one of Napoleon's surgeons, Andre Paré, put it: "I merely dressed his wounds; God healed them." William Osler, the giant of modern medicine, and the founder of scientific medicine at McGill, where so many Island doctors were educated, put the matter this way: "the medicine of the surgeon was better than the surgery of the physician and in the rural areas, of course, the general practitioner reigns supreme."

Island medicine before the twentieth century was also a mixture of science and art, of quackery and skilled judgment. The rural nature of doctor-patient relations meant that doctors were anything but specialized, and they saw a wide range of ailments and diseases. For most patients, rural medicine often meant that God's work proceeded through the calendar of the seasons, with farming and fishing through the six months of April-October, and cutting timber, preparing traps and boats, fixing the farm machinery, and house repair during the winter. Both doctors and patients understood PEI's natural bounty "plenty of fruit, pure water, pure air, and pure food," as one Island doctor put it. Perhaps Voltaire said it best: "The art of medicine consists of amusing the patient while nature cures the disease".

There was also an acute awareness of nature's life cycle, and patients relished the unique power of house calls from a visiting doctor. The industrializing ways of Upper Canada, or to some degree, Charlottetown, changed God's orientation to time and space. Farmers and fisherman spoke of the seasons, the lunar calendar, dawn and dusk, the tides and the wind, the rainy season and The Big Dipper. The Sabbath Day provided the beginning of the week. Each Sabbath was a religious holiday named after a saint. Babies were often given a name that often combined the Saints name and the father's first name for the first son. Families knew that, with many children, the first few months of life were critical.

This natural life cycle reached out to the rural communities in other ways. Most people knew that medicine was a funny business. Doctors knew the old mantra: "Bleed, cup, and blister; purge, physic, and clyster". For the first part of a person's life, doctors took away things from the body - babies from mothers; tonsils, teeth, abscess, fixtures like the appendix, gallstones and amputations of all sorts. They knew that in the second half of the life cycle, doctors added things to the body, from glasses to false teeth, and hip replacements to transplants. The tools of medicine were secondary - from vaccines and antibiotics to the placement of surgery, namely a kitchen table, only later to become a hospital bed. Superstition and mysticism never really disappeared from the early Island immigrants, many of whom were illiterate and uneducated. Religion thus was a close partner to medicine, and became more so as the doctor-patient relation had a simple rule - longevity if possible, pain relief if necessary. Doctors were like the clergy, in that they worked long hours, traveled from farm to farm, and were paid little. Rural doctors might charge $200 per year, and collected only a fraction as cash payment, with food produce being a suitable substitute.

Island medicine has progressed as the medical story of Canada has unfolded. The early years were based around the lone, traveling doctor, of doctors and health professionals, mainly nurses but also religious orders like the Gray Nuns, attempting to deal with God's maladies in a humane fashion. Until recent history, medical practice was a catalogue of enormous judgment of the disease itself and of the patient. There were few instruments available to provide total practice, and the handful of 'medicines' available for dispensary that had known therapeutic advantages. The doctor's tools were often primitive by modern standards, but helped make medical diagnosis more focused, and included the six inch clinical thermometer, the stethoscope (an instrument designed by a French doctor to listen to chest problems, since Etiquette prevented him from putting his ear to a woman's chest!), blood pressure from a sphygmomanometer, microscopes, and chloroform, which became widely accepted when Queen Victoria's fourth son, Leopold, was delivered with chloroform.

During the nineteenth century, the Island population grew steadily, from only 5000 people in 1800 to roughly 80,000 in 1880. More immigrant doctors arrived and were equitably spread out across the three counties and parishes of the Island as they settled into practice. Medicine was never seen as a path to riches, unless, of course, the patient was a man of wealth or royalty. The doctors of King George III, for instance, were notable for their time with *this* patient, on whom they contributed little, except their exceptionally high fees. When King George III at last died, blind, senile, bearded, and spending his last six years 'in a world of his own', the medical bills were an outrageous £271,691 18s, echoing the lines of Hillaire Belloc's poem: "They murmured, as they took their fees; there is no cure for this disease.' These court doctors gave the medical profession a bad name, what today would be considered an inferior brand. Island immigrants seemed to understand this issue; many Islanders were very reluctant to pay their bills.

Until the federal Medicare program became a public institution, most doctors had an exceptionally high level of unpaid bills, usually marked 'accounts receivable'. Despite this, Islanders were receiving all that medical science had to offer. The real problem was that the science of medicine had yet to make many breakthroughs, either through the physical sciences of biology, physics, and chemistry, or in the emerging field of pharmaceuticals with new drugs like penicillin and insulin. As Cyril Sinnott puts it, "Older people still say of their beloved physician, 'he never refused to come, no matter what time it was.' It was good public relations and it was comforting to the patient because after all, that was the most important thing the doctor could do for him. A soothing voice and a sympathetic ear were the best weapons in his armamentarium."

Island doctors were pillars of the Church, and for good reason. However much medical practice had to offer to succour the patient, doctors knew the spiritual side of medicine was real. For many in the medical profession, there was an intricate relationship between medicine and religion. They understood the scientific side of medicine, like the doctors in Edinburgh in the nineteenth century performing autopsies, as well as the art side of medicine, what a doctor can do, and what is best left to nature. Everyday, doctors and nurses – the core of the modern health system – are called to help defeat an external enemy, the bacteria that cause infectious diseases. But they are also called to help the patient heal the body, to heal itself. Wounds, injuries, bone fractures, and even heart attacks or strokes – these medical challenges may be subject to the self-healing properties of the human body if given rest, nutrition, warmth, and time.

These remedies are as old as medicine itself, and were well understood by the aboriginal communities, as well documented by the French explorers. They suggest a *spiritualelement* to the practice of medicine, what the anatomist, John Hunter, called a 'vital spirit' and what William Osler himself called the *vis medicitrix naturae* – the healing power of nature. Modern Islanders understood the three day ritual of religious faith - matching, hatching and dispatching - but doctors well understood that these rituals were the life cycle of medical disorders, especially for children and mothers at birth, disease and disorders at death, and communicable disease for married and unmarried adults. They were also unwitting witnesses to one of the great scams of the North American economy, rum running, prohibition, and the alcohol trade.

****

The modern era of scientific medicine started in the 1950s, when "antibiotics, intervertebral disc disease, Rh factor, cardiac or vascular surgery, transplants, early ambulation or psychosomatic disease" sparked enormous scientific and technological progress, as one Island doctor put it to the McGill School of Medicine, and at first glance seems a long way from alcohol prohibition, the Temperance societies, bootlegging, and rum running. Perversely, there is a linkage. Throughout Island history, alcohol was a standard potion used by doctors to warm the stomach, endure a medical operation, and outlast the nerves of a pulled tooth. In England, workhouse infirmaries for cholera patients allowed nurses better food and more gin for their work, but if there was a corpse to be laid out, nurses received extra glasses of gin, or brandy, a stimulant used in cholera cases. For a hundred years, politicians coped with the distinctions between the wets and the dry, between those who thought access to alcohol was an essential part of British freedom, like a shot of rum aboard Her Majesty's ships, and those who wanted a ban on alcohol sales. Yet there was constant worry about the perverse effects of alcohol consumption, and argued the merits and demerits of these addictions which might corrupt the Island way of life.

Throughout the North American colonies, alcohol production and consumption were prodigious, as was the case in the major cities of Europe. It was an age before refrigeration and sanitation, so food was often stale, putrid or foul. Any visitor was invited to a drink, both in the morning, at noon, or during the night, usually because coffee, tea or soft drinks were not available or inordinately expensive. At the turn of the eighteenth century, alcohol production was probably three gallons per year for every man, woman and child. In war and battle, liquor provided courage and comfort to the injured. As early as 1826, church ministries in Boston organized a group called the American Society for the Promotion of Temperance, which became a mainstay of other temperance crusaders who would seek through lectures, press campaigns, school texts, public speeches, and essay contests to reduce or eliminate the impact of the Demon rum. Pledges were volunteered by asking for a T beside a signature – T stood for Total Abstinence, hence the phrase "Teetotaler".

Alcohol influenced every aspect of Island communities, encompassing their religious outlook, the role of government, political electioneering, what was taught in schools, and the practice of medicine! Traditionally, alcohol had many uses and was therefore widely available. When the British took over the Island in the 18th century, gin was widely available. Indeed, London and smaller port cities like Liverpool and Bristol reeked of gin. The British navy was run on a quotient of seaworthiness, on "measured amounts of rank food and to drink much liquor." In 1819, a Scottish immigrant, John McGregor, operated a merchant business in Charlottetown and advertised in the *Gazette* his intention to sell a stock from Halifax, "largely gin, rum, and dry goods, 'sold cheaply for cash'"

Across the Atlantic seaboard, West Indian rum was widely available, cheap to buy, and easy to store. Even better, Caribbean molasses was also in abundance, shipped in oak barrels, a useful device to skim a portion of the contents to be made into a home-made rum with a small distillery boiler. The merchant class throughout the region, despite their professed religious fervour, had no intention of supporting anything that would restrict the rum trade with the West Indies. In the years surrounding Confederation, there were no shortage of taverns, saloons and general stores which served liquor, and the hotels throughout the Island kept a good stock on hand. The Victorian Hotel in Charlottetown had a reputation for splendour and service, with "the liquids that were exceptionable".

As far back as 1841, there were scattered attempts to deal with alcoholism, insobriety, and related afflictions. The St. Dunstan's Total Abstinence Society, an outgrowth of attempts in Ireland to deal with such issues, the Irish Total Abstinence Movement, was an early organization. By 1877, Bishop Peter MacIntyre, the third Bishop of Charlottetown, sent a Pastoral Letter to the local body on PEI:

> *We seek to establish Total Abstinence Societies in every*
> *Parish in our Diocese, and we desire to serve every*
> *Catholic in the land a member of some one of them;*
> *moveover, we wish to have a bond of brotherly love*
> *linking each society to the other, and unity of action*
> *secured...we rely on your pastoral zeal in carrying*
> *out our wishes. Redouble your labours in the cause*
> *of Temperance, for you will know that drunkenness is*
> *one of the besetting sins of our time....*

In 1898, Canada had a federal plebiscite on prohibition, with large majorities in favour throughout the Maritimes. With weak support in Quebec, Prime Minister Laurier decided not to act. The local temperance forces, strengthened by the Social Gospel movement of the Protestant religions, attempted to change social policies in such areas as labour rights, education, and public morals, in an attempt to address the roots of abuse. Prince Edward Island adopted Prohibition under the local-option provisions of the federal Scott Act of 1878. As Marlene-Russell Clark records, the Prohibition Act of 1900, while bringing the entire province under the terms of temperance legislation, indeed as the first province to embrace prohibition, had other effects, and its enforcement was dutifully lax:

> *The Lieutenant-Governor-in-Council appointed wholesale vendors, who would sell liquor to druggists, chemists, physicians, and clergymen, while government-appointed inspectors would enforce the legislation. Physicians were issued with certificates that indicated alcoholic prescriptions were to be used as medicine and not as a beverage. Maximum daily doses of such medicine were also spelled out in the law, although these ultimate limits were liberally generous. Druggists who sold liquor for these health purposes were obliged to keep records of such sales, while the government inspectors were authorized to examine the prescriptions and records of the local pharmacists...*

> *...Rum-running became a profitable profession, even though its dangers exceeded the boundaries of monetary and penal punishments, for law enforcers used their fire arms to impede offenders. Some medical practioners (sic) readily parted with their government-issued booklets of prescription certificates – for a suitable fee. Local bootlegging thrived in many imaginative ways. The ingenious owners of one country estate, equipped with a crude but effective plumbing system, escaped detection*

*and inevitable prosecution for liquor trafficking:
the water pipes in the bard were filled with stronger
refreshments for the consumption of visitors, rather
than the resident livestock. Many were the fortunes
resting on liquid foundations. And many were the
sick who called on their family doctor for the more
legitimate alcohol prescription – for medicinal
purposes, naturally!*

The Island was influenced by what neighbouring provinces were doing with the liquor trade and what the US was considering, especially with American Prohibition laws and the passage of the *Volstad Act*, which took effect on January 16, 1920. For most Island politicians, alcohol sales, like issues of abortion, capital punishment, gun control, or language legislation, was a no-win situation. There were strong positions on both sides and facts usually gave way to religious beliefs, social causes, or an obstinate refusal to see the consequences. Numerous elections were held on the issue, and there were plebiscites held as far back as 1880. Between 1879 and 1894, Charlottetown alone had five plebiscites.

Regardless of the views of the wet and the dry factions, external factors also played their part. As in most affairs of business and economics, the Americans impacted the whole Continent, from the brothels and gambling joints of Cuba to the lucrative cross-border rum trade from Canada, with the Island and the Maritimes sharing in the wealth. In the end, Americans ended national prohibition in 1933. While it lasted, US prohibition was a godsend to the nefarious bootleggers in Canada, including what was a disproportionately long list in PEI. With the American government banning alcohol sales through national prohibition, an immense industry developed in Canada, ranging from distilleries who manufactured the liquor, whisky and rum in particular, and the schooners who plied the waters of the Gulf of St. Lawrence to deliver the illegal goods to the hotels, bars, speakeasies, saloons, and illegal stores which sold the precious cargo. This was the demon rum trade.

Because drinking was illegal, both the federal government and the provincial governments had to enforce the various acts. It was often a legal circus, a combination of an evening in a jail (a good deal, with free food and a warm bed), lawyers, search warrants, judges and any number of people who patrolled the wharfs. It was a good economic stimulus, financing policemen who patrolled the sheds where the illegal cargo could be stored as evidence, hotels where the Mounties had to be billeted, and the restaurants which provided the food for the "smugglers class" while they waited for the court appearance, fittingly in a warmly heated jail cell. The tales of fishing schooners that plied the waters between ports like Port Aux Basques, Newfoundland, St. Pierre, Sydney, Cape Breton, Lunenburg, and the ports on the St. Lawrence – the *Nellie J. Banks* was one of the most notable – included celebrated court cases focused upon who could pick the right jury, obfuscation of legal boundaries, and choosing the right site for the court case. In PEI, shrewd legal talent like Frank McPhee, Lester O'Donnell, J. O.C. Campbell, J.J. Johnston, and Reg Bell knew how to question evidence, complicate jurisdictions, limit cash bail, and choose jury members on the knowledge that hard-drinking men, unlike a jury of prohibitionists, not to mention their political views, might get their client released.

Prohibition, in fact, was direct economic stimulus in action, an accelerated push of Ottawa's spending through the economic system. American whiskey traders and leading Canadian tradesman, including four members of the Bronfman family (the so-called Montreal Group), all visited the Island, by mean fair or foul, in pursuit of the whiskey trade, by mean legal or illegal. Ottawa's capability to deal with rum-running was a mix of studied indifference, legal confusion, and questionable enforcement, but even so some people were convicted, even if only with a light sentence. As one Judge said of an Island felon,

> *This man has no support, friend or family,*
> *He has no assets, real or personal,*
> *And no hope, here or in the hereafter.*

Of course, despite prohibition, alcohol sales couldn't be abandoned altogether. For one thing, PEI was a Christian province and religious observances, including the Catholic mass, required wine. There were more needs, such as industrial uses for alcohol, for use in purification for instance. To top it off, alcohol was also a medicine. Talk about a loophole! As one letter to the government warned:

> *We the undersigned residents of Cardigan and vicinity voice our protests of the abuse of the present Liquor Law. It now happens that we have no doctor nearer than Montague or Georgetown, and it happens that those doctors have not sufficient scripts to accommodate the people in their respective towns...*

During Prohibition, the government allowed doctors 50 scripts per month. The popular term was chits, a short form for prescriptions. The scripts allowed doctors and vets a monthly quotient, a truly Heaven-sent gift to the medical profession. Clearly, the scripts helped to advance medical science, through abundant investigation of the therapeutic effects of one or more potions of rum, gin, or rye. Three-star brandy was a special treat, a favoured expression used to describe this good stuff. Needless to say, the medical profession was in no mood to have the chits limited by government, especially when so many patients needed quality booze for relief from injuries, various diseases, and odd ailments.

Over the years, politics maintained a virtuous hypocrisy towards the sale of alcohol. By religion, Catholics typically went with the flow, but some Protestant groups, notably Baptists and the Church of Christ, were adamant in their protests. Another group protested to Walter Jones, the Premier from 1943-1953, and left no ambiguity in their position:

> *We the members of the Woman's Missionary Society of the Presbyterian Church of Canada, Alberton, have respectfully requested that your government refrain and if possible strengthen and enforce stringent by the present Provincial Prohibition Law. And we request further that Temperance Education be imported regularly with the aid and a suitable book, in all our public schools.*

In 1945, the government attempted to reform medical prescriptions through a motion known as the Eugene Cullen amendment, where the script would last six months and allow the patient a set remedy to treat his illness, administered through a bottle of spirits, nine quarts of beer, or 104 ounces of wine. Despite its passage in the Legislature, the Lieutenant-Governor, B.W. LePage, refused to sign it. By 1948, a new law was passed that effectively ended PEI's long dry spell. The government established public liquor boards, but alcohol purchases required a "permit". Ever inventive, most Islanders filled out a government form for each purchase with their personal "number"- i.e. the telephone number in reverse order. The quality of Island moonshine was legendary, with Morell Rear in King's country and Holman Island near Summerside renowned as outstanding sites. So were some of the homes of some prominent citizens. In this respect, the former days of scientific medicine came to an end. There was still a great deal of booze available through smuggling, safe houses, and bootleggers. In the 1950s, at one dinner and dance at Government House, the Lieutenant-Governor's liquor supply was seen as a tad light, with the punch bowl laced with more fruit juice than vodka, despite the profusion of liquor stashed in the parked cars of the Charlottetown elite. Not undaunted, a few of the notables conspired to order a proper supply of booze for the guests. They called the local bootleggers and had the liquor delivered by a local taxi to Government House, much like ordering a pizza today.

There was no shortage of beer, sold by the cask, and plenty of whisky, plus home made distilled potato vodka widely known as moonshine. Whisky, of course, was valued as a medicine, a cleanser, and an antiseptic, what Islanders might call a household necessity. Many farmwives were experts at elder-flower wine or fruit preserves, as Lucy Maud Montgomery showed in her novel, *Anne of Green Gables*. Blueberries were found throughout the Island, and there was no absence of a stilled blueberry drink, widely known as a tasty (and abundant) gin drink. Scottish Presbyterians, in particular, took a balanced view towards alcohol consumption, seeing it as 'the product of the earth's bounty', according to Scriptures (Ps.104), and one of God's blessings. Drink in moderation was a sign of hospitality and civility, while drink in excess was a shameful misuse of God's blessing. There was a popular Gaelic saying on the Island about a dram of whisky: the first drink is a welcoming drink; the second drink is a strengthening drink, but the third drink is a shameful drink. In Charlottetown, away from the farm life and the long farm days, there were far too many shameful drinks.

*****

By 1900, virtually all of PEI had access to medical services, either by doctors who lived in local communities, or by doctors whose specialty or experience allowed them to travel to the rural areas to make house calls. In fact, more doctors lived outside Charlottetown than in the city. Medical payment was anything but shared, as doctors clung to their patients and families like a dog to a bone. Obviously, resident location and travel directly conditioned the doctor-patient relationship. For the doctor, a patient was more than a person; it was the entire family as a group, and patients had long memories.

Until after World War II, most individual doctors treated a variety of problems. There was little real specialization on the part of the doctor, although new techniques like eye treatment became a preserve of doctors like J.P. Lantz, who pioneered new procedures in otolaryngology and ophthalmology. His patients included Catholics and Protestants, Liberals and Conservatives. On such matters, what is required is usually never banned. Even in the early half of the 20th century, as more patients were admitted to hospitals, rather than being treated at home, and thus signed in by the doctor on call, it was customary for senior doctors to alter the chart the next morning to denote the family doctor in charge. At this time, senior doctors kept a tight grip on the hierarchy of the profession, including outside nods from government. This pecking order lasted until after 1945, when the older doctors began to die or gave way to their juniors, who may be the most qualified.

Rural house calls were, of course, common, with doctors having a team of horses on call, sometimes with a driver. When the Island railroad opened after 1872, many of the house calls were conducted by rail, with the doctor accompanying the patient on the train to the hospital. To outsiders, the Island may seem small, but until well into the 20th century, most roads were unpaved, and thus impassable for about 6-7 months a year, with rain, mud, ice and snow, not to mention snow drifts, making transportation uncertain for days at a time. Here the doctor was in a bind, as doctors who refused to do house calls suffered from the reputation of unkindness. In turn, the doctors who did do house calls were quickly in demand. As Dr. Gordon Lea puts it, "the fact that he responded to the distress call did not ensure that the family would seek his services under different and less trying circumstances; not until he was once more needed in response to a distress home call, might he hear from them again. In general, however, the vast majority of such calls were very necessary and very genuine and there was no more rewarding experience in medicine than the thanks expressed on such occasion."

For most of the nineteenth century, Island medicine consisted of a mix of kindness, thoughtfulness, home remedies, and the special skills of a surgeon (bone fractures, obstetrics, hernia, tonsillitis, ruptured appendix). It was not scientific medicine, as it was conventionally viewed only a generation later. Island doctors came from the leading medical centers, Edinburgh, Harvard, Toronto, and McGill. The art side of medicine, outside basic surgical procedures for appendicitis, obstetrics, bone fractures, tumours, kidney abscess, and minor operations like tonsillitis, tooth removal, or amputations required a comforting voice, a quiet demeanour, and a steady hand.

The rural life was indeed harsh. Many families had little formal education, and farming and fishing required hazardous chores that caused innumerable accidents. The good news was that medical practice was widespread, for rich and poor, quite independent of social standing. The doctors knew each other by name or reputation, and some doctors were particularly good at sharing information on new procedures and new remedies. New techniques were tried, as often the alternative was immediate fatality. Unlike many other professions, the medical community was not divided by religious practices. Unlike the legal profession, for instance, the medical community shared their experiences, and followed the Hippocratic Oath as the guiding light of the profession, as professed by Osler himself: "No other profession can boast of the same unbroken continuity of ideals that stretch back

281

to the critical sense as established by the Hippocratic school: we may indeed by justly proud of our apostolic succession. There are our methods .. *this our work* – to prevent disease, to relieve suffering, and to heal the sick."

Nineteenth century rural medicine as delivered by doctors in the farm house changed dramatically at the start of the 20th century. It was not yet the Golden Age of Medical Science that came after 1945, but medicine, like industry, was starting a dramatic leap in culture and innovation. Forty years after Confederation, more than 95 percent of all births in Canada took place at home. Tellingly, ninety percent of all Canadian doctors had no college education; instead, they attended so-called medical schools, many of which were condemned in the press and by the government as "substandard." Five leading causes of death were pneumonia and influenza, tuberculosis, diarrhea, heart disease and stroke. Marijuana, heroin, and morphine were all available over the counter at the local corner drugstores. Among pharmacists, there was a common saying: "Heroin clears the complexion, gives buoyancy to the mind, regulates the stomach and bowels, and is, in fact, a perfect guardian of health." Two out of every 10 Canadian adults could not read or write, and only 6 percent of all Canadians had graduated from high school.

Perhaps no event changed the practice of medicine forever in PEI in the same way as the opening of a hospital. In this period, it was not circumstantial that, like Quebec, it was the Catholic Church that took responsibility to build a hospital, with the direct support of the third Bishop of Charlottetown, Peter McIntyre. The facility was called the Sacred Heart Hospital, and opened on September 19, 1879. The first patient was an Irish peddler, James Flynn, who was admitted on October 17 with a laceration of the leg. He was discharged in April 1880. A second hospital with 12 beds opened in March 1883 in Charlottetown, on a non-sectarian basis, for the benefit of the whole province. In those days, hospitals had less impact on doctor-patient relations; a hospital was seen more as a treatment center for the chronically ill. Rural Islanders saw hospitals as a place to die, and thus avoided them.

There was good reason. For one thing, as the flow of European settlers increased by the mid-1850s, spurred in part by the millions of wretchedly poor people who fled Ireland due to the potato famine, immigrants were quarantined on the North American side of the Atlantic Ocean, in Ellis Island in New York, in Boston, in Grosse Île in the St. Lawrence, in Halifax and Pictou, and in Charlottetown. Immigrant ships were grossly unhealthy, poorly equipped, and overcrowded, often with both imported farm animals (horses, sheep, and cattle) and people as passengers. Many immigrants had severe health problems before they reached the immigrant ships, and often carried smallpox and other infectious diseases when they reached the North American shores. On the Island, the government established a marine hospital at Trout Point near the entrance to the Charlottetown Harbour. It was roughly a half mile from *Redcliffe*, the imposing home owned by Rear Admiral Bayfield, which adjoined the Keppoch Farm built by James and Andrew Duncan, two prominent shipbuilders and members of the Family Compact. All ships anchored near the Marine Hospital, for examination of small pox among the passengers and sailors.

It was well into the twentieth century that hospitals - both in Charlottetown and in Summerside (which opened first as a hotel, and then a hospital in 1912) - became medical centers focused around specialized equipment. What changed the medical profession's role in hospitals was the impact of new medical schools and their links to universities. By the turn of the century, McGill University was the preferred choice for Island students who wanted to become doctors, in the same way that Laval University was the preferred choice for Catholic students who wished to take graduate school. The McGill connection was developed almost by accident. As a university, McGill had achieved prominence in Quebec, despite public support for French universities like the Université de Montréal and Laval.

McGill had benefactors, however, in people like Lord Strathcona and Lord Mount-Stephen, and later, Sir William MacDonald from PEI. MacDonald was the grandson of Captain John MacDonald, who brought Highland settlers to PEI in 1772. McGill was founded in 1802, and even operates today as the Royal Institution for the Advancement of Learning, based on a Quebec statute. In 1811, James McGill donated £10,000, plus his family estate. In 1821, McGill received a Royal Charter, but James McGill's will was challenged in the courts. To settle the legal claim, the Royal Corporation incorporated the Montreal Medical Institution and McGill University started as the first medical faculty, incorporating the Montreal General Hospital. By 1823, the first students were admitted, using the curriculum originally developed at the University of Edinburgh. It was the first medical school in North America where teaching was clinical and students had free access to hospital wards.

By reputation, if not in finances, McGill prospered. By the time William Osler reorganized the medical curriculum at the end of the 19th century, McGill was recognized as one of the great centers of medicine, with a curriculum that was emulated by other universities, including Harvard Medical School. Osler's textbook, *Principles and Practice of Medicine*, a 1050 page tome with 270 pages devoted to infectious diseases, published in 1892, revolutionized medical education, not simply because of its clear language, but because Osler understood that medical knowledge was indeed imprecise, and there were uncertainties. His book played the same role that Paul Samuelson's economic textbook, *Economics*, performed in 1948, educating thousands of medical practitioners around the world, including at John Hopkins where he moved in 1888, and then to Oxford in 1905. (As one reviewer noted about Samuelson's textbook, which applied equally to Osler's work, 'having sought fame, now seeks fortune'. Both authors did extremely well from the royalties of their textbooks.) Osler died at Oxford in 1918, perhaps the world's best known physician, of pneumonia, a fatal disease at that time for the elderly, in a world without penicillin.

As already noted, thanks to William Osler at McGill, and its access to the Montreal General Hospital dating back to 1823, Montreal had the first real medical school, modeled on the practices of Edinburgh. The school had 25 students, the teaching was clinical, and it was the first time in North America that the students had open access to the hospital wards. Medicine itself was to become specialized, split into maternity wards, children's wards, infection diseases, tuberculosis, insane asylums, pathology and the like. New medical specialties from the university teaching hospitals and medical schools had profound effects for Canadian healthcare, but in the early days, these were not so evident. Even American medical schools, at least outside Philadelphia and John Hopkins (where Osler had a powerful influence), diagnostic medicine was a bit like cooking, in that it depended on the ingredients. At Harvard, for instance, in 1870, a student could qualify for a medical degree by attending two lectures every four months, proving three years of medical experience, and passing a simple examination. Harvard's President, Charles Elliot, soon insisted on British practice, namely three years of class attendance, together with laboratory and clinical work. In Britain, medical education was equally hap-hazard, and tuition cost about £400, or much less if the apprentice doctor toiled in the hospital wards or worked as a junior to a doctor. Often it was his father or uncle, since Victorian medicine often ran in the family. Everywhere, hospitals needed more than buildings; they needed new forms of equipment, new forms of care (including antiseptic treatment), and new forms of medical personnel.

A close colleague of Osler was the Island doctor, already cited as a literary figure, Andrew Macphail, who graduated from McGill in 1891, with a specialty in pathology, a topic of special concern for Osler. Macphail was a superb writer, and put himself through university as a reporter for the Montreal *Gazette*. He became student editor of the *University Magazine*, a journal which attracted many writers, including Stephen Leacock, who came from the same area outside of Toronto as William Osler. Macphail became editor of the *Montreal Medical Journal*, later amalgamated with the *Maritime Medical News*, a journal which attracted many articles by Island doctors. The new publication was the *Canadian Medical Association Journal* in 1911, with Macphail in charge as editor. A later editorial, with this Editor's clever words, discussing the new *British Health Insurance Act of 1912*, was both direct and prescient:

> *When this state of affairs comes about, a spirit of charity will be replaced by a cold, official atmosphere. When physicians become civil servants, those who*

> *are particularly adapted for healing the sick will*
> *be automatically forced out of the service and into*
> *private practice. The rich will be the gainers and the*
> *last state of the poor will be worse than the first.*

In addition to Macphail, McGill boasted two other Islanders who held influential positions in Montreal: Dr. Alvah Gordon, head of the Department of Medicine at the Montreal General, and Dr. D.W. MacKenzie, head of Urology at the Royal Victoria Hospital. Each in their own way cultivated connections for their native province. Leacock, in the hierarchy of universities, worked with another Islander, Cyrus Macmillan, English Professor and then Dean of Arts and Sciences at McGill. Later he ran for the federal Liberal Party and spent a year as Minister of Fisheries. Dr. W.J.P. MacMillan, a future Island Premier and head of the PEI Medical Society, was a Holmes Gold Medal winner (top student) in 1911, the second Islander to achieve this honour (the first was Dr. Alex MacNeill from Summerside).

Another Islander, to continue the long McGill connection to Island medicine, and the third doctor to win the Holmes Gold Medal, in 1938 (and the Lieutenant Governors Medal) was Dr. Joseph A. McMillan, no relation either to Cyrus Macmillan or Dr. W.J. P. but a colleague at the Charlottetown Hospital. His brother, Frank, also graduated from McGill. A surgeon, he was known affectionately as Dr. Joe, and would become a leading figure in CMA medical circles, turning down a chance to be the President in 1964. He was the first Canadian to receive the CMA Medal of Service, awarded for "service to the profession in the field of medical organization; for service to the people of Canada in raising the standards of medical practice; for personal contributions to the advancement of the art and science of medicine." By 1912, Canada had a new Dominion Medical Council, which issued a diploma and a license usable anywhere in Canada or throughout the British Empire. By 1934, the Canadian Medical Directory listed all the hospitals throughout Canada and the medical faculties - ten in total.

Doctors faced new methods of training, as the lessons of William Osler crept into the medical school curriculum. Hospitals became the new fixture for delivery of medical services, and there were a plethora of new medical instruments, notably the microscope, and new medical specializations, including pathology, cardiology, and neurosurgery. Medicine was just starting the process of discovering new drugs for epidemics, thanks to the vaccines discovered by Louis Pasteur in Paris, scientific work in Berlin, and the new medical schools in Canada and the US. It wasn't too far behind the discovery of the potent wonder drug, penicillin, which opened new paths for laboratory testing. In the US and in Montreal, there were powerful advances in chemistry and biology, and study of diseases like tuberculosis, a terrible affliction that left 100 people dead in PEI alone in 1920. The flu epidemic of 1918, which started in a military camp in Utah, caused 20 million people to die. Even Government House in Charlottetown became a hospital site.

Sectarian concerns in schooling and politics were common on the Island. In medicine, however, at least initially, many doctors practiced at the PEI Hospital and the Charlottetown Hospital, one Protestant, and one Catholic. At one point, Dr. Stephen R. Jenkins became Chief of Staff to both hospitals and was the first Islander to become President of the Canadian Medical Association. Specialization was the key to medical practice at the hospitals, and common treatments such as appendectomies, cholectstectomies, hysterectomies and hernia repairs. From Lister spray units to methods of delivering anaesthetic, hospitals gradually became the focus of acute testing from 1900 onward. Across Canada, hospitals faced a constant process of expansion, better equipment, and new skills as their roles changed. As Dr. Gordon Lea records in his history of Island Medicine, "by the mid-nineteenth century, hospitals were slowly emerging from the role they had performed since the middles ages of being refugees for the dying, to become institutions for the treatment of disease; from being places where death almost always awaits its denizens, to places where recovery and cure could be expected to occur."

Dr. John Theophilus Jenkins, born in Charlottetown, joined the Crimean conflict, where he was decorated by both the British and Turkish governments. He was the first Island-born physician, and first of a three generation medical family. He was educated in London, and became a member of the Royal College of Surgeons, with special interest in eye diseases, and a student of C.J. Guthries at Westminster Ophthalmic Hospital. He practiced on the Island until his death in 1919. One of his sons, Stephen, born in 1858, graduated from medical school at the University of Pennsylvania. His son, in turn, graduated from McGill and interned at the Royal Victoria Hospital, becoming the third generation of physician known on the Island as Dr. Jenkins.

The events in the Crimean War seemed a long way from the Island, but the Government of George Coles proposed a grant of £2000 for the relief of widows and orphans, a staggering sum in those days. The Government motion, presented on February 22, 1855, was accepted, with three members opposing. Edward Whelan's memorial speech to the Legislature on the "Patriotic Fund" outlined in remarkable detail the military and diplomatic events of this Crimean conflict, and led to the presentation to Whelan of a richly-framed engraving of Florence Nightingale, which he kept in his home at St. Peter's.

Nineteenth century medicine was singularly a masculine profession. Surgeons, doctors, pathologists, dentists and morticians, almost without exception, came from the weaker sex. One person alone changed that circumstance. Her name was Florence Nightingale. When England was at war in the Crimea, in 1855, the English War Minister, Sidney Hubert, sent this young girl, the product of an upper class family and formerly a writer, to the Crimea in an official capacity. She quickly organized a permanent base hospital, starting the day before the Battle of Inkerman. By coincidence, this was the same battle attended by the future Father of Confederation, Col. John Hamilton Gray. He was immortalized by a street name off North River Road in Charlottetown, with his splendid home, Inkerman House, where he entertained the delegates at the Charlottetown Conference in September 1864.

With a burning desire to do good, her characteristic organization, a nurse's sense of immediacy, and scanty equipment, Florence Nightingale mobilized her efforts to reduce the death rate at Scutari from 42 per hundred to 22 per thousand men. She had spent time in Germany and France studying training for nurses, visiting

Kaiserswirth, a Lutheran training school, as well as the Sisters of Charity in Paris. She learned much, but England and Victorian Society weren't much interested. However, a breakout of cholera in London, coupled with the splendid articles by William Russell in the *Times* on the inhuman conditions of British soldiers at the hospital at Scutari led to her invitation, or summons, to go to the war zone.

Given the horrible casualties of the utterly futile battles of the Crimean War, when both sides were completely unprepared, there were more than 500,000 killed for Russia, Turkey, Britain and France – a bitter lesson unheeded for future mass wars. Islanders enlisted on the British side, and another large contingent from Nova Scotia fought in the protracted siege of Sevastopol. Florence Nightingale became a beacon among all combatants. When Russia sued for peace (a foretaste of that country's political problems, and one of the reasons the US purchased Aaska for only $7.5 million), the delegates at the Peace Congress in Paris established the Red Cross movement. She emerged as one of the few persons with an enhanced reputation. Additionally, with the Red Cross movement came the Geneva Convention in 1864 which, with updating and refinements, remains even today as the universally accepted code of international conflicts, providing a generally accepted model of medical relief, with field hospitals, medical treatment, and medical personnel, especially for a new profession, nursing.

Unfortunately, while the Crimean War helped produce the nursing profession and the Red Cross, it had another casualty for the cause of better medicine, the emergence of tobacco as a common medical addiction. In Britain, this war was partly disguised as a combination of aristocratic officers behaving like buffoons, and working class poor, mostly Irish and Scots, heading towards their martyrdom, to be immortalized in the famous poetry of the time, such as the *Charge of the Light Brigade*. Eventually, this would lead to the rise of a future British Labour Party, widespread working class consciousness, and an unfortunate new medical ailment, smoking. Tobacco, of course, has a long trans-Atlantic history, introduced to England by Sir Walter Raleigh, but the popularity of smoking grew during the Crimean War.

Russian soldiers had their little scorchers, the *papirosi*, afterwards called *Moscows* in London, and *Tom Thumbs* and *The Whiff*, selling 25 for a shilling. The Assistant Surgeon to Prince Albert's Light Infantry had felt that the decline of the Ottoman Empire arose from Turkey's love of cigarettes. By 1880, a Bristol firm pioneered the first Bonsack cigarette machine, leading to penny cigarettes, cheap smokes, and the medical affliction of the world's working class. As the financier Warren Buffett would later comment, "You make a product for a penny, you sell it for a dollar and you sell it to addicts." Doctors knew the harmful affects of smoking, especially on skin, muscles, and the heart, but it would take the death of King George VI in 1952, who was demonstrably a heavy smoker, to galvanise medical knowledge towards the study of non-infectious diseases caused by smoking, including cancer, strokes, and heart attacks. It would take decades to realize there were other issues, such as people's social behaviour, their nutrition, and even poor sanitation.

Florence Nightingale now stands as a beacon for women throughout the world, not only for her immense, omnipresent influence and high standards, but as a symbol that in the cruelties of war, women do have a role, and through better education, women's colleges, and the voting franchise, women can make a difference. Her *Notes on Nursing*, first published in 1859, continued as a best seller and was printed in several languages. Her passion was for improved healthcare and better nurses: "No man, not even a doctor, ever gives a definition of what a nurse should be other than this – 'devoted and obedient'. It seems a commonly received idea among men ... to turn a woman into a good nurse." As she put it, "there are evils which press much more hardly on women than the want of suffrage." In today's world, a Florence Nightingale slogan would be simple: "if you want something done seriously, call for a woman."

******

With three hospitals in PEI, two in Charlottetown, one in Summerside, Island women entered medical practice with a vengeance. They served in multiple capacities, both as administrators, nurses, members of the Women's League, and as assistants to doctors. In the decade after 1945, Island medicine was to face profound changes. Except for the older doctors, like Dr. Roddie MacDonald in St. Peters and a dozen other family physicians in scattered communities, medicine shifted to the clinics, the hospitals, and slowly to the government. It was becoming urbanized, industrialized, and professionalized. Whether it was better medicine, many would argue. The Department of Health, first set up by Premier W.J.P. MacMillan in 1933 – he was to become Premier in 1940-1943 – became involved in various aspects of public health, including water and sewer treatment, the medically handicapped, containment of infectious diseases, public ambulance services, alcohol abuse (officially, PEI was a dry province until 1948) and purchase of expensive medical equipment. But like any temporary arrangement, the Department of Health was not a permanent fixture in Island medicine. New doctors were becoming scientists, trained in the latest advances of biology, physics, and chemistry, with the resulting plethora of new medical wonders, from EKG heart machines to tuberculosis resting machines, new medicines and vaccines and new specialties, such as orthopedic hip replacements and heart by-passes. The Department of Health was, in turn, slowly moving into the area of medical financing, releasing funds for maintaining the supply of doctors, covering the cost of hospitals, and especially for advanced equipment needs.

Across Canada, the development of hospitals as the primary vehicle for health delivery, coupled with the increased sophistication of hospital equipment, raised serious questions about the new economics of medicine and health care. By 1940, forty per cent of Island babies were still delivered at home. However, health delivery was inexorably moving away from the simple but direct doctor-patient relationship, towards the more complex formula of government-funded care, initially organized in each province and local municipality. Because the BNA Act of 1867 assigned health and welfare to the provinces, health costs for the national government was insignificant. The severity of the Depression in the 1930s, in conjunction with the pending impact of the Second World War, began to put a severe strain on the organization of Canadian healthcare. The Depression forced local hospital boards, charities, and Churches to look to governments, as malnutrition, disease, and weak public health programs instilled public outcries about the new challenges of healthcare.

PEI hospitals had their own Ladies Auxiliary groups of volunteers, including many wives of doctors, and the Island Red Cross became an exemplary community movement to promote the improvement of health, the prevention of disease, and the mitigation of the sick and the suffering. The Red Cross organization was ecumenical, its work was all encompassing, it was strong and efficient, and it was run predominantly by women. First chartered on the Island in 1914 as an extension of the Red Cross, it started as a volunteer organization during World War 1, but soon had two outstanding directors in Amy McMahon, a nurse from Baltimore's John Hopkins's University, and Mona Wilson, a graduate of the Public Health Nurse course in Toronto.

From the beginning, with much help from prominent citizens and medical doctors, the Red Cross extended its activities to blood donor clinics, which started on September 2, 1943. Whole blood was packaged and sent to Connaught Laboratories at the University of Toronto, in order to be processed into a dry serum, an amber colored liquid that, when mixed with boiled distilled water, was used for blood transfusions in hospital. After World War II, the Island's Red Cross became part of the Canadian Blood Transfusion Services. Two technicians, Margaret MacLelland and Joyce MacPhail, operated the Provincial Laboratory. Iphigeni Arsenault, daughter of Premier A.E. Arsenault, served for 50 years with the Red Cross, helping the Island to exceed its quota for blood donations, and extending Red Cross activities in such areas as disaster training, first aid courses, home nursing, sick room equipment loan services, nutrition, small craft safety, and summer camps for crippled children. Water safety programs, first initiated by Evelyn Cudmore, who learned swimming instruction at the pool in the University of Toronto's Hart House, which at the time was an all male preserve at this Waspish-oriented university, became a mainstay at beaches throughout the Island.

The Red Cross had many allies in the search for better health care, improved facilities, and professionally trained people. The Womens' Institute was an extremely effective political voice, as were the efforts of some national groups like the Canadian Anti-Tuberculosis Association, which lobbied the government to build a new Provincial

Sanatorium. The Sanatorium opened in May 1931, spurred by *The Guardian* newspaper's slogan, "Give 'Til It Hurts, the Cause is Worthy". Islanders did give, and with the opening of The San, as it was called, on McGill Avenue, with support from Charles Dalton, the fox rancher from Tignish, and the Canadian Life Insurance Officers' Association, pressure built to organize a new Department of Health. Dr. W.J. P. MacMillan, an early supporter of the Red Cross and a former vice-president of the Anti-TB Society, became the Island's first Health Minister.

It was only fitting that these two sides of medicine – that of the arts and of science – began first to complement each other, and then to collide. Medical diagnosis needed science, and all its tools. It also needed the artist side of medicine, in the doctor-patient relationship, the special needs of the patient, the care of the family, and the longer spells of protracted disease, and possibly the aftermath. These issues were on full display at the 1952 Toronto meetings of the Canadian Medical Association. Toronto, of course, was mostly dry, and certainly was on Sundays, where WASP society imposed its values. But that would hardly hold back a national meeting of doctors, who were displaying their wares, their achievements, and their knowledge. At the Sunday dinner, with everyone fully refreshed by the cocktails in their private suites, bars being forbidden to serve the public, and wearing their finest tuxes and gowns, the doctors proceeded to a long, tedious presentation by each of the provincial medical bodies. Each year, the provincial Medical Societies promoted a prominent nominee who advanced the cause of medicine.

Starting alphabetically with Alberta, the presenters made their case. Each award winner had a stunning list of achievements, including scientific discoveries, research projects, august medical textbooks, hospital fundraising, and scholarships at medical schools. The list was long, the night wore thin, the room was hot, and the tables were dry. It was eventually PEI's turn. The PEI President of the Medical Society was mercifully brief, and straight to the point. "All these great men of medicine presented tonight deserve their honours. They are from the science side of medicine. From Prince Edward Island, it is now time to present a doctor from the arts side of medicine. It could never be said better than the Island mother having her ninth baby, being carried to the delivery room, who praised her doctor:

> *Jesus, Mary and Joseph and me,*
> *There's nothing like having a baby with old J.D.*

The Canadian medical community, recognizing that the art of medicine was still so valid, responded with thunderous applause for the Island's Dr. J.D. McGuigan.

******

The third era of Island medicine took place after the war, actually starting well into the 1950s. For the most part, Island doctors were just that - born and raised on the Island, often from farms, and very often from poor families. Many doctors, like Dr. J. Cyril Sinnott, John Maloney, Francis McMillan, Major F. Burge, and other Islanders who had spent time overseas in the military, usually stationed in England but later working on battlefields in France, Holland, and Germany, knew from direct experience the views echoed by Andrew Macphail, the medical writer from Orwell Corner, PEI. For these wartime doctors, the Second World War had a lasting impact - not the great battles, not the great wartime generals - but in the savagery of combat, the destitute fortunes of fallen comrades, and the sheer waste of human carnage, often with enormous suffering. Some doctors had unkind words for some of the British generals who seemed indifferent to the fate of Commonwealth soldiers.

Andrew Macphail, the Islander doctor who became Professor of the History of Medicine at McGill in 1907 and formed part of lasting links between PEI and McGill – wrote in a little known tract, *Three Persons*, on Sir Henry Wilson, the English liaison officer between the French and British army staffs during the First World War. Wilson, to Macphail, personified the cold indifference of the British officer class to the actual fighting man, his lack of humanity that prevailed among many English officers. Macphail, knighted in 1918 for distinguished service with the 6th Field Ambulance Corps, rose to the rank of lieutenant. Writing, for instance, about the Canadian troops at Ypres in 1915, he had this to say about General Wilson, a sadly tarnished British hero who was killed by Irish nationalists in 1922:

> *In all these 753 pages of (Wilson's) diary this commendation of the German General-staff is the only hint that nearly half a million Canadians were engaged on the western front. Of those at Vimy there is a single line, and yet the terrain they captured must have been familiar, as it had been lost to the Germans by General Wilson himself in May 1916, when he commanded the IV Corps...*

Allied casualties were enormously high in the Second World War, much like the War of 1914-1918, but so too were German and Russian losses, and medical manpower was in short supply. Surgery was the preferred treatment, blood the fodder of war, with prayers and priests the sole hope for salvation. War was a terrible apprenticeship for young Canadians who later graduated from university science programs and entered medical schools at McGill in Montreal and Toronto.

In this period, medical schools were transforming the practice of medicine. A few Canadian schools like McGill and the leading American schools like John Hopkins and Harvard were pushing aside the European order, obviously centered in Berlin, but also in Paris and London. In both world wars, the American industrial war effort, like Canada's, was enormous, but the US had begun to push unparalleled efforts into scientific effort, obviously helped by the brain drain from Europe of mathematicians, physicists, biologists, chemists and psychiatrists. Medical schools were no longer a professional faculty apart from the science faculties - they were part and parcel of the new world of science and medicine, and essential to the practical world of organized health care.

By the start of the twentieth century, much of the Island's economy had not changed, with agriculture and small farms remaining the mainstay of the working population. The practice of medicine was ready to enter a new phase. Most doctors in Canada and on PEI were

Dr. John Mackieson

Photo courtesy of PEI PARC: No 2398/8c

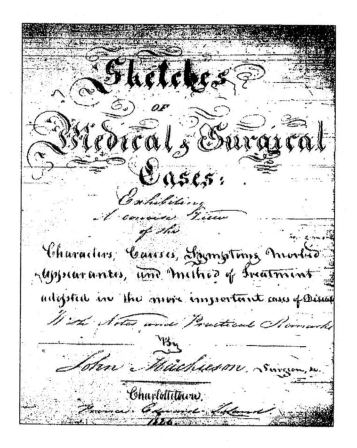

Courtesy of PEI Medical Society

native born and educated in local schools. While Boston remained the intellectual Mecca for many Islanders, McGill was the center for new medical training and teaching. Dalhousie University was far less advanced, and Toronto was facing an uphill battle with new American schools like John Hopkins, where the spirit and teaching practices of William Osler were eventually to make him the world's best known physician. For PEI, the main problem was not to educate doctors; it was to have them return to the Island. The same problem exists today. Fortunately, the new century saw more well-trained doctors return to the Island, and some started a new model of health care, medical clinics.

On July 29, 1925, three enterprising doctors, led by Dr. Wendell MacKenzie, a McGill graduate, opened in Charlottetown a group practice called the Polyclinic. The new partners, Rupert Seaman and Wendall Tidmarsh, both McGill graduates, would practice general medicine, surgery, obstetrics, and gynecology. They also had a nurse who combined chores like bookkeeping, patient records, and even some cleaning. On opening day, the Charlottetown *Patriot* referred to "the Polyclinic as an entirely new departure in medical circles of this city" and that it had "splendidly commodious and luxuriously furnished quarters, with handsome hardwood floors throughout and beautifully finished and furnished, the large waiting room, three roomy offices of the doctors, adjoining examining rooms and laboratory occupy the entire first floor of the building."

Within two generations, the Polyclinic would greatly change the practice of medicine on the Island in ways that weren't always public or openly debated. What became a practice on the Island became a model in other parts of Canada. In fact, within a single generation, there would be three clinics on the Island, the Polyclinic, the Charlottetown Clinic (started in 1941 and incorporated in 1951) and the Summerside Clinic. Outwardly, these clinics changed the locus of doctor-patient relations - slowly, the doctors didn't go to the patients, e.g. to rural, isolated farms, and instead, the patients went to the clinics and the hospitals. Hospitals would no longer be only sixty per cent full, doctors would be off duty in the wards, and the doctor-patient system would become a doctor-family relationship.

Many of the ideas behind the Polyclinic (the name was chosen from a well known institution, the Polyclinic in New York) were learned at McGill, a pioneer in specialized medicine. A few concepts were learned from the Mayo Brothers who formed the famous Mayo Clinic in Rochester, Minnesota, but there were also similar practices in smaller communities, including the Carruthers Clinic in Sarnia, and the Peterborough Clinic in Ontario. What really was at issue was the primacy of the individual doctor to control all aspects of the doctor-patient treatment, not simply diagnosis and prognosis, but the limited degree of any cooperation or individual involvement with other doctors. This meant no fee splitting, no referrals, no joint diagnosis (e.g. heart treatment for new born babies), and no specialization, such as pediatrics vs. obstetrics, or cardiology vs. general surgery.

Clearly, what was driving these changes were the new methods of medical training inspired by the best medical schools, like McGill, and the quality of the best hospitals. Dr. MacKenzie's hospital training, for instance, varied from the Montreal General and two years at the St. Louis Children's Hospital. The Polyclinic was a new model of group practice, with new equipment and techniques introduced to the Island, such as X-rays, laboratory facilities, intravenous therapy, ECG equipment, and even a new specialist, in pediatrics.

Cy Sinnott represented the new order of scientific medicine on PEI. His studies at McGill were a precursor to staggering new treatment of heart patients and the new science of cardiology. His medical thesis, focusing on the rate of oxygen entering the heart muscle, pioneered new laboratory testing using humans, even if, by today's digital standards, the techniques were timeworn, the equipment primitive, and the research financing limited. In order to test the scientific hypothesis, subjects of varying sex, height, weight, age, and medical history were tested. As it turns out, some of the medical guinea pigs used in the McGill studies were not just patients and people from the general public. Medical tests also included members of the Montreal Canadians, the hockey team led by the legendary coach, Hector "Toe" Blake, and including such luminaries as Maurice "Rocket" Richard, Jean Beliveau, Jacques Plant and Doug Harvey. The medical subjects were all monitored, and had to perform running sprints on a standing treadmill, moving at a constant pace by shifting its slope to assess oxygen intake and their heart beat.

The precise medical findings are not the major point for this chronicle. What is relevant is that one of the findings meant that a program of constant physical exercise for heart victims, not a period rest (or lack thereof: in the case of Winston Churchill, who had suffered a mild heart attack at the White House in 1943, the day before he traveled to Ottawa by train to speak to the Canadian Parliament). Instead of rest, running and daily exercise may be the best remedy. The McGill team consisted of prominent physicians at the Montreal General Hospital, and they spent time with the Montreal Canadiens as 'physicians in waiting'. By co-incidence, the prominent CBC play by play announcer for the Canadiens was Danny Gallivan, whose wife Eileen came from Charlottetown and they regularly visited the Island at their cottage in Keppoch, often accompanying players and managers of the Canadiens. Eileen's father, Frank McPhee, was a prominent lawyer, who might have become leader of the PEI Conservative Party, before he succumbed to cancer in 1957. In the heart treadmill race at McGill, no one has ever matched Rocket Richard's record of oxygen delivery to the blood, without an increase in pulse or running faster on the treadmill. This medical device, now greatly perfected, remains a training tool and many popular athletes, including the famed Soviet Hockey Team of 1972, have yet to match the Rocket's heart-oxygen record. Jacques Plant eventually became a coach and sports psychologist advising the Soviet Team, using techniques learned at McGill.

Island medicine in the post war period gradually became a new profession. Doctors had advocated new forms of pre-paid insurance programs as far back as the 1920's, but governments refused to act. Atlantic Canada became a pioneer in moderate forms of prepaid medicine. In 1906, the Dominion Steel Workers' Mutual Benefit Association in Sydney designed a model where coal miners, with an entrance fee of one dollar and a weekly fee of fifty cents, received family coverage for hospital care and nursing treatment for up to $2.50 per day. The following year, the Sisters of Hotel Dieu Hospital in Chatham issued books of 20 admission tickets for $3.00 for coverage of medicines, medical attendance, and room and board at any time during six months after the date of the ticket. But high unemployment and malnutrition in the 1930s and then the Second World War, associated with the rising use of hospitals for medical services, made the methods of payment especially acute.

There were two hospital associations in the Maritimes, with one for New Brunswick, and one for Nova Scotia and Prince Edward Island. As far back as 1934, there were discussions of a Maritime-wide insurance program, inspired by the efforts of Dr. Moses Coady at St. Francis Xavier University, but there were similar efforts across North America, including in Moncton, which had organized a Moncton Group Hospital Plan. Because Nova Scotia and PEI had many hospitals staffed and supported by the Catholic Church, a group headed by two Bishops, Rev. John R. MacDonald of Antigonish and Rev. James Boyle of Charlottetown embarked on a plan to consider health insurance schemes. They were supported by Rev. Mother Ignatius of the Sisters of St. Martha and Sister Anna Seton of the Sisters of Charity in Halifax, plus William Simpson of New Glasgow. At a meeting convened in 1941, the group engaged a high-priced consultant, who eventually reported at another meeting at Pictou Lodge in 1942. This group also listened to Dr. Harvey Agnew of the Canadian Hospital Association and Mr. A. Swanson from the Toronto General Hospital.

The meeting itself was inconclusive, but out of it came one of the few Maritime-wide associations dealing with serious health issues, in the Maritime Hospital Association. It was effectively a merger of both hospital associations into a single group, eventually to be incorporated in Nova Scotia as the Maritime Hospital Service Association. In short, it was the first step to create a Blue Cross program in the Maritimes, a Group Hospitalization Plan, which was enacted in each legislature. Ruth Cook Wilson became the first Executive Director, T. L. (Leddy) Doyle, recruited from Moore & McLeod in Charlottetown, became the first enrolment officer to enlist new members and hospitals, and Dr. J. A. McMillan became the first Chairman. The original Blue Cross contract provided a standard ward care for a single subscriber at 0.50 cents per month, semi-private was 0.75 cents per month, and family coverage for children under 17 years was $1.00 for ward care and $1.50 for semi-private. A notice in *The Maritime Advocate* illustrated the popularity of the Blue Cross Plan:

> *...The thought of securing protection for his family was no doubt one reason why Mr. Lester F. Stewart of South River, Antigonish County, NS recently enrolled under the Maritime Plan for Blue Cross. He could have no idea that within twenty-four hours after his contract became valid his young son, Lester G. (Elgie) would fall and fracture an elbow. Yet that was exactly what happened. Lester was rushed immediately to St. Joseph's Hospital in Glace Bay, where he received meals, dietary service, general Nursing care, use of operating room as often as necessary, routine tests, ordinary drugs, dressings and plaster cast materials – all without cost!...Lester Gerard (Elgie) was the Plan's first patient, his father, the first parent, in the Maritime Provinces to benefit in advance for the hospital Care of his entire family at a cost of less than a postage stamp.*

Blue Cross and the related Blue Shield programs became an immediate success, widely accepted by the Atlantic Premiers and governments, the public at large, and was seen as an appropriate and strikingly efficient measure to deal with the rising costs of hospital services. It was also a stunning success for Atlantic cooperation, with its headquarters based in Moncton, a strong field staff headed by leaders like T.L. (Leddy) Doyle, Ruth Wilson, the two Dr. Joes, J.A. McMillan (serving as first Chairman and Medical Director) and J.A.McDougall (later serving as Mayor of Saint John) and L.G. LeBlanc. The Blue Shield Program was approved on February 12, 1948, partly in response to pressures from the union movement, which wanted a wider healthcare package. The result was now three core plans: hospital only, Hospital-Surgical, and Hospital-Surgical-Medical. When Newfoundland joined Confederation on March 31, 1949, Bill 56 received Royal Assent and, on August 13, 1949, Blue Cross and Blue Shield operated in all four Atlantic Provinces.

By 1957, it was becoming clear that both the federal and the provincial governments were exploring ways to pursue active, direct involvement in the healthcare field. Britain enacted the recommendations of the Beveridge Report, and now had state medicine based around a single payer system. There were two reasons for more active Canadian government involvement. The first was rooted in the medical profession itself, in an unwitting way. Scientific medicine was producing new drugs, techniques, and devices, and these vastly changed public expectations of health care coverage. Scientific medicine promised better health, to be sure, but also greater longevity and the cure of formerly incurable diseases. For instance, the outbreak of poliomyelitis in 1952, and the subsequent discovery of the Salk vaccine in 1954 to deal with this dreadful communicable ailment, helped to force governments of all political stripes to act.

In May 1957, the federal government, only too aware of the dramatically changing Canadian demographics, proclaimed a new initiative. The *Pre-Paid Hospital Care Insurance Act* was to be administered by the provinces by means of a premium tax payable by individuals, or, alternatively, by an increase in the provincial sales tax, which meant that provinces like PEI had to institute what was called a hospital tax. By 1959, all Maritime Provinces introduced new governmental plans for hospital insurance, and medical claimants suddenly jumped six per cent. Canada's slow crawl to inflation-induced government funding was now picking up pace. When the Liberal Government fell to Opposition status in the 1957 federal election, followed by a juggernaut sweep for the Conservatives in the election of 1958, Prime Minister John Diefenbaker responded to these health challenges by establish a Royal Commission on Health Services, and appointed his personal friend from Saskatchewan, Chief Justice Emmett Hall, as Chairman.

At Blue Cross, where total revenues in the Maritimes now passed $100 million in 1968, rising and inflationary costs of health benefits showed that, even with more subscribers, costs were rising faster than benefits. Nationally, it was clear that the Hall Royal Commission was dealing with an uneasy public, a worried health profession, and nervous governments. The chickens were coming home to roost, as medical science was in its Golden Age, with more drugs, better equipment, and better hospital care. But there was a severe imbalance: with uncontrollable costs, doctors no longer controlled the doctor-patient relationship. The era of medical *noblesse oblige* was much like the Big Band era, a thing of the past. The public wanted more of everything, and governments fed these expectations. When the British and the Canadian doctors gathered at a conjoint meeting in Toronto, the Hon. Paul Martin, the federal Minister of Health and Welfare, set out the new philosophy:

> *This brings me to the important distinction that must be made between the technology of medicine and its organization. In technology, we can include all the skills of diagnosis and treatment that constitute the practice of medicine. Organization, on the other hand, embraces all the arrangements, social and economic, by which medical care is brought to the individual. You will agree that the doctor is not alone in possessing the right to determine the nation's medical welfare, particularly when this involves, in addition to medical skill, questions of social organization that are, understandably, usually outside the province of his professional experience.*

By January 1971, all provinces – the last was New Brunswick – joined the national Medicare program as a single payer system, split between the provinces and the federal government. Socialized medicine had arrived. It forced Maritime Blue Cross to give up many of its original programs, and compelled the organization to diversify into new lines of coverage, such as Private Duty Nursing, Prescription Drugs, Dental Care, and Life Insurance, as well as health computer services. On the 40th anniversary of Blue Cross, the President noted the change in mission:

> *We commenced business in 1943 as a community service non-profit organization to help Maritimers finance hospital costs. Today, we are a business underwriting a complete package of employee benefits other than pension plans for employer groups in*

*Atlantic Canada. In addition, we administer benefits
on behalf of these governments.*

As the payment terms of medical practice evolved towards a single payer, government- financed system, there was a small footnote to the Blue Cross story in Atlantic Canada. As noted, Blue Cross had cultivated new activities, including the establishment of insurance plans, known as the Atlantic Mutual Life Assurance Corporation, and programs for the Department of Veteran's Affairs and the RCMP detachments in Atlantic Canada. When T.L. (Leddy) Doyle retired in 1976, he made a significant career change. Originally recruited from the Moore & McLeod store in Charlottetown, he climbed to the top of both the Blue Cross organization and the first President of Atlantic Mutual Life. After his wife died, he entered the seminary and was ordained a Catholic priest, joining his three daughters, all nuns, in the service to God and the Church. On January 27, 1984, he and the co-founders of Blue Cross were awarded with a special medal of service: Rev. T. L. Doyle, Dr. J. A. McMillan, and Ruth Wilson.

****

Emmett Hall's momentous Royal Commission report calling for the establishment of Medicare, as well as many changes to medical education, differed from the official policy of organized medicine, in the Canadian Medical Association. Emmett Hall spent a lot of time in Prince Edward Island, not only because he enjoyed his visits, but because he could see the implications of his report in a small jurisdiction, like his home province, Saskatchewan, which first adopted Medicare in 1962. The Hall Commission Report was an enormously comprehensive policy document, and most of the key recommendations have followed its basic framework, implemented in the Canada Health *Act*.

But what the Hall Report did do was turn the practice of medicine into the science of medicine. In only a few decades - say from 1930 to 1960 - medicine had made more scientific process than in the previous 300 years. The science of medicine shifted back to the doctor-patient relationship, but the patient himself became the rational focus of scientific attention, through the sciences of biology, physics and chemistry. The medical schools themselves became pre-eminent sources of scientific discoveries, often aided and supported by a huge inflow of European scientists, many Jewish. If the first part of the twentieth century was led by sanitation, hospitals, and vaccines like insulin, penicillin and the Salk vaccine, medicine as a science was led by medical schools to seek the eradication of life threatening diseases at birth, especially for vaccine-preventable diseases, ranging from Cholera to small pox, and other risk-threatening diseases, like cancer, heart attacks and hereditary disorders.

Island medicine has a fortunate link to the science of medicine. It is a province without a medical school in a region with a shortage of doctors. But it did have links to one school in particular. Like the Grande Seminaire at Laval University in Quebec, where the Island's Catholic sons entered Holy Orders, Island medicine developed strong links to McGill. Indeed, in days gone by, some Island doctors complained that Island medicine was too McGill-centric. In the 19th century, numerous Island students studied at McGill, as Canadian-based schools took over medical training from European medical schools, Edinburgh most of all. The role of William Osler was the centrepiece of McGill's reputation, but the fact that Islanders were attached to McGill and Montreal was equally important in attracting students.

Medicare has many features, some good, some bad. As a huge health consuming nation, Canadians love Medicare, mainly because it is assumed to be free. As an administrative system, it leaves much to be desired, since the provinces are the locus of organization, and there are massive inefficiencies in care provision - PEI and Atlantic Canada are good examples of such duplication. Some doctors could and have argued that organized medicine, even in the U.S, where a credit card may be as important for hospital admission as a cancer liability, is a system of perpetual inflation, because no one is in charge of costs. Furthur, supply creates its own demand, in the classic law of Jean-Baptiste Say, where better treatment leads to further wants of better drugs, medical machines, or personalized medicine (a quarter of all health expenditure in the USA is devoted to patients in the last six months of life).

Today, Canada has seventeen medical schools: only New Brunswick and PEI don't operate one of their own. Through inter-governmental arrangements, these two provinces share space and schooling slots, much like the system used to order planes from companies like Bombardier and Boeing through a queue system called 'slots'. Visit any medical school in Canada and ask, "Who plans to practice family medicine?" and too few hands will go up. Having competed with thousands to get into these prestigious schools, and already deeply in debt, most of these ambitious young adults feel they cannot afford to become family doctors. Without fringe benefits, and after the expenses of renting a clinic, paying receptionists and nurses, and buying equipment and supplies, a family doctor working forty-hour weeks could expect to take home roughly the salary of a union plumber, auto worker, or skilled bricklayer (around $70,000). But with a few more years of training, medical students can become specialists, virtually guaranteeing them twice the income of a family doctor.

Family medicine is no longer a popular career option. For most residents in a large Canadian city, easy access to a family doctor is a luxury. Family medicine is also a problem for dual-income families, and by extension for small communities, especially for those that cannot provide a job for spouses, or decent schools for kids. Moving to the suburbs often means years of waiting to join local family clinics. In 2004, almost five million Canadians did not have a family doctor, while in Ontario, according to the Ministry of Health, there are 138 communities facing a critical lack of physicians. Island medicine from the earliest days removed the economic stigma of treating the very poor and destitute, providing quality medical care to the entire population, albeit through imposing immense hardships on the medical community.

A report by the Society of Rural Physicians of Canada shows that between 1994 and 2000, the number of family doctors practicing outside our largest cities declined by 15 percent. Furthermore, a 2004 report by the College of Family Physicians of Canada stated that up to 3,800 physicians were expected to retire over the next two years, among them some 1,400 family doctors. Rural General Practitioners

McGill Version of the Oath of Hippocrates

SPONSIO ACADEMICA

In Facultate Medicinae Universitatis

"Ego, ..., Doctoratus in Árte Medica titulo jam donandus sancto, coram Deo cordium scrutatore spondeo:— me in omnibus grati animii officiis erga hanc Universitatem ad extremum vitae habitum persevaturum; tum porro artem medicam caute, casta et probe exercitaturum et quoad in me est, omnia ad aegrotorum corporum salutem conducentia cum fide procuraturum; quae denique iter mendendum visa vel audita silere conveniat, non sine gravi causa vulgaturum. Ita praesens mihi spondenti adsit nomen."

1938   Joseph A. McMillan, Charlottetown, P.E.I.

The following is a free English translation of the Latin version:

The University's Faculty of Medicine

"I, ... about to receive the honour of Doctor of Medicine and Surgery, promise before Almighty God, the searcher of hearts, that I will perform the duties of my profession in a careful, moral and upright manner; that I will diligently minister, as much as in me lies, to the comfort and restoration of the sick entrusted to my care; that I will not divulge, without grave reason, anything that I have seen or heard during my professional attendance, which it may be proper to conceal; and that I will ever seek to promote the interests of this University of which I am now to become a graduate."

SOURCE: Sinnott (1975)

Latin Version of the Oath of Hippocrates

quickly discover that they are not just physicians, but small-business owners as well. Does PEI illustrate the central medical challenge for the organization of modern health care, in combining the needs of general practitioners committed to the complete welfare of familiar patients, and the necessity of a critical mass of specialists, coupled with expensive medical devices and technicians, in large hospital settings? The latter by definition is bureaucratic, impersonal, and closely monitored by government auditors, whose mistakes are quickly censured.

The chronology of Island medicine is a story of sacrifice and duty, both by doctors in the nineteen and twentieth century, and by the enormous contributions of women as nurses, hospital nuns, administrators, and volunteers, who support the Red Cross, the Women's Auxiliary movements, and as unpaid supporters of the old and the infirmed. All too often, Island doctors knew the limits of medical options, the agonizing medical challenge, often amounting to questioning the lesser of two evils. For example, should the physician either recommend the more aggressive ventilator, on which the patient would probably die, or the more passive morphine, from which the patient might slip into death? Doctors are forced to assume risks. The power of a doctor's pronouncement is profound. When a doctor enumerates side effects or offer sketchy statistics, patients can experience fear and despair.

The language of hope has become an excruciatingly difficult issue in the modern relationship between doctor and patient. For centuries, doctors followed Hippocrates' injunction to hold out hope to patients, even when it meant withholding the truth. This false hope is both a hangover from the centuries-old belief that doctors should withhold bad news, and a practice newly infused by the explosion of so many medical treatments and the tenuous promise held out by clinical science. As health care providers struggle with whether, how, and when doctors should speak of hope, a consensus is building on at least two fronts: that what fundamentally matters is that a doctor tells the truth with kindness, and that a doctor should never just say, "I have nothing more to offer you". Island medicine never heeded that loathsome call.

8

Rural Renaissance and the Legacy of Angus MacLean

War Hero * Politics of Rural Renaissance* The Electoral System *
Confederation of the Arts * Higher Education * The Fixed Link *
Again: The Land Question * Heritage Foundation * Immigration*
New Issues – The Barbados of the St. Lawrence

At the Charlottetown airport in 1981, two European ladies decamped
from an Air Canada 727 aircraft, unsure about their final destination,
their daily schedule, or their welcoming party. As it turns out, their
personal reason to visit PEI was for a reunion of sorts with a celebrated
bombardier, a man who belonged to a group called the Comet Line,
an escape route designed during World War II to assist airmen fleeing
from European battle zones to avoid Nazi imprisonment. In that
difficult period, life was only a daily affair, 24 hours at a time: a
breakfast companion could become the evening bereavement. As the
war unfolded, combined Allied efforts slowly broke down traditional
divisions of language, nationality or political cause, and Europeans
lived a torment of fear for six years. The two visitors from Belgium
knew the man they were to meet, a man whose name was a code for
an Amsterdam houseboat, and a disguise for escaped veterans, the
underground, and the specialists of M1-9, known bureaucratically
as Military Intelligence, Section 9. The houseboat code was called
Angus MacLean.

Officially, Baronne Burnadette Greindl and her daughter Clair came to Charlottetown as the guests of the Royal Air Forces Escaping Society. In reality, they were the personal guests of one of Canada's great escape artists during the Nazi occupation. Flying a Halifax bomber, code-named H for Harry, with a crew of seventy-five Canadians, Angus MacLean's first mission was to attack the Krupp ironworks in Essen, Germany. Powerful blue search lights led to fierce ground attacks on the bomber groups. It was the first of many 1000 bomber raids. On the sixth raid over these same works, this time a 300-bomber run, the plane from 405 Squadron was shot down over Holland. The crew of seven men bailed out over enemy territory in the Zuider Zee region of North-eastern Holland. MacLean himself landed in a field of Holstein cows, largely unscathed. Underground movements moved the 20 year old PEI native from Holland to Belgium, and to a meeting with a distinguished gentleman known only by the name Nemo.

Nemo was the head of a Belgian escape organization called the Comet Line. The Nazis, seeking personal information and intelligence, paid a reward of 500 guilders for an officer or 300 for an NCO. Nemo, the Belgian underground chief, was himself later arrested and killed by the Nazis in September 1943. Over 100 soldiers had been arrested by the Nazis. Nemo had interrogated Angus MacLean personally, in search for clues about double agents, Nazi spy plants, and local civilian's helpers for the allied cause. To avoid the detection of allied troops, Nemo kept personal belongings for their safe keeping, as they could incriminate escapees to the Nazis. MacLean happened to be wearing a Masonic ring, numbered C1107, and an identification, *Canada*, both of which he entrusted to Nemo. With the help of the Comet Line, MacLean eventually made it back to England via Gibraltar and the Isle of Skye, by co-incidence, the home of his paternal grandmother.

He was awarded the Distinguished Flying Cross, which was presented by King George VI at Buckingham Palace, and returned via New York on the *Queen Elizabeth* to the Patriation Center in Rockcliffe, Ontario. He later served with the Occupation Forces in post-war Germany before returning to his farm community in

PEI, which happened to be close to the very spot of the original Selkirk settlements in King's County that first began in 1803. This small hamlet would be the base for his future federal political career. Among his military colleagues in London was a young officer of MI 9, also dressed in artillery uniform with several medals, including the Military Cross. His name was Major Airey Neave, and he was one of the first Allied prisoners to escape from Colditz Castle, a German prisoner of war camp.

After the war, MacLean's personal items were retrieved from hidden placements in Belgium, but the only decipherable identity on the Masonic ring was the word *Canada*. As it turns out, Nemo in fact was Baron Jean Greindl, the Belgian underground chief who was killed in an air raid at Etterback in 1943. Now his wife and his widowed daughter were in Charlottetown to visit this airman, who at the time was serving as the Federal Minister of Fisheries, and was a prominent man about town. The Greindls were very impressed, especially when they found that the personal ring, No. C1107, belonged to Angus MacLean, P.C., M.P., and native of Lewis, PEI. Travelling with another escapee helper from Holland, Sir Adrian Ferdinand Van Goelst, head of the secret organization supplying military intelligence to the Allies, remarked to assembled wartime friends, "I did not realize what I started when I supplied a fishing pole for Angus MacLean to carry on his way to Zaltbommel railway station, to help disguise him as a local. The next time I heard of him, he was Minister of Fisheries for Canada."

**

When Angus MacLean assumed the leadership of the provincial Conservative Party, after three consecutive Liberal terms with Premier Alex Campbell, the thinking pundits thought that he was too old, too set in his ways, and too wedded to rural politics during an era of urban élan. Insiders had a different view. For one thing, he deliberately recruited young candidates, including Pat Binns, a young development worker, who was raised in Alberta but born in Saskatchewan. His personal staff was half his age, and he traveled widely throughout the Island, as well as to other provinces. He witnessed for himself the potential challenges of coping with social change and the intellectual model of top down, imposed bureaucratic thinking as the means to impose change. Provincially, the Liberal Government of Jean LeSage, one of the strongest Quebec administrations since Confederation, went down to defeat by Daniel Johnston. In New Brunswick, Richard Hatfield's Conservatives defeated a Liberal Party grown arrogant with big plans for social change. Pierre Trudeau, perhaps the most ostensibly intellectual of all Canadian Prime Ministers, hung on by a hair in 1972 over a re-rejuvenated Tory Party led by Robert Stanfield, the former Premier of Nova Scotia, whose ancestors emigrated to PEI from Yorkshire. MacLean was banking on two political reflexes: the arrogance of power and its time for a change.

On the Island, Alex Campbell's themes for change, represented by the cumbersome and inappropriately named Development Plan, sounded Orwellian to the man on the street. Angus, with his unprecedented eight electoral victories in federal politics, was the first Islander to hold a Cabinet position in Ottawa and then return to PEI and become Premier. His government was sworn in on May 1979. In contrast to Campbell's views on big development, MacLean's ideas came from his platform of rural renaissance, an intellectual takeoff on the economic tract of Edward Schumacher, *Small is Beautiful*. Underneath this slogan, Angus never doubted the electoral outcome: on the Island, when the tide goes out, it is hard to lift political boats. For him, the tide was coming in.

Contrary to some expectations, the new Premier's intention was not to put back the clock, to revive the rural past of the nineteenth century, the ideal rural paradise set out by his neighbour, Andrew Macphail in his book, *The Master's Wife*. MacLean, after all, was part of the activist Diefenbaker government that itself brought wholesale national policy reforms, from advanced technical schools to changes in healthcare, medical education and aggressive expansion of export markets, including to China, much to the chagrin of the American government. But MacLean's primary concern was to maintain the family farm, which he saw as the bedrock of the Island way of life. In addition, he argued that all basic government services, from high schools to hospital care, should be available throughout the Island

and not simply in Charlottetown. He knew, of course, that advanced industrial societies required modern bureaucracies and a respected public civil service, one of the unheralded features of Alex Campbell's Development plan. That required hiring and promotion based on professional merit, not the traditional jobs that all parties, federal and provincial, provided when there was a change of government.

It was never any secret that the highways in the provinces, in addition to CN and the Post Office in the federal bureaucracy, were the mother lode of partisan job creation when governments changed. The national press, with its usual Toronto-centered hypocrisy, suggested that on the Island, the slogans were "if it moves, pension it; if it doesn't move, pave it." What was less well known is how extensive patronage was in both the provinces and Ottawa, albeit not for the working class, but for professionals, especially in the legal community. On the Island, from the earliest governors appointed by Imperial London, Patterson, Fanning, Smith, government represented secure jobs, patronage for family members, and healthy salaries. In time, the rural community came to resent lawyers, magistrates, and judges as parvenus, modern arrivistes whose legal training was questionable at best, and whose goal was a safe and well paid job on the bench. Unlike the clergy or doctors, where the idea of *noblesse oblige* had great currency, the legal profession was often seen differently, a case of public ignorance and legal illiteracy for lawyers' own political ends. To many, lawyers seemed to work as both as judge and jury. It was a small group, with the lawyers too close to the politicians who established the rules and friendly with judges who, with high salaries and healthy promotion prospects, administered them.

MacLean's career had, like many Islanders who fought in Europe, given him a chance to compare. When MacLean was born in 1914, the population of PEI had decreased from 109,000 in 1891, the year when Sir John A. died, to a low of only 73,000. The 1911 census reported an Island population of 94,000 people, which bottomed out at 86,000 in the mid-1920s. Pressure had built to retain the Island's four House of Commons seats, since they were allocated by population, and Ottawa agreed. This was a victory for Premier John A. Mathieson, when the change was enshrined in the BNA Act. Robert Borden was

Prime Minister and PEI, like the Maritimes, was struggling with the economic effects of the post-confederation union. Premier J.A. Matheson strongly argued, in a submission to the federal government, that Ottawa, even with all the subsidies, including transportation (the railway and the new ferry), took a third more in revenues than the province received. Tariffs were high, and generally favoured central Canada. His successor, Premier A.E. Arsenault, recalls in his Memoirs the bitterness felt by the Maritime Provinces over the expansion of the boundaries of both Quebec and Ontario, from the original Confederation settlement, and the expansion of the Western provinces, without compensation to the Atlantic Provinces:

> *The three Maritime Provinces contended that those Northern Lands were part of the public domain and that the Maritimes had a proportionate financial interest in them along with those other Provinces which comprised the Dominion of Canada which the transfer of ownership was made to the other six Provinces by the Federal Government. Since they had been purchased from the Hudson's Bay Company by the Federal Government out of the public monies, these north lands were the common property of the whole of Canada...*

> *Why should our three Maritime premiers not be blamed for their lethargy in respect to the Maritime share of these lands? It is not as though, because they belong to another generation, they are not acquainted with the constitutional aspects of the case... Those Maritime claims are on file in Ottawa. They have never been contradicted. On the contrary, they have been tacitly recognized by such great Parliamentarians as Borden and (Sir Lomer) Gouin. And all that remains to be done is to take them from their pigeon holes, dust them off, and, in the further light of present day information, present them anew...*

The Maritime shipbuilding cycle had reached the end of the Golden Age of Sail. The disappearance of cheap timber, and the introduction of new, disruptive technologies like steam engines, steel hulks, and new mechanical devices, ranging from reciprocating engines to steam turbines, changed this industry forever. In 1917, when everyone assumed the War was going to continue until at least 1920, a government commission recommended grants to revive wooden shipbuilding because of a forecasted steel shortage. An Island politician, John Macdonald (MP, Kings), ordered the last three ocean going schooners ever built on the Island. It was not the case that Maritimers didn't understand the problems – after all, a New Brunswicker, Bonar Law, became the Prime Minister of Britain, another was the media dynamo who would save Churchill and Britain with air plane construction, and a Nova Scotian was the Prime Minister of Canada. The truth was, shipbuilding and all its side effects for the Maritimes was no longer a commercial venture, but rather was driven by governments and imperial defense needs. "By the end of the 19th century," wrote Neihard Hough, "the constructor's of the worlds battleships were having a hard time keeping pace with the irresistible advance of science and technology, which had stymied defense councils into a confusion not to be exceeded until the first propulsion of the fish bomb in 1845."

In the postwar period, as Angus McLean decided to enter politics from his farm life in Lewis, there were other concerns and challenges that faced the Island, no matter who was in power or from what political party. Now known as the rural renaissance, what took form was an automatic response to the embrace of bigness and agglomeration by governments and companies alike, a grassroots "small is beautiful" philosophy. It was only in the 1950s that much of rural Canada gained electric power through Ottawa-sponsored rural electrification programs. Paved roads outside major arterial highways were quite uncommon, and meant easier access to schools and churches, but also commercial centers for shopping and leisure, movie theatres and hardware stores. Population pressures, partly due to immigration, and partly due to the bulging baby boomers, focused on urban issues and the cities. Banking in the post-war period had long since left its local roots and had become nationally-based, in Montreal (Royal Bank, Bank of Montreal) and Toronto (CIBC, Toronto Dominion, Bank of Nova Scotia, despite its nominal headquarters in Halifax), and concentrated in the large population centers. Ontario was the center of insurance, trust companies, and the stock exchange; the only local firms remaining were small coops.

In MacLean's first election, on June 11, 1945, he repeated his father's record, running as a Conservative in the dual riding of Queen's with businessman Chester McLure. He lost. He ran again in the national election in 1949 and lost. Despite his war hero image, it was a tough time for Maritime Conservatives. For much of the twentieth century, and especially from Robert Borden's last ministry in 1915, Ottawa had been Liberal-led. Exceptions were the brief Meighen government in 1926 and the Bennett Conservative government of 1930-1935, which presided over the worst depression of twentieth century capitalism. However, four by-elections in 1951 - two in Manitoba, one in Waterloo, and one in Charlottetown - led to four Conservative wins. All four victors were World War II veterans. Angus MacLean was off to Ottawa.

Of the twenty-six Premiers of Prince Edward Island since 1873, few will ever match his electoral successes, constituting eight federal election victories and only two losses, including his first, and the only federal cabinet minister to become Premier. Uniquely, he is also only one of two to successfully run in two different ridings – Malpeque and Queens. Three Premiers have run federally: Joseph Pope and Louis Davies in the 19th century, and Bennett Campbell in the 20th century, each becoming federal cabinet ministers. (No Canadian Premier has ever become Prime Minister.) Prime Minister Mackenzie King held an Island seat from 1919-1921, in the Prince County Liberal fiefdom. The same riding was later occupied by the War Minister, J.L. Ralston, from 1940-1945. Finance Minister Charles A. Dunning in turn held a Queens County seat from December 1935 to July 1939-40. Few Premiers or federal members from PEI had such a close personal relationship with national political leaders – David Lewis and Tommy Douglas of the NDP, George Drew, John Diefenbaker, and Bob Stanfield of the Conservatives, St. Laurent, Pearson and Trudeau of the Liberals. Because of their shared military experience, Angus McLean remained a close personal friend of René Leveseque, the Premier of Quebec and vaunted *Independiste*.

Angus MacLean

In curious ways, Angus MacLean was a modern politician who, like Sir Andrew Macphail, whose ancestral home was close to his farm in Lewis, detested the modern political ethos of bigger farms, schools, and governments, often using the code word of "amalgamation". In reality, MacLean was an old school politician, a man with a keen sense of farm and community. He well realized that urbanization did not translate easily into community welfare, understanding that industrialization could also mean poor economic conditions, and poor people. He, too, had read John Steinbeck's *The Grapes of Wrath*, and knew only too well that poverty can lead to a poor intellectual heritage, on the Island or anywhere else in Canada. Angus, in short, was a leader who had traveled the world, seen the great cities of Europe, and knew the hardship and economic suffering in post-war Germany. Even though he had received a meal in Buckingham Palace, he also knew that trends and fads, political or otherwise, could be a short recipe for early political retirement.

Angus MacLean brought PEI back to its rural roots. In the 20th century, PEI, like Canada at large, had grown wealthy and prosperous, investing in better education, healthcare, and government services, such as Old Age Pensions, aid for Veterans, and programs for the Aboriginal people. Canada had become an urban country based around large population centers like Toronto, Montreal, Calgary and Vancouver. The 1967 World's Fair had transformed Canada, and became more than a spectacular tourist event, with some 50 million visitors, visiting American TV specials like the Ed Sullivan show, and instilling an immense new pride in the country. MacLean understood, like many of the Canadian elite, that there were new challenges, a fact set out so well by the Carleton University sociologist, John Porter, in his book, the *Vertical Mosaic*.

Canada's model of governance required a fresh but uncompromising revision outside the narrow boundaries of the Golden triangle of Toronto, Montreal, and Ottawa. Politicians needed to reflect on the real meaning of Diefenbaker's message of One Canada, which meant breaking down the powerful divisions between the WASP elite, represented best by the Toronto banking establishments, and the rest of the country. He greatly resented an incident in Cabinet government, when he and his colleagues were presented with a *fait accompli* by Donald Flemming, the Minister of Finance, who wanted to cash $6 billion in war time Victory bonds, paying 3 per cent interest, before they matured, to be converted to new Government of Canada bonds at 4.5 per cent, because they were overhanging the market. What he and the Cabinet were not told at the time was that the Victory bonds were held by the banks and financial institutions, and the conversion led to huge financial gains by these insiders.

The great industries of aerospace and automobiles, computers and pharmaceuticals, were enormous job creators, and attracted the best talents of the poor regions, from both Atlantic and Western Canada. Both the rural areas of Canada and the one-company towns were in serious trouble. Farming in large and small acreages had to struggle for markets. Food processing and large groups like Canada Packers and Swifts were facing ruin. Small communities across Canada were subject to conflicting trends in the ethos of bigger is better, producing scale and efficiency for schools, hospitals, and government services, but at the cost of uprooting communities and severing family ties. CN was closing down entire rail lines, removing all services from PEI and Newfoundland. Air Canada and the CBC were losing their public policy goals of representing all regions of Canada, not just the urban centers. MacLean realized in conservative Alberta, that Peter Lougheed didn't hesitate to 'nationalize' PWA as a Western air carrier run from Calgary because of diffident Air Canada service. Later MacLean would hear Premier LeSage of Quebec, speaking in Charlottetown, arguing for the need of Canadian renewal: "I have no reason to believe, without proof to the contrary, that Confederation, if it were genuinely lived with everything that it calls for in the way of broadmindness and mutual understanding, could not prove to be a success ... to become the progressive and united people that the Fathers of Confederation foresaw."

Of course, urbanization and its resulting turn towards scale-based bureaucratization were not a PEI phenomena only, as it was clear in Britain before and during the war. In turn, it proved to be a North American crisis through the depression era, sparking farm foreclosures, the break up of entire communities, and even the possible bankruptcy of certain US states. It was the economic issue in post-war Germany and Japan. The Soviet Union never did get its agricultural policies right from the 1917 revolution, and Stalin deliberately suppressed and killed the Kulaks. John Diefenbaker pioneered enormous wheat and agricultural sales to the Soviets, and then to China, long before the American started to develop close commercial trade ties after Nixon's trip to Beijing in 1971. But MacLean saw this challenge directly in his small Island province, where scale had a real meaning for small communities, representing more than the celebrated 'Island way of life'.

No two political leaders in modern times stood in greater contrast than the two Premiers, Angus MacLean and Alex Campbell, who dealt with these conflicting forces. PEI has shared many political odd couples: the two Pope brothers during the Confederation era; the two Peters brothers, Fred and Arthur, the only brothers who were both Premiers; two reformist Liberals like George Coles and Edward Whelan, who differed so much on the Confederation terms; the Island's first Acadian Premier, a young, well traveled A.E. Arsenault (who articled in London under the formidable Lord Charles Russell, the agent for Canada in the U.K.) and the Opposition Leader, Benjamin Rogers, a former Lieutenant-Governor who was 78 when he took over the Liberal Party. Even Premier Thane Campbell, who swept every seat in the house in 1935, differed from his son Alex Campbell, who would win four elections. MacLean and Campbell seemed as different as John Diefenbaker and Pierre Trudeau or John A. Macdonald and George Brown, two politicians, grounded in their family and worldly experience, who saw the same facts but reached contrasting conclusions.

MacLean was a seasoned politician, battle-weary with election wins, both federal and provincial. As Federal Fisheries Minister, he had traveled the country, knew Premiers and their Cabinet members, and some national leaders from Europe. As a World War II veteran, he traveled widely, both to Europe, the US, and countries as diverse as Japan and Cuba. He was a true farmer, much more than a passive owner of woods and crops, but an active land owner, and a blueberry grower. He knew trees, birds, animals, and their food habits. He understood Island history, represented different constituency ridings and knew all the tricks of electioneering, from booze for workers to funeral visits. Alex Campbell was a study in contrasts. Young, educated, suave, and a lawyer by training, he was one of the first Premiers to support Pierre Trudeau as Liberal Leader and thus Prime Minister. Campbell was urbane, witty and a political advertiser's dream. In the 1967 era of Canada's coming of age, younger Canadians wanted their own political leaders to be Kennedy-esque, more JFK, less Nixon, more PET, less Diefenbaker-Pearson. Campbell used his father's Liberal Heritage, ties to Trudeau and Ottawa, and his own desire to get the Island moving again to spearhead his victory. As he put it, in an amazingly frank way,

> *We, in this Province, are caught between these two cultures. The culture of the past, with its problems of back-breaking labour, disease, child mortality, premature aging, inadequate medical facilities, and limited educational opportunities and the culture of the future as represented by modern industrialized states.*

In reality, the two leaders were amazingly similar: not in personality, to be sure, but in politics - this is PEI, after all – and the means to achieve their ends. Both seemed similar in their version of the Island in a post-industrial world, where both thought that globalization and technology were uprooting treasured institutions and traditional values. MacLean and his Tory Critics could attack Campbell for his modernization policies. As MacLean himself wrote, "The Liberal government has taken power from hundreds of school boards and given it to five consolidated school units from small communities and given it to regional service centers; from the people, and given it to planners and consultants; from you and given it to someone else." Further, "The watchword of the day was 'amalgamation.' The government seemed bewitched by the notion that "bigger" meant "better" - bigger farms, bigger schools, bigger public institutions. Tragically, this philosophy accelerated the demise of rural districts...."

Campbell's approach to politics - he served longer than any Premier in Island history – was to modernize the machinery of government.

There were the usual policies towards farm and fishing support, industrial projects, high school education reforms and the merger of the two Charlottetown hospitals. But in essence, Campbell's real concern was two fold: he introduced modern methods of accuracy, financial controls, and merit-based mechanisms in the public service and he settled, once and for all, the sectarian conflicts over education. People were reminded of his Father's famous victory in 1935, when Thane Campbell won every seat in the Legislature, defeating the hapless W.J.P. MacMillan, who was a better doctor and physician than politician. The local papers saw the same result but drew different conclusions. In black, bold letters, *the Patriot* proclaimed: "Liberals 30 - Conservatives 0." Another heading noted: "Tories wiped completely off the map of Prince Edward Island. MacMillan government annihilated in yesterday's general elections." *The Guardian*, a Conservative organ, was more direct: "Island votes for Liberal dictatorship." The smaller heading said, "Exploiting depression and unemployment grievances, Liberals yesterday achieved clean sweep in every constituency. Conservative electors deprived of any voice in legislative assembly."

***

Any stranger to PEI must wonder at the Island's electoral system. It is a slow outgrowth of responsible government, granted in 1851. Some might say 'exceedingly slow'. Some would go further, that PEI is the most over-governed jurisdiction on the planet. That is an over statement. Like all provinces except Ontario, there are two electoral maps - one federal, and one provincial. When PEI joined Confederation in 1873, six MPs were granted to the Island - two seats for each of the three counties - Prince, Queens, and Kings. Unfortunately for the Island, this was never fully documented, so the lingering doubt meant that the Island would be subject to George's Brown dictum at the Charlottetown Conference, that the House of Commons would be elected by 'rep by pop', i.e. representation by population. After Confederation, as the Island population steadily declined, with too many young people leaving for greener shores and no Selkirk-style inward immigration, the PEI government received pressure for some kind of settlement, particularly as the Ontario population grew steadily. In 1912, with Canada having nine provinces (Alberta and Saskatchewan were created in 1905), PEI was granted a constitutional agreement of having no fewer members in the House of Commons than in the Senate, i.e. four seats.

In theory, the Canadian Senate represents not the provinces, as in the US (where each state is equal with two Senate members, now elected but once appointed), but the regions, with 24 for the Atlantic region, 24 for Quebec, 24 for Ontario, and 24 for the Western provinces. When Newfoundland joined the Dominion in 1949, six seats were added to the Senate quorum of 96; the Upper Chamber now had 102 appointed senators, chosen by the Prime Minister of the day. Today, there is also one senate seat for each northern territory. In one sense, both at the Charlottetown Conference and at Quebec, this second chamber, an appointed body, was the unwanted stepchild of the Confederation calculus, neither fish nor fowl, representing the four regions when two of the four, the West and the Atlantic region, weren't homogeneous on most matters.

It was at heart a compromise, and proved a useful addition to the Prime Minister's patronage arsenal. Eventually, Senate appointments were also a drawback to the natural forces of centralization, with Ontario gaining the most because of its population, and Quebec losing the least, because it was guaranteed 75 seats, and which are the basis of calculating House of Commons seat counts in the rest of Canada. As Western Canada grew in every respect, including population, economic vitality, utilization of natural resources, and education, it was natural that the West wanted in. This resulted in new suggestions, from the Triple E Senate proposal of the Reform Party of Canada (elected, equal by province, and effective) to outright abolition. Since PEI already had four senate seats, Ottawa and the other provinces guaranteed the four members to the House of Commons, regardless of population changes. Asymmetric federalism at work!

The four House of Commons seats in PEI were divided, with one for Prince County, one for Kings County, and Queens serving as a dual riding with two seats, like the only other dual riding existing in the country, Halifax. (The word riding for a political district comes from the English word, ryding.) From Confederation to 1979, the four House of Commons seats, and four senate seats were quietly divided by custom. Protestant Liberals were matched against Protestant Conservatives, with the exception of Kings County, where there were Catholic Liberal candidates against Catholic Conservatives. In 1965, Mark MacGuigan, the son of a prominent Liberal lawyer and grand nephew of James MacGuigan, an Island priest who became the first English Cardinal of the Catholic Church in Canada, ran as a Catholic Liberal in Queens, and lost to Angus MacLean. He moved to Windsor, Ontario to inherit this safe Liberal stronghold from Paul Martin Sr. He became the Justice Minister in the Trudeau Cabinet in 1968, as perhaps the only Canadian cabinet minister to have two PhDs. Only in Kings County was a Senator also a Catholic, usually on a rotating basis with a Protestant.

The Provincial electoral system was equally complex. Indeed, when the first Island Assembly met in July, 1773, fittingly in Alexander Richardson's premises, the Cross Keys Tavern, the doorman and supposed sergeant-at-arms, Edward Ryan, viewing the mix of Parliamentary procedures and pleasurable libation, was overheard to remark, quite audibly to the assembled, "this is a damned queer parliament." The next morning, Ryan, on his bended knees, was pardoned, but then was fired, losing his five shilling paycheque. That too was appropriate, as firings were a regular part of Canadian political life, with a change of government or an inauspicious remark. The next item of business was also timely - the requirement to have a proper license to sell rum and other liquors in the Colony.

From 1773 until 1893, the Island Assembly consisted of 30 members, chosen from the three counties, with four dual constituencies per county, plus two each from the county capitals of Princeton (now Summerside), Charlottetown, and Georgetown. The Legislative Council of 12 such members was appointed by the Governor. Voting in PEI, as in other Canadian colonies (and in Britain), was in the oral tradition: people voted publicly by naming their preferred candidate. In 1830, Catholics were allowed to hold public office and vote. In 1877, the Davies Government passed legislation, the *Registration and Electors and Ballot Act*, to allow voting by a secret ballot. At this time, elections were especially controversial, mixing a series of policy issues like Confederation and the land question to equally contested skirmishes over religion and bible reading in schools, booze and prohibition, and federal appointments. But a secret ballot required a proper voter's list, as well as proper voting procedures (ballots, voting hours, and places to vote), all of which was an expensive process. More to the point, the Party in power might be able to manipulate the election machinery. In 1879, after much criticism and debate, the Sullivan Government repealed the 1877 *Act* and the oral tradition was restored until 1913, when the secret ballot was finally accepted, and used in the 1919 provincial election. The distrust was alleviated, in part, because ballot voting was used in civic elections, first in Souris in 1910, then in Charlottetown in 1911, and in Georgetown in 1912.

Until 1966, there were 15 dual ridings at the provincial level, with two Liberals facing two Conservatives. True, other parties ran candidates, like the Progressives and the CCF, but with no real chance of victory. J. Walter Jones, later a Liberal Premier, ran first as a Progressive in 1921 with Horace Wright, while John A. Dewar, a Conservative, got elected in 1919 as an Independent. In truth, the Assembly membership is rooted in history, in politics, in religion, or until recently, a mix of them all. From 1893 until 1963, the composition of the Legislative Assembly changed from the system enacted in 1862, as a result of responsible government, with the elected Upper Chamber of 13 members representing property interests, four per county, plus one from Charlottetown. Pressure for change came in 1893, when half of the 30 man Legislative Assembly, consisted of Assemblymen, elected by resident males over 21, and half as Councillors, elected by voters who owned property. If a voter owned property valued at $100 or more outside his own district, he could voted for an Assemblyman; if his property outside his own district was worth $325, he could vote for both an Assemblyman and a Councillor. In this way, the 15 dual ridings included an Assemblyman and Councillor, who sat in a combined House of Assembly. Until 1963, property owners could vote in any riding where they owned land - in theory, they could vote in every riding. Many did.

Pat Binns

Alex Campbell

Within the 15 ridings, there was another unwritten custom. In nine ridings where the voters were primarily Catholic (i.e. First Kings, the Souris area, or First Prince, the Tignish area), a Catholic Liberal and a Protestant Liberal competed against a Catholic Conservative and a Protestant Conservative. In this way, there could only be nine Catholics in the Legislature. Obviously, in the other ridings, there could be two Protestant Liberals against two Protestant Tories. Clearly, as populations within the Island shifted, mainly towards Charlottetown and Summerside, new battle lines would be drawn. In 1966, the Shaw Government added two seats for Charlottetown to the Assembly, although some Conservatives like Dr. J.C. Sinnott thought a better plan was to remove small ridings like Fifth Kings that had been Liberal since Confederation. Undaunted, the Conservatives added the two seats to Charlottetown, losing both, but carried 5th Kings, where Cyril Sinnott beat Arthur MacDonald by three votes on election night. When Sinnott asked his election team how he would do on the recount, he was told: "don't worry, we have four votes preserved in the Georgetown cemetery". After the recount, he won by one vote, and became celebrated as landslide Sinnott.

Unlike the federal Liberal Party which, after Laurier, cleverly rotated Leaders between an Anglophone and a Francophone, there was no formal custom or tradition to support leaders by religion or by sex. The first Catholic Premier and party leader was W.W. Sullivan, who served from 1879-1889, while the first of 28 Premiers since Confederation who was Francophone was A.E. Arsenault, who governed from 1917-1919. There have been five Catholic Premiers on PEI (Sullivan, Arsenault, W.J.P. MacMillan, James Lee and later, Pat Binns). But only W.W. Sullivan was elected, with Arsenault and MacMillan becoming Premier when their leader resigned; both failed to win office on their own. James Lee won office before the Mulroney federal sweep in 1984, completing Angus MacLean's term after the latter resigned in 1981. Lee's victory came in 1982, but he was defeated three years later by Joe Ghiz, the first Premier ever elected in Canada from an non-European background. Many Tories thought that Ghiz, the son of a poor Lebanese family, and a graduate of Harvard Law School, would not appeal to the country ridings. How wrong they were! Lee was also the first modern Island Premier not to have a university degree.

For the first hundred years, Island politics, like much of Canada's, was an exclusively male preserve. Women on the Island weren't allowed to vote until 1922, when the 1893 formula was amended, extending the franchise to finally include both sexes. A side effect was that the change highlighted many of the absurdities of the Island's unique electoral system. Political scientist Marlene-Russell Clark, who is the leading expert on such electoral matters, notes that "... the effect of the 1922 legislation and these later amendments was to heighten the inequalities and absurdities of the whole franchise structure. Henceforth, it was possible for a husband and wife, owning a minimum $4,875 worth of property that was suitably divided among the various ridings, to cast a total of 60 votes in each provincial election." Surprisingly, the first female candidate on the Island who ran (and lost) was Hilda Ramsay, a CCF candidate. Clearly, as a CCF candidate, she had no chance, male or female. The first elected woman, Jean Canfield, ran for Alex Campbell's second Liberal Administration, running as an Assemblyman, and beating Frank Myers in First Queen's 1451 to 1180. This was almost an exact reversal of the 1966 election, when Myers won 1306 to 1143. Ironically, Mary McQuaid also ran in 5th Queen's for the Tories, only to lose to a strong, popular and powerful Attorney General, Elmer Blanchard. This election finally broke the glass ceiling for women in Island politics. Federally, Margaret Macdonald was first elected in a by-election in May 1961, replacing her deceased husband, John A., and retained the seat in the national election of 1962, becoming the first woman in Atlantic Canada to be elected to the House of Commons.

Henceforth, women candidates were not only regular and accepted members of Island caucuses and Cabinets, but also became regular members of election backrooms, fund raising, and party organizations. The first elected female Premier in Canada was Catherine Callbeck, and the first female Leader of the Opposition was Pat Mella, who became Provincial Treasurer. In 1993, the provincial election system was totally changed, switching to 27 independent ridings, with nine per county. At a stroke, this changed the electoral dynamics of the Province, with the Catholic-Protestant divide simply disappearing as an election issue.

Federally, the old boundaries were changed for the 1968 election. The realignment meant that the four guaranteed Island seats were now single member ridings named after PEI's four bays - Cardigan, Egmont, Hillsborough, and Malpeque - with Senate seats attached to each. The religious divisions changed as well, more perhaps by demographics than by law. A century ago, political differences by religion mattered in PEI and across Canada. In the 1990s and into present day, religion simply didn't matter. In 1984, all three political leaders in Ottawa were Catholic; few knew and fewer cared. In 2003, the Prime Minister of Canada, or the Premiers of Ontario, Quebec, New Brunswick, PEI, and Newfoundland were Catholic; again, few cared. Even fewer Islanders now worry that a 'mixed marriage' no longer means a couple that are Catholic or Protestant, or have an ethnic mix. A more serious issue is whether they are Liberal and Conservative. More tellingly, when Pat Binns assumed the leadership mantle from Angus MacLean, not only did the Premier's religion have no bearing, the fact that he wasn't even born on PEI simply went unnoticed.

In the postwar period, there have been ten Lieutenant Governors chosen by the Prime Minister, usually on the advice of the Island Premier and Island MPs. Fortunately there is a neat mix of Anglophone and Francophone placements, which helps to mitigate the traditional Catholic-Protestant religious divide. But since 1945, religion has far less impact then it once did. Many Governors, as they are called on the Island, come from the political field, but there are some exceptions, such as W. J. MacDonald. Curiously, the Governor is not the most sought after patronage appointment until recently, because it didn't pay much. Former politicians often seek the job, but their political coloration fades quickly at the palatial Government House, now fully refurbished with unique Island furniture, antiques, paintings, rugs, and accruements. The Lieutenant-Governor, like the Governor-General in Ottawa, is the unsung hero of the Canadian federal system, often seen but rarely heard, who often gives quiet advice to the Premier but not in command. As Frank MacKinnon details in his treatise, *The Crown in Canada*, "the offices of governor-general and lieutenant-governor are constitutional fire extinguishers with a potent mixture of powers for use in great emergencies. Like real extinguishers, they appear in bright colours and are strategically located. But everyone hopes their emergency powers will never be used; the fact they are not used does not render them useless; and it is generally understood there are severe penalties for tampering with them."

The Island Governor travels widely to schools, hospitals, and charity events, and fills the customary formal roles prescribed by British conventions, such as reading the Speech from the Throne, welcoming foreign visitors, attending Veteran's Day events, and presiding over university convocation with the Chancellor. At its best, the Governor performs a useful, non-partisan role, despite their previous occupation or career. The Governor can be a bridge between rival groups, and this non-partisan role also allows both the Government and the Opposition to welcome members of the Royal Family from London, and a litany of foreign dignitaries. Two recent examples: the Crown Princes of Japan, who received in 2004 an honorary degree at the University of Prince Edward Island and attended opening night at the Confederation Center hit musical, *Anne of Green Gables* and Prince Edward, who received an honorary Doctor of Laws, *honoris causa*, in 2007.

Most Governors have been men, as far back as the first Governor of the young colony, Walter Patterson. The first female was Marian Reid, an exceptionally bright, talented, and innovative Governor, appointed by Prime Minister Brian Mulroney. Her term in office raised the standard for future incumbents, and coincided with another innovation for Prince Edward Island, as for the first time in the British Commonwealth, perhaps in the world, the Island had women controlling the five major powerful positions: the Governor (Marian Reid), Premier (Catherine Callback), Leader of the Opposition (Pat Mella), Speaker of the Assembly, (Roberta Hubley), and the President of the University (Elizabeth Epperly).

****

Despite Prime Minister Diefenbaker's indecisiveness and the decided tendency of his minister's to overrule the civil service, the 1957-1963 period proved to be a very activist period in Canadian history. There were strong new provincial governments, including Jean LeSage's Quiet Revolution in Quebec, strong, new Western Premiers, and three new Maritime Premiers, who broke 30 year Liberal terms and started major initiatives to help Atlantic Canada. Diefenbaker, of course, was a Westerner (but born in Ontario) and he was an instant political success in the four Atlantic Provinces. Even Diefenbaker came to realize how Atlantic Canada helped him in his hour of triumph in 1957. Dalton Camp, himself a former Liberal from New Brunswick, and founding patron of Ontario's Big Blue Machine, led an electoral team of strong and shrewd backroom power players. Together, they combining advertising, communications, and polling for leadership candidates and provincial or national elections, and the group basically consisted of Maritimers like Lowell Murray, Norm Atkins, Findlay Macdonald, and Flora MacDonald, toiling for the Conservative Party in Ontario, on loan as it were. Camp put the matter this way:

> *My own part of Canada – the Maritimes – had contributed so substantially to the result; and because we had wrung from the new rulers of the country substantial commitments to policy, and it seemed certain that Maritime members such as Nowlan, would have positions of considerable influence in the new government ...*

Starting in 1957, all Island MPs were Tories, and Angus McLean became the Fisheries Minister. The new Government, after 32 years of federal Liberal Rule, ushered a series of sweeping reforms that helped the Island economy, including better cost shared programs, more health care funding, support to build a causeway, new vocational schools, modernization of rural roads and electrification, and better highways as part of Dief's slogan, Roads to Resources. In 1959, Walter Shaw, the former deputy minister of Agriculture, took over the provincial Conservative Party, winning a third Conservative sweep after long Liberal rule, and joining New Brunswick, won by Hugh

John Flemming, and Robert Stanfield in Nova Scotia. Clearly, Shaw's enormous victory in the provincial election was part of the coattail effect of his link to John Diefenbaker –the Tories became *the* party of the causeway – and he stayed in office until 1966.

Two core issues continued to plague the Island's political structure. The first was religion, while the second was people, or rather, the lack thereof. Together, these issues plagued the Province, because young people, not so tied to the ways of the past (or the parents) predominantly decided to leave for greener pastures. Young people had choices, and the television age typified that there were indeed greener pastures – not only in the bigger cities, but also in education or new emerging careers like professional sports. Clearly, Shaw's enormous victory in the provincial election made the Tories into the party of the causeway – and they stayed in office until 1966, when mishaps led to a by-election and then a change of Government. In the post-war period, two events dramatically changed the Island. They were more than subtle changes, as they brought a new social life and affected far more than economic issues, simply because the Island economy was increasingly bound by Canadian and North American flows. The first was the Confederation Center of the Arts, and the second was the creation of the University of Prince Edward Island. Both initiatives were controversial, and both brought out the worst jealousies and petty rivalries. At the same time, these initiatives also brought out the best in people, in some sense inspiring almost heroic leadership. Not surprisingly, when viewed after the fact, much like the controversy over the 'Fixed Link', the 13 kilometer bridge to PEI, it is hard to find people who now oppose the landmark changes.

The origin of the Confederation Center of the Arts, a multipurpose complex of an art gallery, a theatre, library, and a restaurant-catering area, is not without mystery and intrigue, almost imitating the way PEI eventually joined Confederation. In the Confederation Foyer, there is a bust of Dr. Frank MacKinnon, the former President of Prince of Wales College, who became the driving force and chief advocate to create this addition to the Island's reservoir of historic buildings. Opened in October 1964, the Center is a fitting memorial to the 1864 Conference, and a tribute to the real founders of Canada.

The celebrations on that day, complete with national and international media, abundant guests, banquets, and parties echoed the past glories of the first days of September 1864 when the famous statesmen decided the new constitutional makeup of the Dominion of Canada.

In 1964, as in 1864, the Island was split on this Arts initiative. The rural folk, reaping the harvests from the fields, had their eye on new cars and winter storage, not the black tie celebrations at the Confederation Center. It was to be built on the site of the old farmers market, which had served Island farmers for 100 years. They were indifferent to this new arts set, or even to tourism generally, seeing people from away as simply those who occupied the beaches, cluttered the roads, imported their own booze, and did little to augment the demand for Island produce. To farmers, the Arts Center was a diversion from limited money that could be better used elsewhere, like propping up the huge Canada Packers plant, the largest in Canada east of Toronto, located only five blocks away. Many farmers agreed with a comment in the Charlottetown *Guardian* that this complex couldn't even store Island potatoes, and needed a whitewash besides! But that is an Island overstatement.

In another sense, the Confederation Center of the Arts represented a massive shift of thinking in the Island story. It was primarily an urban story, a set of new ideas not detracting from the rural economy and the rural mores of Island thinking. This new paradigm was rooted in a new way of examining the urban landscape, the role of cities, and powerful new communication networks taking place across North America, and indeed the world. It was a new era for television, that powerful instrument that foretold, as Marshall McLuhan would remind his listeners, the age of the global village, leaving an impact that would revolutionize all traditional institutions, from the economy to sports, and arts to politics. Television was as yet only ten years old, but it was an age of Ed Sullivan introducing Elvis Presley and the Beatles to international audiences, John Diefenbaker mesmerizing Canadians with his Northern Vision and Roads to Resources, and a young John F. Kennedy demonstrating a new generation and a bold new frontier of American politics, civil rights, space exploration, and new initiatives in arts and culture, embodied by his wife, Jacqueline.

It was a vivid contrast to Kennedy's nemesis, the master of old school politics, with Richard Nixon preaching the gospel of Republican bankers and cold war rhetoric.

Islanders understood these issues. High school and university enrolment was increasing, and many listened to the CBC's superb program, *This Week has Seven Days*, while also seeing the likes of John Kenneth Galbraith and Marshall McLuhan in person. One person who did understand these issues, perhaps because he had two daughters, attempted to use these profound changes to promote the Island. Col. J. David Stewart was Mayor of Charlottetown, an Islander with a distinguished military record in World War II, a merchant, and an entrepreneur. In Charlottetown, he owned the biggest Ford dealership on the Island, selling Fords, Mercurys, and Lincolns on Great George Street, two blocks from Province House. He owned the ferry service, Northumberland Ferries. It was not the giant ferry service operated by the CNR, with its mammoth ice breaker ferries like the *Abegweit,* which plied the Northumberland Straights between Bordon and Cape Tormentine, N.B., a nine mile stretch of water that could be extremely treacherous in winter when the ice flows could freeze the ferries carrying train cars, trucks, and automobiles for up to 24 hours or more. Stewart owned the much smaller ferry run at the east end of the Island, a 14 mile stretch linking Wood Islands in Kings County to Pictou, N.S., with smaller boats that ferried tourists across for the six months of the spring-summer season.

Dave Stewart was a staunch Conservative, a Protestant (to that point, all Mayors of Charlottetown were Protestant), and friends with the four Island MPs, all Conservative. In 1959, the provincial Conservative Party that was likely to win the next election, not only because of the magnetism of John Diefenbaker, but because the two neighbouring parties had become Conservative, turning back Liberal governments that seemed to survive since, well 30 years or so. Stewart's father had been Premier of PEI, winning the 1923 election, but died in office (two other Premiers, Arthur Peters and Walter Lea, died in office). David Stewart had a strong personal presence, a mix of military discipline, entrepreneurial flare, man of the people, and possessed a very pleasing common touch. Dalton Camp, no stranger to Canadian politics and political henchmen, and politicians, wrote this about David Stewart: "He appeared to be a popular Mayor and to enjoy the office, even though he was an unusual politician – blunt, terse, and tough talking – and he was an unusual Islander – worldly, prosperous, and cynical. I had not met anyone like him. ...He was the first under-achiever I encountered in Canadian politics."

The deciding event for Dave Stewart was a major fire at the City Library, located on Queen and Grafton, the site of the old Farmers Market, located near the Post Office, and immediately adjacent to Province House. The old market building, designed by William Critchlow Harris, a gothic building of Island stone, was the fourth structure on this historic site, had to face the classic dread of fire, and on April 29, 1958, burned down, and the entire complex, including not only the Charlottetown Public Library, but the upstairs Robert Harris Memorial Art Gallery, and the home of various artistic clubs, including the Arts Society, the Historical Society, the Drama Society, and the Camera Society.

As Mayor, Stewart had to worry about the costs of the Library's replacement, an important institution that served the citizens of Charlottetown, as well as nearby schools like Queens Square School, with 600 students (the former St. Patrick's School, built in 1855 and expanded after the war), West Kent, and Prince of Wales College. Costs were a factor, because the City was in a rebuilding process, and was focused on replacing the five high schools, including Queen's Square School, which served mostly Catholic boys, St. Joseph's Convent (the site of the same building constructed personally by Bishop Angus MacEachern), Notre Dame Convent, which taught mainly Catholic girls, Kent Street School, and Price Street School. The Library, headed by the notable Miss Jean Gill, had stickers on books that read: "wash your hands before handling this book". Two of several new schools were built, including Queen Charlotte High School in 1955, and Birchwood High School in 1957, which were now combining boys and girls in the same class rooms. Much of the leadership in the Charlottetown School System came from highly-rated principals like Col. B. F. MacDonald, another war veteran, but also Dr. R. G. Lea, Chairman of the School Board (and son of the former Premier, Walter Lea) and Mr. Ken Parker.

Within social and political circles, there was discussion about what steps the Island might take to celebrate the 100th anniversary of the Charlottetown Conference. This issue, of course, was related to what steps the Island might take to celebrate 100 years in Confederation in July 1, 1973. Walter Shaw won the 1959 election for the Conservatives, with David Stewart as a member of the Shaw Cabinet, winning a seat in Charlottetown. Both Governments were riding the winds of change, towards a more urban environment, better schools and hospital care, and improved infrastructure, with John Diefenbaker resurrecting the old canard of a "fixed link" by promising to build a causeway between Borden and Cape Tormentine. The new Shaw Government had a more urban face, with many young professionals, a sweep of the four districts in Charlottetown and Summerside, and a coherent vision of moving the Island into the second half of the 20th century.

David Stewart understood these issues. He had a wide circle of friends, not only in the wealthier areas of Charlottetown, where Catholic-Protestant divisions were breaking down quickly, because many families shared interests in common (like Florida holidays, golf memberships, and summer residences), but also in his direct interest in his Ford dealership, where September purchases by farmers and fishermen correlated exactly with the quality and yields of the summer harvests. Thanks to his ferry service, he realised that more off-Island tourists wanted more than fine Island beaches – they wanted golf courses, restaurants, and other urban pleasures like theatres. It was no accident that his summer cottage was in Cavendish in the National Park, built around the beaches, the home of Lucy Maud Montgomery, and the site of the wreckage of the celebrated *Marco Polo*, the fastest ship in the world.

The push for a theatre and cultural complex evolved from all of these forces, and was reliant on the political support of the Diefenbaker and Shaw Conservative Government, the leadership of Dave Stewart, and the collective interest of a number of Islanders interested in commemorating the Charlottetown Conference. Acting on the suggestion of Mrs. E.B. Ellis, Stewart organized a local committee, which in turn enlisted a nine member national committee, the Fathers of Confederation Memorial Citizens Foundation, including Eric C. Harvey of Calgary, who served as Chairman, Senator Paul H. Bouffard of Quebec City, Sir Brian Dunfield of St. John's, and C.F. Scott of Ottawa. Frank MacKinnon, the only son of a former Lieutenant Governor and a Conservative provincial politician, D.S. (Murdoch) MacKinnon, who was now Principal of Prince of Wales College, took charge of the local initiative, helped by a wide circle of interested parties. The idea of an Arts Complex was not new, either on the Island or across Canada. The Massey Royal Commission on National Development in the Arts, Letters, and Sciences of 1951, headed by Vincent Massey, demonstrated only too clearly that in the area of arts and culture, Canada trailed the industrialized world. Frank MacKinnon, on behalf of the Island, presented a submission to the Massey Commission about an Arts Center in Charlottetown. J. Walter Jones, the Island's premier from 1943 to 1953, who likened himself to be the Farmers' Premier, perhaps spoke for all Premiers when he confided personally with Vincent Massey, "I don't see why the commission should bother with Prince Edward Island at all; it doesn't need any culture."

It took time for the messages of the Massey Report to sink in, but gradually the federal government created new mechanisms to help young artists, re-invigorated the CBC's French and English networks through drama, comedy, and sports, and created the Canada Council, the basis of three new federal funding agencies to support university research in medicine, engineering, and the social sciences. Perhaps more directly, the federal government started to fund universities, which swelled as the baby boom generation flooded campuses, becoming centers of sports, theatre, and cultural events, in addition to academic pursuits. By extension, similar attention was finally being paid to sports and athletics, which had remained until then, a crudely exploitative system of funding for both the Olympics and professional hockey, which was dominated by the six team NHL, where players had little formal education and were under-paid. The universities, unlike in the US, couldn't afford to fund their athletic programs. Thanks to a number of amateur athletic associations in the provinces,

Ottawa initiated the Canada Winter Games and the Canada Summer Games, which served as a catalyst to train Canadian athletes and build a network of quality sports complexes in small communities across Canada, with the Games rotating every two years. Significant contributions to this athletic initiative came from three Islanders, namely David Boswell, Charles Ballem, and Bill Ledwell.

As 1964 approached, Frank MacKinnon assembled this diverse group to promote the idea of an Arts Complex, to be built and located next to Province House to commemorate the Fathers of Confederation. The hope was to get federal support, plus the support of ten provinces. At a meeting with the Prime Minister, John Diefenbaker pledged to support half the total, $15 million, if the other provinces funded their share, roughly 0.15 cents per capita. It was the old game of federal-provincial jostling, the first new industry created at the original Charlottetown Conference. Gradually, the other provinces did commit their share, based on a per capita population basis, with Quebec, led by John LeSage, a prominent hold out. But thanks to a spectacular intervention by Robert Stanfield, Quebec came on side, and the Fathers of Confederation complex was opened on October 5, 1964. All ten Premiers attended, plus the new Prime Minister, Lester Pearson, and Queen Elizabeth II and Prince Philip, their second visit to the Island. As the Queen laid the cornerstone, the Prime Minister spoke words that were prophetic, that the building serves as "a tribute to those famous men who founded our Confederation. But it is also dedicated to the fostering of those things that enrich the mind and delight the heart, those intangible but precious things that give meaning to a society and help create from it a civilization and a culture."

In retrospect, the Confederation complex, housing several theatres, an art gallery, and a library, adjoining the adjacent Province House and the George Coles building, now has one of the best collections of Confederation archives outside Ottawa and stands as a monument to the nation's collective memory, all for an original cost of $15 million. For the first time, the premiers had agreed to provide funding for a national institution outside their own jurisdiction. It was a spectacular success for Prince Edward Island, which gained a new cultural complex, a new tourist attraction, and began a fresh start of a real national awakening of the Island's role in Confederation. During the first summer season at the theatre, under the inspired leadership of Mavor Moore, the Confederation Arts Center launched a spectacular musical, *Anne of Green Gables*, with magical lyrics by Norman and Elaine Campbell and Don Herron, directed by Allan Lund, winning the applause of TV and newspaper critics. Nathan Cohen, the acerbic drama critic for the Toronto *Star*, offered his own assessment: "something wonderful is happening in Charlottetown".

There was a long litany of other performances, like Wayne and Shuster, attracting some of the finest actors and performances to Charlottetown, and equally, drawing newspaper columnists and arts reviewers from media as distant as New York, London, and Tokyo. The entire complex oozed of the 'kindred spirits', to use an *Anne of Green Gables* phrase, of the Fathers of Confederation, each with different backgrounds, personal experiences, languages and religion, toiling by day and deliberating at night, walking the streets of Charlottetown, forming personal friendships, fostering new political alliances, and debating the Confederation terms, with their conscience as their guide.

In Province House, near the tablet showing the crests of the first four provinces in Confederation, and the five statesmen – Macdonald, Cartier, Tilley, Tupper, and the Island's John Hamilton Gray, there is a memorial plaque to describe their work[1]:

> *Providence being their guide,*
> *They builded better than they knew.*

*****

During the Campbell-MacLean era, PEI was going through wrenching changes, rooted in more than simple economic pressures. There were new challenges facing Canada, not just in the rural/urban divide,

---

1 *The world was all before them, where to choose, There place of rest, and Providence their guide.* John Milton, Paradise Lost, Book XII, Line 646. *He builded better than he knew; The conscious stone of beauty grew.* Ralph Waldo Emerson, *The Problem. Stanza 2.*

which deeply affected the legislatures and the political priorities of government. It was, in short, the classic problem of democracy: who gets what, where, when and how, e.g. in education, industrial development, and health care. Canada required more immigrants, and it greatly needed to devote more attention to science and technology, which to the man on the street or the woman on the farm, was not a great vote winner, certainly not when compared to improving local roads and schools. The post-war baby boom was changing the very nature of Canadian society. Cities were the new engine of growth, education was a central policy agenda, and health care was being transformed by innovative new technologies, ranging from antibiotics and pharmaceuticals to new forms of medical specialization. The universities needed money, for faculty, for new science buildings, for engineering labs, and for expensive research. Outside the gerrymandering of political districts around religion, the Island faced a growing problem of higher education, which few people wanted to address, as there were too many old wounds and scars. However, at this time the Diefenbaker government started funding higher education based on a per capita funding formula, so PEI no longer could avoid the university issue.

Education on the Island dates back to the early years of Edmund Fanning as Lieutenant-Governor, who set aside land for a school in 1803. Politics, religion and education proved to be a heady cocktail on the Island, because schools were affiliated with churches (e.g. St. Peter's as an Anglican School, Notre Name and St. Joseph's Convent were Catholic). In 1877, the Public Schools' Act provided for a provincial Department of Education, and consolidated the Normal School and the Model School, St. Dunstan's College was Roman Catholic and privately funded, and Prince of Wales College was funded publicly. Across Canada, most universities were not really state operated secular institutions; they were denominational institutes, tied to one religion. More students lived not only outside the family home but even outside their city or province, and naturally they needed residences. This resulted in a new worry for parents, *in loco parentis:* who looks after the students? But with new federal funding, the Island's Government faced a direct problem, in that it had two institutions, one private and Catholic, with half the Province

341

being Catholic, and one public, which offered only two years of university.

Each institution had a long history, generous Alumni support, and overlapping programs. Prince of Wales College offered degree programs in Arts, Science, Nursing, Education, and two years of engineering, plus the last two years of high school. It also offered preparation courses for provincial teachers' licenses. Several Catholics taught at Prince of Wales, and historically, two or three professors taught at both institutions. A handicap was that Prince of Wales didn't offer four year programs leading to degrees. St. Dunstan's, the successor to St. Andrews, became a University in 1941. As a Catholic institution, it had never received provincial government support. St. Dunstan's had also grown in enrollment, with many off-Island students, mainly from Quebec, the Boston states, and Hong Kong. Aside from the last two years of high school, it offered degree programs in Arts, Sciences, Education, three years of pre-med, and two years of Engineering. Its operations included a large, brick campus and a dairy farm outside Charlottetown. Money was a perpetual problem, and aside from student fees and some Alumni support, St. Dunstan's received enormous clergy assistance. Indeed, both as professors and administrators - about 26 priests and 20 nuns – the Catholic Clergy were paid a pittance, less than a thousand dollars a year, even though almost all the professor clergy had doctorates from some of the best American and Canadian universities.

In 1957, after fifty years of political peace, where two institutions operated in a suspended solitude, the university problem put religion back to the front burner of Island politics. It proved to be an intractable issue that remained in one form or another for two more decades. On May 25, 1955, the Liberal government of Alex Matheson had a sweeping victory, 27-3, a huge majority that contrasted with the 1935 election, when the Liberals won every seat under Thane Campbell. Yet the 1955 victory came at a cost. The provincial Liberals, who had been governing for three decades - both in Ottawa under MacKenzie King and Louis St. Laurent, and on the Island – exhibited internal personality differences. Walter Harris, St. Laurent's Minister of Finance, argued that Ottawa had overpaid PEI by $1.4 m, and wanted the federal money back. That was, to put it mildly, a political mistake. In addition, they then faced John Diefenbaker, the oracle of Prince Albert, whose leadership campaign in 1956 presaged a new era in federal-provincial relations, a corner stone of his 1957 victory. The Island's Conservative delegates, not enamoured with George Drew, were strongly pro-Diefenbaker. Now federal and provincial issues were joined.

In the Island Legislature, the Matheson government introduced a measure to allow university education courses for teacher certification (i.e. additional education courses allowed teachers better salaries). The proposal, introduced by Education Minister Keir Clark, was that only the courses offered by a public institution would be endorsed. It was a clumsy measure, and poorly thought out, but it was too late. Even though there were many Protestant students at St. Dunstan's, and many Catholic students at Prince of Wales, with up to half of the high school teachers on the Island being Catholic, the bill enraged the Catholic community and brought up the notorious Protestant–Catholic battles of the past, which by now were thought to be below the political radar screen. Prince of Wales supporters, knowing that the College offered teachers training courses, were upset. In addition, some Protestants weren't happy that a Catholic university was offering courses for non-denominational high school teachers. A delegation from St. Dunstan's University spoke to the Legislature, meeting in full session, and outlined its own plans to offer a Bachelor of Education program for the increased number of high school teachers. An enormous sectarian division broke out, splitting the provincial Liberal caucus and putting severe strains between Premier Matheson and the Education Minster, Keir Clark, a Protestant with many close friends at PWC, and some members of the Legislature.

For the first time in 75 years, PEI faced an open religious dispute, pitting Catholics against Protestants. In fact, when the SDU delegation appeared, with a fully prepared and well argued brief, the government's position changed overnight, allowing both institutions to offer education courses for advanced teacher training. The religion-education mix remained a simmering cocktail of potential strife, even though many Catholics and Protestants felt immensely uneasy about this festering sore spot, which divided schools, universities, hospitals, and friendships. The days of the Matheson Government were numbered. Curiously, Matheson himself announced his retirement at a political meeting held at St. Dunstan's University.

This incident illustrates that Maritime university history is full of lost opportunities, including a failed proposal by the Carnegie Foundation to fund a federated university for the Maritime Provinces, a structure used in American states like New York and California. Sir William MacDonald, grandson of Captain John MacDonald, who first brought Scottish settlers in 1772, and had funded MacDonald College at McGill University, and started a prototype MacDonald model school near Charlottetown, became interested in the Carnegie proposal. Indeed, he was fully prepared to help support higher education on the Island, starting in 1907 with a plan to make PWC a college of McGill University. Not surprisingly, religion and politics intervened at the highest levels to stall the federated proposal. It was another lost advantage, destroyed when prevarications, weak leadership, and personal animosities entered the policy fray, often all at once. Tragically, for higher education in Canada, the idea of universities with multi-campuses, even in different provinces, was gone for a century.

The new demographics proved to be a financial struggle for both institutions, as the post-war baby boom had arrived. There were real shortages of faculty, and budget problems were at a crisis point. St. Dunstan's, with rising enrollments, new science faculty for the Duffy Chemistry building, and a thriving athletic program, submitted a request for $300,000 in annual funding to the Walter Shaw government in 1963. Unsure of how to proceed, the Shaw government appointed a Royal Commission on Higher Education, a three-man group of distinguished Canadians. The Commission recommended the creation of a single university named the University of Prince Edward Island, with two autonomous colleges: St. Dunstan's and PWC. In the meantime, through cost-sharing arrangements, the federal government now provided financial support to all universities across Canada, including both St. Dunstan's and Prince of Wales College.

Meanwhile, PWC was also on the move. The Principal, Frank MacKinnon, the noted political science professor and author, was quick to implement a key recommendation of the Royal Commision, namely to make Prince of Wales a degree granting institution. In 1964, PWC became a university, with four years of course offerings, and with Lester Pearson, the Prime Minister, receiving the first honorary degree. Simultaneously, MacKinnon announced grand plans for Prince of Wales, including new buildings, affiliations with the Confederation Center, and recruiting prominent architects, all with appropriate funding requirements from both levels of government. Premier Alex Campbell, fully aware of the political pratfalls of linking politics and higher education, knew only too well that a competitive race to support a Catholic institution, when half the population was Catholic, against a public institution that could play the 'Protestant' card, was a dreaded political sink hole. He knew that an elite group of Catholic and Protestants - people who were educated, who knew both institutions, but who knew that their own friends and religious groups questioned their motives - was a potential card he could play. And Campbell himself, a pure old school politician, also had many friends on both sides of the religious divide that would support him in the end. After all, if Trudeau could say that the state had no role in the bedrooms of the nation, why should religion dominate the classrooms of the Island's small academic world?

What policy options faced the provincial government, and could the Premier cope with the political consequences? For instance, how could PEI deal with the funding issues for these two colleges? How could there be specialization, so that duplication could be avoided? How could they fit into a large mix of Maritime institutions (13 in Nova Scotia alone), sharing for instance, engineering offerings with the universities in Nova Scotia or New Brunswick? How would PEI science students become prepared for pre-med instruction at Dalhousie Medical School? Could the province afford the rapidly rising cost of healthcare, now that PEI joined other provinces in sharing the cost of Medicare, introduced nation-wide in 1968? In 1969, the Campbell government merged the two institutions, one of the Island's most dramatic political events of the century. What happened behind the scenes?

In 1969, the Campbell government introduced Bill 57, which established the University Grants commission, a non-partisan administrative body operating in several provinces and countries to offer advice on program funding. The Principal of PWC, Dr. Frank McKinnon, pounced on the bill and launched a massive protest, using the students as political fodder and the media as his polemical weapon. Personally, he had refused to have any dealings with St. Dunstan's University, either formally or informally. While the issue on the surface was based upon the role of Government and the principle of academic freedom, the real problem was intensely partisan and religious - to MacKinnon, Prince of Wales should be the sole Island University. In this heady and sensitive mix, the public policy issue of Higher Education became intensely personal. The general issues of politics and religion were known, accepted, and increasingly taken for granted, at least when serious money was not on the table. But Campbell's choices were few, any option would be very expensive, and every action was now very public. Campbell was young, ambitious, and clearly he was not an academic. McKinnon was older, knew the academic establishment across Canada, and understood that this was his last chance to lead PWC to his promised land. In reality, the issue really centered on two people, Frank McKinnon, an enigmatic academic who could be brilliantly open and forthcoming but who privately could nurse the personal demons of a single child abandoned by his father, and Alex Campbell, the son of a Premier, a politician who did not understand the workings of the academic marketplace, but who wished to lance the boil of this perpetual Catholic-Protestant rivalry in higher education. In the extreme, it was the central problem of democracies: who governs?

The Premier was not acting in a vacuum. As noted, there had been a 1965 Royal Commission on Higher Education, appointed by the Shaw Government in 1964, which effectively proposed a merger of the two institutions into the University of Prince Edward Island, but left open the option that each institution could retain its campus and college offerings. Campbell had other groups on his side, including women's groups, and private citizens representing Catholics and Protestants, pushing the idea of a single institution. The Bishop of Charlottetown, Malcolm MacEachern, who was an outsider from Cape Breton, N.S., was quietly supportive. He recognized that many of the Island's 100 Catholic priests wanted to retain autonomy for St. Dunstan's, including some of the clergy professors at the University, but he knew that the SDU faculty understood an amalgamation was necessary, as did the Catholic Rector at St. Dunstan's Basilica, William Simpson. Through intermediaries, including the Governor, W.J. MacDonald, a Catholic who had taught math at PWC, the Bishop offered to support Frank MacKinnon as the new President of a federated or amalgamated institution. On the other hand, there were many Catholic clergy on the staff of St. Dunstan's who supported a single university, as did the Students Union. On April 2, 1969, before a packed gallery and a full Legislative Assembly, Premier Alex Campbell announced the new policy, what was to become the creation of the University of Prince Edward Island:

> *I have not referred to this new institution by name, since it has none. At the moment the name is unimportant - it is the function and the purpose of this new institution upon which we must focus our attention. In doing so, let us as Islanders constantly bear in mind that it is to be our Island university, designed to meet our needs, and it must be developed to the limits of our capabilities. It must be considered to the university of all religious faiths, the university of each and every ethnic group, in short the university of all Islanders...It will be our University, and our program for the Island. A university can grow as we grow and one that all Islanders can support, utilize and cherish.*

This speech lanced the boil, finally helping to end to this nasty dispute, what historian and former aide to Premier Campbell, Wayne MacKinnon, calls "a pathetic story of petty prejudice, blatant bigotry, false bonhomie, intellectual pretensions, insatiable egos, and unmitigated arrogance." Instead of being the calm before a storm, the quietude came immediately after. The two colleges became the University of Prince Edward Island, and most of the faculty stayed, while the Prince of Wales campus was converted into a technical school, Holland College. Ultimately, the new University became what the founding fathers of both institutions had always wanted, a place of high learning dedicated to the advancement of the Island.

In fact, UPEI has become an engine of economic growth, as the old St. Dunstan's campus was slowly refurbished with new buildings, advanced lab facilities, and the Atlantic Vet College, one of only four in Canada. Rural renaissance, if it was anything, meant survival of the family farm. However, this implied more than financial tokenism, protected markets for produce, and traditional small scale production. Farm life on Prince Edward Island hadn't changed much in 100 years, with most farms producing potatoes, dairy cattle for milk production, and a few exotic crops like beans. In one sense, farm production had moved backwards, as more acreage was devoted to potato production, perhaps up to 120,000 acres at the peak, with too little crop rotation and leaving some of the land fallow. Today, there are about 75,000 total acres in cultivation. This compares to an estimated 110,000 in 1900, with almost 14,000 farms. Increased yields per acre come not from better farm methods per se but from increased use of pesticides and infusion of chemical ingredients.

Many Islanders hold the view that the Province's agriculture should be entirely devoted to organic production, rather than the trend to potato farming fixed on frozen French fries suitable for national fast-food chains. The Canadian Experimental farm, located near the St. Dunstan's campus in Charlottetown, introduced some changes but now remains largely passive. Island farmers and the Department of Agriculture were slow to accept these changes, including better land use, reduction in potato acreage to acceptable levels, and prevention of pesticides near rivers and waterways. Around the world, farming was becoming more scientific, as new Dutch immigrant farmers demonstrated on their large farms in King's County. Better land use and superior agriculture was the familiar lament dating from the days of Lord Selkirk in 1803. Continuous attempts to improve agricultural production through better yields and high value added production usually fell on deaf ears, including the abolition of destructive practices, stemming from the processing industry's demand for long potatoes, which requires leaving the crop in the ground until late

September, and harvesting through October, leaving no time for a winter cover crop to take root.

In 1984, talks in Atlantic Canada raised the on-going issue of agriculture and veterinary medicine, but regional squabbling left open a possible location. Circumstances proved to be opportune for PEI Premier, Jim Lee and federal Agriculture Minister Eugene Whalen, to join forces to provide financial support for Atlantic Canada's first veterinary school, located on the UPEI campus in Charlottetown. The Vet College was an immediate success, with superb facilities, faculty recruited from Canada and abroad, and new measures of Atlantic cooperation to attract students from across Canada, the US, and overseas. In 2005, the AVC, now part of the University of Prince Edward Island, broke ground on a $32-million expansion aimed at making the school a leading force in aquaculture and biosciences. The project is being backed with $18 million from the National Research Council, two million from the province, and a private sector fundraising campaign. The aim is to build on the University's recognized leadership in global animal sciences, and the Island's traditional sectors, farming and fishing, where research and science can create improved value added production for the Atlantic region, in part through network affiliations with universities, the Island's food technology centre, the federal plant health laboratory, and federal research scientists.

******

In the development of innovative ways to celebrate the hundredth anniversary of the 1864 conference, Islanders were particularly fortunate to have the presence of a young historian, a freshly minted PhD from the history department of the University of Toronto. This scholar, who also happened to be a Catholic priest, came from the most prestigious history department in Canada, and studied with two of the very best history professors in the land. These icons of Canadian history wrote magisterial biographies of John A. Macdonald and George Brown. Francis Bolger, born and educated in Stanley Bridge, one of four sons, graduated *summa cum laude* from St. Dunstan's University. He was ordained a priest in 1948, and then toiled in the seminar rooms at the University of Toronto. His research papers at the University of Toronto exposed an intriguing issue: the two best historians of the Confederation period, and the noted authorities on John A. Macdonald and George Brown, actually knew very little about the Charlottetown Conference.

In one sense, Bolger was an anomaly as a historian. His teachers were the finest historians in the country, and included Donald Creighton, Maurice Careless, and other giants at the University of Toronto, the largest academic institution in Canada. The Careless-Creighton duo were exceedingly good teachers, and great scholars of the old school, skilled in the philosophy of history, the mix of personalities, the economic and social context of events, and the use of abundant records, letters, and archival documents. They are accorded to the 'great man' theory of history, the study of dominant figures and how they shaped the decades and centuries of a young country. Like Thomas Carlyle, they saw political personalities for what they are, as great shapers of destiny, people who leave lasting impressions and momentous monuments to their talent. Creighton, with his magisterial two volume study of John A. Macdonald, *The Young Politician* and *The Old Chieftain*, has never been surpassed in Canadian historiography. Bolger proceeded to study the Charlottetown Conference of 1864 and the rest, as they say, is history.

With Creighton as Chairman of the Ph.D. committee, and prompted by Donald Creighton himself, Bolger read every book he could find on the subject, and then started the long, tortuous work of the real scholar, like a Sherlock Holmes in heat, combing libraries, archives, and private homes in Toronto, Ottawa, Charlottetown, and London for material. He studied the tangled correspondence, newspapers, court records, and colonial archives, focusing specifically on the events of 1864. In such efforts, where luck can be the residue of design, Francis Bolger unlocked many secrets of the Charlottetown Conference. It was more than a meeting of politicians, more than a series of fancy parties on the *Queen Victoria*, or what Islanders called the Confederate Cruiser. Charlottetown shaped the destiny of Canada.

Curiously, both authors, Creighton in his history of John A. Macdonald's, and Careless, in his biography of George Brown, John

A's nemesis, had limited access to the records of the Charlottetown meetings, but both felt there was much missing about this historic conference. Creighton was more than Bolger's teacher and Chairman of his PhD thesis. They were both interested in Prince Edward Island as a British colony that became a province, however reluctantly, and both scholars had a keen interest in the events leading up to the Charlottetown conference, including the discussions about Maritime Union, the political personalities in the Maritimes, and the intricate and direct links with nation-building work in Charlottetown. Further, Charlottetown facilitated detailed discussion of the specific clauses that were ratified in Quebec, known as the Quebec Resolutions, which became part of the British North America Act – in short, Canada's constitution.

Bolger, his thesis completed, moved from Toronto to Charlottetown as head of the history department at St. Dunstan's University, and published his opus, *Prince Edward Island and Confederation*, in 1964. His timing was perfect. The Island was in a festive mood, not unlike the Slaymaker's and Nichol's Olympic Circus in 1864, but also celebrating a magnificent new theatre complex in downtown Charlottetown, immediately adjacent to Province House, where the Father's of Confederation did their work and, as the historic plaque says, 'they builded better than they knew'. This grand complex is the lasting memorial to the Canada's Founding Fathers, and Father Bolger's book celebrating the 1864 Charlottetown Conference was the theme of the 100 year Island celebrations in 1964.

Creighton's instincts about the Charlottetown conference were known in small professorial circles, but there were many issues not yet understood or explained. More specifically, the Island conference was not the idle partners meeting often described by many historians. In fact, many of the delegates did not know each other until they came to Charlottetown, including some Maritime delegates who would not be known among the delegates from Ontario and Quebec. Indeed, despite the personal friendships of delegates like George Coles and Ed Whelan, they took issue with many of the terms of union. In fact, in contrast to Macdonald's personal view towards a unitary state, rather than a federal union, Coles led the charge that the provinces, not the federal government, be the stronger power, with all residual powers invested in the provinces, along the lines of the American federal union. While it is easy to say that the Maritime delegates basically listened to Cartier, Macdonald, Brown and Galt, and then posed a few questions, Bolger shows that, in fact, each Maritime legislature had fully debated both Maritime Union, and the issue of a federal union. The Maritime delegates weren't at Charlottetown to be informed: they were there to be won over. MacDonald knew this because he was a fervent listener, which is why he spent so much time with the delegates. Further, it was a credit to the Island delegates, who belonged both to the government and the opposition – Leader George Coles and A.A. MacDonald – that the conference discussed all the terms of the proposed union, including a presentation by Andrew Galt on day two of the federal powers, taxation, and financial issues.

These and other issues were laid out in Bolger's book. He was asked to speak at public forums, conventions, and the Rotary club. Suddenly PEI had a star historian, a colourful, entertaining and, at times hilariously funny story teller, who could regale huge audiences about Island history and the true story of the Charlottetown Conference. Soon Fr. Bolger, as he was affectionately known by Protestants and Catholics alike, had packed speaking tours, not only in PEI, but throughout the Maritimes during 1964. He spoke with passion, elegance, and fervour about Confederation. He challenged the conventional views of Canadian history, recognizing the powerful impact of the work of the Charlottetown Conference, and the personal roles of the Island delegates, especially the strong and instinctive wisdom of George Coles, who directly challenged John A's vision. Bolger admired Ed Whelan's role as an elegant speaker, backroom friend of many delegates, including D'Arcy McGee and, as an Editor of *The Examiner*, his capacity to write as a newspaper editor, with all the editing tools to take down notes. Whelan was, coupled with George Brown's letters to his wife, the author of the closest memoir of the proceedings.

Father Bolger's book was the start of an Island awakening to its own history. Bolger's proselytizing oratory, writings, personal demeanour, and use of sharp wit masked the seriousness of his cause, and his message to take Island and Canadian history seriously. Suddenly, families searched their attics, barns and basements for family records and land documents. Women's Institutes published histories of local communities and authors came forward with histories of local personalities like Cornelius Howett, John Hamilton Gray, and Dr. John Mackieson. New histories on topics ranging from the Island railway story to the land question, and the cooperative movement to the Highland settlers were now re-examined with new documents and personal stories. The province funded a new publication, *The Island Magazine*, now in its fourth decade, and it allows local and national historians to re-examine Island events and personalities, while recording new works on such issues as immigration, shipping, Island politics, and the land issue. There were new and renewed subjects, from compilations of Island poetry led by the works of Frank Ledwell, to studies of the biodiversity of the Island's wildlife, the unique sand dunes, and tidal marshes.

Father Bolger's courses on Island history coupled with his protracted efforts to recruit new faculty and develop the history department at St. Dunstan's and UPEI produced new landmark studies, and influenced other historians to examine Island questions, even the role of small Island economies in the world – the initiative of the Island Studies department at UPEI. He promoted initiatives to engage the Island's professional class – doctors, lawyers, scientists, bureaucrats, nurses, and fellow clergymen – to tell their unique stories of the Island, and Island institutions. And he encouraged politicians to write their own stories, and open their personal archives to other historians. More specifically, he pressed the Confederation Library and the University to build an Island collection of documents, letters, manuscripts, diaries, and priceless archival material to the Provincial Archives and the special section of the Robertson Library at UPEI. His work accumulated in cooperation with librarians and archivists on the Island, skilled people like Nicholos de Jong, Doug Boylan, Harry Holman, Boyde Beck, Simon Lloyd, Brendon O'Grady, and Ed MacDonald.

Perhaps the great upshot of the 1964 celebrations, extended to the 1973 celebrations when PEI celebrated 100 years in Confederation, was a powerful new, historic 'infrastructure' on the Island, in the Public Archives, in the Confederation Center Library and the Island Reserve section of the UPEI Library, the magnificent records of Island history which reside for students, researchers, and historians. Few people understood better than Father Bolger the need to preserve historic papers. During his thesis work, he had met members of the family of Joseph Pope, and saw they possessed some important historic records that many thought had been destroyed. From a historian's perspective, the Island's Joseph Pope is *the* Father of historic archives in Canada. He was, of course, the closest person to John A. Macdonald, and his wife Agnes, and had access to Macdonald's papers to write Macdonald's first biography.

More significantly, first as assistant clerk of the Privy Council under Macdonald, and then under other Prime Ministers, including Wilfred Laurier, Pope recognized that Canadian state papers were not being catalogued properly and indeed, several state papers involving treaties and foreign affairs were kept in London, not Ottawa. Even worse, a dramatic fire in the West block in 1897 almost destroyed public documents. Laurier did act, and appointed a three man study group, led by Joseph Pope and fortuitously, another Islander, Ernest Jarvis, from St. Eleanors. The work was not helped when two civil servants refused to talk to each other. By this time, Pope was equal to this diplomatic challenge, and all three agreed to the final report. Eventually, in 1904, Arthur Doughty was appointed the new Dominion archivist. Canada was starting to grow up! Today, thanks to Father Bolger and a host of historians, librarians, politicians, archivists, and bureaucrats, Prince Edward Island stands second to none as keeper of records.

****

When the baby boom generation initiated the first wave of retirement, the signs of the real demographics of the Island started to show in small ways, for example, in the rising number of Japanese tourists who wanted to move to the Island, the presence of Chinese students at the University who, when they finished their graduate studies, moved back to the Island, and the presence of 'people from away' who worked for the federal government. Ottawa now provided important job creation on the Island, such as the Departments of Veterans Affairs, the RCMP, and the new tax office in Summerside where the GST was collected. More and more people now realized that the Island, and the Maritimes generally, had reached what they faced 200 years ago, a shortage of people.

Across Canada, demographics, that esoteric study of people, their age cohorts, and the shifts in population, affects provinces and regions far more significantly than the ups and downs of the economic cycle. Demography is the study of populations, the age profile of regions and countries, and the changes in births, deaths, and immigration and emigration. Compared to most areas of the social sciences, demography is amazingly accurate, as a person who is 20 years old in 1990 will always be 30 years old in 2000. Demography and its implications have become a huge industry, as the ebb and flow of population greatly impacts industries, technologies, and corporate strategies. The United Nations now widely uses world population data sheets, based upon census studies, for identifying key indicators for some 190 countries, including births, deaths, natural increases/ decreases, infant mortality, levels of fertility, life expectancy, prevalence of HIV/AIDS, contraceptive use, land intensity, etc.. Demographic specialists, called actuaries, are sophisticated experts who use advanced statistical tools and computer models to trace population movements years and decades ahead to see trend lines and policy changes. The problem for the Island is not the more traditional rural-urban shift of the population, but the 'greying effect', caused by too few young, and too many old people, with not enough in the middle, as significant wage earners.

A related problem is that the Maritimes generally, and the Island in particular, are not the destination of the immigrant population. New immigrants to Canada, about 300,000 per year, gravitate towards the big cities – Toronto, Montreal, Calgary and Vancouver – and few come to the Atlantic region, except as potential tourists. In the past 100 years, there have been only two waves of immigration to the Island, mainly as Dutch farmers and the Lebanese community. Both groups had relatives who came in the 1930s or before. Since the vast majority of Islanders trace their ancestry to immigrants from the successive waves of French, Scottish, English and Irish citizens who looked to the new world for land, prosperity, and survival, immigration has never been seen as either an economic challenge or a social crisis. It now is. In the last 100 years, more immigrants have come from other shores, as in Dutch farmers from Holland, for instance, and Lebanese families from the Middle East, from Lebanon, but also from Syria, and the sorted boundaries of Palestine. In recent years, PEI joins other provinces in search of their Pacific heritage, based on the catalogue of tales from immigrants from Asia, including China and Japan, but also South Korea and Hong Kong.

The presence of non-European immigrants is instructive. The first people of Chinese origin to arrive in PEI was in July 1891, according to an article in *The Guardian* on October 9, 1891: "Charlottetown will soon have no Chinese. They cannot find enough work to do... ." A decade later, the official count of Chinese people was four: Jack "John" Ling, James Ling, Joseph Ling and Wylam Ling from the Canton Delta region of China. John Ling actually arrived at the age of 26 in 1896, and started a laundry business in Charlottetown. Others had preceded him, but only John Ling stayed. With the construction of the CPR, there had been a massive influx of Chinese labourers, but after the railway was completed in 1885, anti-Chinese laws were introduced to slow their entry. A Chinese head tax of $50 per person was imposed, and soon was increased to $500, the equivalent of three years wages. Chinese immigration paralleled the experience of the Highland Scots or the Irish, where at home there was a mix of famine, wars, starvation and unemployment, the Malthusian crisis now experienced in African countries. Prejudice was a fact of life for Chinese immigrants. In 1923, Chinese emigration was stopped by the *Chinese Exclusion Act*. On PEI, a special provincial tax was proposed, directed at Chinese businessmen only.

In Summerside, the Royal Cafe opened its doors in 1922 at a time when the silver fox industry was a lucrative endeavour. Restaurants and eateries emerged in the 1920s, but they typically didn't serve oriental fare. While hand laundries were predominately women's work in China, laundries were the most common business choice for male Chinese immigrants. Businesses with names like Sing, Lee,

Ling, Chan and Hop-Wo came and went over the years in P.E.I., each employing an average of four or five people. All were located in Charlottetown or Summerside, with one in Souris. In 1923, the Exclusion Act meant entry to Canada all but ceased, leaving Chinese immigrants on P.E.I. completely cut off from direct links with their relatives and removing any chance of bringing their dependents to Canada. As a result, almost no Chinese women were on P.E.I. until the Act was repealed at the end of the 1940s.

After the War, new Chinese immigrants arrived, and Chinese physicians became part of the staff at the Provincial Sanatorium. In 1956, in response to a shortage of educational institutions in Hong Kong, St. Dunstan's accepted its first Chinese students. In the 1960s, after changes to federal immigration policy, immigrants with professional skills, such as researchers, scientists, medical personnel and university professors, started to arrive. Some students, after graduating from St. Dunstan's, went on to do their doctorates across North America, and then returned to pursue their academic career at UPEI. One Hong Kong Alumnus, Dr. Albert Young, made a major contribution to the Sports Center at UPEI. By 1999, the Chinese Canadian Association of P.E.I. listed 63 families, with more then 200 members.

Historically, Asian immigrants kept a low profile. Wong Fong, for instance, operated the City Cafe in the 1930s, and was the only immigrant known to have a full-blooded Chinese wife in town during that time. Anglicized names were usually assigned to Chinese immigrants upon entry to Canada. Before the Second World War, all permanent Chinese residents in P.E.I. were in the laundry or restaurant business. Rose Ling, 38, passed away in 1940 and was buried in the Catholic cemetery, the earliest known tombstone for a Chinese woman on PEI. The Chinese Exclusion Act was repealed in 1947, but some restrictions still remained. Meanwhile, the Chinese people were starting to merge with the existing European-based P.E.I. population, sometimes marrying local people. However, in the case of John Ling's son, William, he returned to China and married a local woman with whom he had one son. He returned to P.E.I. and after that marriage was dissolved, wed Toni Tolman of

Boston. They have descendants on the Island, including Rose Ling, a past president of the Chinese Canadian Association of PEI. A new trend is also increasing the local Chinese Canadian population, as Island couples adopt babies from the People's Republic of China. Immigrants such as Harry Thom came to Canada in 1910 and settled in PEI, married a woman from Newfoundland, and operated a store in Charlottetown.

Like other immigrants, especially the large Lebanese-Syrian community, they concentrated on business. They were also extremely education conscious, and generally stayed away from the political fray. However, some of the Lebanese community became active politically: Frank Zakem, whose relatives first received a peddler's license from the Province in the nineteenth century, became Mayor of Charlottetown, while Joe Ghiz became head of the PEI Liberal Party and the first ethnic Premier in Canada. His son Robert Ghiz became Premier in 2007, becoming the second father-and-son Premiers in Island history, following the tradition of Thane and Alex Campbell.

****

Prince Edward Island entered the new millennium with optimism. Federal-provincial agreements provided more leverage to deal with the Island's economic priorities, and the province's finances were rated in the middle of the ten provinces, no mean achievement for a province without natural resources (like oil and gas, minerals, or timber), or huge crown lands. New political leaders like Joe Ghiz and Pat Binns had learned much from the Campbell-MacLean transformation, as politics began to focus on the new national agenda, with the primacy of education as the benchmark, exports as the key to wealth creation, and energy conservation as the unheralded saviour of hydrocarbon addiction. Religion was no longer a factor in politics or education, although traces of the old bitterness and rivalry lingered. If anything, notwithstanding the very high weekly attendance at Sunday services, with the Island population now at 140,000, and with some 110 Churches spread across all corners of the province, some churches now had a new ecumenical role as an attraction for tourists, a site of musical concerts, and, thanks to the incredible acoustics of St. Dunstan's Cathedral and William Critchlow Harris's architectural gem, the St. Mary's Catholic Church in Indian River, now a place for international operas, musicals, and classical concerts. Joe Ghiz, the son of Lebanese immigrants, put a new emphasis on Atlantic cooperation, and was a strong backer of a constitutional settlement with Quebec, in the famous Meech Lake Accord. Curiously, he was a powerful and vociferous opponent of the US-Canada free trade agreement, when national tariffs had played such a powerful role in the general decline of the Maritime economy.

Pat Binns was the natural heir to Angus MacLean's legacy. As a politician, he ranks with Alex Campbell as the man with a winning way, tackling such complex issues as educational funding, hospital reorganization, and the environmental challenges of waste treatment, pure water, and raw sewage in a province with limited land and shallow water tables. Binns has three advantages from his political mentors: Peter Lougheed, where Binns was raised in Alberta and educated at the University of Alberta; Brian Mulroney, under whom he spent four years as a federal member from Cardigan; and, of course, Angus MacLean, under whom he served as the Minister of Municipal Affairs and the Environment and learned the Island lessons of rural renaissance.

Brian Mulroney, perhaps the last "Atlantic" Prime Minister, learned much of his politics and economic development ideas from his stints at St. Thomas University and St. F.X. in Antigonish. He witnessed first hand the problems of small communities, one-industry towns, and poor infrastructure so similar to his home town of Baie Comeau and the Quebec North Shore. As Prime Minister, he became a potent ally of Pat Binns on the building of the Fixed Link, the new airport in Charlottetown, long term financial support for the Confederation Center, the location of the GST (Goods and Service Tax) in Summerside, and the transformation of the historic Summerside Airbase, which served so nobly during the Second World War as a Training Center for Commonwealth Pilots, into a hugely successful aerospace industrial park. Part of Binn's lasting legacy was his role in founding the Council of the Federation, an institution of the ten provinces and three territories, to deal with national policies from the perspective of the provinces. The first meeting was held, appropriately, in Charlottetown in December 2004.

The Internet, faxes, and cell phones might be everyone else's bridge to the future. But, on PEI, the defining feature of the Island's identity is the 13km ribbon of concrete - a vast, engineering marvel of steel, cement, and communications wizardry that measures tides, ice flows, wind, air pressure, snow flurries and anything that affects the elements. From New Brunswick, the Confederation Bridge looks like a highway that rises into the horizon. From PEI, it is far more majestic, a sweeping ribbon of 44 suspended pillars reminiscent of a vast Roman Aqueduct, connecting the mainland to the Island.

Transportation has been an Island obsession for over 150 years, from when the first ice boats helped deliver the mail. In 1852, the New York and Newfoundland Telegraph Company installed the first submarine cable in North America, linking Cape Tormentine in New Brunswick and Cape Traverse in PEI. After Confederation, steamer service became a priority – indeed, George Etienne Cartier, on his trip to Charlottetown in August 1869, argued for a strong steamship line for continual communication, and when the Island joined the dominion, the better terms included a pledge for year-round communications. Vast ice breaker ferries like the *Abegweit*, carrying trains, cars, trucks, campers and automobiles, an underground tunnel (championed by Rev. Arthur Burke), and the causeway, promoted by Walter Shaw and John Diefenbaker, were all attempts to deal with this transportation challenge. Finally, the Mulroney government settled the issue with the construction of the engineering marvel, the 13 km Confederation Bridge. The Northumberland Strait, as an extension of the Gulf of St. Lawrence, is a fast-flowing waterway which deceives the eye.

Robert Ghiz (top), Joe Ghiz

Below the water is a staggering diversity of God's marine jewels, ranging from oysters and lobsters to diverse marine life, from small herring to enormous blue fin tuna. Along the Island shores, as Lucy Maud Montgomery so brilliantly described the coastline, there is an unparalleled habitat for sand dunes, secluded beaches, and crescent-shaped bays and inlets, a land pattern unique in North America. From bald eagles, falcons, and blue herons to piping plover, the Island is a giant, protected, sandy park loaded with diverse plants, trees and flowers, some imported from Europe 200 years ago. Springtime is an oasis of wild flowers, contrasting with the greens of trees, shrubs and grass, and with the red soil and water never far away. Treating this mystique of the Island as a protected species - as a giant protected asset - is perhaps a new idea, and one different in meaning but similar in concept to the colonial absent landowners, the entire province as a rural city state. As one Island women put the matter, when asked if she traveled much, replied, "No, didn't have to. I was born here."

In a generation, the Island has changed much, but some would argue, in an echo of comment by a visiting professor at UPEI, Abe Rotstein, the province has much to change if it is to remain the same. A small example illustrates this truism. Back in the 1950s, the medium of television led to a new appreciation of East Coast music and interest in the wider culture of Atlantic Canada. The most celebrated musical figure, a New Brunswicker by birth and an Islander by adoption, was Don Messer, whose musical talents were immense, and whose local reputation was not only widely appreciated but served as a model for young people on the Island. He performed all over Atlantic Canada, and was a natural attraction at political rallies. His first television show, *Don Messer and his Islanders*, featuring Marg Osborne and Charlie Chamberland, was as popular as NHL hockey. Fortunately, the local radio station, CFCY, had a powerful signal and Don Messer and the Islanders were heard as far north as Eastern Quebec and as far south as Maine. The CBC eventually moved his show to CBC Halifax, not only to reach a wider TV audience, but to introduce new talent from the Maritimes. Sadly for the Maritimes, the format of the CBC shifted to a new program, the *Singalong Jubilee*.

On this show, new, young talent came from all over Atlantic Canada, including John Allan Cameron, the Rankin Family, Nancy White, Stompin' Tom Conners, and Teresa O'Neill. One particular star, a young, brash, and immensely talented singer, born in Springhill, N.S., but serving as a physical training instructor in Summerside, was Anne Murray. Anne Murray proceeded to become both a national and international superstar, with best selling albums, TV shows, night club appearances, and Christmas Specials. She was helped in this by her manager and husband, Bill Langstroth, the producer of the Don Messer show in Halifax, and Island songwriters like Gene MacClellan, author of the enormously successful song, *Snowbird*. As a TV star, Anne Murray had the talent, drive, and commercial acumen to reach the top of her form, but also to help other Maritime musicians, song writers, poets, and musical stars to climb the greasy pole to stardom. Anne built superb international contacts, especially in Nashville where Maritimers like Hank Snow were well known, and were close to many fiddlers who knew Don Messer. Many Nashville stars started to come to Atlantic Canada, not only to put on shows and entertain at *Ceidleghs*, but to cultivate local talent. Over the decades, country music was being transformed into a mix of country music, the blues, gospel music, and bluegrass, and this cocktail fitted into Atlantic music, a blend of French, Scottish, and Irish music, with fiddle music at the core.

An example of such visitors was an enormously successful concert in 1966 at St. Dunstan's University of the Irish singing group, The Clancy Brothers and Tommy Makem. The three Clancy Brothers, Tommy, Paddy, and Liam, came from the south, while Tommy Makem came from the North, in Keady, County Armagh. They knew all the rebel songs of Ireland, were steeped in the poetry and music of *that* Island, and performed concert tours in the US and Europe. While staying in New York, Tommy Clancy, with his rich baritone voice, also performed in Broadway musicals, and befriended a young singer in Greenwich Village, named Bob Dylan. Soon, the Clancy Brothers and Tommy Makem were performing with Pete Seeger, Bob Dylan, and Joan Baez, and they appeared on national television shows like Ed Sullivan. In their first of many appearances on PEI in 1966, they were greeted by an awesome snow storm, so their Saturday performance at the St. Dunstan's University Winter Carnival was postponed by a day. Thanks to announcements on CFCY radio and in all the Island's Church bulletins, which gave notice of the delay, undaunted, they performed to a packed audience, representing families who traveled as far as Tignish and Souris, despite the weather. They may have been Irish (reinforced by their glistening Aran sweaters knitted by Mrs. Clancy), but their songs, poems, readings, and banter reflected the Island's own roots, with songs about the Irish troubles, revolutionary history, jokes about the English landlords, and the beckoning call for families who had to leave Ireland's shores. Their closing number, *The Patriot Game*, brought down the full house:

> *Come all you young rebels, and list while I sing,*
> *For the love of one's country is a terrible thing.*
> *It banishes fear with the speed of a flame,*
> *And it makes us all part of the patriot game.*

Not only did the audience love the performance, but the Clancy Brothers and Tommy Makem fell in love with the Province, where they had a chance to hear local talent and their love of Irish music. The group were surprised at the extent of musical talent on the Island and in the East coast, and the fact that Island fiddlers had three generations of family histories, with many prominent names of Island fiddlers, such as Gauthier, Cheverie, Chaisson and Chipman. Needless to say, this visit wasn't their last, nor was it without other gains. Paddy and Tommy Clancy, in their spare time, had business interests, including cattle ranches in Ireland, where they raised a superb French breed of cattle, the Charlais brand. By coincidence, there was a new immigrant farmer on the Island, a Montreal businessman whose son, Norman, was born in Summerside. Howard Webster, the owner of several business ventures, including the historic George Brown paper, the *Globe*, now re-christened as *The Globe and Mail,* a dowager company operating as Canada's national newspaper. Webster had assembled 7000 acres for a cattle ranch, dubbed Dundas Farms, located in King's County near Cardigan. His plan was to raise cattle, preferably Charolais cattle, imported from France. However, there was a health problem with imports, and a quarantine on French cattle. This situation, however, didn't apply to Irish cattle coming to Canada.

This deal embraced Webster and his Dundas Farm to the Clancy Brothers. Eventually, he developed other business ventures, including investments in the Toronto Blue Jays baseball team, which he negotiated with Islander Don McDougall, President of LaBatt's Breweries, to move to Toronto. When Webster and McDougall first met at the Windsor Hotel in Montreal, they didn't know each other, personally or professionally. It didn't take long to ascertain that they both had PEI connections: McDougall, from Kinkora, was born a Conservative, a former Conservative candidate in London and his sister was a future leader of the Island Conservative Party; Webster, in turn, was the owner of Dundas Farms, his son Norman born and raised in Summerside and the former China correspondent for the *Globe and Mail*. They spent three hours discussing everything under the sun, including Island history and their links to that fabled province. The Blue Jay investment? That deal was decided in about 4 nanoseconds. Norman Webster eventually became the Chancellor of UPEI, the Island now has regular visits from Nashville performers, and the province's Eminent Islanders continue to cultivate their contacts around the globe. In the end, all politics is local, and when you look for it, all history has an Island connection.

9

Eminent Islanders – A Place to Be

Thomas Carlyle, that eminent recorder of European history, the author of the best profile of his fellow Scotsman, Robert Burns, loved heroes. He was a master of the Great Man theory of history, which is more than the tale of everyday lives. The Europeans, of course, cultivated their heroes into a mythology. Frederick the Great of Germany, to cite one example, was a beast of a man who learned cruelty from his father because his father was cruel to him, waged many wars, suffering losses of 600,000 men in some battles. In 1945, Joseph Goebels read the tales of Frederick the Great to Adolf Hitler in their final hours in the bunker in Berlin. In Britain, there are more than 600 biographies of Horatio Nelson. Winston Churchill, no mean hero himself, wrote a history of his father, Lord Randolf Churchill, glorifying him as a hero. Europe's heroes are encased in giant warehouses, close to their god: Westminster Abbey, the Pantheon, the Kremlin, the Vatican.

Despite their preference for norms of equality - the guiding light of the Founding Fathers - the Americans have their heroes in the great Presidents like Washington, Lincoln, and Roosevelt. The military heroes and robber barons are transformed into saintly do-gooders, such as Andrew Carnegie, John D. Rockefeller, and Henry Ford. Mount Rushmore symbolizes the tradition of American hero worship. Despite the media and academic attempts to downsize these great men of history through delicious gossip and salacious rumours, the bon mot and tantalizing whisperers of incompetence, great men do survive and get immortalized as great do-gooders. Within the American Empire, every President, good, bad, or forgettable, in the

White House or out of office, is called Mr. President. Only at a US Presidential Press Conference is a foreign leader called by his or her first name.

The history of North America, of Canada or the United States, is a mix of economics, politics, and social events. The US propounds the Turner Frontier theory of history, with the slow exodus beyond the Atlantic Coast to the frontier plains and the Pacific, where cowboys, and the discoveries of Lewis and Clark are celebrated as American heroes, which notably leaves out a lot, including the fact that British explorers like Francis Drake and James Cooke, not to mention the Spanish conquistadors, had been there before. In Canada, Harold Innis developed the St. Lawrence as his frontier thesis, moulding how trade and communications patterns combine to promote economic growth in products as diverse as cod, wheat, and the fur trade. In this mix, the Americans have used their heroes to create an image of the democratic ideal, where elections, competition, constant change, and novelty disguise the bloodiness and awful cruelty of the American experience, ranging from the early slave trade to the treatment of immigrants, the civil war, and the grinding poverty in this very affluent society. Heroes dominate the American landscape because the American media, including Hollywood and its star system, want heroes, which serve to sell papers, books, and movies, and to promote to non-Americans that they can adopt American heroes as part of their own. Not only do Americans often indulge in American exceptionalism, but because of recent history, much of the rest of the world conspire in a curious history to maintain it.

So what causes what? Do heroes create the circumstances that define history, or do circumstances define the conditions that make heroes? In the same way, as Carlyle noted in his work of 1841, heroes leave history with unintended consequences, and many heroes inspire writers to take up causes far different from the hero worshipper. Carlyle's writings, for instance, inspired social reformers such as John Ruskin, Charles Dickens, John Burns, William Morris, and even Karl Marx, a German, who wrote his works in the British museum. Such works also inspire historians to think anew about past events, not only because new documentation appears, but because there is value in accepting fresh evidence that was once heretical, or rethinking theories and practices formerly seen as dogma. In general, Canadians don't espouse hero worship, certainly not like the Americans. But there are many Canadian heroes, and there are many Island heroes. Napoleon argued that history is written by winners of wars and battles. To some degree this truism is correct, but often it is not. Heroes stand because these people respected the lives of their citizens. Islanders are especially proud of their heroes, in their own quiet way.

Hero worship now goes beyond the tracing of great events and great heroes. Today, historians now like to pose 'what if' questions to see how events might have produced different outcomes. What if the Spanish Armada, the first of three massive invasions planned for the British Isles (Napoleon in 1803, Hitler in 1940) had succeeded? What would this mean for the evolution of Britain, its Parliamentary Government, and the Reformation and the Church of England? What if Hitler and the appeasers in the British Government had made a peace pact in Europe, forgoing Churchill as Prime Minister and allowing Hitler's domination of Europe from the Atlantic coast to the Urals? What if the American civil war had been postponed, and the aggressive and imperial side of the American experience had moved north and west into the Prairies and Pacific coast of what is now Canada - who would have stopped them?

Canadian history is full of great 'what if' questions. The nation serves as a full child of North America, built on east-west lines, like the United States, but it could have easily been an Atlantic seaboard country, isolated from the Pacific, because foreign countries sought to dominate these lands – Spain, Britain, France, and even Russia, a vast Empire that once owned Alaska, which was sold to the Americans after the Crimean War, making the United States keen on northern acquisitions. When Britain had taken possession of the northern half of the Continent in 1763, with a greater Quebec extending southward into the Ohio Valley, its hold over the three "Canadian" colonies, Quebec, Acadia, and Newfoundland, plus the 13 "American" colonies, looked impregnable, and sufficient militarily to keep Spain isolated to the southwest in Mexico, Texas and California.

By 1803, two generations later, Napoleon was ready to invade Britain and wondered about his North American Empire. What if, through a merger of greater Quebec, the vast Louisiana Territory, and the Bourbon-controlled Spanish colonies, Napoleon had abandoned or held off eastward Continental acquisition in Europe and turned to North America? But Napoleon did not seize that challenge: if he did, would North America be a French-speaking territory? History records that his mighty battalions had to wait for sea battles, and then there was the Battle of Trafalgar, led by Horatio Nelson, with North American history changed forever.

By 1864, with the American Republic torn asunder by civil war, what was Britain to do with *her* British North American colonies? The Imperial Government of William Gladstone was at best totally indifferent to Britain's colonial empire, and Little Englanders spoke as though the colonies represented a vast financial burden, a budget drain, which fitted Gladstone's passion for tax relief, cost cutting, and a passive caution in military matters. Britain, of course, enjoyed a staggering lead in wealth creation and a rising moneyed class, thanks to being first in the industrialization march, aided mightily by the lucrative slave trade. By 1867, Britain's financial class ran out of places to spend domestically, so British capital invested not only in her own colonies, but in her potential commercial rivals, including the United States. In London, the new Dominion of Canada had its constitution, the BNA Act, and received token congratulations, a speedy passage with unanimous consent, while in the upper chamber, the House of Lords returned to discuss a bill of great importance, on the legality of divorce!

History is determined by the march of sweeping events, the legacy of technological forces, and the impact of the unintended consequences that no one controls. Together they produce new leaders and new heroes, and thus the great men, and often women, of history. Great men influenced Island history, and some great men were Islanders. If history, to some, is the sum of great biographies, great biographies can also be the sum of little men doing great things that make history.

Charles Calonne

Thomas Carlyle, 19th Century Author from Scotland,
On Heroes and Hero Worship

Prince Edward Island had both, and they made history, a unique story in the larger canvas of the Canadian experience. And of course, the Island had its own 'what ifs' in the chronicle of great events. Consider three 'what ifs' for Prince Edward Island.

1. The Land Question: 'What if' towards Prosperity?

Historians seem as one on two questions. The first is the basic mediocrity of the political administration around George III, although history now leaves open the view of the King himself, who wanted to retain the American colonies. Certainly, his personal views and policies towards the treatment of his French Canadian subjects in Quebec, as expressed in the treaties of 1774 and 1791, were ennobling and judicious, and made the French subjects in Quebec lasting monarchists and intensely loyal. Americans never understood this question in the past, and perhaps don't even to this day. While not perfect, this French question owes much to titans like George-Etienne Cartier, who taught his political colleagues the importance of minority rights, this perhaps being the single defining strength of enduring Canadian values.

The second issue is the great lottery scheme, for Prince Edward Island, where all the land – 67 lots of roughly 20,000 acres – was auctioned off for a song and left to a group of absentee landlords, much like cheap share options in today's stock market. The result was both greed and hubris on the part of the landowners, coupled with much corrupt and mendacious behaviour committed by the Island's Governors, who wanted a piece of the action. This created an intense economic burden for incoming immigrants, who often came without a penny to their name. At the time, property rights were a mix of landed inheritance, legal theft, imposed patronage, or wartime booty. People who owned land saw only one side of the equation, namely the entitlement of the land owner, and not the other side, in the protection accorded to the landowner when he follows what is prescribed. But more importantly, what if the landowner doesn't?

It is easy to forget, as Professor J.S. Bumsted constantly records, that there were two conditions on the lottery winners in 1767 - to populate their property either with incoming Protestants from Europe or from residents already in North America, at roughly one settler per 200 acres, and further, to collect annual quitrents at a rate of two shillings per hundred acres for poor land, with six shillings for good land. The proprietors agreed in writing to these terms. At this rate, good settlements would have provided over time abundant revenues to maintain the Island's government, which was separated from Nova Scotia in 1769.

So what if the scheme had been better managed from the start? After all, the theory behind the scheme had merit. Sell the land cheap, since North America at large had land aplenty, with few people. There was also merit in the Malthusian challenge of Great Britain at the time, with too many people, too little food, and too few economic prospects. Ignoring for a moment the way the internal administration of Britain was managed, with both the stupendous wealth and land holdings for the aristocracy, and the crippling waste of Ireland and the Highlands of Scotland, the colonial policy of Britain could be justified. In short, let the landowners manage the land, allow the local government to administrate, and through local finance (from taxes and selling or leasing of land), finance the administrative costs of the colony, such as policing, the ports and administering the Navigation Act, the courts, and the Governor.

In theory, this was in fact the policy on PEI, where administrative costs were, initially at least, about £1400.00 per year. This included the Governor's salary and that of other officials, both military and administrative. Assuming minimal costs, say 20 years of government, real total costs combined amount to only £28,000, less than half the cost of a good battleship. Even the outright sale of 1400 acres of land, at £10 per acre per year, with a small portion going to finance the local government, would have increased the economic value of the rest of the land remaining for sale or lease. But it was not to be! The landowners, with a few exceptions like Captain John MacDonald or Lord Selkirk, refused to accept their agreed terms. New landowners, especially the ship builders, preferred the narrow definition of property rights without accepting their own liabilities. It took over 100 years to sort out these fundamental errors of judgment, and the ensuing political battles, including the need for responsible government, scarred the landscape with fights to correct past mis-judgments. Few Islanders now, or at the time, appreciate fully how radical and forward-looking the Land Purchase Act was, and how it fundamentally made Island farmers into land owners, rather than tenured land farmers, a problem which still exists in so many countries around the world.

In this sense, the protracted and painful uprising of the Tenant League, which produced one of the few examples of rebellion and death on the Island colony, instilled in the people of Prince Edward Island immensely strong political will, and a careful husbanding of political loyalty. On the Island, loyalty is not easy to get, and it cannot be assumed. But once gained, it is there for ever. Islanders have a deep suspicion of outsiders, not because they are inherently against people from away, but because history records that too many outsiders take, but don't give in return.

2. Charles Calonne - 'What if Calonne Had Come to PEI?'

When Charles Calonne escaped to London, horrified by the amazing turn of events in Paris which he had helped start, in the call of the Notables, the Estates General, and the start of the French Revolution, he almost came to Prince Edward Island. Many leading figures in French Society did come to North America, including Charles Talleyrand, but George III's grant of 500 acres in Lot 65 near Charlottetown raises a fascinating 'what if'. The Island was then run by a small political elite, more interested in their personal fortunes and careers, and dependent upon the favourable support and good graces of Imperial London. But what if Charles Calonne, his brother Joseph, and a large group of French émigrés had come to Prince Edward Island, together with their personal effects and treasure?

What if they had come into contact with Lord Selkirk and Angus MacEachern? Certainly, from his arrival in 1790 to his death in 1835, Angus MacEachern was one of the most educated, politically astute, and generally trusted people on the Island, at home with both Protestants and Catholics, and accepted by the Colonial Government, landlords, and tenant farmers. According to his memoirs, Selkirk sought out MacEachern's advice for his settlers' housing, requesting his opinion on size, materials, and tools. Sadly, he and Selkirk never met. But these three men, so different in background, personality, and upbringing shared similar aspirations. They also differed in their experience with governments, Calonne with the French monarchy, Selkirk with Imperial London, and MacEachern with the Island's colonial powers. Calonne, vainglorious, egotistical, and awesomely smart, was at the very center of power in Imperial France, where he cultivated many outstanding and very bright people. Selkirk, an aristocrat who came to believe in the democratic ideals of the French revolution, was personally ambitious, erudite, and paradoxically a man of the people, wished to alleviate the Malthusian horrors of over-population, hunger, and personal want of his fellow Scots. More to the point, he had what the Island needed, and owned a precious asset in liquid cash from the sale of an estate in Scotland. MacEachern, a saintly priest, needed no lessons from English authorities on the treatment of the poor, and reached out to all who could help *his* mission, which was both worldly and rooted in the things that were God's.

Together, they would have been an incredible threesome, each sharing a Trinitarian goal of emigration, education, and freedom from tyranny, with each to pursue their private wishes for personal wealth, political ambition, and God's good fortune. They were unencumbered by direct Imperial patronage, so they could share in the need for education, public works, improved farms, and community economics, from crafts to carpentry. Furthermore, they understood why the sea and marine life were a powerful export supplement. Irish and Scottish peasants, relatively unskilled in farming, knew the value of the sea, the marine life, and realised the worth of kelp, seaweed that was rich in protein fertilizer. Indeed, prices reached £12 a ton, which is substantial for a product which spills onto the shoreline from the restless oceans, requiring no planting and no cultivation, just people. But it was not to be: Selkirk and MacEachern never met, and Calonne's brother, Abbé Joseph the priest came to PEI, an intellectually strong but politically and ambitiously weak substitute. Together, they would have been a powerful second front to the colonial elite which perpetuated two generations of largely inept administrative rule and held back the new values of education, ambition, and self-reliance that characterized the colonies to the South.

3. Maritime Union – 'What if the Maritimes Acted as One in 1864?'

In 1864, the three Maritime colonies collectively had about the same population as Lower Canada, while Upper Canada had slightly more but was growing rapidly. According to Professor Peter Waite's calculations, the combined population of the Atlantic Provinces, including Newfoundland, was 848,000, compared to a total of 1.15m in Canada East. George Brown's principal preoccupation, indeed his *modus operandi*, was representation by population. When Brown first joined the Cabinet of John A Macdonald, and when he came to Charlottetown and then to the Quebec Conference in 1864, he argued for an elected House of Commons on the British model, knowing full well that Ontario would grow the fastest of all the colonies. Professor Underhill recalls the advantages of Confederation for Upper Canada, with a population of 1.5 million and the advantages espoused by George Brown, the Toronto *Globe*, and the Grit Party:

> *The Grits had been campaigning for 'rep by pop' for a dozen years before 1864, and in the new constitution they rightly considered themselves victorious. In the new federal Parliament, Ontario because of its population, would have the largest delegation, and could look forward to a dominant influence in the making of national policy. It had been a favourite occupation of the Toronto Globe before 1867 to indulge in elaborate statistical reports about the growth of Upper-Canadian population and wealth as compared with what was taking place in the other colonies, and to argue that its constituents could count on the day when Ontario, shortly after the census of 1871, would have majority of the whole population of Canada.*
>
> *It was thoughts of this kind that overcame doubts about the division of powers between federal and*

*provincial governments. What did this matter when
the federal government would be under the firm
leadership of Ontario?*

Originally, the Charlottetown Conference was planned to discuss Maritime Union, not the wider vision of a union of all the British Colonies. Before this meeting, attended, as history shows, by the delegates from Upper Canada, Lower Canada, and the three Maritime colonies, the British Government advocated, mainly on grounds of coastal defence, a measure of cooperation among the Atlantic Colonies. The New Brunswick Governor was anything but an idle advocate of Maritime Union. D'Arcy McGee and about 40 members of the Canadian legislature toured Saint John and Halifax to meet the local Boards of Trade. Two relevant topics were an Inter-colonial railway and a federated union, perhaps as a way to cope with the rise of industrialism in the small, separate provinces, each themselves dispersed into three regions, and no central coordination around a commercial center, as in Upper or Lower Canada.

Prince Edward Island, from the earliest time when it became an independent colony from Nova Scotia, argued strenuously for autonomy, against the wishes of the Duke of Kent and Lord Durham (who both argued for re-unification with Nova Scotia) or for formal cooperation in inter-colonial free trade or navigation rules. Even a proposal to have a union between the Magdalen Islands and PEI was rebuffed in 1845. Both in Charlottetown and in Quebec, the Island delegates like Palmer and Coles left little doubt that they were against any proposals to dilute PEI's sense of exclusion. D'Arcy McGee, who so enraptured the citizens of Charlottetown, and himself no stranger to wit and repartee, warned the PEI delegates: "Now don't you be too boastful about your little Island, don't let us hear so much about it, or we will send down a little tug boat and draw you up into one of our lakes, where we will leave you to take care of yourselves."

After Confederation in 1867, various proposals were advanced to foster Maritime Union, including a new Conference proposed by Nova Scotia in 1877. As far back as 1865, Charles Tupper revived the idea of Maritime Union, in part to save the Confederation calculus in his home province of Nova Scotia, only to be scorned by the

Executive Council in Prince Edward Island. Even interventions by the British Government, in this case by Edward Cardwell, the Colonial Secretary, to deny the salary of the Island's Lieutenant Governor, was crude, clumsy, and unwarranted, and given the circumstance, quite an unhelpful gesture. But by then, the cast was set, hardened, and ready to stand. In PEI, the cards were stacked against Confederation, and Nova Scotia itself was no sure thing. Joseph Howe's oratory and brilliant writings were in full flight.

In reality, it was too late. One of the great what if questions asks what if the first part of the Charlottetown Conference in September 1864 was devoted to a simple proposition that the three provinces would speak as one, in equal measure to Upper Canada and Lower Canada. It is easy to forget that both in Charlottetown and in Quebec, there was never any resolution or opposition to the concept of a federal union. At Charlottetown, where all the basic details were forged, there were no formal votes. Even in Quebec, Macdonald was careful to avoid formal voting, province by province, because he at least was thinking ahead to obtain agreement in London. Consider the point made by one of the eminent writers on the period, Professor Francis Bolger, following the records of Edward Whelan:

> *The Maritime delegates presented resolution after resolution aimed at giving a larger membership, but their arguments were weakened by their failure to base them on principle rather than upon expediency. Why did they not assert their demand for larger representation as a right based on provincial sovereignty. A.A. MacDonald of Prince Edward Island made the strongest bid for provincial equality. He stated that he 'considered each province should have equal representation in the Federal Upper House', and he instanced the different states of the Union, which, however diversified in area, were each represented by two Senators, in the General Government.*

It is also easy to dismiss much of the writings that suggest the Maritimes were not opportunistic in Quebec, or mired in local parochialism. The Island delegates, for instance, were particularly well traveled, and knew that what caused the American civil war wasn't the issue of equal treatment of each state, as Macdonald had argued, but the fact that the slave states equalled the number of free states, which was a very different issue. It is equally easy to dismiss what Goldwin Smith, a man with a distinguished name, a skilful pen, yet a writer who ended up on the wrong side of most things, including Canada's annexation with the Americans, called Maritime politics, "the smaller the pit, the fiercer the rats."

Macdonald himself saw in Charlottetown the natural political opposition facing his Confederation vision. Ontario wanted one primary goal, that being rep by pop. Quebec through Cartier had one primary goal, a system that preserves the French culture, language, and legal system (their gains from 1791). The Maritimes had three potential strengths to bargain their way for better terms in their Atlantic location, the key to naval defence against the Americans; the Atlantic fisheries, which New England desperately wanted; and equal representation in both the House and the Senate. George Coles was the only deliberative Maritime politician who argued forcefully against the Canadian legislators, and Alexander Galt's offer of six seats for PEI, while proffered, fell on deaf ears. Macdonald, ever the wily negotiator, knew that five personal allies were central to his scheme: Brown and Cartier from Canada, Tilley from New Brunswick, Tupper from Nova Scotia, and William Pope from PEI. On these stars, John was prepared to roll the dice, and thus hope that his opponents wouldn't railroad his Confederation calculus. For the Maritimes, Macdonald was prepared to buy time, meaning that he could ignore the anti-Confederation opponents, especially Howe in Nova Scotia and Coles in PEI. In the end, Macdonald won, but the Maritimes lost, although not because they were parochial, hadn't traveled, or fell prey to the older members rather than the younger 'visionary' Fathers. On the central issues, they would not be 'railroaded,' to use Professor Peter Waite's delightful aphorism, to accept Canadian terms.

Perhaps some measure of Maritime cooperation was simply not in the cards. Not only did the Maritime provinces have three distinct political cultures, they were divided by three distinct internal regions. They remain so today. New Brunswick, separated by two great rivers, the Saint John and the Miramichi, splits its economic base between the United Empire Loyalist culture of the southern industrial stratum and the north-western Acadian farm and timber area, with the middle part of the province straddling both sides, but with no real urban center. Nova Scotia has three diverse political cultures in Cape Breton, the large, urbanized commercial center of Halifax, and the mainland. Prince Edward Island, tempered by the land issue, immigration patterns, and economic wealth, has three distinct counties in Prince, Queens, and Kings, a point the Island delegates argued at the Quebec Conference when offered five seats in the House of Commons: five divided by three isn't an easy political equation!

What if the Maritimes had united on a point of principle on the key question of equal representation? What if these three proud colonies, and their mix of delegates at Charlottetown and Quebec, had fought for the basic principle of equality among the colonies - would it have been too much? Would the visiting delegates from Canada, uneasy with the evolving Confederation calculus, simply return to their original bargain, a federal scheme between Upper and Lower Canada? Would the Maritime colonies seek membership in the Great Republic? In retrospect, it remains a great 'what if' question. Frank MacKinnon argues as follows: "had the Islanders been joined with the small neighbouring provinces in the 1860s, as the Maritime Fathers of Confederation originally discussed, a plan which was the reason for their 1864 Conference, and had the three entered Confederation together as one substantial province, the future might have been kinder."

In September 1864, when John A. left Charlottetown, on his way to Quebec City on the *Queen Victoria*, in his own mind, he faced a short distance race because time was his enemy. He knew the Americans, knew full well what Imperial London was thinking, and *he* knew the Confederation calculus was shaky at best. But from the Maritimes, the great 'what if', knowing all this, is what if the Maritimes had argued as a single group for better terms, and the legislative strengths that other provinces eventually were conceded. Even Sir Wilfred

Laurier, who had little sympathy for Sir John A. and his Tory Party, willingly conceded, in a speech to the House of Commons on March 26, 1912, the particular case of Prince Edward Island: "The one reason only which has impressed me – and it is not a constitutional reason, it is not a legal reason, it is simply a reason of equity – is the fact that Prince Edward Island has not profited by Confederation."

From 1867 to modern times, Atlantic Canada has struggled with the Confederation terms. The Atlantic Provinces surrendered to the federal government, in the name of national unity, most of the control over the region's natural bounty, including the fisheries, the oceans and sea, and its trade relations, just as industrial and technological circumstance diminished what provincial power was left, with an obviously decreased revenue base, and from lack of crown lands. To its own discredit, the Atlantic region has made its own mistakes, and pays a huge burden for its self-inflicted misfortunes. But today, thanks to globalization, the entire region's fortunes have never been better, thanks to increased education, a willingness to work, and the pull from other regions, especially in Western Canada, where the bonds with Atlantic Canada are so strong. In Alberta, building on the Atlantic Canadian struggles for property rights, local ownership of land and resources, both private sector and governments are only too willing to hire Atlantic workers, with their powerful work ethic, personal and family integrity, and the powerful legacy of their historic immigrant past, that innate sense of self-reliance and natural equity.

PEI – A Place to Be

For some four hundred years, from early explorers and the descriptions of Jacques Cartier, and from the early founders of PEI, not just the colonial governors, military adjutants, and men of the quick buck, but also the people who saw in the Island's beauty and serenity the possibilities for freedom and health, the Island took shape and fostered its prospects, mostly with little conflict and bloodshed. Lord Selkirk, Laird MacDonald, Bishop Angus MacEachern, Edward Whelan, John Mackieson, William Pope, Louis Davies, Lucy Maud Montgomery, Andrew Macphail, Joseph Pope, and a host of Island-born leaders saw in the Island's future great possibilities. These were highly educated people who believed in the welfare of the inhabitants, with their fertile soil, speckled shores, and little in the way of natural resources except its people. No one today needs to be briefed on the rich grandeur of the Island, its past, or its future. These Eminent Islanders have made their mark, who, like the Confederation delegates meeting in Conference at Charlottetown in 1864 "builded better than they knew."

Song writers, and perhaps Shakespeare, can tell the real meaning of words like alright and all right. PEI is alright, which is far better than all right. As the lexicographical writer Aaron Brown notes in the New York *Times*, it means far more; it means the best, the greatest, the tops. All right conveys the meaning of satisfactory, average, or mediocre. In the world of music and poetry, according to Sasha Frere-Jones, the pop music critic at the *New Yorker*, "When alright comes up in rock 'n' roll, it's often in a poetic sense, where it means that something is really good, much better than the vernacular all right." PEI, as Lucy Maud Montgomery notes incessantly, as an Island, is like poetry: it is alright.

The history of PEI, by some standards, doesn't fit into the conventional theories of economic development, since the province did not face the massive impacts of industrialization, where the problems of economics of scale, heavy machinery, and the difficult challenges of a very large work force collectively meant an enforced political and economic culture. On the other hand, some might argue that Prince Edward Island neatly fits into the stages of a growth model of economic development. From its inception as a European-discovered outpost to its colonial development, first under the French explorers and settlers in the reign of Louis XIV, the Roi du Soleil's long, long reign (1640-1715), second under the British, starting with George III, PEI expanded its population but set the seeds for discord and troubles as settlers sought to control their destiny, own their land, and cultivate their lives without rule and domination from Europe, either through Paris or London. As the population increased in the nineteenth century, as agriculture and shipbuilding created a wealth producing economy, PEI, like other British colonies in Canada, sought a real form of home rule in a nascent elected government structure that eventually led to the formation of Canada as an independent country and which later became the basis of responsible government for all former British colonies.

The shift from colonial government to provincial status had its own rewards and punishments, and as more economic power shifted to Ottawa, industries became part of a Canadian defensive expansion from Atlantic to the Pacific, and then later under free trade, from North to South. As a province, PEI is now subject to forces that increasingly prevent real provincial economic control, as federal spending, priorities, and handouts slowly lock the province into a time warp as a glorious vacation spot, a province steeped in history, and a demographic profile that has too many youth and too much senior citizens for its working population. Despite party differences, politicians struggle to maintain the Island way of life, often by gaining some financial advantages with federal largesse, but slowly surrendering economic decision-making, either to Ottawa or to the larger forces of globalization. Successive Island politicians rightly want to maintain PEI's political autonomy, with its fierce democracy and independent judgment.

Islanders are proud of their history, and the work of Eminent Islanders who have made their mark, who like the Confederation delegates who met in Charlottetown in 1864, never doubted the larger vision either in the abstract or in practical circumstance. In PEI, history and geography act together. Bruce Hutchinson, that avid and able chronicler of Canada and her people, knows that Canadians may not have the dreams of revolutionary escape from tyrants, or the heroism of a space walker, or even the majesty of monarchical rule. If Canada has too much geography and too little history, it must protect its history with a vengeance, because once gone, it is difficult to get back. In that sense, Prince Edward Island, despite its size, glories in a long and important history, including its proud placement as the Cradle of Confederation. But it does have a home to dream, "building something of his own, no better than other men's work, possibly not as good, but still his own" of Prince Edward Island, this insular but vehement democracy:

It must be, indeed, the most democratic system in the nation, or perhaps anywhere because it is small enough and intimate enough to keep government in daily and hourly touch with all the people and well able, as larger units of government are not, to argue, to understand and master its own business strictly by the democratic process.

This, I begin to see, is the key to the Island's private riddle. It has mastered its own business. It has accomplished nothing grand but the grandeur of contentment. It has built nothing of note but the quality of its life. It can never be wealthy like some of their provinces because it lacks the materials of wealth, and it cannot be poor because it is assured of a steady livelihood. It cannot have more than a moderate portion of what men call progress and cannot lose that tranquility which most progressive regimes have mislaid in their truth. Its only achievement is perfection.

References and Bibliography

Prince Edward Island is fortunate in having librarians and archivists who are both helpful and knowledgeable about their subject, and cultivate a collection of books, monographs, official documents, newspapers and periodicals, biographies, government records and reports that trace the story of the Island's history. The two main collections are in the PEI Section of the Robertson Library at the University of Prince Edward Island, and the Library in the Fathers of Confederation Center. In addition, there is an abundance of material in the various short biographies in the multiple volumes of the *Dictionary of Canadian Biography*, published by the University of Toronto Press, and the Island Register has a collected and easy to use access (Islanders in the "Dictionary of Canadian Biography"). See also www.biographi.ca for the Dictionary of Canadian Biography. In addition, the 40 year collection of *The Island Magazine* is must reading for topics, biographies, family stories, immigration, the land question, political questions, and Island institutions.

Preface

Bigger, H.P., *The Voyages of Jacques Cartier*. Ottawa, 1926.

Bragg, Melvyn, *The Adventure of English*. London: Hodder & Stoughton, 2003.

Brooke, John, *King George III*. St. Alban's, Herts., U.K.: Panther, 1974.

Burt, Alfred LeRoy, *The Evolution of the British Empire and Commonwealth from the American Revolution*. Boston: D.C.Heath, 1956.

Clairborne, Robert. *Our Marvelous Native Tongue: The Life and Times of the English Language*. New York: Times Books, 1983.

Carlyle, Thomas, *On Heroes And Hero Worship And The Heroic In History* (London, 1841).

Rayburn, Alan. *Geographical Names of Prince Edward Island* (Ottawa: Department of Energy, Mines, and Resources, 1973).

Chapter One – A New British Colony

Blanchard, J.-Henri, *The Acadians of Prince Edward Island.* Charlottetown, 1964.

Bolger, Rev. F. W. P. (Ed.), *Canada's Smallest Province: A History of Prince Edward Island* (Charlottetown: Centennial Commission, 1973).

Campbell, Duncan, *History of Prince Edward Island.* (Charlottetown: Bremner Brothers, 1875).

Champion, Helen Jean, *Over on the Island.* Toronto: Ryerson Press, 1939.

Clark, Andrew Hill, *Three Centuries and the Island: A Historical Geography of Settlement and Agriculture in Prince Edward Island, Canada* (Toronto: University of Toronto Press, 1959).

Cotton, W. L. Moore, *Chapters In Our Island Story.* Charlottetown: Irwin, 1927.

Harvey, Daniel Cobb (Ed.), *Journeys to the Island of St. John or Prince Edward Island.* (Toronto: Macmillan, 1955).

Johnston, Walter. *Travels in Prince Edward Island in the Years 1820-21.* Edinburgh: Chalmers and Collins, 1823.

MacDonald, Hubert T. and Margaret MacDonald, *The Lords of the Isles and Their Descendants.* Winnipeg, 1944.

MacKinnon, D. A. and A.B. Warburton (Eds.), *Past and Present in Prince Edward Island.* Charlottetown: F. Bowen, 1905.

McLennan, J.S., *Louisberg: From Its Foundation To Its Fall, 1713-1758*. London: MacMillan, 1918.

Meachem, & Co., J. H., 1880: *Illustrated Historical Atlas of The Province of Prince Edward Island*. Charlottetown:J.H. Meacham & Co., 1880.

Pollard, James B., *Historical Sketch of the Eastern Regions of New France, also Prince Edward Island: Military and Civil* (Charlottetown: John Coombs, 1898).

Stewart, John, *An Account of Prince Edward Island*. London: 1806.

Warburton, A. B. *A History of Prince Edward Island, 1534-1831* (Saint John: Barnes, 1923).

Chapter Two – Early Settlements and the Colony of Lord Selkirk

Alexander, Caroline, *The Bounty*. New York: Penguin, 2003.

Bolger, F.W.P. (Ed.), *Canada's Smallest Province: A History of Prince Edward Island* (Halifax, Nimbus, 1991).

Bumsted, J.M., The *People's Clearance: Highland Emigration in British North America, 1770-1815*. Edinburgh: Edinburgh University Press, 1982.

Bumsted, J.M., Land *Settlement and Politics in Eighteenth Century Prince Edward Island*, Kingston: McGill Queens, 1987.

Bumpsted, J.M. "Settlement by Chance: Lord Selkirk and Prince Edward Island", *Canadian Historical Review*, 59:2 (June 1978).

Bumstead, J.M. "The Origins of the Land Question on Prince Edward Island, 1767-1805," *Acadiensis, XI:1 (Autumn 1981)*.

Campey, Lucille H., "A Very Fine Class of Immigrants": Prince Edward Island's Scottish Pioneers 1790-1850. Toronto: Natural Heritage Books, 2001.

Hill, Douglas, *Great Emigrations: The Scots to Canada London: Gentry, 1972.*

MacDonald, Norman H., *The Clan Ronald of Lochaber: A History of the MacDonalds or MacDonells of Keppoch* (Edinburgh: 1978).

MacQueen, Malcolm. *Skye Pioneers and "The Island".* Winnipeg: Stovel Company Ltd., 1929.

Newman, Peter C., *Caesars of the Wilderness.* Toronto: Penguin Books, 1987.

Putman, Ada MacLeod, *The Selkirk Settlers and the Church They Built at Belfast* (Toronto: Presbyterian Publications, 1939).

Reid, W. Stanford (Ed.), *The Scottish Tradition in Canada.* Toronto: McClelland and Stewart 1976.

Russell, Phillips, *John Paul Jones: Man of Action.* New York: Brendano's,1928.

Selkirk, Thomas Douglas. *Observations on the Present State of the Highlands, with a View of the Causes and Probable Consequences of Emigration.* (London: Johnson Reprint Corp., New York, 1969).

The Arrival of the First Scottish Catholic Emigrants in Prince Edward Island 1772-1922. Memorial Volume (Summerside: Journal Publishing, 1922).

White, Patrick Cecil Teford (Ed.), *Lord Selkirk's Diary 1803-04.* (Toronto: The Champlain Society, 1958).

Chapter Three – The Missionary Priest

Bambrick, John, "Days of Bishop McEachern," *Prince Edward Island Magazine*, 3 (June 2001), pp. 148-153.

Blair, Bernard. *Things that Are Above: The Gothic Art and Architecture of St. Dunstan's Cathedral Basilica.* Charlottetown: Island Offset, 2004.

Bolger, Rev. Dr. Francis, "The First Bishop," in Michael Hennessey (Ed.), *The Catholic Church in Prince Edward Island*. Charlottetown: William and Crue, 1979, pp. 22-57.

Burke, Alfred E. "The Life of A.B. MacEachern," Unpublished Manuscript, (Charlottetown: Diocese of Charlottetown, n.d.).

Fraser, Antonia, *Marie Antoinette: The Journey.*Toronto: Anchor Canada, 2002.

Lacouir-Goyet, Robert, *Calonne: financière, reformateur, contre-revolutionaire, 1734-1802* (Paris, 1963).

Loménie, Louis de, *Beaumarchais And His Times*. New York, 1857.

MacDonald, Edward, "The Good Shepherd: Angus Bernard MacEachern, First Bishop of Charlottetown," *The Island Magazine*, 16 (Fall-Winter 1984), pp. 3-8.

MacDonald, Edward, "Angus MacEachern", *Dictionary of Canadian Biography*.

MacMillan, Rev. John. C., *Early History of the Catholic Church in Prince Edward Island* (Quebec: L'Evénement, 1905).

Mapp, Alf J. Jr, *Thomas Jefferson: Passionate Pilgrim*. (New York: Madison Books, 1991).

Mossiker, Frances. *The Queen's Necklace*. London: Phoenix, 2004.

Pineau, Rev. J. Wilfred, *Le Clergé Français dans L'Ile-du-Prince-Edouard 1721-1821* (Québec, Editions Ferland,1967).

Price, Munroe, *The Road from Versailles. New York: St. Martin's Giffin, 2002.*

Rogers, Irene L., Charlottetown: The Life in its Buildings. Charlottetown: The Prince Edward Island Museum and Heritage Foundation, 1983.

Schama, Simon, *Citizens: A Chronicle of the French Revolution.* New York: Vantage Books, 1988.

Chapter Four – Towards Responsible Government

Bolger, Rev. Francis W.P., *Prince Edward Island and Confederation, 1863-1873* Charlottetown: St. Dunstan's University Press, 1964.

Bowers, Patrick, *Edward Whelan* (Charlottetown, 1868).

Careless, J., Maurice S., *Brown of the Globe*. Toronto: MacMillan,1963.

Cotton, W. L. "The Press in Prince Edward Island, " in MacKinnon and Warburton.

Creighton, Donald, *John A. Macdonald*, Vol. 1 & 2. Toronto: MacMillan, 1952, 1955.

Harvey, D.C., "The Centenary of Edward Whelan," in G.A. Rawlyk (Ed.), *Historical Essays on the Atlantic Provinces* (Toronto: McClalland and Stewart, 1971).

McCourt, Peter, Ed., *Biographical Sketch of the Honourable Edward Whelan*. Charlottetown: McCourt, 1988.

Robertson, Ian Ross, (ed.), *The Prince Edward Island Land Commission of 1860* (Fredericton: Acadiensis Press, 1988).

Robertson, Ian Ross, "Edward Whelan", in *Dictionary of Canadian Biography,* 9, 828-835.

Waite, Peter, *The Life and Times of Confederation* (Toronto: University of Toronto Press, 1962).

Chapter Five – The Post Confederation Era

Armsworthy, Cassanda, "Offering Opportunity – Sir William C. Macdonald and Prince Edward Island, *The Island Magazine*, 57 (Spring-Summer, 2005), pp. 34-39.

Arsenault, Hon. A.E., *Memoirs*, Charlottetown, 1953.

Arsenault, Georges, "The Acadians in Island Politics," *The Island Magazine*, 43 Spring-Summer 1998), pp. 13-24.

Burns, A. Byron, *The Narrow Gauge Steam Railroad on Prince Edward Island.* Summerside: William & Crue, 1996.

Forbes, E.R. andD.A. Muise (Eds.), *The Atlantic Provinces in Confederation.* Toronto: University of Toronto Press, 1993.

Greenhill, Basil and Anne Giffard, *Westcountrymen in Prince Edward's Isle* (Toronto: University of Toronto Press, 1967).

Holman, H.T., "James Bardin Palmer," *Dictionary of Canadian Biography*, 6, 565-569.

Hornby, Ian, *Black Islanders: Prince Edward Island's Historic Black Community.* Charlottetown: Institute of Island Studies, 1991.

MacDonald, Edward, 'And Christ Dwelt in the Heart of His House:' A *History of St. Dunstan's University – 1855-1955.* Charlottetown, 1990.

MacKinnon, Frank, *The Government of Prince Edward Island.* Toronto: University of Toronto Press, 1951.

MacLelland, Jean M., *From Shore to Shore: The Life and Times of the Rev. John MacLennan of Belfast, P.E.I.* (Edinburgh: John Knox Press, 1977).

O'Grady, Brendan, *Exiles & Islanders: The Irish Settlers in Prince Edward Island* (Montreal: McGill-Queen's University Press, 2004).

O'Shea, Rev. Art, *A.E. Burke.* Charlottetown: Clarke Printing, 1993.

Robertson, Ian Ross, *The Tenant League of Prince Edward Island, 1864-1867.* Toronto: University of Toronto Press, 1996.

Underhill, Frank H. *The Image of Confederation.* Toronto: CBC Publications, 1964.

Chapter Six – Island Artisans

Bolger, Francis W.P., *The Years Before Anne* (Charlottetown, PEI Heritage Foundation, 1974).

Hennessey, Catherine G., The Arts in Charlottetown,: A Pre-Confederation Center View (Charlottetown: Unpublished Manuscript, 2003).

Reid, Dennis. *A Concise History of Canadian Painting.* Toronto: Oxford University Press, 1988.

Rubio, Mary and Elizabeth Waterston, *The Selected Journals of L.M.Montgomery,* Vols.1-4. Toronto: Oxford University Press.

Weber, Ephraim, "L.M. Montgomery's Anne," *Dalhousie Review*, 22 (October 1942), pp. 300-310.

Westin, H.M. Peter, *An Act of Faith: The First Fifty Years of St. Peter's Cathedral.* Charlottetown: St. Peter's Publication, 1994.

Williamson, Moncrieff, *Robert Harris (1849-1919)*, Ottawa: The National Gallery, 1973.

Williamson, Moncrieff, *Island Painter: The Life of Robert Harris (1849-1919).* Charlottetown: Ragweed Press, 1983.

Chapter Seven – Nature's Helpers – Island Medicine

Baldwin, D. and T. Spira, Eds., *Gaslights, Epidemics, and Vagabond Cows.* Charlottetown, 1988.

Lea, R. G., *History of the Practice of Medicine in Prince Edward Island.* Charlottetown: Prince Edward Island Medical Society, 1964.

Macphail, Andrew, "Medicine in Canada," in W. Stewart, *Canada Yearbook*, Vol. 4 (Toronto: University Associates 0f Canada, 1936).

McMillan, Joseph A., "1938-1963 – What Has Become of the Doctor?" McGill University, *Montreal General Hospital* (October 18, 1963).

Mullally, Sasha, "Dr. Roddie, Dr. Gus & The Golden Age of Medicine," *The Island Magazine*, 42 (Fall-Winter 1997), pp. 3-12.

Pincombe, C. Alexander, *40 Years Under the Blue: A History of Blue Cross in Atlantic Canada* (Moncton: Centennial Press, 1985).

Rogers, Irene, "John Mackieson", *Dictionary of Canadian Biography*.

Shephard, David, *Island Doctor.* Montreal: McGill-Queen's University Press, 2003.

Shillington, C. Howard, *The Road to Medicare in Canada* (Toronto: Del Graphics Publishing, 1972).

Sinnott, Cyril, *A History of the Charlottetown Clinic* (Charlottetown, 1975).

Trainer, Alice, and the Alumnae of the Charlottetown Hospital School of Nursing, *History of the Charlottetown Hospital School of Nursing and the Charlottetown Hospital.* Charlottetown: Irwin Printing, 1991.

Whelan, William L., "The Jenkins of Charlottetown," *CMA Journal,* 155 (August 15, 1996), pp. 445-447.

Chapter Eight – Angus MacLean

Callbeck, Lorne C. *The Cradle of Confederation: A Brief History of Prince Edward Island from Its Discovery in 1534 to the Present Time.* Fredericton: Brunswick Press, 1964.

Cameron, Silver Donald, "Charlottetown," *Canadian Geographic* (August-September, 1984), pp. 8-18.

Camp, Dalton, *Gentlemen, Players, and Politicians.* Toronto: McLellan & Stewart, 1967.

Campbell, Alex, "Recalling the Birth of a Great Small University," *The Guardian* (September 5, 2003), p. A7.

MacDonad, Edward, "The Origin of the Confederation Center of the Arts (Charlottetown: Unpublished Manuscript, October 2003).

MacKinnon, Wayne, *Two Solitudes*. Charlottetown, 2005.

MacLean, Angus, *Making It Home: Memoirs of J. Angus MacLean*. Charlottetown: Ragwood Press, 1998.

Macquarrie, Heath, *Red Tory Blues A Political Memoir*. Toronto: University of Toronto Press, 1992.

Moore, Mavor, *Reinventing Myself: Memoirs* (Toronto: Stoddart Publishing Co. Ltd., 1994).

Porter, J., *The Vertical Mosaic* (Toronto: University of Toronto Press, 1965).

Reid, Marion, *These Roots Run Deep*. Charlottetown: Transcontinental, 2005.

Smith, Denis, *Rogue Tory: The Life and Legend of John G. Diefenbaker*. Toronto: MacFarlane, Walter, & Ross, 1995.

Smitheran, Vernon et al., (eds.), *The Garden Transformed: Prince Edward Island, 1945-1980*. Charlottetown; Ragweed Press, 1982.

Zakem, Frank, *The Neighbourood Family Run Corner Store Experience*. Charlottetown: 2002.

Chapter Nine – What ifs

Hutchison, Bruce, *Canada, Tomorrow's Giant (Toronto: Longmans, Green, and Co., 1957)*.

MacKinnon, Frank, *Church Politics and Education in Canada: The PEI Experience*. (Calgary: Detselig Enterprises, 1995.)

Roberts, Andrew, *What Might Have Been: Leading Historians on Twelve 'What Ifs' of History*. (London: Orion, 2004).

Strawson, John, *If By Chance*. (London: Pan Macmillan, 2004).

Underhill, Frank H., *The Image of Confederation.* (Toronto: Canadian Broadcasting Corporation, 1964).

Waite, Peter, *The Life and Times of Confederation* (Toronto: University of Toronto Press, 1962).

Index

population 216
Post Office 195
prohibition 258, 275–278
railway 142, 146, 148, 164–165, 174, 177–182, 190, 195, 200, 208, 241, 312, 315, 353, 356, 377
religions 7–9, 21, 36, 275
religious controversies 161
School 38
shipbuilding 52, 72, 134–135, 153, 168, 182, 190, 209, 216–217, 315–316, 382
tourism 334
Transportation 360
Prince of Wales College 229, 253, 333, 336, 338, 341–342, 345
Prohibition
American 276
Canada 276
PEI 276
Provencher, Joseph-Norbert 99

Q

Quebec Act of 1774 73
Quebec Conference 1864 200, 257, 376, 380
Quebec House 164
Quebec Resolutions 163, 172, 174, 351
Queen Charlotte 4, 20, 42, 90, 336
Queen Elizabeth 311
Queen Square School 211
Queen Victoria 155, 163, 171, 177, 350, 380

Quesnay 78
Quit Rent Act 55

R

Ralston, J.L. 317
RCMP 305, 355
Ready, John 187, 256
Red Cross 289, 292–293, 309
Reform Bill, 1832 29
Reid, George 233
Reid, Marian 331
Richards, William Buell 195
Richelieu, Cardinal 84
Riel, Louis 203
Ritchie, J.H. 169
Roberts, Charles G.D. 225
Robertson, Ian 114
Robertson, James 116
Rodgers, Sir Frederick 172
Rogers, Benjamin 321
Rotstein, Abe 362
Royal Gazette 67, 108, 116, 128
Royal Scots College 69, 106
Russell, Charles 321
Russell, Lord John 124, 127
Russell, William 289
Ryan, Edward 325

S

Saint-Pierre, Comte 19
Say, Jean-Baptiste 306
Schurman, Jacob Gould 229
Scott, Walter 38, 46, 49, 221
Scripts 278
Seaman, Rupert 298
Senate, Canadian 324